CAREER OPPORTUNITIES IN ADVERTISING AND PUBLIC RELATIONS

Fourth Edition

SHELLY FIELD

Foreword by
HOWARD J. RUBENSTEIN

Ferguson Publishing
An imprint of Infobase Publishing

This book is dedicated to my parents, Ed and the late Selma Field,
who taught me that if I reached
high enough for a star, I would be able to catch one;
and to my sisters,
Jessica and Debbie, who helped me reach.

Career Opportunities in Advertising and Public Relations, Fourth Edition

Ferguson
An imprint of Infobase Publishing
132 West 31st Street
New York NY 10001

Library of Congress Cataloging-in-Publication Data
Field, Shelly.
   Career opportunities in advertising and public relations/Shelly
Field; foreword by Howard J. Rubenstein.—4th ed.
      p. cm.
   Includes index.
   ISBN 0-8160-6245-5 (alk. paper)
   1. Advertising—Vocational guidance. 2. Public relations—Vocational guidance. I. Title.
   HF5828.4.F54 2005
   659′.023′73—dc22   2005040041

Ferguson books are available at special discounts when purchased in bulk quantities for businesses, association, institutions, or sales promotions. Please call our Special Sales Department in New York at (212) 967-8800 or (800) 322-8755.

You can find Ferguson on the World Wide Web at http://www.fergpubco.com

Cover illustration by Art Parts/Ron and Joe, Inc.

Printed in the United States of America

VB Hermitage 10 9 8 7 6 5 4 3 2 1

This book is printed on acid-free paper.

CONTENTS

ACKNOWLEDGMENTS

I thank every individual, company, corporation, agency, association, and union that provided information, assistance, and encouragement for this book.

First and foremost, I acknowledge with appreciation my editor, James Chambers, for his continuous help, encouragement, and guidance. I am thankful to Kate Kelly, who, as my initial editor, provided the original impetus for this book as well as for a number of my other books. Thanks also to Randy Gill and Neal Maillet for their help. I gratefully acknowledge the assistance of Ed Field for his ongoing support in this and every project.

Other organizations and individuals whose help was invaluable include: the Academy of Hospital Public Relations; Ellen Ackerman; Advertising Club of New York; Advertising Council; Advertising Research Foundation; Advertising Women of New York, Inc.; Julie Allen; American Advertising Federation; American Association of Advertising Agencies; American Society for Hospital Marketing and Public Relations; Art Directors Club, Inc.; Association of National Advertisers; Association of Theatrical Press Agents and Managers; Dan Barrett; Lloyd, Barriger, Barriger and Barriger; Debra Barnes; Allan Barrish; Warren Bergstrom; Eugene Blabey, WVOS Radio; Robert Boone, Isle of Capri Casinos; Theresa Bull; Business/Professional Advertising Association; Liane Carpenter; Earl "Speedo" Carroll; Eileen Casey, Superintendent, Monticello Central Schools; Casino Career Center; Mary Cawley; Anthony Cellini, Town of Thompson Supervisor; Patricia Claghorn; Andy Cohen; Bernard Cohen, Horizon Advertising; Dr. Jessica L. Cohen; Lorraine Cohen; Norman Cohen; Jan Cornelius; Crawford Memorial Library Staff; Margaret Crossley, Nevada Society of Certified Public Accountants; Meike Cryan; Direct Marketing Association, Inc., Mark Di Raffaele, Direct Marketing Educational Foundation, Inc.; Joseph Doucette, General Sales Manager, Middletown Honda; Dan England; Dress Barn; Michelle Edwards; Scott Edwards; Valerie Esper; Ernest Evans; Field Associates, Ltd.; Deborah K. Field, Esq.; Edwin M. Field; Lillian (Cookie) Field; Mike Field; Robert Field; Selma G. Field; Finkelstein Memorial Library Staff; David Garthe, CEO, Graveyware.com; John Gatto; Shelia Gatto; Sam Goldych; Alex Goldman; Grey Advertising; Gary Halcott; Joyce Harrington; Hermann Memorial Library Staff; Joan Hezza; Joan Howard; Jo Hunt; International Council of Shopping Centers; Julia Jacobs; Jimmy "Handyman" Jones; Margo Jones; Dave Kleinman; Janice Kleinman; Dr. John C. Koch, Sullivan County Performing Arts Council; Bruce Kohl, Boston Herald.com; Tom Lagrutta; Karen Leever; Liberty Public Library Staff; Lipman Advertising; William Little, Jr.; Dorothy Marcus; Robert Masters, Esq.; McCann Erickson; Judy McCoy; Lois McCluskey; Phillip Mestman; Rima Mestman; Beverly Michaels, Esq.; Martin Michaels, Esq.; Monticello Central High School Guidance Department; Monticello Central School High School Library Staff; Monticello Central School Middle School Library Staff; Sharon Morris; Ellis Norman, UNLV; Dorothy Olim; The One Club; Outlet Bound; Ed Pearson, Nikkodo, USA; Barbara Pezzella; Public Relations Society of America; Doug Puppel; Harvey Rachlin; Ramapo Catskill Library System; Doug Richards; John Riegler; David Rosenberg, Human Resources Manager, Grey Advertising; Howard Rubenstein; Diane Rudd; Saatchi & Saatchi Advertising; Joy Shaffer; Raun Smith; Society of Illustrators; Laura Solomon; Laurie Spar; Parke Spencer; Aileen Spertell; Matthew Strong; Tom Sutton; Thrall Library Staff; Marie Tremper; Brian Vargas; Kaytee Warren; Carol Williams; John Williams; John Wolfe; WTZA-Television; WSUL Radio; WVOS Radio.

My thanks also to the many people and companies who provided material for this book who wish to remain anonymous.

FOREWORD

It's exciting to pick up the new edition of Shelly Field's guide to *Career Opportunities in Advertising and Public Relations* and discover that the book's relevance has only grown in recent years. Of course there've been changes in the landscape of new media since the third edition was published, but career opportunities in PR and advertising have kept pace and there remains a strong need for creative individuals who can shape the message to bring about bottomline results.

The explosion of online information, whether through Web sites complementing traditional news outlets or through blogs and other digitized formats, has only enhanced the role of media in our culture. It sometimes seems as if everybody's plugged into one news source or another all the time. What this means for people looking to enter the fields of public relations and advertising is that the pace of everything has increased—but so has the number of places in which to communicate a client's message. Our job as professionals in the communications industry is to plunge into the fray and recognize that while strategies and formats might change, the basics of the business remain the same. You still need to develop strong writing and oral presentation skills. You still have to be able to think on your feet and work hard. And you still have to make integrity and honesty an absolute priority in everything you do. In order to acquire these assets, a good guide to the business is essential.

I've always seen three main tracks of activity at the core of any information service business: creating a brand identity; managing the flow of information to all types of audiences; and shaping public perception of both the brand and the information flow. Those essentials haven't changed in the digital age. As publicists and advertisers, we're still the people who stay out of sight creating the message that meets the public eye.

Fifty years ago, I began my own public relations agency. Probably from my father's strong influence—he was a police reporter—the firm developed and has grown to function a good deal like a newsroom. On any given day, we're interviewing newsmakers for quotes, writing, sharing ideas between colleagues, following the breaking news on the wires and doing our best to channel all this information firing at us into stories that enable our clients to achieve their goals. Just like in a newsroom, you can never be sure of the developments that the next half-hour will bring, let alone the next day. But whatever comes at you, you've got to draw on all your skills to communicate the client's message. You've always got to remember that you have your own story to break; and wherever possible, other stories should be feeding into the one you're trying to tell.

I think Shelly Field's *Career Opportunities in Advertising and Public Relations* is a terrific road map for anyone either entering the field for the first time or contemplating a move to a new firm. Not only does she do a great job of explaining the opportunities out there today, she gives readers the necessary resources to translate her lessons into new strategies to meet the inevitable changes that will come as the fields evolve. Both advertising and public relations are now such broad industries that you need a guide like never before to find your way around. With Shelly's book in hand, you'll make your way through the maze just fine.

Howard J. Rubenstein
President
Rubenstein Associates, Inc.
Public Relations

HOW TO USE THIS BOOK

Purpose

The advertising and public relations industries offer a myriad of careers. Thousands of people want to work in these interrelated industries but have no idea how to go about getting jobs. They are not aware of the career opportunities, where to find them, or the training required to be successful in their quest.

Until the first edition of this book was published in 1989, there was no single reliable source describing the major job opportunities in the advertising and public relations industries. Four editions later, this book still serves as a guide for all those seeking a career in these industries. The 2006 edition of *Career Opportunities in Advertising and Public Relations* includes all the updated information you need to prepare for and find an exciting and rewarding job in these fields.

This book was written for everyone who aspires to work in any aspect of advertising and public relations but doesn't know how to start. It was written to help you get a great job and climb the career ladder to success.

The 88 jobs covered in this book encompass careers in agencies and in the corporate world. There are very few types of organizations in the country, or in the world for that matter, that do not need or use advertising and public relations in some form. Opportunities exist in a wide array of companies and businesses, not-for-profit organizations, television and radio stations, publications, political parties, schools, and governmental entities as well as online businesses and Web sites.

Advertising and public relations are multibillion-dollar industries whose growth continues with a multitude of career opportunities. The advertising and public relations industries need a variety of people with many different talents. Secretaries, receptionists, accountants, executives, salespeople, publicists, press agents, copywriters, computer technicians, artists, writers, designers, Webmasters, and others are required. The trick in locating a job is to develop your skills and use them to get your foot in the door. Once in, learn as much as you can, work hard, and climb the career ladder into other positions.

This fourth edition includes updated information necessary to prepare you and help you find an exciting and rewarding career in these fields.

Sources of Information

Information for this book was obtained through interviews, questionnaires, and a wide variety of additional sources. Some information came from personal working experience. Other data were obtained from business associates and colleagues in various positions in advertising and public relations.

Among the people interviewed were men and women in all aspects of the advertising and public relations industries. These included people in the corporate world, colleges, trade associations, not-for-profit organizations, newspapers, magazines, radio and television stations, politics, and government. Also interviewed were publicists, public relations counselors, advertising agency owners and employees, hotel, nightclub, and restaurant owners and managers, Web site marketers, freelancers, and businesspeople. Employment agencies were contacted as well as recruiting firms, schools, personnel offices, unions, and trade associations.

Organization of Material

Career Opportunities in Advertising and Public Relations is divided into nine general employment sections. These include: Corporate and Industry; Agencies; Radio and Television; Sports and Entertainment; Hospitality and Tourism; Nonprofit Agencies; Publishing; Freelance and Consulting; and Miscellaneous Opportunities. Within each of these sections are descriptions of individual careers.

There are two parts to each job classification. The first part offers job information in a chart form. The second part presents information in a narrative text.

In addition to the basic career description there is information about unions and associations, as well as tips for entry. Seven appendixes, a glossary, and a bibliography are offered to help locate information you might want or need to get started looking for a job in the field. E-mail addresses and Web sites are included when available for companies listed in the appendixes. This should make it even easier to obtain additional information.

Your career in advertising and/or public relations can be exciting, glamorous, and fulfilling. Whichever facet of the business you choose to enter, your work can be far-reaching in terms of its effects on individuals, the community, and even a worldwide audience.

This book will help you prepare for a great career you will love. It will give you the edge over other job seekers. The jobs in advertising and public relations are out there waiting for you. You just have to go after them.

Shelly Field
www.shellyfield.com

INTRODUCTION

The advertising and public relations industries are multibillion-dollar businesses. Thousands of people work in these industries. One of them can be you!

Advertising and public relations coupled together can have a significant effect on people. Every time you make a decision to buy a product, choose a vacation spot, vote for a political candidate, watch a television show, go to a movie, read a story about an entertainer, celebrity, new product or business, or even choose a Web site search engine you are feeling the effects of both of these disciplines.

We are surrounded by advertising on a daily basis: television commercials, radio spots, advertisements in the newspaper or magazines, highway billboards, bright pylon signs on buildings, mass transit posters, or even banner or pop-up ads on the Internet. We are similarly surrounded by public relations campaigns that attempt to provide us with opinions, often trying to influence us to change the ones we have now.

A career in advertising and public relations can be challenging and demanding. It can also be glamorous, fun, and very rewarding.

As you read the various sections in this book, searching to find the job you have always dreamed about, keep in mind that there are many ways to get into advertising and public relations. I have provided you with the guidelines. The next step is yours.

Within each section of this book you will find all the information necessary to acquaint you with the important jobs in both industries. A key to the organization of each entry follows.

Alternate Titles

Many jobs in advertising and public relations, as in all industries, are known by alternate titles. The duties of these jobs are the same, only the names are different. The title varies from company to company and from agency to agency.

Career Ladder

The career ladder illustrates a normal job progression. Remember that in the advertising and public relations industries there are no hard-and-fast rules. Job progression may occur in almost any manner.

Position Description

Every effort has been made to give well-rounded job descriptions. Keep in mind that no two agencies or compa-

nies are structured in exactly the same way. Therefore, no two jobs will be precisely the same. For example, note the figures on the following pages. These illustrate tables of organization for a typical advertising and public relations agency and a typical communications department within a corporation. However, as no two companies are set up the same way, other agencies and corporations might have different tables of organization. The company might have people reporting to other executives. The company might also eliminate some positions on the chart or add others.

Salary Range

Salary ranges for the 88 job titles in the book are as accurate as possible. Salaries for a job will depend on the size and location of a company as well as the experience and responsibilities of the individual.

Employment Prospects

If you choose a job that has an EXCELLENT, GOOD, or FAIR rating, you will have an easier time finding a job. If, however, you would like to work at a job that has a POOR rating, don't despair. The rating means only that it is difficult to obtain a job—but not totally impossible.

Advancement Prospects

Try to be cooperative and helpful in the workplace. Don't try to see how little work you can do. Be enthusiastic, energetic, and outgoing. Do that little extra that no one asked you to do. Learn as much as you can. When a job advancement possibility opens up, make sure that you are prepared for it.

Education and Training

This book outlines the minimum training and educational requirements, but this does not mean that it is all you should have. Get the best training and education possible. A college degree does not guarantee a job in either advertising or public relations, but it will help prepare you for life in the workplace.

Experience, Skills, and Personality Traits

These will differ from job to job. However, any job will require a lot of perseverance and energy. You will also have to be articulate. An outgoing personality helps. Contacts are important in all facets of business; make as many as you can. These people will be helpful in advancing your career and helping you network.

Best Geographical Location

Most major agencies are located in cities such as New York, Atlanta, Los Angeles, Chicago, Detroit, Boston, Minneapolis, Pittsburgh, Washington, Dallas, and Cleveland. This does not mean that these are the only locations in which to look for employment, however. Smaller agencies or those found in other cities will often offer easier entry into the advertising and public relations world.

Jobs in television, radio, publishing, hospitality, tourism, and entertainment may be located both in large cities and in less populated areas. While government or political positions may be located in Washington, D.C., or in any of the state capitals, they might also be found in other areas. Opportunities in corporate and nonprofit organizations may be found almost anywhere in the country.

Unions and Associations

Unions and trade associations offer valuable help in getting into the advertising and public relations industry, obtaining jobs, and making contacts. They may also offer scholarships, fellowships, seminars, and other beneficial programs.

Tips for Entry

Use this section for ideas on how to get a job and gain entry into your area of interest. When applying for any job, always be professional. Dress neatly and conservatively for interviews. Don't wear sneakers. Don't chew gum. Don't smoke in the reception area before an interview or during an interview. Don't wear heavy perfume or cologne. Always have a few copies of your résumé with you. These should look neat and professional. Have résumés typed and well presented. Make sure you check and recheck for errors in grammar, spelling, and content. Don't just rely on your computer's spelling and grammar checker.

If you are applying for a creative job such as artist or copywriter, put together a portfolio of your best work. Make it neat and imaginative. This will help illustrate your potential. Bring this with you to all interviews.

Use every contact you have. Don't get hung up on the idea that you want to get a job by yourself. If you are lucky enough to know someone who can help you obtain the job you want, take him or her up on the offer. It will be up to you to prove yourself at the interview and on the job; nobody can do that for you.

Use the Internet to help you research companies, look for jobs, get ideas, and keep up with trends. If you don't have Internet access at home, most schools, colleges, and public libraries generally offer free on-site access.

Be on time for everything. This includes job interviews, phone calls, work, meetings, sending letters, and answering e-mails. People will remember when you are habitually late, and this will work against you in advancing your career.

Learn something positive from every experience. Don't burn bridges. Don't criticize prior bosses, clients, or jobs. The advertising and public relations world is a small one. In short do your best at all times. A good professional reputation will follow you throughout your career.

Have fun reading this book. Use it. It will help you find a career you will truly love. The world of advertising and public relations can be both glamorous and exciting. You will wake up and go to work every day knowing that the results of your job will be influencing others.

Don't get discouraged. People rarely get the first job they apply for. You may have to knock on a lot of doors, send out many résumés, and apply for a lot of jobs, but you will eventually find the job of your dreams. When you do get it, share your knowledge and help others get into the business too.

We love to hear success stories. If this book helped you in your quest for a job and you would like to share your story, go to www.shellyfield.com and let us know.

Good luck!

ORGANIZATION—TYPICAL ADVERTISING AND PUBLIC RELATIONS AGENCY

ADMINISTRATION

- CEO
- PRESIDENT COO
- ADMIN. ASSISTANT
- EXEC. VP & TRES.

ACCOUNTING / DATA PROCESSING

- VP FINANCE
- ACCOUNTING COOR-DINATOR
- BILLING COOR-DINATOR
- BILLING COOR-DINATOR
- BILLING COOR-DINATOR
- RELIEF RECEP-TIONIST/CLERK
- DATA PROCESSING MANAGER
- SYSTEMS OPERATOR
- DATA PROCESSING PROGRAM-MER
- ACCOUNTING SECRETARY

RECEPTION

- RECEP-TIONIST

WORD PROCESSING

- WORD PROCESSING LEAD OPERATOR
- WORD PROCESSING OPERATOR

CREATIVE DEPT. COPY, ART, BROADCAST PRODUCTION

- SR. VP CREATIVE DIR. ART
- SR. VP CREATIVE DIR. COPY
- VP ART DIRECTION
- VP COPY
- SENIOR ART DIRECTOR
- SENIOR COPY-WRITER
- ART DIRECTOR
- COPY WRITER
- ART DIRECTOR
- COPY WRITER
- ART DIRECTOR
- ART DIRECTOR
- ART DIRECTOR
- BROADCAST PRODUCTION
- BROADCAST CREATIVE COOR-DINATOR
- BROADCAST CREATIVE ASSISTANT

PRINT PROD, GRAPHIC CENTER, FINAL ART

- VP PRINT PRODUCTION
- PRINT PRODUCTION MANAGER
- PRINT PRODUCTION ASSISTANT
- GRAPHICS CENTER
- FINAL ART MANAGER
- FINAL ARTIST
- FINAL ARTIST
- FINAL ARTIST

RESEARCH

- RESEARCH DIRECTOR
- RESEARCH ASSISTANT

ACCOUNT RESEARCH

- SR. VP MARKETING
- SENIOR VP CLIENT SERVICE
- ACCOUNT SUPERVISOR
- ACCOUNT COOR-DINATOR
- ACCOUNT EXECUTIVE
- ACCOUNT SUPERVISOR
- ACCOUNT COOR-DINATOR
- ACCOUNT COOR-DINATOR
- ACCOUNT EXECUTIVE
- ACCOUNT COOR-DINATOR
- ACCOUNT EXECUTIVE
- ACCOUNT SERVICES SECRETARY
- ACCOUNT EXECUTIVE
- ACCOUNT COOR-DINATOR
- ACCOUNT COOR-DINATOR
- ACCOUNT EXECUTIVE
- ACCOUNT EXECUTIVE
- ACCOUNT COOR-DINATOR
- ACCOUNT EXECUTIVE
- ACCOUNT COOR-DINATOR
- ACCOUNT EXECUTIVE

MEDIA

- MEDIA DIRECTOR
- MEDIA SECRETARY
- ASSOC. MEDIA DIRECTOR
- TRADE MEDIA DIRECTOR
- MEDIA COOR-DINATOR
- MEDIA PLANNER BUYER
- MEDIA COOR-DINATOR
- MEDIA PLANNER BUYER
- MEDIA COOR-DINATOR
- MEDIA PLANNER BUYER
- MEDIA COOR-DINATOR
- MEDIA PLANNER BUYER
- MEDIA BUYER
- MEDIA AUDITOR

PUBLIC RELATIONS

- PR MANAGER
- PR ACCOUNT EXECUTIVE
- PR ACCOUNT EXECUTIVE
- PR ACCOUNT EXECUTIVE
- PR ACCOUNT EXECUTIVE
- PR ACCOUNT EXECUTIVE
- PR ACCOUNT COOR-DINATOR
- PR ACCOUNT COOR-DINATOR

ORGANIZATION—TYPICAL COMMUNICATIONS DEPARTMENT
WITHIN A CORPORATION

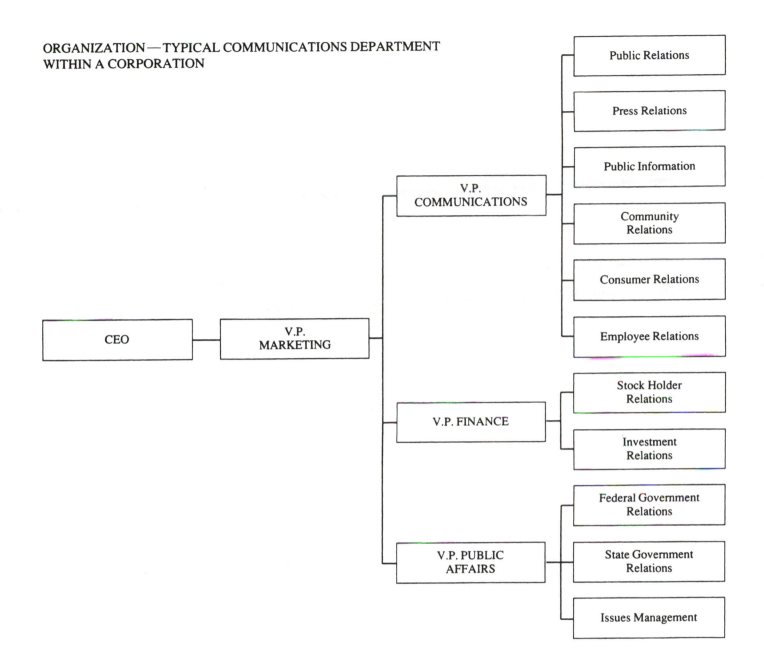

CORPORATE
AND INDUSTRY

BRAND MANAGER, CORPORATE/INDUSTRY

CAREER PROFILE

Duties: Develop, direct, and implement marketing efforts for a specific brand or product; identify key markets and potential customers; develop pricing and distribution strategies

Alternate Title(s): Brand Marketing Manager; Product Manager

Salary Range: $30,000 to $150,000+

Employment Prospects: Good

Advancement Prospects: Good

Best Geographical Location(s): Positions may be located throughout the country; greatest number of opportunities will exist in cities with many large corporations or manufacturers.

Prerequisites:

Education or Training—Minimum of bachelor's degree in marketing, communications, liberal arts, advertising, public relations, or related field

Experience—Experience in marketing and branding

Special Skills and Personality Traits—Creative, communication skills; detail-oriented, motivated, decision-making ability; people skills; supervisory skills

CAREER LADDER

```
┌─────────────────────────────────┐
│   Brand Manager for a Larger, More   │
│   Prestigious Brand or Corporate     │
│      Marketing Director              │
└─────────────────────────────────┘

┌─────────────────────────────────┐
│         Brand Manager            │
└─────────────────────────────────┘

┌─────────────────────────────────┐
│ Assistant or Associate Brand Manager, │
│   or Brand or Product Executive      │
└─────────────────────────────────┘
```

Position Description

Many large corporations often comprise a number of smaller companies or divisions, each with their own brand. Mars, Inc., for example, is the parent company of many brands, including 3 Musketeers, M&Ms, Skittles, Snickers, Mars, Milky Way, and an array of others. Similarly, the Sara Lee Corporation not only has its own Sara Lee brand, but also well-known brands such as Hillshire Farms, Kiwi, Jimmy Dean, and Playtex.

While there generally is a corporate marketing director, many companies with multiple brands also have specific Brand Managers. These are the individuals responsible for developing and implementing marketing campaigns for their particular brand.

Depending on the structure of the company, Brand Managers can have an array of responsibilities. Individuals are expected to develop both long- and short-term strategic marketing plans for the brand. These might include marketing initiatives, special packaging, and/or point of purchase pieces for the specific brand, as well as promotions, sweepstakes, contests, giveaways, and coupons.

The Brand Manager is expected to develop budgets for his or her department. In doing so, the individual determines how best to spend the monies allocated in order to increase sales. Should more monies go toward research? What about advertising? How about changing the packaging? The decisions of the Brand Manager can affect the bottom line of the brand.

Brand Managers often work with the research and development team. This might be necessary, for example, to determine how products within the brand can be improved. Would customers purchase more if products were offered in single-serve packages? Is a sauce too spicy? Does the packaging need updating? Do consumers purchase a product once and then not again? The Brand Manager works with the research and development team to determine not only why, but what can be done to turn the problem around.

An important function of the Brand Manager is locating key markets and potential customers. To do this, he or she might deal with the advertising department or the advertising agency in charge of the brand not only to locate these markets, but also to find ways to reach them.

Will advertising in a new media increase sales? Will it pay off? Can the Brand Manager fit the new advertising campaign into his or her budget? There are always questions that need to be looked into, researched, and answered.

The Brand Manager is always on the lookout for the best way to pitch the brand or product to the consumer. In order to gauge the consumer's reaction, he or she works with the market research departments. The Brand Manager also works with members of the production, packaging, promotion, distribution, advertising, and sales departments in developing the most effective packaging, promotional materials, advertisements, and commercials. He or she is also expected to develop pricing and distribution strategies. The Brand Manager does everything possible to make the brand competitive in the marketplace.

When new products in the brand are introduced, the Brand Manager also works closely with the public relations department and/or agency in launching a media blitz and coordinating public relations activities. He or she is expected to monitor and control all advertising and promotions within the brand. As part of the job, the individual is also responsible for keeping up with industry trends and the competition.

The Brand Manager is essential to the success of the brand. His or her decisions and expertise can make the difference between a brand or product "making it" and one that ultimately falls between the cracks. For those who enjoy being in the forefront of the corporate industry, this might be the ideal career choice.

Salaries
There is a wide range of salaries for corporate Brand Managers. Individuals in this field generally earn from $30,000 to $150,000 or more annually. Factors affecting earnings include the size, prestige, and geographic location of the company in which the individual works. Other factors include the experience and professional reputation of the Brand Manager. In many cases, individuals also receive bonuses based on increased product sales.

Employment Prospects
Employment prospects are good for talented Brand Managers. Positions may be offered in a variety of companies hosting multiple brands, including those that manufacture products as well as companies that provide services. Individuals may need to relocate to find a position.

Advancement Prospects
Advancement prospects are fair for Brand Managers. Those who prove themselves will have no trouble moving up the corporate career ladder. There are a number of ways individuals working in this area can advance their career.

The common forms of career progression are either finding a similar job in larger, more prestigious company or being promoted within the same agency to handle a more prestigious brand. Some individuals climb the career ladder by becoming corporate marketing directors for large companies.

Education and Training
Most companies require a minimum of a bachelor's degree for this position. Helpful majors include marketing, advertising, communications, or a related field.

Seminars and workshops in market research, branding, marketing, and advertising will be useful in honing skills.

Experience, Skills, and Personality Traits
Brand Managers working in the corporate world need experience in branding and marketing. This experience is generally obtained by working in the marketing department.

The most successful Brand Managers are highly motivated, ambitious, energetic individuals. Excellent written and verbal communication skills are essential. Individuals should be detail-oriented and have the ability to multitask without getting flustered. The ability to prioritize and organize is vital.

Creativity and innovation are a must. Interpersonal skills and the ability to understand people's thought patterns are helpful. Excellent analytical and quantitative abilities are crucial.

Unions and Associations
Brand Managers working in the corporate world may belong to a number of associations that provide career guidance and professional support. These include the American Marketing Association (AMA), the Direct Marketing Association (DMA), the Marketing Research Association (MRA), and the Advertising Research Foundation (ARF), among others.

Tips for Entry
1. If you're still in school, look for an internship. These are valuable in providing experience and helping you make important contacts.
2. Take classes, workshops, and seminars in marketing, brand management, and consumer research. In addition to honing your skills, they provide excellent networking opportunities.
3. Positions may be advertised in the classified section of newspapers under heading classifications such as "Brand Manager," "Product Manager," "Marketing,"

"Corporate and Industry," or in specific corporate company advertisements.

4. Jobs may be advertised in trade journals

5. Don't forget to check out openings on the Web. Start with some of the more popular career and job sites like Hotjobs.com or Monster.com and go from there.

6. Corporate Web sites often list job openings. Visit the sites of companies you might be interested in working for.

ASSISTANT ADVERTISING MANAGER, CORPORATE/INDUSTRY

CAREER PROFILE

Duties: Assist advertising director in the development and implementation of corporate advertising campaigns; create advertisements; perform research; assist in the development of annual advertising budget

Alternate Title(s): Assistant Advertising Coordinator

Salary Range: $23,500 to $58,000+

Employment Prospects: Fair

Advancement Prospects: Fair

Best Geographical Location(s): Positions are located throughout the country.

Prerequisites:

Education or Training—Four-year college degree required

Experience—Experience in advertising is usually required

Special Skills and Personality Traits—Understanding of the advertising industry; creative; innovative; copywriting skills; knowledge of layout and graphics; persuasive

CAREER LADDER

```
┌─────────────────────────────────┐
│      Director of Advertising     │
└─────────────────────────────────┘

┌─────────────────────────────────┐
│   Assistant Advertising Manager  │
└─────────────────────────────────┘

┌─────────────────────────────────┐
│      Advertising, Promotion,     │
│      or Marketing Assistant      │
└─────────────────────────────────┘
```

Position Description

The Assistant Advertising Manager of a corporation works with the advertising director to develop an advertising program for the company. The individual will assist the director of the department in estimating and/or developing an annual budget and implementing the program.

In some corporations there are large advertising departments filled with artists, copywriters, researchers, and media buyers. In others there might be just a director of advertising or a director and an Assistant Advertising Manager. Depending on the size and structure of the corporation and the advertising department, the individual will have varied duties.

It is part of the responsibility of the Assistant Advertising Manager to develop advertising campaigns and programs that are both effective and cost-efficient. He or she has to know the company and its products inside out. With this information the individual can create innovative ads and promotions that will attract consumers and sell products.

In certain corporations the Assistant Advertising Manager is responsible only for the advertising of a specific product. For example, the individual may work for a corporation that produces women's cosmetics, men's hair products, and a line of vitamins. The Assistant Advertising Manager may just be responsible for developing the advertising program for the women's cosmetic line.

If the corporation is not very large or the company does not have its own researchers, the Assistant Advertising Manager may be expected to do research. He or she may research the company's prior advertising campaigns and their effectiveness or may delve into consumer buying trends. The individual may do profiles on those who use the company's products in order to develop better advertising programs. He or she might also evaluate secondary research done by others. The Assistant Advertising Manager may be required to write questionnaires for consumer information files or supervise research interviews.

The Assistant Advertising Manager works with the director of the department in preparing annual media budgets. The individual is often required to do a lot of the legwork associated with this function. He or she may have to obtain rate cards, discount information, and demographics from various media, as well as meet with media representatives. Media costs can then be estimated for the coming year. In some companies the advertising department reviews the advertising expenditures of competitive companies. This responsibility usually falls to the Assistant Advertising Manager.

Depending on the size of the corporation and the advertising department, the Assistant Advertising Manager may be responsible for writing copy, creating graphics, and doing layout for print ads. He or she might also create storyboards and scripts for television or radio commercials or oversee their production and taping. Conversely, the individual might supervise others in the department who are performing these tasks or may be required to hire freelance or outside people.

The Assistant Advertising Manager is often required to place ads, purchase space or time on television or radio, and come up with promotions. In certain corporations the advertising department carries out functions of promotion and marketing. In others the department develops advertisements for promotions that have been created by the promotion or marketing department.

The Assistant Advertising Manager may be responsible for checking billing, authorizing payments, and keeping accurate records. He or she might be required to make sure that copy for ads is accurate, that all ads are reviewed by the director or other proper people, and that ads and commercials are delivered to the media in time for placement.

The Assistant Advertising Manager in the corporate world is often expected to assist with the development of ideas for new products and new product names. He or she may be required to meet with the advertising director, promotion manager, public relations director, or marketing manager to discuss new ideas for advertising and implementation of company products.

The Assistant Advertising Manager is responsible to the director of the advertising department. In certain corporations there is no advertising director. Instead, the marketing director is the immediate supervisor of those working in the advertising department.

The Assistant Advertising Manager is required to work normal business hours, as well as overtime when projects need to be completed or deadlines must be met.

Salaries

Earnings for Assistant Advertising Managers working in the corporate world vary greatly, depending on the job description and location. Individuals can expect salaries to range from $23,500 to $58,000 plus.

Variables in compensation include the size, location, and prestige of the corporation and the experience and responsibilities of the individual. Those working in smaller companies average salaries between $23,500 and $27,000 a year. Mid-size companies may pay Assistant Advertising Managers between $26,000 and $40,000 annually. In larger corporations individuals in this position may earn up to $58,000 or more.

Employment Prospects

Employment prospects are fair for those seeking employment as Assistant Advertising Manager in corporations. Individuals may find job opportunities located throughout the country.

More and more corporations today are using in-house advertising departments instead of advertising agencies. This trend is expected to continue in the coming years.

Individuals with limited experience may find employment prospects better if they look into smaller corporations.

Advancement Prospects

Advancement prospects are fair for Assistant Advertising Managers. Some people may advance by keeping the same job title but moving to a larger, more prestigious corporation that provides increased earnings. Others climb the career ladder by becoming the director of the advertising department.

In order to advance, individuals must be conscientious, creative, and innovative while performing their jobs.

Education and Training

Most corporations require that individuals hold four-year college degrees. Good choices for majors for those interested in working in corporate advertising include advertising, marketing, public relations, communications, liberal arts, English, or business.

Graduate degrees are often useful to those who seek rapid advancement.

Experience, Skills, and Personality Traits

The Assistant Advertising Manager working in a large or mid-sized corporation is usually required to have experience in advertising. This might come through an internship or training program. Other individuals obtain experience working in the advertising, marketing, or promotion departments. On occasion smaller companies might hire someone right out of college if his or her résumé looks good and the individual shows talent. Working in a smaller company is also a good way to gain experience.

Assistant Advertising Managers should be creative and innovative people. A complete understanding of the advertising industry is necessary. Individuals should have copywriting skills as well as a knowledge of graphics and layout.

The successful Assistant Advertising Manager is articulate, aggressive, personable, and persuasive. He or she should have a working knowledge of all advertising techniques, processes, and policies.

Unions and Associations

Assistant Advertising Managers working in corporations do not belong to any union. They may belong to a number of trade associations. These groups provide members with informational and educational seminars, conferences, and materials. They also provide a forum for individuals working in the advertising industry.

These groups include the American Advertising Federation (AAF), the Direct Marketing Association, Inc. (DMA), the Advertising Club of New York, the Advertising Research Foundation (ARF), Advertising Women of New York, Inc. (AWNY), Business Marketing Association (BMA), and the Association of National Advertisers, Inc. (ANA).

Individuals might also be members of trade associations that are specific to their particular corporations.

Tips for Entry

1. Large corporations may offer internships or training programs. These are useful because they give you hands-on experience and help you make important contacts.
2. Join trade associations—especially those that offer student memberships. These groups can often provide you with job information and leads.
3. Read the trades. These magazines frequently advertise job openings and keep you up on current trends in advertising. If you can't find them in your local library or magazine store, write to the publisher about a short-term subscription.
4. Jobs are also advertised in the newspaper classified section. Look under category headings of "Business," "Advertising," or "Corporations."
5. Attend seminars in all phases of advertising. Not only will you hone your skills, but you will also make more professional contacts.
6. Check out job opportunities online. Many companies have job openings listed on their Web site.

COPYWRITER, CORPORATE/INDUSTRY

CAREER PROFILE

Duties: Write copy for internal and external publications; develop copy for print advertising, broadcast commercials, and outdoor media

Alternate Title(s): None

Salary Range: $23,000 to $60,000+

Employment Prospects: Good

Advancement Prospects: Good

Best Geographical Location(s): Positions are located throughout the country.

Prerequisites:

Education or Training—Four-year degree required, with major in public relations, English, journalism, communications, marketing, advertising, or liberal arts

Experience—Writing experience helpful, but not required in all positions.

Special Skills and Personality Traits—Good writing skills; creative; articulate; good grammar, spelling, and word usage; ability to work quickly and accurately

CAREER LADDER

```
┌─────────────────────────────┐
│    Publications Manager      │
└─────────────────────────────┘

┌─────────────────────────────┐
│        Copywriter            │
└─────────────────────────────┘

┌─────────────────────────────┐
│  Journalist Position, Intern,│
│      or Entry Level          │
└─────────────────────────────┘
```

Position Description

Copywriters working in corporations and industry have varied responsibilities depending on the structure of the company and the department they are working in.

Individuals may be responsible for writing the copy for any of the internal or external publications the corporation produces and/or the copy for corporate ads and commercials. The Copywriter may be required to write news releases, feature articles, newsletters, brochures, leaflets, annual reports, letters, and memos. He or she might also be responsible for writing stockholder reports, annual reports, proposals, speeches, scripts for audiovisual material, instructional booklets, giveaway sheets, and promotional materials.

In order for the Copywriter to do his or her job accurately, he or she generally has to do some sort of research to obtain the required facts. This research might include anything from talking to a department head to obtain information on a press release to using the library to obtain needed facts. It is imperative that all information used by the Copywriter is accurate.

Copywriters who write speeches for corporate executives usually have to spend some time with the executives. The individual must write speeches in an informative, interesting, and often witty manner. He or she meets with an executive and decides what topic must be covered. The Copywriter then tries to write in the "voice" of the speaker.

Speech writing is difficult for most people. The speaker often has ideas in his or her mind that are not communicated immediately to the Copywriter. The Copywriter may have to change the speech many times before getting to a final, accepted draft.

The Copywriter may get assignments from a number of sources. These include the publication manager, if there is one; the public relations, marketing, promotion or consumer affairs director; or the advertising manager. The individual may be responsible to any of these people, depending on the structure of the corporation. After the assignment is completed the individual usually has the project approved by the appropriate superior.

The Copywriter may have ongoing assignments, such as weekly internal newsletters, weekly press releases for the media, monthly feature articles for a newspaper or magazine.

If the Copywriter is working in the advertising department, he or she may be responsible for developing innovative, creative copy for both print advertisements and radio or television commercials. The individual may also be required to write copy for billboards and other outdoor advertisements.

He or she may be required to write headlines, body copy, or both. Depending on the structure of the advertising department, the Copywriter may be responsible for developing the entire theme of an ad or series of ads or may work with the theme provided for him or her by the advertising director.

The individual may be responsible for writing copy for other things, including direct mail pieces, sales letters, promotional materials, manuals, and posters.

The Copywriter working in a corporate setting usually works normal business hours. He or she may, however, take work home or come up with ideas for copy at night or on weekends. It is hard to turn off creativity. When projects need to be completed or advertising deadlines are near, he or she may be required to work overtime.

Salaries

Salaries may differ greatly for individuals in this job. Factors for this include the skills, experience, and responsibilities of the Copywriter. Other differentials include the size and location of the corporation.

Earnings may begin as low as $23,000 and go up to $30,000 annually for individuals just entering the job force. Experienced, creative Copywriters who carry a lot of job responsibility in a large corporation may earn up to $60,000 or more a year.

Employment Prospects

Employment prospects are good for individuals seeking employment as Copywriters in corporate businesses. There are thousands of corporations that hold employment possibilities located all over the country.

There is also a high turnover in this position due to advancement and promotion. This is especially true at the entry level.

Advancement Prospects

Advancement prospects are good for Copywriters working in corporations. An individual can take a number of different paths in climbing the career ladder. The Copywriter may become a publications manager. He or she might advance to be assistant director of public relations. An individual may also stay a Copywriter but locate a position in a larger, more prestigious corporation or possibly an advertising or public relations agency.

Education and Training

Most corporate positions for Copywriters require a four-year degree. Good choices for majors might include English, journalism, public relations, marketing, communications, advertising, or liberal arts.

Additional courses and seminars in all facets of writing, advertising, publicity, and public relations will prove useful to the individual.

Experience, Skills, and Personality Traits

Copywriters must enjoy writing. Whether they are writing copy for advertisements, press releases, brochures, audio or audiovisual scripts, or newsletters, they must be able to do it in an interesting, creative, clear, factual manner. The individual must have a working knowledge of grammar, word usage, and spelling.

Copywriters should have the ability to work quickly and accurately. They must know how to research information for articles and check details for accuracy. Typing, word processing, and/or computer ability is necessary for most positions.

The Copywriter should be able to communicate effectively in person as well as on paper. This is especially important for those who want to climb the career ladder rapidly.

Many Copywriters working in corporations entered the job market right out of college. Others worked in journalism positions as reporters or columnists.

Unions and Associations

Copywriters working in the corporate world may belong to a number of trade associations that help bring them together with others in the same line of work. The associations also offer conferences, seminars, courses, and professional guidance.

Depending on the individual's duties, he or she may belong to any of the following organizations: the Public Relations Society of America (PRSA), the American Advertising Federation (AAF), the American Marketing Association, the Advertising Club of New York, the Advertising Research Foundation (ARF), Advertising Women of New York, Inc. (AWNY), the One Club, the International Association of Business Communicators (IABC), the Association for Business Communications (ABC), and the Association for Women In Communications (AWC).

Tips for Entry

1. Get as much experience writing as you can. Volunteer to write press releases, newsletters, and advertising copy for local civic and nonprofit groups.
2. Join your school newspaper. This will give you valuable hands-on experience.
3. Consider finding a summer or part-time job at a local newspaper or magazine as a reporter or columnist.

Work experience always looks good on an entry-level résumé.

4. Take courses and seminars on all varieties or writing. Hone your skills.

5. Put together a portfolio of your work that has appeared in print. If you have nothing, put together a portfolio of samples of different kinds of writing. For example, include press releases, photo captions, feature articles, ad copy, etc.

6. Join trade associations and attend their meetings, conferences, and seminars. These can help you learn more about your craft and help to build a list of professional contacts.

7. Many large corporations offer internships and training programs. Try to locate one of these and ask to work in the publications, public relations, or advertising department.

8. Don't forget to check out job openings on company Web sites.

9. Job possibilities might also be located on job and career Web sites such as Monster.com and Hotjobs.com.

ASSISTANT ART DIRECTOR, CORPORATE/INDUSTRY

CAREER PROFILE

Duties: Assist art director of corporate advertising department formulating advertisements and ad campaigns; create ads

Alternate Title(s): Junior Art Director; Art Director Assistant; Associate Art Director

Salary Range: $25,000 to $55,000+

Employment Prospects: Fair

Advancement Prospects: Fair

Best Geographical Location(s): Positions may be located throughout the country.

Prerequisites:

Education or Training—Art school training or college degree in fine art, commercial art, graphics, communications, or advertising preferred

Experience—Experience working in advertising or art departments is useful, but not always required.

Special Skills and Personality Traits—Creative; artistic ability; understanding of the advertising industry; working knowledge of graphics, layout, pasteups, photography, typefaces, and desktop publishing

CAREER LADDER

```
┌─────────────────────────────────────┐
│            Art Director             │
└─────────────────────────────────────┘

┌─────────────────────────────────────┐
│       Assistant Art Director        │
└─────────────────────────────────────┘

┌─────────────────────────────────────┐
│ College Student, Entry Level of Artist │
└─────────────────────────────────────┘
```

Position Description

The Assistant Art Director working in the advertising department of a corporation can have varied responsibilities depending on the size and structure of the company he or she is working in. In some corporations the individual might be responsible for advertisements from the initial concept through completion. In others, he or she may be delegated responsibilities to complete only certain phases of the advertisement.

The individual may create ads for any type of media, including newspapers, magazines, billboards, direct mail, packaging, promotion, posters, books, or broadcast.

In very large corporations the individual is responsible for helping the senior art director supervise artists, designers, copywriters, and illustrators. In smaller industries the Assistant Art Director may function as an artist, illustrator, and copywriter.

The Assistant Art Director working in the advertising department of a corporation may be required to design advertisements and commercials that are eye-catching and effective. He or she assists in the development of the graphics, typography, photography, color, illustration—the entire look and layout of the advertisements.

If the corporation is small, the Assistant Art Director may choose or design type styles, sizes, and colors for both the headlines and the body copy. If the company is larger, the Assistant Art Director may recommend or review the suggestions of the other artists working in the department. The Assistant Art Director may sketch or draw art and graphics to be used in advertisements, or he or she may just offer suggestions to the artists to render or produce.

The Assistant Art Director is often at a "shoot" when a photographer is taking a picture for an advertisement. The assistant tells the individual exactly how he or she wants the finished photo to look, and what should be emphasized, in order to make the advertising effective.

If the corporation is working with television broadcast commercials, the Assistant Art Director has additional duties. He or she may be responsible for locating freelance people to work on a commercial, including producers, directors, camera people, set designers, etc. The individual may sketch out storyboards indicating the way the set should be designed, photographed, and lit. The Assistant Art Director is also responsible for having design work done for any graphics and type to be used in the television commercial.

The Assistant Art Director may work with the corporate graphic designers developing the art, graphics, and layout for company logos, packaging, corporate identity, promotional or sales materials, brochures, leaflets, or booklets. Depending on the size of the department, the structure of the company, and the individual's duties, he or she may also be responsible for doing the actual designing and developing of ideas.

The individual is often assigned the task of finding outside or freelance people to perform various functions, including airbrushing, type design, photography, and illustration. In addition to locating these people, he or she may have to negotiate fees, make sure payments are made promptly, supervise workers, and approve their work.

The Assistant Art Director is required to attend meetings with the senior art director and directors or managers from the promotion, marketing, public relations, and sales departments. He or she may also attend meetings with executives and owners of the company to obtain feedback, concepts, and ideas for advertisements.

The Assistant Art Director is responsible to the senior art director in the advertising department. He or she must get used to working with the pressure and stress of meeting deadlines. While the individual may work normal business hours, he or she is often required to work overtime to develop ideas, finish advertisements, or attend meetings.

Salaries

Salaries for Assistant Art Directors working in the corporate world differ from job to job depending on the company and its size, prestige, and location. Salaries also depend on the individual's experience level and his or her responsibilities and duties.

Earnings can range from approximately $25,000 for an individual with little or no experience or one working in a small company to $55,000 or more for one with more experience, with more responsibility, or in a large corporation.

Employment Prospects

Employment prospects are fair for individuals seeking employment as Assistant Art Directors in corporate settings.

Opportunities will get better in the coming years, as more and more companies are taking charge of their own advertising, eliminating the use of advertising agencies.

There are numerous corporations located throughout the country that have internal advertising and art departments and therefore offer this position. Individuals can often get a job as an Assistant Art Director in a smaller company right after graduation from college without a great deal of experience.

Advancement Prospects

Advancement prospects are fair for Assistant Art Directors. There is a lot of turnover in all departments in the corporate world. The advertising and art departments are no different.

Individuals may climb the career ladder by becoming the Assistant Art Director in a larger, more prestigious corporation or by obtaining a position as a full-fledged art director.

Education and Training

The Assistant Art Director is usually required to hold a bachelor's degree in either fine arts or commercial art. While many creative art positions do not require formal training, most corporations prefer that individuals in executive positions hold at least a four-year college degree.

Although the individual may just be supervising other artists, letterers, photographers, and pasteup people, he or she must also be able to perform these tasks if need be.

Courses and seminars on advertising as well as graphic arts, pasteup, layout, and photography are useful in honing skills.

Experience, Skills, and Personality Traits

The Assistant Art Director working in a corporate setting must have management skills. He or she may be in charge of the work of freelance and corporate artists, graphics people, and photographers. The individual must know how to set priorities and be able to meet deadlines without getting flustered.

The Assistant Art Director should be creative, artistic, and fully able to perform most art tasks. A working knowledge of pasteup, layout, typography, sketching, drawing, painting, photography, mechanicals, computer graphics programs, and desktop publishing is necessary. A sense of style and design is imperative.

The individual must have the ability not only to visualize an advertisement, but to communicate ideas as well. The Assistant Art Director must be articulate and personable. He or she often meets with management and directors of other departments.

While many Assistant Art Directors with little experience find employment just after graduation, the individual is usually required to present a portfolio of work and ideas for review.

Unions and Associations

Assistant Art Directors working in corporations do not belong to any union. Individuals may, however, be members of a variety of trade associations. These groups often offer educational guidance, and the chance to get together with others in the same field. Some of these organizations include the American Advertising Federation (AAF), the Art Directors Club, Inc. (ADC), the One Club, the Society of Illustrators, the Graphic Artists Guild (GAG), and the American Institute of Graphic Arts (AIGA).

Individuals might also belong to trade associations specific to their industries.

Tips for Entry

1. Put together a portfolio of your best work. If you have no real experience, include work you have done while in school. Make sure, however, that nothing in the portfolio is of mediocre quality and that it is creative, imaginative, versatile, and neat.
2. Many large corporations offer training programs and internships. Write and inquire.
3. Job openings are often advertised in trade journals and classified sections of the newspaper. Look under heading classifications of "Advertising," "Artist," "Art Director," or "Corporations."
4. Join trade associations. Many offer student memberships. Some provide job guidance and will even review your portfolio and make suggestions as to what will make it better.
5. Work on school publications to get experience with layout, type styles, headline sizes, and graphics.
6. Consider a part-time or summer job in the advertising or art department of a newspaper or magazine. It will give you hands-on experience.
7. Don't forget Internet companies when job hunting.

GRAPHIC DESIGNER, CORPORATE/INDUSTRY

CAREER PROFILE

Duties: Develop graphics for corporation; design packaging; design corporate graphics

Alternate Title(s): Graphic Artist; Artist

Salary Range: $23,000 to $50,000+

Employment Prospects: Good

Advancement Prospects: Fair

Best Geographical Location(s): Positions may be located throughout the country.

Prerequisites:

Education or Training—Four-year college degree with major in art required in most positions; art school helpful in others

Experience—Art and advertising experience is helpful but not always required.

Special Skills and Personality Traits—Understanding of advertising; creative; artistic ability; knowledge of pasteups, mechanicals, typography, color, and photography; drawing and illustration skills; knowledge of computer graphics software and desktop publishing

CAREER LADDER

```
┌─────────────────────────────┐
│    Assistant Art Director    │
└─────────────────────────────┘

┌─────────────────────────────┐
│      Graphic Designer        │
└─────────────────────────────┘

┌─────────────────────────────┐
│ Entry Level, College or Art School │
│ Student or Freelance Commercial    │
│      or Graphic Artist             │
└─────────────────────────────┘
```

Position Description

The Graphic Designer working in a corporate or industry setting in responsible for filling the function of designing and developing graphics for a variety of the company's artistic and publication needs. The individual in this position is usually part of the advertising and promotion department. He or she consults with the research and sales departments as well as with management during the course of carrying out his or her job.

It is the responsibility of the Graphic Designer to develop graphics that are creative, innovative, appealing, and memorable. The individual has varied duties depending on the type of business he or she is working in and the structure of the company. Graphic Designers working in corporations can work in almost any type of industry, from manufacturers of consumer-oriented products and food companies to book publishers and record companies.

One of the main functions of the corporate Graphic Designer is to develop designs for the company's packaging. Package design is important to all companies. It is another form of advertising for the product. When the product is on the shelf in the marketplace, the package must catch the eye of the consumer in order to sell. He or she will be responsible for developing the creative concept, which might include the most effective shape and color or the artwork appearing on the outside of the box or packaging.

If the Graphic Designer is working for a book publisher, for example, he or she may be responsible for designing the way the interior of books look and choosing the correct type, book jackets, and book displays. This completed work helps sell the product in the store. Individuals working as Graphic Designers in record companies may be responsible for designing record jackets. Whatever the industry, the job is similar.

The Graphic Designer may be required to develop corporate graphics. These could include logos, stationery, envelopes, order forms, labels, sales tags, and calendars. Designs are not limited to paper products. The individual may have to design the logos and messages on the sides of company trucks that will be moving the corporation's merchandise.

The whole purpose of this creative effort is to design something that represents the company in a positive manner. The individual constantly tries to develop designs that will make people think of and remember the company name and what it represents.

Graphic Designers are often responsible for developing the design of brochures, booklets, pamphlets, posters, billboards, or the art in advertisements. The individual may be required to design promotional material. This could include items that help to advertise, market, or promote products or services. Examples include point-of-purchase promotions, signs, display racks, and shelves.

In designing all advertising and promotional pieces, logos, and packaging, the Graphic Designer must always try to keep the image of the company prominently identified. He or she usually tries to keep the design of all product names, graphics, and logos closely tied together so that customers will relate the design to the company. If, for example, Campbell's soup constantly changed its logo and the color of its soup cans, customers might not identify the right brand of soup—or, worse yet, might not be able to locate the brand on the shelf. That is why so many store or generic brands look similar to nationally marketed brands. Advertising departments tell Graphic Designers to design labels that look the same as those of publicized brands in the hope that customers won't notice the difference.

Often, the Graphic Designer is required to come up with a number of different package designs, logos, or advertisements. The research department takes the samples and test-markets them. After the results are in, the Graphic Designer finalizes the sample that tested the most effectively.

Depending on the size of the corporation, there may be only a single Graphic Designer in the company, or there may be a large pool. The Graphic Designer works normal business hours. He or she may work late or develop designs at home when a project is due. The individual is usually responsible to the art director of the corporate advertising and promotion department.

Salaries

There is a wide range in salaries for corporate Graphic Designers. Individuals entering the corporate world in this position may earn from $23,000 to $30,000 annually. Talented Graphic Designers who have a great deal of responsibility and those working in larger corporations may earn up to $45,000 a year. Individuals who have proven themselves by developing outstanding logos and graphics that are identified with the company may earn $50,000 or more.

Employment Prospects

Employment prospects are good for Graphic Designers who want to work in corporations and industry. There are companies, large and small, located throughout the country that offer job possibilities. Many of the larger corporations have a dozen or more individuals working in the department.

Individuals may often obtain jobs by demonstrating that they have the skills, if not the experience. This is done by exhibiting samples of work in the form of a portfolio.

Advancement Prospects

Advancement prospects are fair for Graphic Designers working in the corporate world, depending on how the individual wants to climb the career ladder. The Graphic Designer may become the assistant art director for the advertising department in the same corporation where he or she is currently working, or possibly at another company. The individual may want to advance his or her career by remaining a Graphic Designer but locating a position in a larger, more prestigious corporation with additional responsibility and a higher salary. The Graphic Designer might also move up the career ladder by seeking a higher-paying position in an advertising agency.

Education and Training

Education requirements for this job differ from position to position. Many, if not most, corporations require a four-year college degree with a major in art. There are a few jobs that only require art school training. In order for the individual to advance in his or her career it is often necessary to have the college degree.

Courses in all facets of graphic design are necessary. Other helpful courses and seminars include package design, advertising, photography, and corporate identity.

Experience, Skills, and Personality Traits

Graphic Designers working in corporations should be creative, artistically talented people with an innate sense of design. Individuals must be skilled in all facets of art. These include sketching, drawing, and painting. The Graphic Designer should have a working knowledge of pasteups, mechanicals, typography, color photography, computer graphics software, and desktop publishing.

An understanding of the type of industry the individual is working in is necessary. The Graphic Designer often relates to management and other departments within the framework of his or her work. It is imperative that he or she be articulate and have good communication and interpersonal skills.

Unions and Associations

Graphic Designers working in corporations do not belong to a union. Individuals may be members of a number of trade associations that can put them in touch with others in their field, often provide training and seminars, and offer professional guidance. These might include the Graphic Artists Guild (GAG), the Art Directors Club, Inc. (ADC), the One Club, the Society of Illustrators, the American Advertising Federation (AAF), or the American Institute of Graphic Arts (AIGA).

Tips for Entry

1. Put together a portfolio of your best work. Make sure it is neat and creative. To get almost any job in this field, you will need this portfolio.

2. Join trade associations. Many of them offer to critique your portfolio and give constructive criticism on making it better.

3. Try to locate an internship or training program. These are most often found in the very large corporations. Write and inquire.

4. You might consider a part-time or summer job working in a corporation, manufacturing plant, or other business. This will give you hands-on experience with corporate life. While working there you will be able to see the way corporations run from the bottom up.

5. Make sure you're comfortable using a variety of computer graphics programs.

6. Check out openings on the Web.

MARKETING ASSISTANT, CORPORATE/INDUSTRY

CAREER PROFILE

Duties: Assist the manager or director of marketing with plans and campaigns; perform clerical duties; input data into computers; research information

Alternate Title(s): Marketing Representative

Salary Range: $23,000 to $38,000+

Employment Prospects: Good

Advancement Prospects: Fair

Best Geographical Location(s): Job possibilities may be located throughout the country.

Prerequisites:

Education or Training—Four-year college degree required

Experience—Marketing, promotion, public relations, or advertising experience helpful, but not always required

Special Skills and Personality Traits—Creative; innovative; energetic; excellent communication and writing skills; ambitious; aggressive; high motivation; computer ability

CAREER LADDER

```
┌─────────────────────────────────┐
│  Marketing Manager, Coordinator,│
│      or Assistant Director      │
└─────────────────────────────────┘

┌─────────────────────────────────┐
│      Marketing Assistant        │
└─────────────────────────────────┘

┌─────────────────────────────────┐
│      Entry Level or Trainee     │
└─────────────────────────────────┘
```

Position Description

The Marketing Assistant working in a corporation helps the marketing manager fulfill his or her duties. Depending on the individual's experience level, he or she may be responsible for anything from performing secretarial duties to assisting with the development of a corporate marketing plan.

The marketing director is responsible for developing the concepts and campaigns that detail how the company's products will get to the consumer. The Marketing Assistant helps in this endeavor. The marketing department in a corporation works in conjunction with the sales, promotion, advertising, and public relations departments. Marketing decides how much and what type of advertising, promotion, public relations, and selling will be most effective. It also decides matters such as the most effective techniques to market the company, its products, and its services, and the viability of introducing new products. The marketing department may try to market a new product, only to find

out that buyers are not really interested in it or that the product isn't financially viable for the company.

The Marketing Assistant assists the marketing director in the planning and coordination of all the company's marketing goals and objectives. He or she is expected to help plan and organize projects and become involved in promotions and presentations.

The Marketing Assistant works closely with the marketing director on a variety of projects, providing clerical and other types of support. He or she may be required to type letters, reports, proposals, and memos. The Marketing Assistant often makes phone calls on behalf of the marketing director in order to obtain information. He or she may answer phones to free the director, who may use his or her time to work on special projects.

The Marketing Assistant is required to keep track of all ideas and concepts the director is involved with. He or she may be expected to write preliminary proposals on marketing campaigns outlined by the director. The individual may also be responsible for writing memos or other informational data to keep other departments aware of new marketing plans and campaigns that are taking place within the corporation.

The Marketing Assistant may help coordinate and implement special events and other programs the marketing director has developed. He or she may serve as a liaison with other corporate departments to ensure that a project goes smoothly and according to schedule.

Depending on the experience of the Marketing Assistant, he or she may be responsible for researching facts and data or may just assist the director with a research project. Almost any subject could be researched by the marketing department, including information about potential purchasers of the company's products, individuals who use competitor's products, and the effectiveness of certain advertising or promotions. The individual may work with the corporate research department (if there is one), trade associations, or libraries. He or she may develop questionnaires or conduct interviews to obtain the required information. The assistant may tabulate the data or may just input the information into a computer for review by the director.

The Marketing Assistant may help the director develop and implement promotional ideas, advertising concepts, or new ways to sell. For example, a company's product may always have been sold in retail outlets. Through marketing research, information may be developed that indicates that people purchasing the product would rather purchase it through the mail. The Marketing Assistant may help write sales promotion letters or direct mail pieces in order to initiate the new concept.

Other duties may include the preparation of promotional brochures, press releases, or newsletters and attendance at trade shows, conventions, and fairs on behalf of the company.

The Marketing Assistant is directly responsible to the marketing director, coordinator, or manager, depending on the structure of the company. While the individual works normal business hours most of the time, he or she may often be required to work overtime on projects, special events, and promotions.

Salaries

Marketing Assistants can earn between $23,000 and $38,000 or more annually, depending on the corporation they work for and their responsibilities and duties.

Employment Prospects

There is a large turnover in marketing due to career advancement, individuals leaving for jobs in other corporations, and the general mobility of people who enter this field.

Employment prospects, therefore, are good for Marketing Assistants who are seeking jobs in the corporate world.

Almost every midsize or larger company has a marketing department and often at least one assistant. Job opportunities can be located throughout the country in metropolitan and suburban areas.

Advancement Prospects

Advancement prospects are fair for Marketing Assistants. Individuals who work hard, learn marketing concepts, and have the ability to implement them will climb the career ladder. The next step up for the Marketing Assistant is the position of marketing manager, coordinator, or assistant director, depending on how the company is structured.

While many individuals find career advancement through promotion within the company, some find it easier to seek advanced positions by moving on to other corporations.

Education and Training

Most corporations require that their Marketing Assistants hold a minimum of a four-year college degree. Good choices for majors include marketing, public relations, advertising, business administration, liberal arts, or communications.

Courses should also be taken in English, psychology, sociology, research, and statistics.

Experience, Skills, and Personality Traits

The Marketing Assistant needs to be articulate, with excellent communication skills. He or she should be both creative and innovative. The ability to write well is necessary. The Marketing Assistant should have a good command of spelling and word usage. Computer competency is essential.

The assistant should be ambitious, aggressive, highly motivated, and energetic. He or she needs the ability to handle many details and a variety of projects at one time.

The individual must have the ability to perform clerical and secretarial duties such as typing, filing, making calls, and responding to phone calls. It is imperative that the Marketing Assistant knows how to use a computer to input information and is comfortable working with it.

A working knowledge of research techniques is a plus in this field.

Unions and Associations

Marketing Assistants working in the corporate world do not belong to any union. They may, however, belong to a number of trade associations. These organizations provide extensive literature about the marketing field and offer seminars and professional and career guidance. Some of these associations are the American Marketing Association (AMA), the Association of National Advertisers (ANA), the Direct Marketing Association (DMA), Business Marketing Association (BMA), the American Advertising Federation (AAF), Association for Women In Communications (AWC) the Marketing Research Association (MRA), Sales and Marketing Executives International (SMEI), and the Association for Business Communication (ABC).

Tips for Entry

1. There is an abundance of marketing seminars given throughout the year. You can locate these through the various trade associations, business organizations, and trade journals. These are helpful for both the educational value and the opportunity to make professional contacts.

2. Join the trade associations. They will be valuable to you in searching for internships, scholarships, and training programs. They also offer a wealth of helpful literature.

3. Jobs may be advertised in trade journals as well as the classified sections of newspapers. Look under the heading classifications of "Marketing," "Market Research," "Public Relations," "Promotion," or "Advertising."

4. Consider sending your résumé and a cover letter to a number of corporations. There is a big turnover in this field. Ask that your résumé be kept on file.

5. You may want to consider a part-time job as an interviewer for a research firm. These jobs are relatively easy to obtain and will give you experience in interviewing and research techniques.

MARKETING DIRECTOR—WEB SITE

CAREER PROFILE

Duties: Develop and implement marketing plans and campaigns for company's Web site, Web store, etc.; handle day-to-day marketing functions; plan and implement special events; oversee advertising and public relations program

Alternate Title(s): Web site Marketing Director; Internet Catalog Director of Marketing; Marketing Manager

Salary Range: $26,000 to $85,000+

Employment Prospects: Fair

Advancement Prospects: Good

Best Geographical Location(s): Jobs may be located throughout the country.

Prerequisites:

Education or Training—College degree preferred, but not always required

Experience—Marketing, merchandising, publicity, public relations, advertising experience, and Internet experience necessary

Special Skills and Personality Traits—Creative; good verbal and written communication skills; Internet savvy; computer skills

CAREER LADDER

```
┌─────────────────────────────┐
│   Marketing Director at Larger, │
│   More Prestigious Web site,    │
│      or Marketing Director      │
│        in Other Industry        │
└─────────────────────────────┘

┌─────────────────────────────┐
│  Marketing Director at Web site │
└─────────────────────────────┘

┌─────────────────────────────┐
│   Assistant Marketing Director  │
│      or Marketing Director      │
│        in Other Industry        │
└─────────────────────────────┘
```

Position Description

A wide array of businesses and organizations maintain Web sites. Whether a business provides products, services, or information, it is becoming increasingly important to have a presence on the Web.

There are literally thousands of Web sites on the Internet. Some represent companies whose names and reputations were well known even before they established their Internet presence. Others are less well known. The Internet has made it possible for people in almost any part of the world to set up a company as small or large as they like. No matter what the company's size, the site is available to the public.

With so many sites available, how does a Web site attract visitors? As in traditional business, a Web site must market its presence.

The Marketing Director of a Web site has a very important job. He or she is responsible for finding ways to market the site to potential customers. The manner in which this is done can be the success or failure of the site.

The Marketing Director is responsible for developing the concepts and campaigns which will determine how the site will be marketed. The director is expected to determine the most effective techniques and programs to market the site and its contents.

As part of this job, the Marketing Director must plan and coordinate all of the site's marketing goals and objectives. How will people know the Web site exists? How will they know the Web address? Who will the site be marketed toward? Who is the company trying to attract? Marketing a Web site is slightly different than marketing a traditional business, because visitors to online businesses can come from virtually anywhere in the world.

It is essential that the Marketing Director find ways to include the store's Web address in as many places as possible. In some situations, the company may have a traditional "real world" presence that can make it easier to let people know of a new Web site.

The Marketing Director must be sure that the company's Web address is added to all television commercials, print advertisements, and packaging. This helps get the name and address of the online store in front of the public.

The Marketing Director's job becomes more challenging if the company's name isn't recognizable. In this case, he or she must find ways to bring the store to the public's attention, and may utilize a variety of programs to help attract customers and bring people to the company's site.

The Marketing Director must decide which of these programs and services are most viable for his or her specific audience. Often, Marketing Directors advertise the site. They may do this in print, on television, or via banner ads on other sites. Banner ads are the advertisements commonly seen on a Web site where an individual need only click on the banner and it takes the person to the site of the advertiser.

The Marketing Director often does research to obtain information about current and potential customers. He or she may prepare questionnaires or surveys to be placed on the site. In order to entice people to answer questionnaires, the Marketing Director may offer a gift, a percentage off future orders, or free shipping, if the company is selling products.

Marketing Directors must develop innovative ideas to attract new visitors to the site. In many situations, online store Marketing Directors utilize sweepstakes and contests for this purpose. Once people log on to the Web site to enter the contest, the hope is they will return to the site to browse and buy. To accomplish this, many Marketing Directors run contests that visitors can enter daily. This means users may visit the site daily and hopefully see something of interest.

Web site Marketing Directors also use sweepstakes to help build mailing lists. When people enter contests they usually provide their names, addresses, phone numbers, and email address. Additional information may be gathered as well which may be helpful in targeting the site to visitors.

Marketing Directors also use contests to build lists for email newsletters. These newsletters inform customers about company business, store specials, merchandise, and promotions.

The Marketing Director who implements innovative and creative ideas might get the attention of journalists or others doing articles or stories on interesting Web sites. The individual may, for example, contact a television talk or news show to do a segment on an interesting product being sold on the site. Depending on which show a story ends up on, it can lead to thousands of Web site hits.

Depending on the size and structure of the Web site, the Marketing Director may work with an advertising and public relations director. In some situations, the Marketing Director may also be responsible for handling the public relations and advertising functions. In some cases, the Marketing Director may either sell space to other businesses on the site or have salespeople handling this task.

Additional duties of a Web site Marketing Director might include:

- Supervising marketing, public relations, and advertising staff
- Developing marketing budgets
- Designing and developing marketing materials
- Conducting market research
- Developing and providing advertising content.

Salaries

Annual earnings for Web site Marketing Directors range from approximately $26,000 to $85,000 or more. Variables affecting earnings include the size and prestige of the specific site as well as the experience and responsibilities of the individual. Many dot-com companies also offer stock options to their employees as part of their employment package.

Employment Prospects

Employment prospects are fair for this position. As more companies get on the Web, prospects will improve. Jobs can be located throughout the country. Individuals who have a proven track record are most employable.

Advancement Prospects

Marketing Directors in this industry have a number of options for career advancement. Some get experience, prove themselves, and move on to positions at larger or more prestigious sites for increased responsibilities and earnings. Often, companies try to recruit the Marketing Director from a successful Web site.

Other individuals may climb the career ladder by moving into positions as Marketing Directors in other industries. Still other individuals strike out on their own and start their own marketing firms.

Education and Training

Educational requirements vary for Web site Marketing Directors. Smaller or lesser-known sites may prefer a college degree, but do not always require it. Generally, larger, more prestigious, or better-known Web sites will require their Marketing Directors to hold a minimum of a four-year college degree. Good choices for majors include public relations, advertising, business, journalism, marketing, liberal arts, English, communications, and business.

Courses and seminars in marketing, public relations, publicity, promotion, the retail industry, and Web marketing are also helpful.

Experience, Skills, and Personality Traits

Marketing Directors in this industry must be Web savvy. Communications skills, both written and verbal, are essential. Individuals should be creative, innovative, ambitious, articulate, and highly motivated. Marketing Directors also need to be energetic, with the ability to handle many details and projects at one time without getting flustered and stressed.

A knowledge of publicity, promotion, public relations, and advertising, as well as research techniques, is also necessary. Computer skills are essential.

Unions and Associations

Marketing Directors may belong to a number of trade associations that provide support and guidance. These might include the American Marketing Association (AMA), the Marketing Research Association (MRA), the Public Relations Society of America (PRSA), Electronic Retailing Association (ERA), and World Organization of Webmasters (WOW).

Tips for Entry

1. Positions may be advertised in the classified section of newspapers. Look under headings including "Marketing," "Marketing Director," "Web Store," "Web site Marketing," "Corporate Marketing," "Online Store," or "E-Tailing," "E-Commerce."
2. Send your résumé and a cover letter to corporations, companies, stores, and catalogs for which you are interested in working. Ask that your résumé be kept on file if no vacancies are available.
3. Join trade associations. These will help you in searching for internships, scholarships, and training programs in marketing.
4. Jobs may also be advertised in trade journals.
5. Look for jobs online. Check out sites such as www.hotjobs.com and www.monster.com to get started.
6. Take seminars and courses in marketing, promotion, public relations, publicity, and Web marketing. These will give you an edge over other applicants and help you hone your skills and make valuable contacts.

PROMOTION COORDINATOR, CORPORATE/INDUSTRY

CAREER PROFILE

Duties: Develop, create, and implement promotions of corporation's products and services

Alternate Title(s): Promotion Representative

Salary Range: $23,000 to $46,000+

Employment Prospects: Fair

Advancement Prospects: Fair

Best Geographical Location(s): Positions may be located throughout the country.

Prerequisites:

Education or Training—Four-year college degree required

Experience—Publicity or promotion experience required in some but not all jobs

Special Skills and Personality Traits—Creative; innovative; communication skills; ability to deal with many projects and details; good writing skills; personable

CAREER LADDER

```
┌─────────────────────────────┐
│   Director of Promotion,     │
│ Public Relations, Marketing, │
│      or Advertising          │
└─────────────────────────────┘

┌─────────────────────────────┐
│   Promotion Coordinator      │
└─────────────────────────────┘

┌─────────────────────────────┐
│ Publicity or Promotion Assistant │
└─────────────────────────────┘
```

Position Description

The Promotion Coordinator working in a corporate setting is responsible for developing, creating, and implementing promotions and promotional campaigns to help spotlight a company's product or service. The individual works with the corporation's advertising, public relations, marketing, sales, and advertising departments in order to fulfill this function. The Promotion Coordinator may have varied responsibilities depending on the structure of the particular corporation.

The Promotion Coordinator seeks promotional opportunities in both the retail and wholesale fields to promote the corporation's products. The individual may develop sweepstakes or contest promotions to be used in conjunction with the company's consumer advertising campaign or to attract more wholesale customers. For example, a food company might run a recipe contest for professional chefs who use their product in creating dishes. The company might also run a similar contest for the home consumer. Once the contest has been concluded, the Promotion Coordinator might give away cookbooks with the top recipe entries included. Since all recipes would use the company's product and people usually don't throw away cookbooks, the Coordinator would have created a long-lasting promotion.

The Promotion Coordinator is also required to develop point-of-purchase programs. These are the promotions generally used in stores. They usually have some type of display set up in the same location as the company product. The displays might include giveaways, coupons, or promotional products with the company logo. The individual may develop a program in which customers could send in a number of labels from the product and receive in return a camera or a set of mugs. There may or may not be a charge added depending on the program the individual developed. The Promotion Coordinator usually tries to run promotions that are cost effective for the consumer and the company. The important thing is to continually come up with programs that keep the company's name in front of the buyer.

At times the Promotion Coordinator is required to attend and exhibit at trade shows, conferences, and conventions.

The individual may be responsible for designing the booth, display materials, contests, and giveaways that are part of the exhibit. He or she may participate in wholesale shows as well as fairs where the general public comes to buy or become acquainted with products and/or services.

The individual may put together tie-in programs such as the sponsorship of an athletic event like the Olympics or a rock star's worldwide tour. He or she has to work out all the details so that every time the product is advertised it will be tied into the event. The Promotion Coordinator also makes sure that all programs and promotional material contain the name of the product as well as the company logo.

It is the responsibility of the Promotion Coordinator to constantly look for and find new markets for the company's product and new ways to obtain exposure. The individual may use direct mail as a method of marketing or promoting the company's products. He or she may offer samples, coupons, rebates, or discount prices in order to stimulate a consumer to try and buy a product.

He or she might be required to write sales letters, promotional material, and display copy. He or she may also be responsible for developing press releases about promotions and other events.

The Promotion Coordinator may work with the community relations department developing promotions that will attract attention to the company and also help the community. The individual may work with or put together programs such as the sponsorship of nonprofit events and/or make donations of the company's product to worthwhile causes.

These types of programs are used to help keep the company's name and image in the public eye. They are used for advertising as well as public relations and goodwill purposes.

Depending on the structure and size of the company there may be more than one Promotion Coordinator in the department. The individual may be responsible to the promotion director, if the company has one, or to the public relations or marketing director. While the Promotion Coordinator is supposed to work normal business hours, he or she is often required to work overtime to finish projects or implement promotions.

Salaries

Annual earnings for Promotion Coordinators may range from $23,000 to $46,000 or more depending on the responsibilities and experience of the individual as well as the size of the corporation.

Promotion Coordinators who do not have a lot of on-the-job experience will earn between $23,000 and $30,000. Individuals working in larger corporations, with more experience and handling additional responsibilities, have salaries averaging between $27,000 and $35,000. There are some Promotion Coordinators in the corporate world who are earning $46,000 or more a year.

Employment Prospects

Employment prospects for Promotion Coordinators in corporations are fair. While there are thousands of corporations located throughout the country, usually only the midsize and larger companies hire someone for this position. The smaller corporations often expect an individual in the marketing, public relations, or advertising department to perform the functions of the Promotion Coordinator.

Advancement Prospects

Advancement prospects are fair for Promotion Coordinators. Individuals may climb the career ladder in a number of ways. The coordinator may advance to become the director of promotion if the company is structured with this type of position. He or she might become a Promotion Coordinator in a larger, more prestigious company. The individual might also advance by becoming a director or assistant director of public relations, marketing, or advertising.

Education and Training

Most corporations require that Promotion Coordinators have a minimum of a four-year college degree. Good choices for majors include marketing, public relations, communications, advertising, or business.

Seminars on promotion, publicity, advertising, and writing are also useful.

Experience, Skills, and Personality Traits

Promotion Coordinators need to be creative and innovative. They should have the ability to develop ideas that will be unique and attract attention. Individuals should be able to handle details and work on many different projects at once.

The individual should be articulate with good verbal and communications skills and have a pleasant phone manner. He or she will often meet with salespeople, buyers, department heads, and upper management people. The ability to write well is also necessary. The Promotion Coordinator may write preliminary proposals, reports, press releases, and letters.

An ability to get along with others is imperative. The individual in this position needs an abundance of energy and should not mind traveling. He or she may have to go to other locations for trade shows, fairs, and conferences to promote the company.

Unions and Associations

Promotion Coordinators working in corporations do not belong to bargaining unions. Individuals may belong to a number of trade associations including the Advertising Club of New York, Advertising Women of New York, Inc. (AWNY), the American Advertising Federation (AAF), the Business Marketing Association (BMA), the Public Relations

Society of America (PRSA), the American Marketing Association (AMA), the Promotion Marketing Association of America (PMAA), Sales and Marketing Executives International (SMEI), and the Direct/Marketing Association (DMA). These organizations bring individuals in the same field together for seminars, conferences, and training as well as offering professional and educational guidance and literature.

Tips for Entry

1. Join a number of trade associations, especially the ones that offer student memberships. These will give you an opportunity to make professional contacts by attending seminars and conferences as well as providing tips on finding employment.

2. Try to obtain some hands-on experience working in a part-time or summer job doing publicity, promotion, or advertising for any type of business, local radio or television station, or newspaper.

3. There are a good number of internships and training programs in this field. These are offered or sponsored by the larger corporations as well as certain trade associations. Write and inquire.

4. Trade journals often have ads for openings as Promotion Coordinators or representatives.

5. Job possibilities are sometimes advertised in the display or classified advertisement section of the newspaper. Look under heading classifications of "Promotion," "Marketing," "Public Relations," or "Advertising."

ASSISTANT PUBLIC RELATIONS DIRECTOR, CORPORATE/INDUSTRY

CAREER PROFILE

Duties: Assist director of department in fulfilling public relations and publicity functions; help write and produce internal and external communications; promote corporation and enhance its reputation and image

Alternate Title(s): Assistant PR Director; PR Assistant

Salary Range: $25,000 to $55,000+

Employment Prospects: Good

Advancement Prospects: Good

Best Geographical Location(s): Positions may be available throughout the country.

Prerequisites:

Education or Training—Four-year degree in public relations, communications, journalism, liberal arts, or English required

Experience—Writing experience necessary; graphics experience helpful

Special Skills and Personality Traits—Good writing and communication skills; knowledge of graphics, typography, photography, and layout; computer capability; personable; good phone skills; organized

CAREER LADDER

```
┌─────────────────────────────────────┐
│      Public Relations Director       │
└─────────────────────────────────────┘

┌─────────────────────────────────────┐
│  Assistant Public Relations Director │
└─────────────────────────────────────┘

┌─────────────────────────────────────┐
│  Journalist Position, Intern, Trainee,│
│           of Entry Level             │
└─────────────────────────────────────┘
```

Position Description

The Assistant Public Relations Director working in a corporation is responsible for helping the public relations director perform the company's public relations and publicity functions. Duties vary depending on the structure of the company and other corporate departments.

The individual is responsible for assisting the director of the department in relaying information and communications internally to staff employees as well as externally to the outside community and media.

This information exchange might be accomplished through the use of press releases, letters, memos, and reports. The Assistant Public Relations Director or PR assistant, as he or she might be called, is required to both develop and write the press releases, letters, memos, and reports. If the corporation does not have a publications manager, or if the responsibilities

of that job lay in the public relations domain, the individual may be called on to write feature articles, annual reports, newsletters, brochures and leaflets.

The Assistant Public Relations Director is responsible for developing and maintain accurate media and mailing lists. These lists are used to send releases and articles. The individual will also get to know various media personnel and maintain close business relationships. In this way he or she can call the correct person with a story that should be covered or an article in which the media might be interested.

The assistant must be comfortable dealing with the media. He or she may just talk to reporters about a story or actually have to go on television or radio as the corporation spokesperson. It is important that the individual understand corporate policies and follow them to the letter. If information is confidential and the PR assistant lets it leak out, he or she may lose his or her job.

The individual may be required to set up or assist in the setting up of television and radio interviews for people within the corporation. This process is often used to earn goodwill or may be instituted for informational purposes. For example, a corporation that manufactures and distributes cosmetics may want one of their spokespeople to do a media tour touting a new type of makeup. The public relations assistant may call or write to guest coordinators in order to place the spokesperson on various shows. He or she may accompany the corporate spokesperson to the interviews. The individual may also work with the spokesperson, helping him or her come up with flowing answers to the questions that usually are asked.

The individual may screen calls for the director of the department and be required to take care of everyday public relations problems. Depending on whether the company has a customer relations or consumer affairs department, the individual may deal with customer complaints and problems. To do this, he or she may talk to the person who has the complaint and smooth the problem over with a telephone call. The Assistant Public Relations Director may write a letter of apology or explanation to the customer. If the complaint cannot be resolved by the PR assistant, he or she will be responsible for bringing it to the attention of the public relations director to rectify.

The Public Relations Assistant constantly tries to promote the company and enhance its reputation and image. He or she may be asked to meet with community and civic groups as well as to attend luncheons, cocktail parties, and dinners on behalf of the corporation.

Depending on the size of the public relations department, the PR assistant may supervise others. He or she may work with copywriters, graphics people, artists, printers, and photographers. At times the assistant may be required to edit copy or supervise the layout of publications.

In smaller public relations departments, or in situations where the individual is just entering the work force, he or she may be responsible for secretarial-type duties including answering the phones, addressing envelopes, typing press releases, or inputting data into computers.

Individuals may be required to plan or assist with the planning of press conferences, press parties, and news conferences. The assistant can be required to hand-deliver invitations, make arrangements for the room and food, and call people to see if they are planning on attending.

The PR assistant might also be responsible for attending corporate functions that will later be reported in internal newsletters or other communications. He or she may be required to write press releases, take photographs, or arrange for a professional photographer to be on hand at the event.

The Assistant Public Relations Director is responsible to the director of the public relations department. He or she will work normal hours most of the time. When special projects or problems crop up, or a deadline must be met for a news release, annual report, or other publication, the individual will be required to work overtime.

Salaries

Earnings for Assistant Public Relations Directors working in corporations may range from $25,000 to $55,000 plus depending on a number of factors. These include the experience and responsibilities of the individual and the size and location of the corporation.

Employment Prospects

Employment prospects are good for those seeking positions as Assistant Public Relations Directors in corporations and industry. Individuals may have to begin in smaller businesses in order to obtain experience.

There are thousands of corporations throughout the country. Almost every one of them has a public relations department. While jobs may be found in almost any location, individuals may have to relocate in order to find the job of their dreams.

Advancement Prospects

Advancement prospects are good for Assistant Public Relations Directors. The next step up the ladder for these individuals is public relations director or manager.

While most corporations like to promote from within, individuals may have to locate a job in another corporation if the job of director of the department is not vacant.

Education and Training

A minimum of a four-year college degree is required for the job of Assistant Public Relations Director in the corporate world. Good choices for majors include public relations, journalism, communications, marketing, English, or liberal arts.

Seminars relating to public relations skills, publicity, and marketing will also be helpful.

Experience, Skills, and Personality Traits

Assistant Public Relations Directors should be creative, articulate people. Individuals should be personable and enjoy working with people. They should demonstrate both good judgment and common sense.

Good writing skills are necessary. Individuals should be able to write clearly, factually, and quickly in a creative manner.

The ability to speak in public is required in most positions, as well as the ability to communicate on the telephone in a polite, friendly, and effective manner. Assistant Public Relations Directors must also be comfortable talking to media.

Individuals should have a knowledge of graphics, typography, photography, and layout. The ability to type and use word processors and computers is imperative.

Unions and Associations

Individuals working as an Assistant Public Relations Director in a corporation do not belong to a union. They may, however, belong to trade associations specific to their industry as well as to public relations and communications. These organizations provide seminars, conferences, and courses to help individuals hone their skills and make important professional contacts.

Trade associations might include the Public Relations Society of America (PRSA), International Association of Business Communicators (IABC), National Federation of Press Women (NFPW), and the International Public Relations Association (IPRA).

Tips for Entry

1. Obtain hands-on experience in publicity and public relations. Volunteer to be the publicity chairperson for a local civil or nonprofit group.
2. Work on your school newspaper. All writing experience is helpful.
3. Consider a part-time or summer job working on a newspaper.
4. Try to locate an internship in public relations or publicity in a corporate or nonprofit situation.
5. Take all the courses and seminars you can find on public relations, marketing, and publicity. These can help you hone skills as well as make professional contacts.
6. Public relations positions are often advertised in trade journals' "marketplace" or help wanted section. Remember to look in both PR trade journals and other trades specific to the industry you are interested in working in.
7. Job openings are also advertised in display and classified sections or newspapers. Look under heading classifications of "Public Relations," "Publicity," "Communications," "Marketing," and "Promotion."
8. There are employment agencies that deal specifically with public relations jobs. Before you get too deeply involved with these, check to see who pays the fee when you find a position. In some cases, the employee pays. In others, the employer absorbs the cost.
9. Check out employment Web sites such as www.monster.com and www.hotjobs.com.

PUBLICATIONS MANAGER, CORPORATE/INDUSTRY

CAREER PROFILE

Duties: Develop, write, and complete internal and external publications for a corporation

Alternate Title(s): Publications Coordinator; Publication Manager

Salary Range: $25,000 to $55,000+

Employment Prospects: Good

Advancement Prospects: Fair

Best Geographical Location(s): All locations may offer job possibilities.

Prerequisites:

Education or Training—Four-year college degree with major in English, public relations, communications, journalism, or liberal arts

Experience—Writing or other experience working with publications necessary

Special Skills and Personality Traits—Good writing and editing skills; communication skills; understanding of layout and graphics; working knowledge of grammar, spelling, and word usage; computer capability; supervisory skills

CAREER LADDER

```
┌─────────────────────────────────┐
│   Director of Public Relations  │
└─────────────────────────────────┘

┌─────────────────────────────────┐
│      Publications Manager       │
└─────────────────────────────────┘

┌─────────────────────────────────┐
│   Copywriter, Journalist,       │
│   Intern, College Student,      │
│   or Entry Level                │
└─────────────────────────────────┘
```

Position Description

The Publications Manager working in a corporate or industry setting is responsible for the development and completion of both internal and external publications. Depending on the structure of the corporation, the Publications Manager may work with the public relations, marketing, promotion, advertising, and/or consumer affairs departments.

He or she may be required to do the research, writing, graphics, and layout of material or may work with researchers, copywriters, and artists. The Publications Manager is responsible for estimating budgets for publications and making sure that projects come in at or under that budget. He or she may write or call for several quotes on a specific project in order to obtain the best price.

It is also up to the Publications Manager to set timetables for projects. These include projection schedules for printers, graphic artists, copywriters, photographers, and any others who might be involved in the preparation of the publication. The manager must see to it that projects are finished when they are supposed to be. A late publication may throw off the timing on anything from an upcoming promotion to having new product information books available to include with product distribution.

The Publications Manager must know a great deal about the printing industry. He or she will be responsible for choosing the correct paper stock, type styles, and graphic formats for a publication. This is an involved project, as there are many different types, weights, and colors of paper available, as well as thousands of different varieties of type to choose from.

The individual must also be aware of the various sizes in which publications can be printed. While paper can be cut into almost any size, certain sizes and shapes will be more economical. For example, a publication for which consumers write to the company would probably be best if it fit into a standard #10 business envelope. While a square or oversized shape might look more creative, it could pose problems in the mailing process.

The Publications Manager may be required to write specific publications for the company or may be asked by the various departments to develop a publication for which they have an idea. The individual may be responsible for writing proposals and outlines for publications or may farm this task out to an assistant or copywriter.

The Publications Manager may be responsible for a great variety of publications depending on the type of corporation or industry in which he or she is working. These could include internal and external newsletters, brochures, pamphlets, letters, leaflets, annual reports, and press releases. Other written materials might include speeches, feature articles, stockholder reports, and scripts for audio or audiovisual materials. Individuals might also be required to develop consumer-oriented instructional booklets and giveaway sheets, as well as sales books and other promotional materials.

If the individual is working with writers on a project, he or she will be responsible for editing the copy and checking it for accuracy. When working with graphic artists or photographers the individual will be responsible for explaining exactly what he or she wants artistically and graphically.

Before a publication is actually printed the Publications Manager will usually be required to have it reviewed for accuracy, content, and possibly even style. This is generally done by the department head who will be using the publication. In some cases the publication also has to be reviewed by a vice president of marketing or promotion or even the chief executive officer.

With the current popularity of computerized desktop publishing, the Publications Manager may find that more and more projects are prepared "in-house" instead of at commercial printers. Desktop publishing allows the Publications Manager to have copy typed into a computer and then laid out in a graphically pleasing format. Photographs, scanned artwork, logos, computer clip art, and graphics can be put directly into the computer and placed in the publication. Computer graphic artists can even design artwork and special graphics.

What all this means is that the Publications Manager can now easily produce printer-ready mechanicals. It also means that the Publications Manager must be computer-capable. He or she may be responsible for the input of data and graphics and layout or may delegate these task to other individuals. The Publications Manager must be able to train others on the machine, using the various computer programs needed to put together publications.

The Publications Manager usually works normal hours. If a project is near completion or a deadline must be met, he or she will be required to work overtime. Individuals may be under pressure or stress in this position. Projects must constantly be developed, designed, written, and completed.

Depending on the structure of the corporation in which the individual is working, he or she may be responsible to the director of public relations, marketing, or promotion. He or she might also be responsible to a vice president or even the corporation's CEO.

Salaries

Annual earnings for Publications Managers working in corporations and industry can range from $25,000 to $55,000 plus, depending on a number of factors. These include the size and location of the corporation and the experience and responsibilities of the individual. Smaller businesses in general offer lower salaries.

Employment Prospects

Employment prospects are good for individuals seeking employment as Publications Managers in the corporate world. Very large corporations may have a person in this position in a number of different departments. For example, there may be a Publications Manager in public relations, another in promotions, and yet another in consumer affairs.

Other corporations may have just one individual on staff. In some businesses the public relations department is expected to handle publications and writing functions in addition to their other responsibilities.

Jobs may be located almost anywhere in the country in this field. Corporations and other industries in every location may offer possibilities.

Advancement Prospects

Advancement prospects are fair for Publications Managers. Individuals may climb the career ladder by becoming director of public relations or possibly director of consumer affairs. Career paths can take off in different directions.

Individuals might also advance their career by locating a position as a Publications Manager at a larger corporation. This usually results in more responsibility and an increased salary.

Education and Training

Most corporations require a minimum of a four-year degree for this position. Good choices for majors include public relations, communications, journalism, English, and liberal arts.

Seminars and courses relating to all phases of writing, desktop publishing, computers, graphics, and layout should prove to be extremely useful to the individual.

Experience, Skills, and Personality Traits

Individuals in this position should have had some experience working with publications. This might include working on a school paper or yearbook, and local civic or non-profit group newsletter. Many Publications Managers have worked as reporters for newspapers or as publicity or public relations assistants.

Individuals should be able to write clearly, quickly, and accurately in an interesting manner. The Publications Manager should have a working knowledge of grammar, spelling, and word usage. Editing capabilities may be necessary.

Publications Managers need a sense of graphic style and layout. A working knowledge of the printing industry, including the various typefaces, and varieties and weights of paper is useful. Computer capability is currently required in many positions. The ability to handle desktop publishing is a plus.

Individuals need good communication skills. They should be personable, articulate, able to work quickly and accurately, and should have good supervisory skills.

Unions and Associations

Publications Managers working in corporations do not usually belong to any union. Individuals may be members of a number of trade associations that provide training, seminars, conferences, and professional guidance. These might include the Public Relations Society of America (PRSA), the International Association of Business Communicators (IABC), and Association for Women In Communications (AWC). Individuals might also belong to trade associations specifically related to their industries.

Tips for Entry

1. Work on your school newspaper or yearbook. Try to experience all types of jobs, from reporting to layout and editing.

2. A part-time or summer job on a local newspaper gives you hands-on experience.

3. Volunteer to produce a civic or nonprofit group's newsletter for them. Once again, the hands-on experience will be invaluable.

4. Large corporations often offer internships and training programs. Locate one of these and ask to work in the publications, public relations, or marketing departments.

5. These positions are often advertised in trade journals' "marketplace" or help wanted sections.

6. Openings might also be advertised in newspaper display or classified ads. Look under heading classifications of "Publications," "Writer," "Editor," "Communications," or "Public Relations."

7. Jobs may be listed on company Web sites.

8. You might also want to check out some of the Web's more popular employment sites.

COORDINATOR OF CONSUMER AFFAIRS, CORPORATE/INDUSTRY

CAREER PROFILE

Duties: Supervising and coordinating consumer affairs, customer services, customer relations; assisting consumers in solving problems they have with the company's products or services; training customer relations representatives

Alternate Title(s): Coordinator of Customer Services; Consumer Affairs Director; Customer Relations Manager; Director of Customer Relations

Salary Range: $25,000 to $56,000+

Employment Prospects: Fair

Advancement Prospects: Fair

Best Geographical Location(s): Positions may be located throughout the country.

Prerequisites:

Education or Training—Minimum of four-year college degree

Experience—Experience working in customer services, customer relations, consumer affairs, or public relations necessary

Special Skills and Personality Traits—Supervisory skills; good interpersonal skills; ability to remain calm; empathy; articulate; writing skills

CAREER LADDER

```
┌─────────────────────────────────────────┐
│  Public Relations or Marketing Director  │
│    or Coordinator of Consumer Affairs    │
│  in Larger, More Prestigious Corporation │
└─────────────────────────────────────────┘

┌─────────────────────────────────────────┐
│      Coordinator of Consumer Affairs     │
└─────────────────────────────────────────┘

┌─────────────────────────────────────────┐
│     Customer Relations Representative    │
└─────────────────────────────────────────┘
```

Position Description

The Coordinator of Consumer Affairs working in a corporation supervises and coordinates the consumer affairs, customer services, and customer relations services. The individual in this position will be responsible for everything that happens in the department.

The consumer affairs department has a number of functions. The department is responsible for making sure that customers are satisfied with the company's products and services. It is also responsible for resolving any complaints and problems that the customer has. A third function of the department is to supply customers with useful information about the company and its products. The Coordinator of Consumer Affairs is responsible for seeing that all these functions are carried out.

The Coordinator of Consumer Affairs, who also might be called the director of customer relations, works with the public relations department as well as upper management in creating corporate policies as they pertain to consumers. He or she is required to understand and be able to explain policies to customers and customer relations representatives. The individual sees to it that state and federal regulations as they apply to company products and services are adhered to.

The Coordinator of Consumer Affairs is responsible for training customer relations representatives. The individual may hold one-on-one training sessions for each new employee or may hold group sessions at periodic intervals. The coordinator may also be expected to write and develop training manuals for both consumer representatives and others working in the company.

The individual is responsible for explaining how consumer calls and letters should be handled, answered, and taken care of. The coordinator explains what information should be taken from consumers and how to maintain files.

The Coordinator of Consumer Affairs is not usually responsible for answering routine calls from customers. However, the individual is responsible for dealing with phone calls or letters from consumers who are extremely upset, irate, or irrational. The coordinator is also expected to handle any major consumer problems. For example, if a customer calls the company about a problem and suggests that a lawsuit will follow unless he or she is satisfied, the Coordinator of Consumer Affairs will step in.

The coordinator finds out what the problem is and determines what will resolve the situation in the customer's mind. Often a replacement will take care of the situation. Sometimes the consumer just wants someone to agree with him or her. At other times the problem must be discussed with the public relations or marketing director or possibly upper management. The coordinator must know enough about human psychology to have the ability to calm people down so that problems can be resolved.

The coordinator is responsible for writing letters to consumers who have written or called. The individual may develop stock letters for different situations and write personal letters where the stock letters are not applicable. He or she may also be required to prepare periodic reports dealing with the number of calls and letters the department has received and the number of and nature of complaints, and to explain to management how problems were resolved.

In the event of a product recall the Coordinator of Consumer Affairs has yet another responsibility. He or she must train the representatives to deal with consumers who call up frightened and angry. The individual meets with upper management and the advertising, public relations, and marketing departments to decide what steps to take to keep customer confidence in the company and to alleviate any additional problems that may occur.

The coordinator must decide the best way to tell consumers about the recall. Depending on the product and the severity of the recall, the consumer affairs office may just call or write to people who have sent in their product warranty cards. The coordinator may be required to write press releases or give information on the recall to people in the public relations office. National and local news and wire services may be informed of the situation in order to get the word out quickly. This is important. If the product recall concerns food or a children's toy, promptness might be life-saving.

The Coordinator of Consumer Affairs is required to let consumers know what to do with the faulty product. He or she must decide if the product should be brought to a store for a refund, sent back to the company for repair, replacement, or refund. The individual is responsible for coordinating the entire recall effort.

The coordinator may also be responsible for developing and writing consumer-oriented materials. These materials could include product information and instructional books, leaflets, booklets, and flyers. The individual might also be expected to prepare consumer newsletters.

The Coordinator of Consumer Affairs is responsible to the director of public relations or marketing or to the chief executive officer of the company, depending on the structure of the corporation.

Salaries

Salaries for Coordinators of Consumer Affairs may range from $25,000 to $56,000 plus annually depending on a number of variables. These include the specific corporation, its location, and its size. The individual's responsibilities and experience level are also variables.

Employment Prospects

Most midsize and larger companies have a Coordinator of Consumer Affairs position. It may be called customer relations manager, director of consumer relations, customer services coordinator, or one of a host of different names, but the position is still relatively the same.

Employment prospects are fair for an individual seeking employment as a Coordinator of Consumer Affairs in a corporation. Positions may be located throughout all areas of the country.

Advancement Prospects

Advancement prospects are fair for a Coordinator of Consumer Affairs. The individual may climb the career ladder by becoming the director of public relations or marketing. The coordinator may also find a similar position in a larger, more prestigious corporation, which would result in increased earnings.

Education and Training

The Coordinator of Consumer Affairs working in the corporate world is required to have a minimum of a four-year college degree in public relations, marketing, advertising, English, communications, liberal arts, or business administration. Many individuals in this position have a graduate degree.

Experience, Skills, and Personality Traits

Supervisory skills are a must for the Coordinator of Consumer Affairs. The individual must have a working knowledge of company policy and the corporation itself. Experience working as a customer relations representative is usually necessary, although experience in public relations might also be acceptable.

The coordinator of this department should have good interpersonal skills. The ability to deal well with subordinates, superiors, and customers is imperative. The Consumer Affairs Coordinator will often be called in when the consumer relations representative cannot resolve a problem. At this point the consumer might be either irate or irrational. The ability to handle problems and situations with empathy, sympathy, and calm is required.

The individual must be articulate, with good communications skills. He or she should also be adept at developing and writing a variety of different types of materials.

Unions and Associations

The Coordinator of Consumer Affairs working in a corporation may belong to the Society of Consumer Affairs Professionals in Business (SOCAP). This organization holds seminars, training sessions, and conferences and offers written material on effective ways to deal with consumer problems in business. Individuals may also belong to private and voluntary consumer organizations created to advocate specific consumer interests.

Many Coordinators of Consumer Affairs are also members of the Public Relations Society of America (PRSA) and the International Association of Business Communicators (IABC).

Tips for Entry

1. Become a member of SOCAP, the industry trade association, as well as the PRSA and other relevant organizations. These organizations provide educational and professional guidance in addition to the opportunity to make important contacts.

2. Volunteer your time to work with a consumer organization. This will give you valuable hands-on experience and look good on your résumé.

3. Job openings are advertised in newspaper display and classified sections. Look under heading classifications of "Consumer Affairs," "Customer Service," "Customer Relations," "Public Relations," "Advertising," or "Marketing."

4. There are many employment agencies that deal specifically with jobs in public relations. Before you get involved, determine who will pay the fee when you locate a job. In some agencies the applicant pays, while in others the employer is responsible for the fee.

5. Jobs may also be located on company Web sites. Look for the employment section.

CUSTOMER RELATIONS REPRESENTATIVE, CORPORATE/INDUSTRY

CAREER PROFILE

Duties: Obtain answers to customer questions; assist consumers in solving problems with company products or services

Alternate Title(s): Consumer Relations Representative; Public Affairs Representative; Consumer Affairs Representative; Customer Service Representative

Salary Range: $20,000 to $35,000+

Employment Prospects: Good

Advancement Prospects: Fair

Best Geographical Location(s): Positions may be located throughout the country.

Prerequisites:

Education or Training—Four-year college degree required by most corporations; others require high school diploma

Experience—Experience dealing with people is preferred, but not necessary.

Special Skills and Personality Traits—Personable; good phone manner; articulate; ability to communicate; writing skills

CAREER LADDER

```
┌─────────────────────────────────────┐
│   Coordinator of Consumer Affairs,   │
│ Assistant Customer Relations Manager,│
│  or Coordinator of Customer Relations│
└─────────────────────────────────────┘

┌─────────────────────────────────────┐
│   Customer Relations Representative  │
└─────────────────────────────────────┘

┌─────────────────────────────────────┐
│     Entry Level or Sales Position    │
└─────────────────────────────────────┘
```

Position Description

A Customer Relations Representative working in a business is responsible for answering customers' questions, obtaining answers to those they don't know, and assisting consumers in resolving problems with company products or services.

The main function of the Customer Relations Representative is to make the customer feel that he or she is important and that any difficulty with the product or service can be resolved. The customer relations department works in conjunction with the public relations department in trying to make sure that customers are satisfied. Many corporations feel that word of mouth is the best advertising. A pleased customer will tell his or her friends about the product, and they may purchase the product, too.

The Customer Relations Representative or consumer relations representative, as he or she may be called, has varying duties depending on the structure of the company and his or her specific responsibilities.

Before the Customer Relations Representative begins to deal with customers, he or she usually goes through a training period. During this time the individual learns all about the company, its products, and its policies. He or she will most likely be required to read and study policy books and other written material about the company. The individual will probably use the company's products in order to become totally familiar with them.

The Customer Relations Representative answers phone calls made by consumers. The consumer may call the company for a number of different reasons. He or she may want to obtain information on a product or may need an explanation of how to use or put together the product. The consumer may need warranty information or instructions on how and where to service a faulty or broken item. The customer may also get in touch with the company to complain about a problem with a product or about poor service.

The Customer Relations Representative is responsible for answering the consumer's questions. If he or she does not know the answer, the individual will be expected to find it. The individual may call a superior or someone in a specific department in order to find the correct information. He or she will then be responsible for calling or writing the customer.

In some companies, the individual is required to keep extensive records on all people who call. This information may be handwritten or may be typed into a computer terminal. The Customer Relations Representative usually needs the person's name, address, and phone number and a short explanation of the question or problem. He or she may also get product code numbers, and dates and places of purchase.

The Customer Relations Representative is responsible for taking calls of irate customers. These phone calls may come in for any number of reasons. The consumer may have purchased a faulty product, received bad service, or may just be complaining about an area that is totally out of the control of the company.

The individual tries to get to the root of the problem and determine if he or she can handle it directly or if the call should be forwarded or referred to a supervisor. The Customer Relations Representative must know company policy. In many situations the company will offer to replace or repair a product at no charge just to keep a customer satisfied, even if the company was not at fault.

Depending on the corporation, the individual may also be called upon to take orders, check on the status of orders, or do billings.

The individual is often required to write letters to consumers to apologize for a problem, to explain a situation, or to offer a solution. The Customer Relations Representative may also have additional writing responsibilities. He or she may be expected to write leaflets, booklets, or newsletters aimed at helping the consumer and keeping him or her aware of company products or the usage of products.

If a product recall occurs, the Customer Relations Representative may become involved in the recall procedure. He or she may take the calls from customers who have already purchased a product and explain the replacement or refund process. The individual may also phone or write customers who have sent in warranties to make them aware of the problem.

The Customer Relations Representative works normal business hours. He or she is responsible to the customer relations manager or director.

Salaries

Salaries can range greatly for Customer Relations Representatives depending on their experience and responsibilities and the size, structure, and location of the company.

Individuals who have limited experience and responsibilities or those working in smaller businesses may earn between $20,000 and $25,000 plus a year. Others who have more experience and more responsibility and are working in larger companies in metropolitan areas may earn up to $35,000 or more annually.

Employment Prospects

Employment prospects are good for Customer Relations Representatives. Jobs may be located throughout the country in all types of businesses, large and small.

Midsize and larger corporations usually have more than one Customer Relations Representative on staff. In large businesses there might be 20 people or more holding down this position.

Advancement Prospects

Advancement prospects are fair for Customer Relations Representatives. The next step up the career ladder for the Customer Relations Representative is to become an assistant customer relations manager, director of customer relations, or coordinator of consumer affairs, depending on the structure of the company.

Depending on his or her qualifications, the Customer Relations Representative might also advance by becoming an assistant director of public relations.

Individuals need a good educational background to advance their careers. They must also be willing to relocate to find a position if one does not open in their current company.

Education and Training

Most positions for Customer Relations Representatives require that the applicant have a four-year college degree. While some positions do not require anything but a high school diploma, higher education is necessary in order to advance the individual's career.

Any type of major may be acceptable. Good course options might include psychology, sociology, English, public relations, marketing, advertising, writing, and communications.

Experience, Skills, and Personality Traits

The Customer Relations Representative should be articulate with good communication skills. He or she should also have a pleasant phone manner. A lot of the individual's time is spent on the telephone talking to customers with questions or problems.

The individual should have the ability to display empathy when dealing with a problem. He or she should be able to handle many details at one time without getting flustered. Computer capability is a plus in many positions.

The Customer Relations Representative must be personable. He or she should be able to deal with an irate consumer in such a way that the customer calms down so that the problem can be effectively solved. The Customer Relations Representative must never let his or her temper show.

In some positions the Customer Relations Representative is expected to fulfill writing functions. He or she may be required to write letters, reports, customer service pamphlets, or booklets. A working knowledge of the English language, letter writing, spelling, word usage, and grammar is necessary.

Unions and Associations

Customer Relations Representatives may become members of the Society of Consumer Affairs Professionals in Business (SOCAP). This organization holds seminars on effective ways to deal with consumer problems in business. Individuals may also belong to private and voluntary consumer organizations that advocate specific consumer interests.

Tips for Entry

1. Jobs for Customer Relations Representatives are often advertised in the classified sections of newspapers. Look under heading classifications of "Customer Service," "Customer Relations," "Public Relations," or "Consumer Affairs."

2. Consider sending your résumé and a cover letter to the personnel or human resources director at a number of different companies. Ask that your résumé be kept on file. There is a high turnover rate in these positions. You might be called in for an interview sooner than you think.

3. Get some hands-on experience dealing with customers in a summer or part-time job as a salesperson.

4. If you are still in school, think about joining an organization or club that deals with the handling of student affairs and problems. This will give you valuable on-the-job training.

5. Offer to write an "Action-Line" column for your school or local newspaper. This is a column in which people write in with consumer problems and the columnist searches out answers for them. This will look good on your résumé and may help you climb the career ladder once employed.

COMMUNITY RELATIONS COORDINATOR, CORPORATE/INDUSTRY

CAREER PROFILE

Duties: Coordinate relationship between corporation and local agencies, civic, and community groups; represent company in beneficial community activities

Alternate Title(s): Community Relations Representative; Community Affairs Coordinator; Community Affairs Representative

Salary Range: $23,000 to $56,000+

Employment Prospects: Fair

Advancement Prospects: Fair

Best Geographical Location(s): Areas that have large industries and corporations offer more opportunities.

Prerequisites:

Education or Training—Four-year college degree required

Experience—Experience working with community and nonprofit groups helpful

Special Skills and Personality Traits—People skills; creative; good written and verbal communication skills; public speaking ability; organized

CAREER LADDER

```
┌─────────────────────────────────────┐
│   Community Relations Director or    │
│ Manager or Public Relations Director │
│             or Manager               │
└─────────────────────────────────────┘

┌─────────────────────────────────────┐
│   Community Relations Coordinator    │
└─────────────────────────────────────┘

┌─────────────────────────────────────┐
│    Community Relations Assistant,    │
│      Public Relations Assistant,     │
│             or Journalist            │
└─────────────────────────────────────┘
```

Position Description

A Community Relations Coordinator working in the corporate or business sphere has an interesting job. In this position the individual coordinates the relationship between the corporate business and local agencies, civic groups, schools, community groups, political entities, and governmental agencies. The Community Relations Coordinator is required to plan and design programs that will both help the local community and promote the image of the corporation in a positive way. While performing these tasks the individual must continue to be sensitive to the local community and its needs.

The individual is responsible for representing the corporation in beneficial community activities. He or she may work with the sponsorship of programs including sporting events, cultural events, and community-related programs. For example, the Community Relations Coordinator may arrange company sponsorship of Girl Scout or Boy Scout troops or local sports teams.

The Community Relations Coordinator may develop programs or work with local community groups such as the United Way or Red Cross on specific projects. The Community Relations Coordinator, as an example, may act as a liaison between the United Way and employees of the corporation in programs in which monthly donations are taken out of participating employees' paychecks. The individual may work with the Red Cross in a program where a select day is set up for employees of the corporation to donate blood.

The individual may also be required to develop new or innovative community relations programs. These might include events in which the company can take leadership, such as marathons, fairs, art auctions, and parades. An example of this technique is the Macy's Thanksgiving Day Parade, which is aired on television every year. These events will keep the corporation favorably in the public eye. Programs such as these also indirectly help market the corporation's products or services to the public.

The Community Relations Coordinator may be required to be the representative of the company on nonprofit organization boards and committees. The individual may also be asked by the corporation to become an active member of civic and community groups.

He or she may work with other departments in the corporation coordinating functions and handling details. These might include public relations, advertising, marketing, and promotion.

Depending on the structure of the company, the individual may be responsible for writing press releases and feature articles on various community relations projects. He or she might also be responsible for taking photographs during corporation-sponsored community events or arranging to have a professional photographer present.

At times the Community Relations Coordinator may be asked to give speeches on behalf of the company. The usual procedure is for the community relations person to point out in the speech a tie-in with a community project in which the company is currently involved. He or she may be required to appear on local public service television and radio interview shows to promote the corporation's community projects as well as to make sure the company maintains a good public image.

The Community Relations Coordinator usually has a good working relationship with the media. In this way, when the corporation is sponsoring a local team or helping to raise money for a worthwhile cause, the company reaps the benefits of press coverage.

The Community Relations Coordinator often takes community groups on tours of the company plant. He or she may arrange teas, luncheons, or dinners for these groups so that they can learn more about the corporation and its community programs.

Individuals in this position may often have to work after normal business hours to attend civic, nonprofit, and community group meetings, to make speeches, or to represent the corporation at an event.

The Community Relations Coordinator may be responsible to the community relations director, if there is one. He or she may also be responsible to the public relations director of the company.

Salaries

Earnings for this position may range from $23,000 to $56,000 or more depending on the specific corporation and the responsibilities and experience of the individual.

Many larger corporations hire people with limited experience and pay a relatively low salary at the beginning. Individuals who have more experience or handle extensive responsibilities may have annual earnings averaging in the mid-thirties.

Employment Prospects

Employment prospects are fair for individuals seeking Community Relations Coordinator positions. It should be noted that not every corporation hires someone specifically for this job. Instead, many expect someone from the public relations department to be responsible for the functions of a Community Relations Coordinator.

Advancement Prospects

Advancement prospects are fair for a Community Relations Coordinator. An individual may take a number of different career paths in climbing the ladder of success. He or she may locate a similar position in a larger, more prestigious company that would result in higher earnings. The individual may also advance by becoming a community relations director or manager. This may be difficult, however, because relatively few corporations have this position available. The individual might find more opportunities by climbing the ladder and landing a job as a corporate public relations director or a manager or assistant director of marketing.

If he or she has developed a good working relationship with a nonprofit organization that is seeking a director, the individual may be considered for the position.

Education and Training

Community Relations Coordinators working in corporations are usually required to have a minimum of a four-year college degree. While majors might vary, emphasis should be placed on courses in publicity, public relations, marketing, advertising, journalism, English, communications, writing, psychology, and sociology.

There are numerous seminars on working with nonprofit groups, community relations, public relations, and publicity that will prove useful to the individual in obtaining a position and being successful at it.

Experience, Skills, and Personality Traits

Individuals working in community relations should enjoy working with people. They should be community-minded and have an understanding of nonprofit, civic, and community groups.

Individuals in this profession are the type of people who are always the first to volunteer to help when someone has a problem. They like to solve problems and help others.

Community Relations Coordinators should be outgoing, personable, aggressive, and articulate. Good writing, organizational, and planning skills are necessary. The individual must have the ability to speak in front of large and small groups without getting flustered.

Community Relations Coordinators may have advanced to their present job in a variety of ways. They might have had experience working in a nonprofit organization as a publicity or community relations assistant or as an administrative assistant in the publicity, marketing, or community relations office.

Unions and Associations

Community Relations Coordinators working in the corporate world do not usually belong to any type of union. They may belong to trade associations specific to the industry in which they are working. Individuals often belong to local civic groups, nonprofit organizations, and service clubs and attend their meetings as part of their job duties.

Tips for Entry

1. Join civic and nonprofit groups and volunteer to be on committees. This will give you hands-on experience working in this type of situation.

2. This job often entails a great deal of writing. You might want to take some extra courses or seminars in writing techniques. Local newspapers and chambers of commerce often offer courses in writing and publicity especially for people working with community groups.

3. Community relations positions are often advertised in local newspaper display and classified advertisements. Look under the heading classifications of "Community Relations," "Community Affairs," or "Publicity."

4. Many large corporations offer internships and training programs in various departments. Try to locate one of these.

5. You might want to send your résumé and a cover letter describing the type of job you want to some of the larger corporations. While you won't usually start at the top, you might find an entry level position in the department.

6. Be sure to check out company Web sites. Many list job openings. Start on the home page and look for an employment link.

EMPLOYEE RELATIONS COORDINATOR, CORPORATE/INDUSTRY

CAREER PROFILE

Duties: Handle communications between management and employees in a corporation; develop internal publications; obtain information about needs and interests of employees; create and implement events for employees

Alternate Title(s): Employee Relations Representative; Employee Communications Coordinator

Salary Range: $25,000 to $56,000+

Employment Prospects: Fair

Advancement Prospects: Good

Best Geographical Location(s): Jobs located throughout the country.

Prerequisites:

Education or Training—Minimum of four-year college degree

Experience—Experience working in publicity, public relations, employee relations

Special Skills and Personality Traits—People skills; good writing skills; good communication skills; public speaking ability; knowledge of negotiation, arbitration, and group dynamics

CAREER LADDER

```
┌─────────────────────────────────────┐
│   Employee Relations Coordinator     │
│  in Larger Corporation or Director   │
│ of Public Relations or Personnel Director │
└─────────────────────────────────────┘

┌─────────────────────────────────────┐
│   Employee Relations Coordinator     │
└─────────────────────────────────────┘

┌─────────────────────────────────────┐
│    Employee Relations Assistant      │
│            or Publicity              │
│     or Public Relations Position     │
└─────────────────────────────────────┘
```

Position Description

The Employee Relations Coordinator working in a corporation is responsible for handling communications between upper management and employees. This type of job is usually found in midsize and larger corporations and industries. In smaller corporations the functions of the Employee Relations Coordinator might be assigned to the public relations or personnel department.

The purpose of the employee relations department is to keep employees informed of happenings within their jobs and the company as well as keeping them satisfied with their jobs. In this way employees will be more productive and effective when performing their work.

The Employee Relations Coordinator acts as a liaison between management and employees. He or she is responsible for bringing employee problems to the attention of man-

agement. The individual may also be responsible for communicating management policies to the employees.

In order to fulfill these functions the Employee Relations Coordinator will have a number of responsibilities. The individual has frequent meetings with the personnel director and top management during which they will discuss both new policies and changes in existing policies. During these sessions the coordinator also finds out if there are any messages or information that should be communicated to employees. This information can encompass anything from major policy changes, such as reductions in employees' pay or fringe benefit changes, to something relatively trivial, such as the date of a company baseball game or the prizes for the company's bowling league.

The Employee Relations Coordinator is responsible for finding the most effective way to make employees aware of the information. In some situations the individual finds that writing memos to department heads is the answer. The department head can then pass the information on to employees. In other situations each employee may receive a personal memo or notice.

The coordinator may decide to use other forms of written internal communications such as flyers, posters for bulletin boards, and newsletters. The individual is responsible for developing, creating, and writing these materials. He or she may do this or pass the task on to an assistant. In the event that an assistant does the writing, the coordinator will be responsible for editing and checking the information for accuracy.

The Employee Relations Coordinator may have special times set aside in which employees can come and discuss problems with the company, their job, or policies. The individual will then try to arrive at a solution or take the situation to upper management to resolve.

He or she might also conduct informational surveys of employees to obtain their opinions, needs, and interests so that management can better respond to them. For example, the coordinator may find through surveys that a large group of employees would be willing to pay for child care in the company building. The individual would take this information to upper management, who might then respond by opening a company-run child care center.

The Employee Relations Coordinator is often responsible for creating and implementing employee events to boost morale. The individual may, for example, develop company softball teams, bowling leagues, or basketball teams. He or she may plan picnics, parties, and other special events for employees and their families.

The Employee Relations Coordinator may arrange and implement seminars, conferences, or meetings for employees. These may be used for a variety of purposes, from honing skills and training to bringing employees together. The individual will often use these functions to have top management give out awards or special honors and single out employees for outstanding service to the company.

The coordinator works with other departments while performing his or her functions. He or she may inform the director of the public relations department of employee honors or achievements so that press releases can be written and sent to the media. The individual may work with the community relations director when employees are sponsoring an event for a local charity or nonprofit organization.

In the event of corporate layoffs, the Employee Relations Coordinator may work closely with the personnel department. The individual might be expected to explain and help implement management's plans for programs for laid-off employees. For example, he or she may work on a program offering résumé writing classes. The individual may also be expected to explain to employees the problems that created the layoffs. He or she may do this through written communications or by speaking to employee groups.

The Employee Relations Coordinator constantly strives to learn employees' needs, opinions, and interests and to discuss the possibilities and methods of responding to them with management. His or her main function is to have employees perceive the company and its management in a positive way.

Depending on the structure of the corporation, the Employee Relations Coordinator may report directly to the president, vice president, or chief executive officer. The individual might also be responsible to the public relations director or the personnel director.

Salaries

Earnings for Employee Relations Coordinators vary from job to job. They may range from $25,000 to $56,000 or more depending on the corporation. Generally, the larger the corporation and the more the responsibility of the individual, the higher the salary will be. Earnings will also be higher for those working in large metropolitan areas.

Employment Prospects

Employment prospects are fair for individuals seeking a job in employee relations and will improve in the years to come. There are currently many midsize and larger corporations that employ a person for this position. More companies are beginning to follow the trend of using employee relations in order to create a more satisfied work force and therefore more effective and productive workers.

Employment possibilities may be located throughout the country.

Advancement Prospects

The Employee Relations Coordinator may advance his or her career in a number of ways. The individual may locate the same type of position in a larger, more prestigious corporation, which would result in increased earnings.

The Employee Relations Coordinator may climb the career ladder by becoming the director of public relations in a corporation. The individual may also move into the position of personnel director or director of human resources.

Education and Training

Employee Relations Coordinators are required to have a minimum of a four-year college diploma. There are a number of positions in which graduate degrees are preferred.

A broad educational background is useful to individuals in this field. Courses in public relations, marketing, communications, journalism, English, business, writing, psychology, group dynamics, negotiation, and arbitration are helpful.

Experience, Skills, and Personality Traits

Employee Relations Coordinator should genuinely like people. They should be personable, with an understanding of people.

The individual needs the ability to fulfill all public relations functions. He or she should be able to write clearly, factually, and creatively. The Employee Relations Coordinator may have to develop and write memos, letters, releases, proposals, newsletters, posters, and flyers. A good command of word usage, spelling, and grammar is necessary.

The Employee Relations Coordinator should have good communications skills. He or she must be articulate and have the ability to speak to large groups of people. The individual should be equally comfortable speaking to management and to employees.

The Employee Relations Coordinator needs a total understanding of both employee attitudes and those of management. He or she should be persuasive, have the ability to negotiate and arbitrate, and understand group dynamics.

Unions and Associations

Employee Relations Coordinators working in corporations may often work with various bargaining unions of which employees are members.

Individuals may also be members of a number of trade associations for those working in the public relations and employee relations field. These include the International Association of Business Communicators (IABC), the Public Relations Society of America (PRSA), and the National Association of Manufacturers (NAM).

Employee Relations Coordinators might also belong to trade associations specific to their industry.

Tips for Entry

1. Become familiar with negotiating, arbitrating, and group dynamics by taking seminars and courses.
2. Obtain writing experience. Consider becoming a reporter for your school or local newspaper.
3. Obtain experience working with groups of people by becoming a member of your school student government.
4. Locate an internship in employee relations or public relations. The hands-on experience will be valuable.
5. If you can't find an internship, consider working as an administrative assistant, clerk, or secretary in either the employee relations department of a corporation or in the offices of upper management. This will give you an overview of the management/ employee situation.
6. Positions may be advertised in the classified section of newspapers. Look under heading classifications of "Corporate," "Employee Relations," "Worker Relations," "Staff Relations," or "Public Relations."
7. Be sure to check some of the career and employment Web sites for openings.

TRADE SHOW REPRESENTATIVE, CORPORATE/INDUSTRY

CAREER PROFILE

Duties: Act as company's representative at trade shows and conventions; demonstrate product or service; staff booth

Alternate Title(s): Trade Show Rep

Salary Range: $23,000 to $100,000+

Employment Prospects: Good

Advancement Prospects: Fair

Best Geographical Location(s): Openings may occur wherever there are large corporations and industries; positions may also be available in cities where there are large convention centers and arenas.

Prerequisites:

Education or Training—College background not always required, but helpful

Experience—Experience working with the public is helpful.

Special Skills and Personality Traits—Neat; articulate; dependable; personable; detail-oriented; enjoy traveling

CAREER LADDER

```
┌─────────────────────────────────────┐
│          Trade Show Manager          │
│         or Sales, Marketing,         │
│  or Public Relations Assistant Manager │
└─────────────────────────────────────┘

┌─────────────────────────────────────┐
│       Trade Show Representative       │
└─────────────────────────────────────┘

┌─────────────────────────────────────┐
│    Entry Level or Public Relations,   │
│     Marketing, or Sales Assistant     │
└─────────────────────────────────────┘
```

Position Description

A Trade Show Representative goes to conventions and trade shows. The individual's main function is to help sell the company's product or service by acting as the company's representative in the field. The Trade Show Representative may travel to different cities around the country (or the world) to perform this function.

The Trade Show Representative can have varied responsibilities ranging from just demonstrating a product at the trade show booth to overseeing the setup of the booth, selling a product, and scheduling the manning of the booths. It all depends on the structure of the company.

The individual demonstrating a company's product at a trade show must know as much as possible about that product. The representative usually spends a great deal of time with company salespeople, technicians, and marketing people to obtain this information. He or she also reads all literature and watches films, videotapes, and advertisements about the company.

The individual may make arrangements to have everything shipped to the venue as well as shipped back to the company headquarters or on to the next trade show. The Trade Show Representative may oversee the actual booth shipment as well as all of the equipment needed to run the booth. This might include booth displays, audiovisuals, signs, giveaways, promotional material, literature, and the product itself.

The Trade Show Representative may also work with unions in the various venues where the shows are located. In many convention centers and halls, union representatives must set up and break down trade show booths and hook up the electricity and lights. In other centers the Trade Show Representative has to set up the booth alone or hire workers to do the setup and breakdown procedures.

Depending on the structure of the company the individual works for, he or she may be responsible for making the travel and lodging arrangements for all staff attending the show. The Trade Show Representative also has to do the scheduling arrangements for all those working in the booth. The individual may work alone or may work with other Trade Show Representatives, salespeople, or even company owners and managers.

As rental prices for trade show space are usually quite high, the Trade Show Representative must check that the exhibit promoter has provided all the equipment and space that the company has contracted for. This might include the physical convention-style booth, chairs, tables, table coverings, signs, electrical outlets, and audiovisual equipment.

Once the individual has seen to the booth setup so that it is both pleasing to look at and easily accessible for people to come in to talk, the representative has other duties.

He or she must arrive at the trade show before it opens to the public. Once people begin to come in, the individual mans the booth, demonstrate the product or service, and answers questions from prospective customers. The representative often conducts contests to try to attract as many potential visitors to the booth as possible. The individual may also give away promotional samples or items with the company's logo such as mugs, T-shirts, or balloons.

The Trade Show Representative often meets with prospective clients after show hours to explain the product in more detail. Many companies hold informal get-togethers or cocktail parties for potential clients after the show. In these instances the individual is expected either to host the event or to be on hand to try to set up sales meetings or presentations.

Some Trade Show Representatives are also responsible for writing orders at the show, while others are just responsible for taking names, addresses, and phone numbers and setting up meetings for company salespeople.

Trade Show Representatives often represent the company on television or radio interview shows in the area in which the trade show takes place. The individual may also do print interviews for magazines, newspapers, or trades at the convention location.

After the trade show has concluded the representative may meet with advertising sales managers, marketing managers, or the public relations department to discuss the questions of customers and clients, make suggestions for future trade shows, or find better ways to increase the effectiveness of the booth display and layout.

Much of the life of Trade Show Representatives is spent on the road. People in this field must like to travel and not mind "living out of a suitcase."

Stress can be a problem for Trade Show Representatives who are required to sell products or services. For others, however, this type of position offers the individual a different way to work, meet a lot of new people, and travel extensively.

Depending on the structure of the company, the Trade Show Representative may be responsible to the marketing manager, advertising manager, sales manager, or public relations manager.

Salaries

Salaries for Trade Show Representatives can range from very low to very high depending on the company the individual is working for and his or her responsibilities.

For those people who are just responsible for manning a booth or demonstrating a product, salaries may begin in the $23,000 to $28,000 range. Representatives who have more responsibility, however, may earn salaries of $27,000 to $38,000 plus. Trade Show Representatives may also receive commissions on sales. These individuals may earn $100,000 or more.

Employment Prospects

Employment prospects are good for Trade Show Representatives. Most companies, corporations, and industries attend trade shows and conventions on a regular basis and need people for this position. More openings may be available in areas where larger corporations are headquartered.

Many companies also use the services of freelance Trade Show Representatives.

Advancement Prospects

Advancement prospects are fair for Trade Show Representatives. Individuals can move up the career ladder in a number of ways. Many Trade Show Representatives find positions working for trade show companies as trade show managers. Others stay in the corporate world and become advertising, sales, marketing, or public relations assistant managers.

Education and Training

There are many jobs as Trade Show Representatives that don't require a college education. However, a college degree is often needed in order to move up the career ladder.

Those considering college should take courses in sales, marketing, business, advertising, English, public relations, and communications.

Experience, Skills, and Personality Traits

Trade Show Representatives need to be neat, articulate, and personable. They need to be detail-minded and able to handle more than one project at a time.

Since the individual travels extensively, he or she should not mind living out of a suitcase and being on the road for long periods of time.

Unions and Associations

Depending on their duties, Trade Show Representatives might be members of the Public Relations Society of America (PRSA), the American Advertising Federation (AAF), the Business/Professional Advertising Association (B/PAA), or the Association of National Advertisers, Inc. (ANA). Individuals may also be members of associations specific to their industries.

Tips for Entry

1. There are often freelance or part-time positions open for Trade Show Representatives. Contact the personnel department of major corporations. Send a letter and résumé.
2. You might also find a freelance position by contacting the major convention centers in your area. Find out when various shows are arriving and write to the show promoters. They should be able to supply you with a partial list of exhibitors you can contact with a cover letter and résumé.
3. Positions are often advertised in the classified section of newspapers under "Trade Show," "Demonstrator," "Advertising," "Public Relations," or "Marketing."
4. Positions may be located online. Check out company Web sites as well as some of the more popular employment sites.
5. If you live in an area with a convention center, contact their management to see if they know of any openings.
6. Look at company Web sites to see if they list job opportunities.

SPECIAL EVENTS COORDINATOR, CORPORATE/INDUSTRY

CAREER PROFILE

Duties: Develop and implement special events and promotions on behalf of a corporation for employees and the community

Alternate Title(s): Special Events Director

Salary Range: $25,000 to $56,000+

Employment Prospects: Fair

Advancement Prospects: Fair

Best Geographical Location(s): Areas that have large industries and corporations offer more opportunities.

Prerequisites:

Education or Training—Bachelor's degree with major in communications, public relations, English, liberal arts, advertising, business, or journalism required

Experience—Publicity, public relations, and special events experience helpful

Special Skills and Personality Traits—Detail-oriented; creative; imaginative; innovative; good writing and verbal communication skills; people skills

CAREER LADDER

```
┌─────────────────────────────────────────┐
│  Public Relations or Marketing Director  │
└─────────────────────────────────────────┘

┌─────────────────────────────────────────┐
│        Special Events Coordinator        │
└─────────────────────────────────────────┘

┌─────────────────────────────────────────┐
│       Special Events Assistant           │
│    or Public Relations Assistant         │
└─────────────────────────────────────────┘
```

Position Description

Special Events Coordinators working in corporations or industries usually work in the marketing or public relations department. The individual's main function is to formulate special events and promotions to enhance the image of the company as well as to make it more visible. Special events and projects may be developed and conducted for employees or may be implemented and executed for the community.

The Special Events Coordinator of a corporation may plan events and promotions for a variety of purposes. The three main ones are to keep up employee morale, to build better public relations, and to obtain publicity and promotion for the company. For example, the individual might execute a special event to highlight the achievement of one or more employees, such as the highest-producing salespeople in the company. This would boost employee morale. He or she could run a promotion to raise funds for a community

cause or charity. This would help build better community relations, leading to better public relations. A special event spotlighting the introduction of a new product would help the company obtain publicity and sales.

Special Events Coordinators have a great deal of responsibility. They must come up with innovative ideas and then take them from inception to fruition. All this must be accomplished within a budget and a time frame. Individuals might plan any type of event, from a Christmas party for employees to a celebration for a corporation that has been in business for fifty years.

The individual begins the process by being notified that a special event or promotion is required in the company. This is usually initiated by someone in the public relations, marketing, or advertising department or by upper management within the corporation. The Special Events Coordinator must then determine general information about the program. This includes the type of event that will be planned, whom it is for, and the purpose, size, time frame, and proposed budget.

The Special Events Coordinator is responsible for developing an appropriate event. The goal is to come up with a novel, workable idea. He or she might come up with this alone or may brainstorm with management or members of the public relations, marketing, advertising, or promotion department. After a number of rough ideas have been developed, the Special Events Coordinator sits down and works out the details and writes a basic plan for the event. If approval is received, the individual can move forward and put the promotion into action.

The individual is responsible for devising a budget for the project and keeping to it. It is his or her duty to locate people, places, and items necessary for making the event a success. The coordinator may have to hire entertainment, talent, caterers, hosts and hostesses, and costumers. Other people may have to be hired and supervised to implement every aspect of the program. He or she might have to locate tents, chairs, stages, promotional items, gifts, and special food. The individual has to scout out locations, dates, and times. Every detail of the entire event becomes the responsibility of the Special Events Coordinator.

The individual may have writing functions, including the preparation of press releases and other publicity on the upcoming event as well as post-publicity on portions of the program that have already occurred. The individual may be required to write, design, and/or lay out programs, booklets, flyers, leaflets, and/or brochures about the program. Writing reports on the status or the result of promotions and events is usually necessary.

At times the Special Events Coordinator may function as a public relations person. He or she may call the media and arrange interviews, articles, feature stories, photo opportunities, and broadcasts. The individual also has to set up and execute press conferences, cocktail parties, luncheons, and dinners.

The Special Events Coordinator is expected to be present at most if not all promotions and events. Days are long. Events often take place in the evening or on weekends. Individuals usually work on many projects at one time.

The Special Events Coordinator is often judged by his or her last event. The individual can execute one hundred successful programs, but if one is deemed a failure, people remember that one. This can be stressful for some people.

Depending on the organization of the corporation in which the individual works, he or she might be responsible to the marketing director, the public relations director, or one of the company vice presidents.

Salaries

Earnings for Special Events Coordinators vary greatly between one corporation and another. Salaries depend on the responsibilities and experience of the individual as well as the type of business and its size, location, and prestige. Compensation will also be dependent on how important the company considers this particular position.

Annual earnings for those working in corporations and industries can begin at $25,000 for an individual with limited experience working in a small corporation. Salaries go up to $56,000 or more for those who have experience and are working in major corporations. Special Events Coordinators who have created extraordinary events and promotions may earn even more. Individuals working in corporations usually have their salary enhanced by various benefit packages.

Employment Prospects

Employment prospects are fair for people seeking positions as Special Events Coordinators. There are countless corporations and industries located throughout the country. It should be noted, however, that not every company has this position. Smaller industries and corporations often make public relations, marketing, or advertising departments responsible for planning and implementing special events and promotion functions.

Advancement Prospects

While there are a number of ways to advance the career of a Special Events Coordinator working in a corporation or another industry, prospects are only fair.

The individuals could move into the position of marketing director or public relations director of the company where he or she is working. In order to do this, however, the current public relations or marketing director would have to be promoted or leave for a better position. Individuals might also move up the career ladder by locating a position in a larger, more prestigious company where salaries would be higher.

Education and Training

Individuals seeking positions in special event coordination need a college degree. Possible majors include communications, public relations, English, liberal arts, advertising, business, and journalism.

Any courses or seminars dealing with special events, promotions, public relations, and publicity will be useful.

Experience, Skills, and Personality Traits

Special Events Coordinators should like working with people. Good interpersonal skills are important. The individual should have the ability to supervise others and delegate responsibility. He or she should be detail-minded and capable of working on many different projects at once without getting flustered.

Those working in special events coordination should be creative, imaginative, and innovative. Individuals need good communication skills, both verbal and written. A good understanding of the business or industry in which they are working is necessary.

Experience in any form of publicity, special event promotion, marketing, and public relations is useful in helping the individual not only obtain a job but be successful at it.

Unions and Associations

Special Events Coordinators may belong to associations and organizations directly related to the industry in which they are working. Individuals in this type of position might also belong to trade associations such as the Public Relations Society of America (PRSA), Business/Professional Advertising Association (B/PAA), or the International Communications Association (ICA). These organizations may offer ideas, seminars, guidance, trade journals, and professional support.

Tips for Entry

1. Get some experience by volunteering to run or coordinate special events and programs for community groups.

2. Try to locate a corporation that offers internships or summer employment in various departments. This will get your foot in the door and give you experience.

3. Many large industries and corporations have internal training programs. These take you straight from college graduation into entry level positions and move you up through the ranks in the department that interests you.

4. Job openings may be advertised in the classified section. Look under the heading classifications of "Promotion," "Advertising," "Marketing," "Public Relations," or "Special Events."

5. You can also send a letter with your résumé to the human resources or personnel directors of major corporations and ask for an interview. Request that your résumé be kept on file even if a position is not currently available.

6. Check out possible openings on employment and career Web sites such as Monster.com and Hotjobs.com.

SPECIAL EVENTS ASSISTANT, CORPORATE/INDUSTRY

CAREER PROFILE

Duties: Assist in the development and implementation of special events and promotions on behalf of a corporation for its employees and the community

Alternate Title(s): Special Events and Projects Assistant

Salary Range: $22,000 to $32,000+

Employment Prospects: Fair

Advancement Prospects: Good

Best Geographical Location(s): Areas that have large industries and corporations.

Prerequisites:

Education or Training—Bachelor's degree with major in communications, public relations, English, liberal arts, advertising, business, or journalism required

Experience—Special event experience helpful, but not required

Special Skills and Personality Traits—Detail oriented; creative; imaginative; innovative; good writing and verbal communication skills; people skills; typing skills; organization

CAREER LADDER

```
┌─────────────────────────────────────┐
│     Special Events Coordinator       │
└─────────────────────────────────────┘

┌─────────────────────────────────────┐
│      Special Events Assistant        │
└─────────────────────────────────────┘

┌─────────────────────────────────────┐
│   Clerical or Secretarial Position   │
│  in Department, Intern, Trainee,     │
│           or Entry Level             │
└─────────────────────────────────────┘
```

Position Description

The Special Events Assistant working in a corporation assists in the development and implementation of special events, promotions, and projects. These might be planned on behalf of the corporation for its employees or for the local community.

Special events and promotions are executed for a number of reasons. It is important for all corporations to enhance the public image of their company and to make it more visible in a positive manner. Companies also like to build the morale of their employees, honor them for special achievements, and give them incentives for doing even better work.

The Special Events Assistant has varied duties in his or her job. The individual may be required to sit in on planning sessions when the coordinator and management decide that a special event or program will take place. He or she may then brainstorm individually or with the group and come up with a variety of ideas and concepts for events.

The individual is often responsible for writing a preliminary proposal for the events that will take place. He or she will probably be required to do research in order to accomplish this. The individual may call or write to obtain a variety of price quotes on locations, decorations, supplies, and food. The assistant may go to libraries, trade associations, and bookstores to find information on similar events or to get fresh ideas for new or innovative projects.

The individual may have to search out possible locations for parties or other programs. He or she may make calls, write letters, or physically visit a variety of locations. Depending on whether the event will be held locally, in another city, or possibly even in another country, the individual may have to do quite a bit of traveling. Once a number of locations are chosen, the individual may have to check which are available for the dates and times of the events.

The coordinator often gives the assistant a checklist of duties to perform for each event. These might include checking on invitations, decorations, speaker's podiums, lighting, and audiovisual equipment.

The assistant may help coordinate all activities of events from their inception through the planning stage and up to the time of the actual event. Even then the individual's duties may not end. He or she may be responsible for writing or assisting in the writing of a report on the effectiveness of the event.

Individuals might be required to help plan any type of program from a press conference to a holiday party. He or she might also plan receptions for employees who have been honored, gala dinners, sales meetings, conferences, and conventions.

The Special Events Assistant does a lot of the legwork for the coordinator in planning a function. He or she may be responsible for finding people, places, and items necessary for making the event a success. This could include caterers, hosts, hostesses, costumers, and props. The individual may help the coordinator locate and rent or buy chairs, tents, and stages.

Depending on the type of function, the individual may have to find gifts and incentive awards for participants. They may have giveaways such as T-shirts, watches, and mugs designed with the corporate logo.

The assistant may screen entertainment and help the coordinator choose the best talent. He or she may be responsible for checking to make sure that all contracts contain the appropriate information and are sent or delivered, returned signed, and filed properly.

At times the assistant may be required to write press releases about the event. These may be written prior to and after the program. Depending on his or her experience and responsibilities, the assistant may also arrange for media interviews, feature stories, articles, and photo opportunities during all parts of the event.

The individual may also be responsible for assisting with the copy, graphics, or layout for programs, booklets, flyers, leaflets, and/or brochures about the program.

Everything that the assistant does is designed with the intention of helping the coordinator put together an outstanding, novel, and creative event that will be received and remembered favorably.

The assistant often puts in long days. He or she is usually expected to attend all special events, projects, and promotions. These might take place at night or on weekends.

The individual rarely receives a great deal of recognition for his or her part in the promotion. If it is a success, most of the credit will go to the coordinator. The Special Events Assistant is responsible to the special events coordinator, if there is one. If not, he or she might be responsible to the director of public relations, marketing, or promotion, depending on the structure of the company.

Salaries

Earnings for this position may range from $22,000 to $32,000 annually. Factors in salary variance include the experience, skills, and responsibilities of the individual and the size, location, and prestige of the corporation.

Large corporations often start an individual with a relatively low salary and increase it after he or she has proven him- or herself.

Employment Prospects

Employment prospects are fair for Special Events Assistants. Many corporations that do not hire directors for this position may rely on people in public relations, marketing, or advertising to perform the duties of the job. They then hire an assistant to do the legwork.

Individuals who are truly interested in landing a position in this field will have to look for positions in very large corporations.

Advancement Prospects

Advancement prospects are good for Special Events Assistants, depending on how they want to move up the career ladder. Individuals may move up by becoming an assistant director of public relations, marketing, or promotion.

Prospects are more difficult for an individual trying to advance to become a special events coordinator. Those positions are scarce, and there is not a great deal of turnover.

An individual who has experience as an assistant will probably receive priority for this type of job over an applicant who just has publicity, promotion, or marketing experience. Individuals who show creativity and have helped produce extraordinary events will also improve their advancement prospects.

Education and Training

Positions such as this require a four-year college degree. Good choices for majors include public relations, communications, English, liberal arts, advertising, business, and journalism.

Any courses or seminars dealing with special events, promotions, public relations, or publicity will be useful. Art or design courses might also be helpful when the individual is working on decorations for parties and events.

Experience, Skills, and Personality Traits

Special Events Assistants are required to run around a lot. The person in this position needs an abundance of energy. The individual should have the ability to handle all kinds of details without getting flustered. He or she should be totally organized and be able to work without constant supervision.

Special Events Assistants will often help develop ideas for special events, parties, and projects. They should be innovative, imaginative, and creative.

The individual should have good verbal and writing skills. He or she might be required to write letters, invitations, and press releases. The assistant must also have good phone skills, as he or she will often make contacts and arrangements on the telephone.

The Special Events Assistant who is artistically inclined is especially valuable. The individual can sketch out ideas for decorating rooms, artwork, booklet covers, or invitations.

Typing, word processing, and computer skills are necessary in almost every position.

Unions and Associations

Special Events Assistants working in corporations do not belong to any union. Individuals may belong to a number of different trade associations depending on their areas of responsibility and interest. These organizations often offer seminars, conferences, and meetings during which individuals can exchange ideas or hone skills. These include the Public Relations Society of America (PRSA), Business Marketing Association (BMA), and the International Communications Association (ICA).

Individuals might also be members of specific organizations directly related to the industries in which they are working.

Tips for Entry

1. Hands-on experience is valuable in a position like this. Try to obtain skills by working on school parties and proms or by volunteering to work in special events for a nonprofit or civic group.
2. There are a great many books available in your local library and bookstore about planning special events and promotions. It will be worthwhile reading up on the subject before an interview.
3. You might also want to look into magazine and newspaper articles on the subject.
4. Keep a file of special events, projects, and promotions you read about or see to give you ideas and inspiration.
5. You might consider putting together a portfolio of promotions or special events including suggestions for running the programs and budgets. If you have participated in putting any of these together, keep a notebook and photographs.
6. There are many freelancers who plan special events and parties. A part-time job with one of these individuals is another good way to get hands-on experience.

SHOPPING CENTER/MALL ADVERTISING MANAGER

CAREER PROFILE

Duties: Plan, develop, and implement advertising campaigns for shopping center or mall

Alternate Title(s): Shopping Center Ad Manager; Mall Ad Manager; Director of Mall Advertising; Mall Advertising Coordinator

Salary Range: $24,000 to $48,000+

Employment Prospects: Fair

Advancement Prospects: Fair

Best Geographical Location(s): All locations throughout the country may have job possibilities.

Prerequisites:

Education or Training—Bachelor's degree required in advertising, business, journalism, public relations, marketing, liberal arts, English, communications, or business

Experience—Experience in some facet of advertising necessary

Special Skills and Personality Traits—Creative; ability to handle details; knowledge of retail industry; articulate both verbally and on paper; knowledge of copywriting, graphics, and layout

CAREER LADDER

```
┌─────────────────────────────────────────┐
│  Director of Shopping Center/Mall        │
│  Marketing, Promotion,                   │
│  or Public Relations                     │
│  or Advertising Manager in Larger,       │
│  More Prestigious Mall                   │
└─────────────────────────────────────────┘

┌─────────────────────────────────────────┐
│  Shopping Center/Mall Advertising        │
│  Manager                                 │
└─────────────────────────────────────────┘

┌─────────────────────────────────────────┐
│  Advertising Assistant                   │
└─────────────────────────────────────────┘
```

Position Description

The advertising manager working in a shopping center or mall is responsible for planning, developing, and implementing advertising campaigns and individual ads for the facility. He or she may work with the mall's promotion director if there is one, the public relations manager, corporate headquarters of stores in the mall, private shop owners, and the shopping managers and owners.

The advertising manager is responsible for planning and developing the annual advertising budget for the mall. When doing this, he or she will call and write to the media to get rate sheets, demographics, and informational sheets. The individual also meets with various representatives of the advertising media to learn more about their publications or broadcast stations. As people often come from long distances to shop, the Mall Advertising Manager must decide

where his or her advertising dollar would be best spent. Choices might include local or regional newspapers, magazines and other publications, television stations, radio stations, cable stations, and billboards.

After the ad manager has developed the budget, he or she takes it to either the mall marketing director (if there is one), the mall management, or the mall owners for review. If the budget is acceptable, there is no problem. If it comes in too high, the individual must make adjustments.

The advertising manager must also develop ad campaigns for the entire year. These campaigns sometimes include advertising for individual holidays, promotions, special events, and sales programs.

Shopping centers and stores feel that as long as they have people walking and browsing, they will have shoppers. They may not make immediate purchases but will buy at some later date. The advertising manager works with the marketing, promotional, and public relations departments to come up with ads and campaigns that will help make as many people as possible aware of what the mall offers. The objective is to attract shoppers and browsers.

The individual often works with the corporate headquarters of stores and private shops in the mall to put together group or cooperative ads. These are advertisements in which a number of mall stores will advertise special sales together at a given time. There might also be some occasions when the mall puts ads in publications advertising all of its stores, shops, and food locations.

The advertising manager may be required to put together a shopper's guide of all the businesses located in the mall. The individual may have to contact corporate headquarters of chain or national stores to do this, as many of the stores cannot advertise without corporate permission. The individual might also help stores design ads for the guide. In some instances, the advertising manager will farm this project out to a local newspaper or magazine publisher who puts the publication together and deals directly with the businesses in the shopping center.

The advertising manager is responsible for advertising all special events and promotions the mall is hosting. These could include craft, antique, and home shows, petting zoos, celebrities, circuses, performers, and demonstrations. The individual may also have to come up with promotions or may just advertise those that either promotion or public relations people have developed.

The advertising manager may be required to do actual copywriting, graphics, layout, and production for advertisements or may work with freelance copywriters, graphic artists, and producers. He or she might also lay out rough ideas for advertisements and have the publication's or broadcast station's advertising department put the ads together.

He or she is responsible for deciding what media to place ads in or on, what section of a publication to have ads inserted in, and when to schedule broadcast commercials. The advertising manager is responsible for making sure all advertisements and commercials have accurate copy and graphics and are mailed or delivered to the correct media before deadline.

He or she must then track tear sheets, clippings, visual cuts, and audiotapes to make sure that everything has gone according to schedule. The advertising manager is also usually required to check bills for placement, send or authorize payment to the correct party, and keep records.

The advertising manager working in a mall or shopping center generally works normal business hours. The individual may be under pressure at times to finish ads before deadline or to come up with creative concepts for advertising campaigns.

Depending on the structure of the shopping center, the individual in this position may be responsible to the marketing director, the mall management, or the owners.

Salaries

Salaries for advertising managers working in malls and shopping centers may range from $24,000 to $48,000 or more annually. Individual salaries depend on the size of the mall, its location and prestige, and the amount of its advertising budget. In some situations the advertising manager receives bonuses when sales increase in a given period. Earnings also depend on the responsibilities and experience of the ad manager.

As a rule, the smaller the mall or the less experience the advertising manager has, the lower the salary. Larger shopping centers with bigger annual advertising budgets usually offer higher salaries. Malls with more prestigious stores and shops also usually offer salaries on the higher end of the scale.

These positions may augment earnings with liberal fringe benefit packages. In addition, most shopping centers offer employees substantial discounts when making purchases in the mall stores.

Employment Prospects

Employment prospects are fair for those interested in locating positions in shopping centers and malls and probably will improve in the years to come. Malls are located throughout the country, and more and more of them are springing up annually.

Almost every mall of any size has someone on staff to fill this advertising function. They may, however, delegate the advertising responsibilities to someone in mall management, public relations, or marketing.

There is also a great deal of turnover in these positions due to career advancement and the mobility of the profession and population.

Advancement Prospects

Career advancement for advertising managers working in malls or shopping centers is fair. Individuals can move up the ladder of success in a number of ways. The advertising manager may find a similar position in a larger, more prestigious mall. This will result in a larger salary and increased responsibilities.

The individual might find work as an advertising manager in another industry. He or she could also become a mall public relations, marketing, or promotion manager or might even move into mall management.

Education and Training

Most malls and shopping centers require the person in this position to have a four-year college degree. Good major choices include advertising, business, journalism, public relations, marketing, liberal arts, English, communications, and business.

Any additional courses or seminars in advertising, copywriting, business, or retail management would also be helpful.

Experience, Skills, and Personality Traits

Advertising managers working in malls and shopping centers should have experience in advertising. This includes knowing how to put together ads as well as understanding how to place them. Knowledge of copywriting, graphics, and layout is necessary. Understanding how to read and interpret rate cards is also a priority.

The individual in this position needs to be creative to come up with ad ideas as well as entire campaigns for the mall. The ability to communicate both verbally and on paper is necessary. The ad manager should be able to handle working with many details at one time while dealing with the stress and pressure of developing ads and placing them to meet deadlines.

The advertising manager should also have an understanding of the inner workings of the retail industry in order to be able to plan successful, effective ads and campaigns.

Unions and Associations

Advertising managers working in malls and shopping centers do not belong to any union. Individuals may belong to a number of trade associations that will provide support and guidance. These include the American Advertising Federation (AAF), the Business Marketing Association (BMA), and the International Council of Shopping Centers (ICSC).

Tips for Entry

1. Obtain advertising experience by working for a local newspaper, magazine, or television or radio station in the advertising department.
2. Take as many seminars and courses as you can in advertising, promotion, public relations, or publicity. If you can find seminars in retail management, mall management, or shopping center development, take these, too. These will give you added knowledge in the field as well as helping to build a contact list.
3. Larger malls and shopping centers often offer internships in the management office. Others may have summer jobs as assistants.
4. Positions are often advertised in the classified sections of newspapers. Look under heading classifications of "Advertising," "Promotion," "Malls," "Shopping Centers," or "Retail."
5. As there is quite a bit of turnover in these positions, it might be worth your while to send your résumé and a cover letter to a number of malls and shopping centers in the area you are interested in. Ask that your résumé be kept on file. Try to send your letter to the mall owner or developer.
6. Look for openings on employment Web sites such as Monster.com and Hotjobs.com.
7. Shopping center Web sites may also advertise employment opportunities.

SHOPPING CENTER/MALL PUBLIC RELATIONS MANAGER

CAREER PROFILE

Duties: Develop and implement shopping center and mall public relations and marketing campaigns; take care of day-to-day public relations functions; develop goodwill between the mall and the community; plan and implement special events

Alternate Title(s): Mall PR Manager; PR Director; Public Relations Director

Salary Range: $24,000 to $65,000+

Employment Prospects: Fair

Advancement Prospects: Fair

Best Geographical Location(s): All locations may hold employment possibilities.

Prerequisites:

Education or Training—Bachelor's degree required in public relations, English, journalism, communications, advertising, business, marketing, or liberal arts

Experience—Publicity or public relations experience or training necessary

Special Skills and Personality Traits—Creative; good writing skills; articulate both verbally and on paper; ability to handle details; personable; knowledge of retail industry

CAREER LADDER

```
┌─────────────────────────────────┐
│  Director of Shopping Center/Mall │
│   Marketing or Public Relations   │
│        Manager in Larger,         │
│       More Prestigious Mall       │
└─────────────────────────────────┘

┌─────────────────────────────────┐
│     Shopping Center/Mall         │
│    Public Relations Manager      │
└─────────────────────────────────┘

┌─────────────────────────────────┐
│     Public Relations Assistant   │
└─────────────────────────────────┘
```

Position Description

The public relations manager at a shopping center or mall is responsible for developing and implementing all mall public relations and marketing campaigns. The individual works with the mall advertising department and the advertising directors of the various shops to promote the mall and its image, campaigns, and events.

The public relations manager is responsible for taking care of the day-to-day public relations functions at the mall. These include writing press releases and weekly or monthly calendars about mall events and special promotions and making sure that they are sent or delivered to the media. The individual may be responsible for developing a media mailing list or updating an old list. Depending on the situation, the individual may do the typing, word processing, and addressing of envelopes or may have an assistant handle the task. The individual also prepares feature stories and special-interest articles for the news and other available media. The public relations manager must be able to write clearly and concisely in a factual manner. He or she should have the ability to come up with unique "hooks" or angles that make the story or release interesting.

The individual may be responsible for producing internal or external communications, booklets, pamphlets, posters, and newsletters. He or she may do the actual writing and layout or may work with graphic artists, copywriters, and printers in getting projects completed.

The PR manager may be required to take photographs of special events that occur in the mall or may be responsible for hiring professional photographers. After an event has taken place the individual is usually responsible for sending out captioned photos to the press. The public relations manager must always try to get as much positive publicity and exposure as possible.

The public relations manager also tries to take care of any problems that may develop with mall customers or shop owners or managers. He or she might make calls to people who have had problems or write letters to stabilize problems and situations.

The public relations manager handles contact with the media to let them know about special events that should be covered. The individual is expected to answer calls that the media makes to the mall seeking information. The P.R. manager must be comfortable speaking on radio and television and to reporters. Often, he or she is asked to be the spokesperson for the mall. The individual must maintain a good business relationship with all media to help ensure that press releases get placed in papers and special events are covered by newspeople.

The Mall Public Relations Manager is responsible for developing, planning, and implementing unique special events and promotions that help draw people into the mall. These might include contests, weddings in the mall, taste tests, petting zoos, craft shows, antique shows, and old car shows.

If one of the stores is having a special event, the mall P.R. manager helps promote it. For example, if a store is having a huge birthday celebration, the individual may write press releases, call the media to cover the event, and develop other promotions to coincide with the birthday celebration.

The mall PR manager is responsible for creating goodwill between the shopping center and the local community. He or she may invite local or civic groups such as the 4-H, Red Cross, American Heart Association, Girl Scouts, or Boy Scouts into the mall to demonstrate activities, pass out literature, or raise money. These groups may hold bake sales or other events to help achieve their goals.

In some shopping centers the mall PR manager may be responsible for attracting bus tours, shopping tours, or other group events. He or she may be required to design and develop promotional material for the mall, escort tours, or pass out giveaways with the mall logo.

The Mall Public Relations Manager usually works normal business hours. When a special promotion or event is planned, the individual may have to stay overtime to plan and implement the activity. He or she may have to work at night as well as on weekends.

The mall PR manager may be responsible to the marketing director, if there is one, the mall management, or the owners, depending on the specific structure of the shopping center.

Salaries

Salaries vary greatly for this position depending on the size, location, and prestige of the mall and the experience and responsibilities of the individual public relations manager. Those just entering the job market with little or no experience, or working in a small mall, may earn $24,000 or more annually. Individuals with more experience, working in larger, more prestigious malls, can earn up to $65,000 or more.

Most malls and shopping centers also provide liberal fringe benefit packages. As an added bonus, mall employees often receive discounts on purchases made in the shopping center.

Employment Prospects

Employment prospects are fair for this position. An individual seeking employment as a public relations manager can look in almost any part of the country and find at least one if not more malls and shopping centers. New shopping centers are opening every year. Most of these facilities employ a public relations manager. Many employ assistants.

There is also a fair turnover rate in these positions due to advancement and the general mobility of people today.

Advancement Prospects

Advancement prospects are fair for individuals in this position. The public relations manager has a few different options when moving up the career ladder. He or she may land a position at a larger or more prestigious mall. This will result in bigger salaries. The individual might also become the mall's director of marketing or the mall manager.

Education and Training

Most mall owners and managers require the public relations manager to have a college degree. Good major choices include public relations, communications, journalism, marketing, English, advertising, business, or liberal arts.

In order to have as much of an edge as possible when applying for a job and to be as effective as possible, it is important to attend seminars in public relations, marketing, publicity, promotion, and the retail industry.

Experience, Skills, and Personality Traits

Public relations managers working in shopping centers and malls need to communicate effectively both verbally and on paper. Individuals need the ability to deal well with people. The PR manager will often have to soothe customers or shop owners or managers who have had problems.

The public relations manager should have good writing skills with the ability to turn out a variety of press releases, proposals, memos, and letters. Creativity is essential, not only for writing and coming up with "angles" and "hooks" for releases, but for promotional ideas as well.

The individual is often forced to handle many different projects at once. The ability to do this without getting flustered is imperative. The individual should also be able to handle details smoothly and efficiently.

At times the public relations manager may have to implement an entire project with no help at all. At other times the individual may have to delegate duties. Being personable and having the ability to work well with others is a plus.

Knowledge of publicity, promotion, and the retail industry will help the public relations manager working in this type of setting excel in his or her job and move up the career ladder.

There are public relations managers who have landed jobs right out of college. Depending on the size of mall and its requirements for this position, the job may be entry level. Other malls may want an applicant to have had experience either as an assistant or doing publicity in some other capacity.

Unions and Associations

Public relations managers working in malls and shopping centers do not usually belong to any union. They can, however, belong to a number of trade associations providing educational guidance, support, seminars, and information to members. These might include the International Council of Shopping Centers (ICSC) or the Public Relations Society of America (PRSA).

PR managers working in this type of setting might also be members of local and civic nonprofit groups.

Tips for Entry

1. Try to get some experience in publicity or promotion. This could include experience in anything from a summer job to volunteering to handle publicity for a school project or local civic group.

2. Join the student group of the Public Relations Society of America. This association provides many services that will help you hone your skills as well as offers an opportunity to make valuable contacts.

3. Positions may be advertised in public relations trade journals or in mall and shopping center trade journals. If you don't have access to these through your local library, you can write to the trade associations and ask about sample copies or short-term subscriptions.

4. Positions may also be advertised in newspaper classified sections under heading classifications of "Malls," "Shopping Centers," "Public Relations," or "Promotion."

5. You may consider sending your résumé and a cover letter to malls in the area in which you are seeking employment. To find the correct address, look in the phone book under malls and shopping centers. Call the main office to get the address and the name of a person to whom you can send your résumé. There is a lot of turnover in these positions. Ask that your résumé be kept on file.

6. There are employment agencies that deal specifically with finding employment positions in public relations. Check to see if you pay a fee if they find you a position or if the company hiring you bears the expense.

ART DIRECTOR, RETAIL OUTLET

CAREER PROFILE

Duties: Develop, design, and create advertisements for retail stores and outlets; design and create advertising sales flyers, posters, show cards, and promotional materials

Alternate Title(s): Advertising Art Director; Retail Art Director

Salary Range: $23,000 to $58,000+

Employment Prospects: Fair

Advancement Prospects: Fair

Best Geographical Location(s): Positions may be located throughout the country.

Prerequisites:

Education or Training—A four-year degree in fine arts or commercial art is required for some positions; others may not have any specific educational requirement

Experience—Experience working in advertising or art department in any industry helpful, but not always required

Special Skills and Personality Traits—Creative; artistic ability; understanding of retail advertising industry; copywriting skills; knowledge of graphics, layout, paste-ups, photography, typography, mechanicals, and desktop publishing

CAREER LADDER

```
┌─────────────────────────────────┐
│      Art Director in Larger,    │
│ More Prestigious Store or Art   │
│   Director in Other Industry    │
│            Title                │
└─────────────────────────────────┘

┌─────────────────────────────────┐
│          Art Director           │
└─────────────────────────────────┘

┌─────────────────────────────────┐
│             Artist              │
└─────────────────────────────────┘
```

Position Description

The Art Director working in a retail store may work in a number of different job situations. He or she may work for a small or large department store, a supermarket, a regional retail chain, or a national retail chain. The Art Director might also work for a cataloger, which is a retail chain that may or may not have actual stores but sells its products or services through catalogs.

The individual's responsibilities vary depending on the size and structure of the retail outlet. The Art Director in the retail world may also perform the functions of a copywriter and an advertising director. In some stores he or she is referred to as the advertising art director.

In a small retail store the Art Director may be the only person in the advertising department. The individual performs the tasks of a sketch and graphic artist, layout and mechanical person, and letterer. The owners of the store may offer their advice and suggestions. The individual is then responsible for developing, creating, and in some cases actually placing the ads. The advertising art director may also be in charge of choosing which media to advertise in.

In larger retail situations the Art Director may supervise a staff of artists, layout and mechanical people, and copywriters or may work with outside or freelance people. He or she is still usually responsible for coming up with the advertising concepts and designing the ads.

The Art Director is often responsible for designing the store posters and flyers used for advertising weekly specials and sales. He or she may locate and work with outside printers. The individual may be responsible for negotiating prices or getting bids for the printing of large quantities of flyers and advertising sales pieces.

The retail Art Director is required to design and create advertising show cards and counter signs. These are the cards or pieces seen on the countertops or windows or hanging from the ceiling advertising new products, price breaks, and sales specials. As these cards change frequently, the individual usually letters them by hand with markers, paints, or ink or electronically prints them with the use of a computer or other printing mechanism.

The Art Director is in charge of designing promotional material for the retail store. Depending on the size and structure of the outlet, he or she may just do the designing or may be responsible for the development, writing the promotional copy, and creating the artwork.

Much of the artwork and advertising for large retail chains may be done by an agency. However, the stores often put out local advertisements and catalogs. The Art Director may be responsible for the layout and all graphics for these advertisements, sales flyers, and catalogs.

When creating advertisements, posters, flyers, show cards, and counter signs the Art Director will have to make sure that everything used in advertising and promoting the store will retain a unified identity and image. That means that while every ad may be advertising a different weekly special, each must look somewhat like the others. Logos must remain the same and be in a similar position on the ad each time. The store name must always look the same. In this way, when customers read and see the ads and promotional material they will think of the store and make a connection.

The Art Director usually works normal business hours. During periods when catalogs must be completed, ads need to be finished, or deadlines have to be met, the individual will have to work overtime.

The Art Director may be responsible to the store owners, if the outlet is a small one, or to a director of marketing, if the outlet is larger. He or she often works under the pressure of deadlines and the stress of designing creative, innovative ads that will draw buyers into the store.

Salaries

Salaries for the Art Director of the advertising department working in retail stores vary greatly depending on the job. The range may begin at $23,000 and go up to $58,000 or more.

Smaller retail stores usually offer lower salaries. The Art Director at this level may be a person with little or no experience at all. Earnings are also lower as a rule in smaller cities.

Larger retail outlets compensate individuals with higher earnings but usually require a higher experience level. The Art Director in these situations also has more responsibilities.

Employment Prospects

Employment prospects are fair for Art Directors working in the advertising departments of department and chain stores and are getting better. There are more and more retail stores following the current trend toward in-house advertising departments. These positions may be located throughout the country.

While major chain stores usually require prior experience, individuals may often be hired in smaller department stores for this position with little or no job experience.

Advancement Prospects

Advancement prospects are fair for Art Directors working in advertising departments in the retail world. Individuals can move up the career ladder in a number of ways. The most common is to become the Art Director for a larger, more prestigious store. An individual might advance his or her career by becoming the advertising or art director in a large corporation, depending on his or her qualifications. The individual might also locate a position as an art director in an advertising agency.

Education and Training

Most employers in larger department stores and chains will require that an applicant have a four-year college degree in fine arts or commercial art. Taking courses and seminars in advertising is a plus.

Smaller retail stores may or may not have the college degree requirement. Certain stores may accept an applicant with art school training or even a self-taught individual who can demonstrate that he or she possesses the required skills.

Experience, Skills, and Personality Traits

Art Directors working in the advertising departments of retail stores need to understand the concepts of retail advertising and art. In smaller stores the individual may be the only person working in the advertising department. If he or she doesn't know how to design and develop advertisements that attract buyers, they will not be effective.

The Art Director must be creative and artistic. In many positions he or she comes up with concepts for advertisements, designs them, and brings the ads to fruition. The individual must be able to sketch, draw, pasteup, lay out, put together mechanicals, and choose type. They must also have a working knowledge of desktop publishing and graphics software.

Many Art Directors working in retail stores must also write the copy for advertisements. It is, therefore, important that the individual have good writing skills.

A portfolio made up of the individual's best work is necessary in order to show samples and illustrate skills.

Unions and Associations

Art Directors working in the advertising department in a retail setting do not belong to any bargaining union. The individual may, however, belong to a number of trade associations that will offer professional guidance, education, and information as well as bring other Art Directors and artists together. Some of these include the American Advertising Federation (AAF), the Art Directors Club, Inc. (ADC), the One Club, the Society of Illustrators, the Graphic Artists Guild (GAG), and the American Institute of Graphic Arts (AIGA).

Tips for Entry

1. Put together your portfolio. Make sure it includes at least some work relevant to the retail advertising field.
2. Join trade associations. Many have student memberships. Others offer critique sessions on improving your portfolio. All of them will help you make important contacts.
3. A number of retail chain stores offer internships and training programs. Contact the company headquarters or ask the manager in your local store of the chain about where to get more information.
4. Obtain experience working in a newspaper advertising department. In addition to gaining experience, you will begin to make contact with local advertisers who might have a job opening down the line.
5. Positions (especially entry level ones) are often advertised in the display or classified sections of the newspaper. Look under the classification headings of "Retail," "Art Director," "Advertising," or "Store."

AGENCIES

ACCOUNT EXECUTIVE

CAREER PROFILE

Duties: Maintain a good relationship between the agency and the client; oversee an entire client account; plan advertising and/or public relations campaigns

Alternate Title(s): Account Manager; Account Representative; Service Representative; Executive in Charge; Contact Person; AE

Salary Range: $32,000 to $200,000+

Employment Prospects: Fair

Advancement Prospects: Fair

Best Geographical Location(s): Major cities such as New York, Los Angeles, Chicago, Atlanta, and Washington, offer the biggest agencies. Other cities may offer additional opportunities.

Prerequisites:

Education or Training—College degree in business, marketing, advertising, journalism, or liberal arts preferred

Experience—Agency experience preferred

Special Skills and Personality Traits—Good writing skills; articulate; creative; confident; aggressive; ability to work under pressure

CAREER LADDER

```
Account Supervisor

Account Executive

Junior Account Executive
```

Position Description

When a new client begins working with an agency, he or she is usually assigned an Account Executive. An Account Executive's main responsibility is to maintain a good working relationship between his or her agency and the client. The Account Executive is the individual who is totally responsible for overseeing a particular account. Account Executives may handle one or more accounts at any given time.

As an Account Executive, the individual acts as a liaison between every department at the agency and the client. When the Account Executive gets a new account he or she has long discussions with the client about program directions. In these meetings, the client discusses the product (event, service, etc.), budget, goals, and campaign ideas. The two also discuss how to best reach the goals. They talk about types of advertisements, various media, publicity, and promotions.

An Account Executive has a lot of responsibility. It is his or her duty to keep a client happy with the agency and satisfied with the services it provides. The Account Executive, who might also be called an account manager, account representative, service representative, AE, executive in charge, or contact person, is in charge of administering every aspect of the account.

While most of the Account Executive's job is administrative, at times it must also be creative. He or she is responsible for planning the kind of advertising that will be most beneficial, the timing and placement of ads, and the use of public relations, publicity, and special promotions. The entire campaign plan is usually the brainchild of the Account Executive. After coming up with the all-important advertising plan or program, the Account Executive must execute the plan. To do this, he or she will work with all the various departments in the agency.

The Account Executive meets with the creative department to explain exactly what the client wants. This includes both the AE's concepts and the thoughts of the client. Creative decisions are ultimately the Account Executive's.

The Account Executive also has to supervise media selection. He or she works with the media directors to do this. Without the correct media, even a good ad won't draw the right public to use the product. The individual must decide if it would be more beneficial to use print media, broadcast media, or both. He or she must make sure that a budget is designed and that the media department keeps to that budget.

The Account Executive meets with the client either formally or informally on a constant basis. At these meetings he or she pitches new ideas and gets approvals and suggestions from the client.

Much of the Account Executive's time is spent in conferences with various people from the agency and the client's office. On any given day the individual might have meetings with people from public relations, media, production, editorial, copywriters, artists, and research. He or she constantly coordinates the activities of various departments in order to run a successful advertising campaign for a client. The individual provides the departments with the information required to complete their work for a client. The main concern of the Account Executive is always the client and his or her campaign.

Account Executives, like most others who work in agencies, usually have to keep time sheets to account for the work accomplished for a client in a given period. This way, clients can be billed for the time actually spent on their campaign.

In certain agencies the Account Executive is also responsible for bringing in new business.

The life of an Account Executive can be rather stressful. If the client is not satisfied with a campaign, the advertising, the results, or anything else, he or she usually blames the agency, which in turn usually blames the Account Executive. In many instances, when a client leaves an agency, the Account Executive is terminated, too.

While the Account Executive is responsible to the client, he or she is ultimately responsible to the account supervisor or vice president of accounts, depending on how the agency is structured.

Salaries

Salaries for Account Executives vary drastically from individual to individual. Annual earnings may span from $32,000 to $200,000 or more depending on experience, type of client, or size of agency.

Larger salaries are usually found in metropolitan cities that have bigger agencies and better-known clients. Employees working in agencies also have their earnings supplemented with fringe benefit packages.

Employment Prospects

Employment prospects for Account Executives are fair. There are many agencies located in major cities, and a rea-

sonable number of agencies even in smaller locations. Chances of employment are better in New York, Chicago, Atlanta, Los Angeles, Detroit, Minneapolis, Boston, Pittsburgh, Dallas, and Cleveland. Turnover is high as a result of individuals leaving for promotions or other positions.

Advancement Prospects

There are a number of ways for an Account Executive to advance his or her career. One way is to find work at a bigger agency. Or the individual might stay at the same agency and obtain larger clients. Another way an Account Executive can move up the ladder is to become an account supervisor or a vice president. The Account Executive might also eventually open up his or her own agency.

Education and Training

While there are Account Executives who have no college background, a college degree in business, marketing, advertising, journalism, or liberal arts is usually required. Many of the Account Executives who are currently in the job market have been there for years. The people who are now moving up from other parts of the advertising agency generally have an education. Master's degrees are useful in obtaining jobs and moving up the career ladder.

Seminars, conferences, and meetings are also important to attend, not only to learn more about an everchanging field but also to network and make contacts.

Experience, Skills, and Personality Traits

An Account Executive must have a lot of confidence in him- or herself. He or she must be creative, well-spoken, articulate, and have a lot of energy. Hours are long in this job. It is not usually a nine-to-five position. Account Executives may work long into the night. Many times, even when an individual is home, he or she is thinking about the campaign or working with the client. The Account Executive must be diplomatic. He or she must be able to tell clients in a nonoffending way that their idea won't work. The individual must not be timid. The Account Executive must be able to come up with a unique idea for an account and not be afraid to present it to the client. Basically, he or she must be a risk-taker.

Most Account Executives have worked in advertising agencies in some form prior to this position. Many worked as junior account executives or executive assistants. Others worked in different sections of management at the creative end, in media, or in research.

Unions and Associations

Account Executives may belong to professional trade associations providing support and guidance as well as networking possibilities. These include the Advertising Club of New

York, the Advertising Research Foundation (ARF), Advertising Women of New York, Inc. (AWNY), and the American Advertising Federation (AAF).

The agency that the individual works for might additionally belong to the American Association of Advertising Agencies (4A's) or the Association of National Advertisers, Inc. (ANA).

Tips for Entry

1. Attend as many conferences, seminars, and meetings as possible. Networking is very important in this field.

2. Subscribe to advertising and public relations journals and periodicals. Many have job openings advertised.

3. Look for employment agencies specializing in advertising and public relations careers.

4. Look in the Sunday classified section of newspapers for openings under heading listings such as "Advertising," "Public Relations," or "Account Executives."

5. Openings may be listed online. Check out some of the more popular employment Web sites such as www.monster.com and www.hotjobs.com.

ASSISTANT ACCOUNT EXECUTIVE

CAREER PROFILE

Duties: Assist account executive with duties; learn how to handle clients and their accounts; obtain and check information

Alternate Title(s): Junior Executive; Jr. Account Executive; Jr. AE; Assistant Executive; AAE

Salary Range: $28,000 to $48,000+

Employment Prospects: Fair

Advancement Prospects: Fair

Best Geographical Location(s): Major cities such as New York, Los Angeles, Chicago, Atlanta, Washington, Pittsburgh, Dallas, and Cleveland offer the biggest agencies. Other cities may offer additional opportunities.

Prerequisites:

Education or Training—Bachelor's degree required

Experience—Agency experience is valuable whether it is an internship or a trainee position.

Special Skills and Personality Traits—Organization; ability and eagerness to learn; understanding of people; good writing and communication skills; ability to accept criticism

CAREER LADDER

```
┌─────────────────────────────────┐
│       Account Executive         │
└─────────────────────────────────┘

┌─────────────────────────────────┐
│  Assistant Account Executive    │
└─────────────────────────────────┘

┌─────────────────────────────────┐
│  Trainee or Entry Level Position │
└─────────────────────────────────┘
```

Position Description

Assistant Account Executives assist the account executive with his or her duties. They are responsible for doing a great deal of the tedious work of the account executive.

Assistant Account Executives often attend a variety of seminars and meetings, learning the ways that the agency does things as well as their policies and methods. Many agencies don't let their new Assistant Account Executives do anything major at first. They prefer them to watch the account executive do his or her job. Then they start by giving the individual limited duties. After the Assistant Account Executive has been at the agency for a while, he or she will begin assisting the account executive more and more.

While the account executive spends a great deal of time with clients, the Assistant Account Executive usually has only limited client contact. He or she may attend client meetings to obtain information. The individual may also attend strategy or planning meetings.

The Assistant Account Executive usually works on the same accounts as the account executive. The individual may, therefore, be working on one account or on many.

He or she may assist the executive in planning an entire advertising campaign or may assist in the development of just one commercial or promotion. The individual may also be asked to come up with ideas that might be beneficial for an account.

The Assistant Account Executive may do a lot of research on the companies he or she is working with. The individual might go over a client's previous advertising campaigns and then give the account executive his or her opinion of what worked well and what didn't. He or she may additionally delve into the client's advertising problems.

Getting to know all the people that work at the agency in the various departments is also necessary for the Assistant Account Executive. He or she works with them daily as more and more responsibilities are granted.

At times the Assistant Account Executive may act as a glorified secretary. He or she makes phone calls for the account executive, answers his or her calls, types memos, and answers correspondence.

At other times he or she may be asked to write reports for clients on the progress of their campaigns or direct memos to account supervisors on the effectiveness of an ad. He or she studies copy, makes suggestions for ads, does research, reviews media selections, and works on advertising budgets. The Assistant Account Executive will eventually assist the account executive in every facet of a client's campaign. He or she might even come up with the all-important "great idea" for a client. It could be a slogan or a new advertising concept. Whatever it is, it will help the Assistant Account Executive advance his or her career.

Assistant Account Executives work long hours alongside the account executive. Advertising is a tough business with a lot of competition. Everyone appears to want everyone else's job. While Assistant Account Executives do not have the stress of making final client decisions, the job is stressful nevertheless. Assistant Account Executives are responsible directly to the account executive with whom they work.

Salaries

Salaries for Assistant Account Executives vary greatly depending on the experience of the individual and the size and location of the agency. Salaries can range from $28,000 to $48,000 or more depending in experience, type of client, and type and size of agency. Larger salaries are usually found in cities that have bigger agencies and better-known clients. Assistant Account Executives working in agencies have their earnings supplemented by fringe benefit packages.

Employment Prospects

Employment prospects for Assistant Account Executives are fair. Agencies are looking for bright, motivated people to assist account executives. Positions are more available in New York and Chicago, as well as in the other cities where agencies are prevalent including Atlanta, Los Angeles, Detroit, Minneapolis, Boston, Pittsburgh, Dallas, and Cleveland.

Advancement Prospects

Advancement prospects for Assistant Account Executives are fair. While employment can often be located for this position, the individual must really work at the job and not slack off. He or she must remain interested, motivated, and willing and able to do more than the next person. Advancement for the Assistant Account Executive can be attained by becoming an account executive at the same agency where he or she has been working or finding an account executive position at another agency.

Education and Training

Assistant Account Executives are usually required to have at least a bachelor's degree in advertising, business, marketing, English, or journalism. An MBA or other master's degree is helpful not only in obtaining the job, but in moving up the career ladder.

Experience, Skills, and Personality Traits

Assistant Account Executives must be willing to learn. Individuals should be creative, well spoken, and articulate and should have a lot of energy. Hours are long in this job, especially if the individual is trying to advance his or her career.

The Assistant Account Executive should be able to come up with unique ideas for an account and should not be afraid to present them to his or her supervisor. He or she must be a risk taker. On the other hand, the individual must be able to accept the fact that some may not like or agree with his or her idea. The ability to deal with constructive criticism is a must. Aggressiveness and ambition are key to advancement.

Good writing and communications skills are necessary. Graphics, artistic skills, and any advertising experience is also helpful.

Many Assistant Account Executives worked in trainee or internship positions prior to their current job.

Unions and Associations

Assistant Account Executives do not belong to any bargaining union. However, they usually belong to professional trade associations to make contact with others in their field and to obtain support and guidance. These groups include the Advertising Club of New York, the Advertising Research Foundation (ARF), Advertising Women of New York, Inc. (AWNY), and the American Advertising Federation (AAF). The agency that the individual works for might also belong to the American Association of Advertising Agencies (4A's) or the Association of National Advertisers, Inc. (ANA).

Tips for Entry

1. Try to find agencies that offer internships or trainee positions. Once an agency puts time and effort into training a person, they usually are glad to have them continue working.
2. Join advertising trade associations. Go to their meetings, seminars, and conventions. You will meet people, have the opportunity to talk one on one, and collect business cards. A few days after the seminar, write letters and send them with your résumé to people you have met.
3. Seek out employment agencies that specialize in locating jobs in advertising. Remember, however, that these agencies often charge large sums to locate jobs.

4. Send your résumé to the personnel directors of advertising agencies. If a résumé looks good or a person looks interesting, the agency will call or write to set up an interview.

5. Jobs can often be located by checking the Sunday papers in cities where the major advertising agencies are located. Look in the classified section under "Advertising," "Marketing," "Public Relations," or "Account Executive" headings.

6. Look for jobs on the Internet. Check out some of the more popular Web sites such as www.monster.com and www.hotjobs.com.

COPYWRITER

CAREER PROFILE

Duties: Write advertising copy for print, broadcast, and out-door media; develop advertising concepts to sell products

Alternate Title(s): None

Salary Range: $26,000 to $90,000+

Employment Prospects: Fair

Advancement Prospects: Fair

Best Geographical Location(s): Positions located throughout the country. Jobs in major agencies are located in cities such as New York, Atlanta, Los Angeles, Chicago, Detroit, Minneapolis, Boston, Pittsburgh, Dallas, and Cleveland.

Prerequisites:

Education or Training—College degree required

Experience—Copywriting experience necessary

Special Skills and Personality Traits—Good writing skills; creativity; articulate; persuasive; knowledge and understanding of advertising industry

CAREER LADDER

```
┌─────────────────────────────────────────┐
│  Senior Copywriter or Copy Supervisor    │
└─────────────────────────────────────────┘

┌─────────────────────────────────────────┐
│              Copywriter                  │
└─────────────────────────────────────────┘

┌─────────────────────────────────────────┐
│          Junior Copywriter               │
│   or Copywriter in Another Industry      │
└─────────────────────────────────────────┘
```

Position Description

The Copywriter's words are what sells a product or service to the public. A Copywriter working in an agency is responsible for writing the copy for advertisements. He or she may write headlines, body copy, or both. Duties include developing the ideas and concepts that will sell the products. The Copywriter may also develop a central theme of an advertising campaign, tying together ads and commercials for the same product or product family.

Copywriting in an agency is a team effort. The Copywriter might begin by meeting with the client and/or the account executive. During this meeting he or she learns about the concept and direction the ads will take. The Copywriter may then do research on the product or work with the research department of the agency. The goal is to come up with some new piece of information about the product that helps show its uniqueness or presents a new angle to persuade people to purchase the item. The Copywriter has to understand the research done on a product and find a way to present it concisely and persuasively. He or she then works together with the art or creative director designing the most eye-catching ad possible.

The Copywriter must have the ability to formulate campaigns and concepts while following client guidelines. After the Copywriter has come up with a rough draft of the ad or campaign, the individual must get client approval. If the client is happy with the way the copy is progressing the Copywriter can go on. He or she makes any necessary changes and revisions. If not, it's back to the drawing board for another idea or concept.

One of the interesting things about the copywriting profession is that the individual does not necessarily have to write thousands of words for an ad to be effective. He or she might write a five-word headline and have a very effective ad that millions of people see every day. Many Copywriters feel it is very gratifying to see their ad in print, or to hear their words on television or radio commercials.

The Copywriter may also write the copy or scripts for television commercials. He or she may do this with a storyboard or a sheet of paper with spaces that resemble TV screens. Pictures of graphics are put into the TV screens. The dialogue is typed under each picture. In this way, the Copywriter can illustrate the action that will take place when people are talking. The Copywriter might set the commercials up in a way that resembles television or movie scripts, where the dialogue is on one side of a sheet of paper and the action is on the other. When doing copy for TV the individual may also work with producers, directors, production staff, and actors as well as the art and/or creative director. He or she may have to change the words as shooting or taping of the commercial progresses.

Another function of the Copywriter is to write scripts for radio commercials. He or she is responsible for coming up with the concept for the commercial and writing the copy, and then he or she may also choose the talent to do the announcing. Depending on the structure of the agency with which the individual is working, he or she may act as producer or may be responsible for locating one.

A Copywriter may also write the copy for billboards or other types of outdoor advertising. While a Copywriter working in an agency usually does the copy for all types of advertisements, the individual may also write copy for other things, including direct mail pieces, sales letters, promotional material, booklets, manuals, brochures, and posters.

Individuals may write the copy for all types of media or may just be responsible for copy for print, broadcast, or billboards.

Copywriters may work on more than one account at the same time. Individuals may work long hours, often taking their work home with them. They must constantly think of creative ways to say things in writing. There is a fair amount of pressure for individuals in this field due to tight deadlines and the constant need for creativity. Copywriters may run into dry spells where it seems that they will never be able to think of a good, creative way to develop copy. Luckily, however, these periods usually pass in a short time.

Copywriters may be responsible to the art director, the creative director, the senior copywriter, or the group head, depending on the structure of the agency.

Salaries

Annual earnings for the Copywriter working in an agency depend on the experience of the individual as well as the size, location, and prestige of the agency and client he or she is working with.

Individuals may begin their careers earning $26,000 annually. Those working in larger agencies and with more experience and responsibility may have salaries that range from $30,000 to $90,000 or more annually. Agency employees usually receive fringe benefit packages to supplement their income.

Employment Prospects

While all jobs in advertising are competitive, Copywriters have a fair chance of finding employment. An amount of luck is involved, as well as a lot of perseverance.

Individuals can increased their chances of landing positions in the cities where major agencies are located, such as New York, Atlanta, Los Angeles, Chicago, Detroit, Minneapolis, Boston, Pittsburgh, Dallas, and Cleveland.

Advancement Prospects

Advancement prospects are fair for the Copywriter working in an agency. He or she may become a copy supervisor or a senior copywriter. The individual may move up in his or her own agency or may seek a better position in another agency.

A lot of advancement in this type of position is dependent on the individual's creativity. If the Copywriter comes up with a spectacular ad, he or she may advance by handling more prestigious clients, which will in turn mean a higher salary.

Education and Training

An individual who wishes to be employed as a Copywriter in an agency needs a college degree. Majors might be in advertising, journalism, communications, English, public relations, or business.

Seminars and additional courses in writing and advertising are helpful to hone the skills of the Copywriter.

Experience, Skills, and Personality Traits

A Copywriter working in an agency needs excellent writing skills. He or she should have good grammar and spelling skills. The individual also should have the ability to write and think creatively. A basic understanding of advertising is necessary.

The Copywriter needs to be articulate and persuasive. He or she should be able to think clearly and present information concisely. Experience writing and/or copywriting in an advertising or public relations agency, or for some other type of business, is necessary. Many individuals gain this experience in trainee or intern programs. Others work in the advertising departments of newspapers, magazines, or department stores.

Unions and Associations

Copywriters who write commercials for television or radio may belong to the Writers Guild of America (WGA), a bargaining union for television, radio, and film scriptwriters. They may belong to a number of trade associations that can put them together with other creative people, help them advance their career, and offer seminars and courses. These include the Advertising Club of New York, the Advertising Research Foundation (ARF), Advertising Women of New York, Inc. (AWNY), the American Advertising Federation (AAF), the One Club, or the Public Relations Society of America (PRSA).

Tips for Entry

1. Write as much as you can. Practice by developing the copy for sample ads and advertising campaigns.
2. Put together a portfolio of the best work you have done. Prospective employers will want to see this book. If you haven't had any real experience, use sample ads. Make sure the book is neat and creative.
3. Look at a lot of magazines and newspapers and study their ads. You might also want to read trade periodicals such as *Adweek* and books on the advertising industry.
4. Call advertising agencies (you can get their numbers from the *Advertising Red Book*) and try to set up interviews. You can also knock on doors and try to get appointments. Remember always to bring your portfolio and résumé.
5. Get a list of advertising agencies where you'd like to work and send them a cover letter and your résumé. Send to the creative director, art director, group head, or even the president of the company. Get someone's name to send it to. Remember that you are trying to sell yourself as a creative writer. Put some thought into the cover letter. Make the person reading it want to meet you and see your samples.
6. You can often obtain experience as a copywriter in places other than agencies. For example, you may find a job in a department store advertising department or in the ad department of a newspaper or magazine.
7. Join an advertising trade association and go to their meetings and seminars. Ask people who have made it for their help.

JUNIOR COPYWRITER

CAREER PROFILE

Duties: Writing copy for advertisements, fact sheets, promotional material, etc.

Alternate Title(s): Jr. Copywriter; Assistant Copywriter

Salary Range: $24,000 to $35,000+

Employment Prospects: Fair

Advancement Prospects: Good

Best Geographical Location(s): Positions located throughout the country. Jobs in major agencies may be found in cities such as New York, Atlanta, Los Angeles, Chicago, Detroit, Minneapolis, Boston, Pittsburgh, Dallas, and Cleveland.

Prerequisites:

Education or Training—Bachelor's degree with major in advertising, journalism, communications, English, public relations, or business required

Experience—Writing experience helpful

Special Skills and Personality Traits—Good writing skills; ambitious; creative; articulate

CAREER LADDER

```
┌─────────────────────────────────────┐
│            Copywriter               │
└─────────────────────────────────────┘


┌─────────────────────────────────────┐
│         Junior Copywriter           │
└─────────────────────────────────────┘


┌─────────────────────────────────────┐
│  Intern, Trainee, or College Student │
└─────────────────────────────────────┘
```

Position Description

Junior Copywriters working in agencies write copy as well as assisting other copywriters with their projects. As a rule, the individual is not responsible at this point in his or her career for developing major advertising campaign ideas or themes.

The Junior Copywriter or assistant copywriter, as he or she might be called, is usually assigned a senior copywriter to work with. The individual helps the copywriter and does a lot of the grunt work involved.

His or her writing duties might include preparing copy for ads. The senior copywriter may write the headline for an ad and then give it to the individual to complete the body copy. The Junior Copywriter may also write promotional pieces, articles, bulletins, sales letters, direct mail pieces, booklets, manuals, brochures, and fact sheets. All of the material on which the Junior Copywriter works must be approved by the senior copywriter.

After the Junior Copywriter gains some experience, he or she may have the opportunity to offer some input into advertising campaigns and projects on which the senior copywriter is working. The individual may come up with some headline ideas or concepts that are shared with the senior copywriter.

The Junior Copywriter is also responsible for helping the senior copywriter with research for a client account. The individual may conduct interviews, search out advertising trends, and review consumer surveys or other data that help the copywriter develop the advertisement or campaign concept.

Many times the Junior Copywriter feels like a "gofer." He or she is expected to go for the coffee, the research results, the newspaper, and memos from other departments. The individual might also be required to do some typing, answer phone calls, make calls, and carry out secretarial duties.

Junior Copywriters at agencies usually stick to writing copy for print media. Additional experience is required before they begin writing television or radio commercials. They may, however, help the senior copywriter in rewrites of these types of ads or may assist him or her with the production.

In certain agencies the Junior Copywriter is required to attend training sessions or seminars where he or she is instructed in policies, different departments in the agency, the advertising industry, and/or job training.

There is a fair amount of pressure for the Junior Copywriter to advance his or her career. The individual may be asked to stay after hours to complete a project he or she is working on or may stick around to learn and do more than is required. The Junior Copywriter is responsible directly to the senior copywriter to whom he or she has been assigned.

Salaries

Earnings depend on the individual's experience and education. Other variables include the size and location of the agency for which the Junior Copywriter is working. Salaries in this position can start low, sometimes beginning around $24,000, and may go up to $35,000 plus. Junior Copywriters at agencies usually have fringe benefit packages added to their earnings.

Employment Prospects

Junior Copywriters have a fair chance of finding employment if they look in cities where the major agencies are. These cities include New York, Atlanta, Los Angeles, Chicago, Detroit, Minneapolis, Boston, Pittsburgh, Dallas, and Cleveland. Smaller agencies often hire only full-fledged copywriters because they don't have the time or money to train junior people.

Advancement Prospects

A Junior Copywriter advances his or her career by becoming a full-fledged copywriter. Advancement prospects are good for the individual who is eager to learn and capable of producing creative work. The Junior Copywriter may attain this advancement in the agency where he or she is currently working or may advance by seeking a Copywriter position in another agency.

Education and Training

Individuals aspiring to start their careers as Junior Copywriters should have a bachelor's degree in advertising, journalism, English, communications, public relations, or liberal arts.

Any seminars and/or courses taken in the advertising, writing, or communications fields are helpful.

Experience, Skills, and Personality Traits

A fondness for writing is essential to a Junior Copywriter. The individual should also have excellent writing skills, a good style, and knowledge of grammar and spelling. He or she should be able to write crisp, clear copy. The Junior Copywriter needs to be creative with an ability to express him- or herself well verbally and on paper.

The Junior Copywriter should be aggressive and persuasive. He or she should possess a willingness to learn and do more than is expected of him or her. The ability to work under tight deadlines is necessary.

Any writing experience at all is beneficial. Working on a school or community newspaper is helpful.

Unions and Associations

Junior Copywriters may belong to a number of trade associations that can put them together with other people in their profession. These trade associations give them the opportunity to make valuable contacts, may help them climb the career ladder, and offer valuable seminars and courses. Associations and organizations include the Advertising Club of New York, the Advertising Research Foundation (ARF), Advertising Women of New York, Inc. (AWNY), the American Advertising Federation (AAF), the One Club, and the Public Relations Society of America (PRSA).

Tips for Entry

1. Try to locate an internship or trainee program in an agency. This type of opportunity will get you in the door.
2. If you are still in school, consider finding a summer job in an agency. While working in the creative department would be ideal, any experience will be worthwhile.
3. Join appropriate trade organizations. If you are in school, many of the groups have student divisions. You will make contacts that will be useful in obtaining your first job and may even help you up the career ladder of success.
4. Put together a portfolio of your best work. You will need this portfolio to illustrate your writing talent for potential employers.
5. Use any contacts you have to get your foot in the door of an agency. If your mother's cousin has a friend who is employed at an agency, ask for help in setting up an interview.
6. Attend seminars on copywriting and advertising. They will help you hone your skills as well as put you in a situation with others in the advertising industry.

COPYWRITER, DIRECT RESPONSE ADVERTISING

CAREER PROFILE

Duties: Write copy for direct response advertising; prepare copy for brochures, sales letters, marketing pieces, etc.

Alternate Title(s): None

Salary Range: $24,000 to $80,000+

Employment Prospects: Good

Advancement Prospects: Good

Best Geographical Location(s): Positions are located throughout the country. Jobs in major direct response agencies are located in cities such as New York, Los Angeles, Chicago, Boston, Pittsburgh, and Philadelphia.

Prerequisites:

Education or Training—College degree required

Experience—Writing experience helpful; experience as junior copywriter, intern, or trainee useful

Special Skills and Personality Traits—Excellent writing skills; good command of English language; persuasive; knowledge and understanding of direct response advertising

CAREER LADDER

```
┌─────────────────────────────┐
│      Copy Supervisor        │
│  or Copywriter in Larger,   │
│   More Prestigious Direct   │
│      Response Agency        │
└─────────────────────────────┘

┌─────────────────────────────┐
│     Copywriter, Direct      │
│    Response Advertising     │
└─────────────────────────────┘

┌─────────────────────────────┐
│ Junior Copywriter, Intern, or Trainee │
└─────────────────────────────┘
```

Position Description

Copywriters working in direct response advertising agencies are responsible for writing copy for direct response advertising and literature. Depending on the experience of the individual, he or she may be responsible for simple copy such as headlines or may write the copy for entire mailings, advertisements, or promotional packages.

Buying products via direct response advertising is becoming a hot trend today. More and more people are shopping through catalogs, television, and specialty marketing pieces.

There are a number of differences between working as a Copywriter for a regular advertising agency and performing the job in a direct response advertising agency. The individual writing for direct response agencies must zero in on specific people or markets that are interested in a product instead of large groups that may or may not be potentially interested in the product. The Copywriter prepares the majority of the copy for direct mail and response selling instead of mass market advertising, such as commercials and advertisements on national television or in national print publications. The individual also writes copy to advertise a product that is available mainly through mail or phone orders instead of retail outlets.

There are numerous examples of direct response advertising. One might be an ad or sales letter sent through the mail selling a product that can be ordered by either phone or mail. Another is the literature received in monthly credit card statements selling merchandise. This is called "piggy-backing." An additional type might be the ads seen on television selling old records via a toll-free telephone number.

One of the oldest direct response advertising concepts is the catalog, while the newest innovation in direct response selling is the home shopping service seen on cable television. People see a product, hear a short sales spiel, and then order.

The Copywriter must write ads that make the consumer want to pick up his or her phone at that very moment and order using a credit card, check, or C.O.D. It is imperative that people look at and read the sales letters, advertisements, and literature and directly order merchandise or services. Many times Copywriters insert a coupon into advertising or promotional pieces in order to stimulate quick and immediate responses. This is why the method has been named direct response.

The advertisement may be sent in the mail, advertised in a specialized publication, or seen during a television program that zeros in on specific categories of people.

Copywriters working for direct response agencies may be responsible for preparing copy for a number of different items. These might include print advertisements, sales letters or brochures, marketing pieces, or copy for a television or radio advertisement. They might also write copy for catalogs or scripts for those selling products on home shopping networks.

The Copywriter is responsible for developing both advertising and sales concepts. He or she may come up with an idea to use as the selling point: the low price, the money-back guarantee, or a trial period. The point of the advertisement is to get people to call or write in at that moment and order.

One of the interesting things about writing copy for direct response pieces is that the results of an ad campaign can be seen almost immediately. People usually either order the product, call the toll-free number and charge it, or throw away or forget the piece. If a sales letter or advertisement does not draw orders, it can then be rapidly changed.

Copywriters working in this type of agency often work long hours trying to develop the perfect selling piece. Those who are successful are in demand.

Individuals are responsible to either the copy supervisor or the account executive, depending on the organization and structure of the agency.

Salaries

Earnings for Copywriters working in direct response advertising agencies vary from job to job depending on a number of variables, including the location and size of the agency and the experience and responsibility of the individual.

Copywriters who are just entering the field with little experience may start out with salaries between $24,000 and $28,000 annually. Copywriters working in small agencies in less metropolitan areas may earn between $24,000 and $40,000 a year, depending on their skills. Experienced individuals working in major direct response agencies may earn up to $80,000 plus per year.

Employment Prospects

Employment prospects are good and getting better. The field of direct marketing advertising is opening up throughout the country. The majority of these agencies are located in New York, Chicago, Los Angeles, Boston, and Philadelphia. There are, however, agencies located throughout the country.

There are entry level positions for those just coming into the workforce after college in both large and small agencies.

Advancement Prospects

Advancement prospects are good for Copywriters working in direct market agencies. This field is growing rapidly. Individuals may advance their careers by becoming copy supervisors. They might also be responsible for bigger and more interesting projects or locate a job in a larger, more prestigious agency, resulting in increased earnings.

Individuals who consistently write copy that elicits a good response will have no trouble climbing the career ladder.

Education and Training

Direct response agencies usually require that a Copywriter has at least a four-year degree. Good choices of majors include advertising, marketing, public relations, English, liberal arts, or communications.

The individual should take as many different advertising and writing classes as possible. These will give him or her the necessary background to hone advertising writing skills.

There are also seminars offered throughout the country on direct mail/market copywriting and the industry in general. These, too, will prove useful to the individual both for their educational value and to make important professional contacts.

Experience, Skills, and Personality Traits

The Copywriter working in a direct response advertising agency should have a complete understanding of the way direct market advertising works. Individuals need excellent writing skills. It is important in this field that the individual be able to write creatively as well as clearly, concisely, and to the point.

The Copywriter will have to prepare material that will catch people's eyes before they throw it in the trash. He or she must be able to write attention-grabbing headlines and persuasive body copy. A working knowledge of word usage, grammar, and spelling is necessary.

Unions and Associations

Copywriters working for direct response advertising agencies usually belong to the Direct Marketing Association (DMA). They might also be members of the American Advertising Federation (AAF), the Advertising Club of New York, the Advertising Research Foundation (ARF), Advertising Women of New York, Inc. (AWNY), the American Telemarketing Association (ATA), or the Mail Advertising Service Association (MASA).

These organizations offer educational guidance, literature, professional seminars, trade journals, and help in job placement.

Tips for Entry

1. Get as much experience as possible in all facets of writing. This will help prepare you for your writing career.
2. Collect samples of letters and promotional material that advertise products using the direct mail approach. Work on mock letters for advertising product via direct mail.
3. Put together a portfolio of writing samples. You may include a variety of different samples as long as there are some that illustrate your talents writing ad copy and direct response materials.
4. Contact trade associations to see which ones offer student memberships and join them. Ask for any materials or literature they provide about the field of direct marketing advertising. Some of these organizations also offer scholarships or internships.
5. Job openings are advertised in newspaper classified sections. Look under such headings as "Advertising," "Direct Mail," "Direct Response," "Copywriters," "Junior Copywriters," or "Agencies."
6. Don't forget to check out employment Web sites such as Monster.com and Hotjobs.com.
7. Company Web sites may also advertise job openings.

MEDIA PLANNER

CAREER PROFILE

Duties: Plan the media that will be most cost effective and produce the best results, and recommend the selected media to agency clients

Alternate Title(s): Media Specialist; Planner; Media Representative

Salary Range: $25,000 to $68,000+

Employment Prospects: Fair

Advancement Prospects: Fair

Best Geographical Location(s): Major cities such as New York, Los Angeles, Chicago, Atlanta, and Washington offer the biggest agencies. Other cities may offer additional opportunities.

Prerequisites:

Education or Training—Bachelor's degree in advertising, merchandising, marketing, business, management, or liberal arts

Experience—Agency experience, internship, or training program required

Special Skills and Personality Traits—Understanding of the advertising industry and media; math and statistics skills; negotiating skills; good written and oral communication skills; computer ability; ability to work under pressure

CAREER LADDER

```
┌─────────────────────────────────┐
│   Media Director or Supervisor  │
└─────────────────────────────────┘

┌─────────────────────────────────┐
│         Media Planner           │
└─────────────────────────────────┘

┌─────────────────────────────────┐
│    Intern, Trainee, or Junior   │
│         Media Planner           │
└─────────────────────────────────┘
```

Position Description

The Media Planner working in an agency operates in the planning section of the media department. He or she is responsible for recommending the portions of the advertising budget that should be spent on selected media. The individual determines if the client's advertising budget will be spent on television commercials, radio time, newspaper ads, magazine ads, outdoor billboards, Web sites, or a combination of media.

While this seems easy, the decision cannot be haphazard. It must be based on continuous research and careful planning. The individual must also determine the best, most cost effective areas within the specific media selection in which to place the advertising. If, for example, the Media Planner decides to use television time, he or she must evaluate whether to use national, local, regional, or cable television.

Once that decision is made, the Media Planner will have to ascertain what type of programming will be most effective for the product. Other decisions might include choosing the best times during the day, week, and year to advertise a particular product. If the Media Planner recommends buying space in magazines, he or she must find the right type of publication and then decide which of the publications in that genre are potentially most effective. He or she must also decide on ad placement. This might include whether the ad should go on the inside front cover, inside back cover, outside back cover, or in the run of the publication.

Throughout the entire planning process the Media Planner must keep cost effectiveness in mind. However, cost is of little value if the Media Planner recommends ad placement in ineffective media. The individual must constantly seek the right target audience and then find the cost of reaching that audience. His or her main function is to determine the least expensive advertising that will produce the best results. This can lead to stress on the job. It is often difficult to judge exactly which is the best choice in media planning.

In order to help with the choices, Media Planners work closely with the research department of the agency as well as working with outside research companies. Through this research process, the individual can find what age groups would purchase a certain product; what type of media (television, radio, magazines, newspaper, billboards, etc.) potential buyers read, pay attention to, and respond to; and specifics on people who have purchased similar products in the past. This information is important in helping the Media Planner choose the best advertising media.

The individual in this position should have a good understanding of research. He or she may be responsible for recommending to clients where to test-market products. The individual also has to recommend which regional advertising media should be used for the test.

In certain agencies the Media Planner also has the function of developing the ultimate media objectives. He or she may have to determine exactly what the client will end up with if he or she utilizes certain advertising strategies.

The planner may recommend media to the client and then give the information to a media buyer to negotiate. In other agencies, the planner may also function as the buyer and negotiate personally for the best prices of ads and placement of commercials. The planner may also be responsible for keeping to the budget that has been set up for the client.

The Media Planner could also be responsible for analyzing the results of specific advertising campaigns and reporting this to the department head, the account executive, or the client.

Media Planners can specialize in various kinds of media. The individual may be a broadcast Media Planner or may specialize in magazine, newspaper, or outdoor advertising. In smaller agencies, however, Media Planners are less likely to specialize and will have to become experts in recommending advertising in all media fields.

Depending on the organization of the media department, Media Planners are responsible to the media director, media supervisor, or media group head.

Salaries

Salaries for Media Planners depend on the experience of the individual, his or her responsibilities, and the size, location, and prestige of the agency he or she works with.

Those with limited experience can earn between $25,000 and $30,000 annually. Media Planners with more experience have salaries that range from $28,000 to $65,000 or more. Those working in agencies have their earnings augmented with fringe benefit packages.

Employment Prospects

Employment prospects for Media Planners are fair. There is a lot of competition in this end of the advertising industry. However, if individuals are persistent and good at what they do, they can find employment. Prospects will be more plentiful in the cities where there are more advertising agencies, such as New York, Atlanta, Chicago, Los Angeles, Detroit, Minneapolis, Boston, Pittsburgh, Dallas, and Cleveland.

Advancement Prospects

Opportunities for advancement are fair for Media Planners. Individuals can advance their career by becoming media directors or supervisors. Other individuals advance by becoming media group heads. Another option for advancement is to find a position in a larger, more prestigious agency.

Education and Training

A college degree is necessary for the position of Media Planner. Degrees can be in almost anything. Useful majors might include advertising, merchandising, marketing, business, management, or liberal arts.

Seminars in any aspect of advertising and marketing are also helpful.

Experience, Skills, and Personality Traits

Media Planners should have a basic understanding of the advertising industry and media in general. Individuals in media planning also need to have good negotiating skills. They should be good with math, statistics, and numbers. A knowledge of bookkeeping is a plus. Computer skills are becoming more and more important in all phases of advertising. Individuals should be articulate and confident and have good communications skills. Media Planners should have the ability to work under pressure and deal with stress.

Unions and Associations

Media Planners are not required to belong to any bargaining unions. Individuals, however, may belong to trade associations such as the Advertising Club of New York, the Advertising Research Foundation (ARF), Advertising Women of New York, Inc. (AWNY), American Advertising Federation (AAF), and the Business Marketing Association (BMA).

Tips for Entry

1. Try to find an agency that offers an internship or trainee program. This will get you in the door. Then it's up to you.
2. A summer job in an agency will also get you in the door. While there, learn as much as possible and do more than you're asked. It will pay off in the future.

3. Knock on the door of agencies with your résumé in hand. Remember to dress appropriately. You can ask to see someone in personnel or the media director or media supervisor. Be persistent.

4. You might send your résumé to the personnel director, the media director, the media supervisor, or even the agency president with a letter asking for an interview.

Try to get people's names before sending a letter. Don't just send a letter to "Media Supervisor," send it to "Mr. John Jones, Media Supervisor" instead.

5. Jobs may be located online. Check out some of the more popular employment Web sites such as www.hotjobs.com and www.monster.com.

MEDIA BUYER

CAREER PROFILE

Duties: Help clients find the most effective advertising space for their advertising dollar; compile information on cost, audience, and markets of various advertising media; negotiate for prices, broadcast time, and advertisement location in print media; buy advertising space

Alternate Title(s): Media Analyst; Media Specialist; Time Buyer

Salary Range: $25,000 to $60,000+

Employment Prospects: Fair

Advancement Prospects: Fair

Best Geographical Location(s): Positions may be found in cities where major agencies are located, such as New York, Atlanta, Los Angeles, Chicago, Detroit, Minneapolis, Boston, Pittsburgh, Dallas, and Cleveland. Other positions are located throughout the country.

Prerequisites:

Education or Training—College degree required

Experience—Agency experience necessary

Special Skills and Personality Traits—Good mathematical, organizational, and analytical skills; knowledge of media and advertising; computer literacy; articulate; ability to negotiate

CAREER LADDER

```
┌─────────────────────────────────┐
│    Media Director or Planner     │
└─────────────────────────────────┘

┌─────────────────────────────────┐
│          Media Buyer             │
└─────────────────────────────────┘

┌─────────────────────────────────┐
│      Assistant Media Buyer       │
│       or Billing Estimator       │
└─────────────────────────────────┘
```

Position Description

A Media Buyer working in an agency has one main function: to help the client find the most effective advertising space for his or her advertising dollar and buy the space. Since there are virtually thousands of places for a client to advertise his or her product or service, and advertising is expensive, the Media Buyer must choose the best place to buy ads. For example, the individual must decide whether a client should advertise in a newspaper or magazine, on radio or television, on a Web site, or through the use of billboards. He or she has to decide what types of publications, stations, Web sites, and programs will be effective, what advertising costs are, and what the projected advertising budget is.

Depending on the size of the agency and the organization of the media department, the Media Buyer might be in charge of collecting, organizing, and analyzing data on various media available. He or she might hand the information over to a media planner who will decide what media will be most effective for a client's advertisements. In smaller agencies, however, the Media Buyer might additionally act in the position of the media planner and recommend where clients should advertise.

The individual must know enough about the media to be able to recommend cost-effective advertising. A lot of research is done by the Media Buyer in order to locate just the right advertising for clients. Advertising costs for a certain medium might seem cheap. However, if they don't reach the right audience, they are valueless. Media Buyers must therefore check out all information thoroughly. If clients advertise nationally, this can be an extensive chore. The Media Buyer must contact television stations, radio stations, Web sites, magazines, and newspapers in every area in which a client will advertise. He or she must obtain rates as well as audience demographics and other pertinent information.

The Media Buyer at an agency works with others in the media department as well as with account executives assigned to specific clients. Together they plan media recommendations for clients. To do this, media and market information must be compiled, keeping budgets in mind through the entire process. The Media Buyer might also be responsible for preparing advertising budget proposals for client campaigns as well as keeping to budget.

The Media Buyer must find out what media are available to clients at the time that they wish to place ads. For example, if a client wants his or her advertisement to appear on the back page of a magazine and it is already promised to another advertiser, it would not be available. The Media Buyer would then have to recommend another part of the magazine, a different publication, or to wait until the back cover becomes available.

The Media Buyer gives the media information he or she has compiled to media estimators, who estimate the costs of advertising in the specific markets and media. If approval is given by the client, the Media Buyer starts talking to salespeople (also called space or time reps) from the media where time or space is being purchased. At this time the individual has the opportunity to negotiate and bargain for better prices and good broadcasting times or publication positions. This is also the time when the Media Buyer does what his or her title implies and buys the media space.

Every week reps from newspapers, magazines, television stations, and radio stations visit the Media Buyer to try to get him or her to buy space with their media. The Media Buyer must go through all the information on costs and audience size, type, desirability, and decide if the media is proper for clients. If it is not right at the time, it will be filed away for future reference.

Media Buyers are often invited to cocktail parties, luncheons, dinners, and other affairs put on by publications and broadcast stations. At these functions executives and salespeople try to sell the Media Buyer on their publication or space. It is their hope that the Media Buyer will then go back to clients and recommend the publication or broadcast station as a viable advertising source.

Media Buyers meet with newspaper and magazine publishers, editors, television producers, and radio station owners. In this way the Media Buyer will learn more about availability of specific media. At times these individuals call the Media Buyer to let him or her know about special shows and magazine issues where specific clients can target their market. It is important that the individual understand as much as possible about advertising possibilities in order to recommend the best places to advertise for each client.

The buyer is responsible for locating the most suitable audience for the product or service the client is selling, gathering information, and negotiating the best price. One of the most important functions of a Media Buyer is to have a good working relationship with advertising salespeople. If clients are not happy with a specific advertising medium, they will not advertise again. If there is a give and take between the Media Buyer and the salesperson, the Media Buyer will purchase more space and the salesperson will in turn sell more time. For example, if a client paid thousands of dollars to have his or her commercial aired during a televised sports event that normally had high ratings and the ratings were not up to par, the Media Buyer might be able to obtain a rebate for the client in the form of money or additional ads at no cost.

Depending on the size and the organization of the agency, the Media Buyer may specialize in just one type of media, such as television, or may buy the advertising space and time for all media.

The Media Buyer puts in long hours. Much of his or her work is done long after everyone else has gone home. There is also a lot of stress caused by people changing their minds about what they want and the pressure of meeting deadlines. Depending on the structure of the agency, the Media Buyer is responsible directly to the media planner or the media director.

Salaries

Salaries for Media Buyers working in agencies can vary greatly depending on the size of the agency, its location, and the type of clients it represents. Earnings will also be dependent on the experience of the individual and his or her responsibilities. Salaries can start at $25,000 annually for Media Buyers in smaller agencies. Earnings may go up to $60,000 or more annually plus a benefit package for those working in cities where the major agencies are located.

Employment Prospects

Employment prospects in this field are fair. As in all agency jobs, there are more positions available in large cities where the major agencies are located. These cities include New York, Atlanta, Los Angeles, Chicago, Detroit, Minneapolis, Boston, Pittsburgh, Dallas, and Cleveland. This does not mean that these are the only locations to find a job. It just means that there are more opportunities.

Advancement Prospects

Advancement prospects for Media Buyers working in an agency are fair. Advancement may be attained by becoming a media director or media supervisor. Individuals can also advance by moving to a larger, more prestigious agency.

Many Media Buyers hope eventually to get into account management.

Education and Training

Most agencies require Media Buyers to have a college degree. Acceptable majors include marketing, communications, economics, advertising, or business.

Seminars and workshops in advertising, media, and marketing are also useful.

Experience, Skills, and Personality Traits

Media Buyers should have good mathematical, organizational, and analytical skills. They should have a general knowledge of media and an understanding of marketing and the advertising business. Computer literacy is becoming necessary.

Media Buyers must know how to read advertising rate books such as Standard Rate and Data as well as rate cards. They must also be good negotiators. Individuals should have good speaking and writing skills.

Many Media Buyers started out as salespeople in small-market radio, television, or newspapers.

Unions and Associations

There are no unions to which Media Buyers in agencies must belong. Individuals may, however, belong to professional trade associations including the Advertising Club of New York, the Advertising Research Foundation (ARF), Advertising Women of New York, Inc. (AWNY), American Advertising Federation (AAF), and the Business Marketing Association (BMA).

Tips for Entry

1. There are a number of agencies that give media training programs. Write to some of the bigger agencies to see which companies offer these programs.

2. Attend as many seminars as possible. You will make the contacts you need to find out where there are openings in the media department. If there are not openings at the moment, people will often remember that you were looking.

3. This is the type of job where you can just send your résumé to as many advertising agencies as you want and ask for an interview. If they have an opening, they might call you. Remember to ask that your résumé be kept on file.

4. Join any advertising-related trade associations you can. These associations offer seminars, journals, workshops, and information for finding jobs and climbing the career ladder.

5. Job openings may be located on the Internet. Start by looking at the more popular employment Web sites such as www.hotjobs.com and www.monster.com.

ASSISTANT MEDIA BUYER

CAREER PROFILE

Duties: Assist media buyer in finding the most effective advertising space for a client's advertising dollar; compile information on cost, audience, markets, and demographics of various advertising media

Alternate Title(s): Assistant Media Specialist; Junior Media Specialist; Junior Time Buyer; Junior Space Buyer; Assistant Space Buyer; Assistant Media Analyst

Salary Range: $28,000 to $40,000+

Employment Prospects: Fair

Advancement Prospects: Fair

Best Geographical Location(s): Positions located throughout the country. Jobs in major agencies are located in cities such as New York, Atlanta, Los Angeles, Chicago, Detroit, Minneapolis, Boston, Pittsburgh, Dallas, and Cleveland.

Prerequisites:

Education or Training—College degree mandatory

Experience—Agency experience or training program required

Special Skills and Personality Traits—Number skills; organizational and analytical skills; knowledge of media and advertising; computer literacy; articulate; aggressive

CAREER LADDER

```
┌─────────────────────────────┐
│        Media Buyer          │
└─────────────────────────────┘

┌─────────────────────────────┐
│    Assistant Media Buyer     │
└─────────────────────────────┘

┌─────────────────────────────┐
│        Media Trainee         │
└─────────────────────────────┘
```

Position Description

The Assistant Media Buyer in an agency works in the media department assisting the media buyers with their duties. In some agencies the assistant is assigned to a senior media buyer and works exclusively on his or her accounts. In others, the individual works where needed most.

Assistant Media Buyers do a great deal of legwork in the selection and purchase of media time and space. The individual is responsible for searching out all types of media information and research. In order to accomplish this, the Assistant Media Buyer must determine whether the advertising and/or marketing plan is going to be a national, regional, or local campaign. This information is usually supplied by the senior media buyer or the account executive. The individual must also ascertain what type of media campaign is being planned. Television, radio, newspaper, Internet, magazine, and outdoor media are all options.

The Assistant Media Buyer is then responsible for researching the various types of media available in the chosen markets. He or she must obtain rates and demographics. This is done in a number of ways, including checking Standard Rate and Data books, calling and writing to publications, talking to broadcast time salespeople, reading rate cards, and reviewing data files that have been collected by the agency. Once the information has been obtained, it must be recorded and either analyzed or given to the senior media buyer or planner for analysis.

Depending on the agency, the Assistant Media Buyer may actually do the research or may work with the research department to locate information on potential markets and how they can best be reached. He or she also finds out where both the client and competitors have advertised previously.

The individual is responsible for tabulating prices of possible media buys for potential campaigns. Other functions might include calling specific media salespeople to determine if certain broadcast times or print media locations are available and what the rates would be. For example, the individual may want to find out if an inside front cover of a publication is available. He or she might also ascertain what type of discounts might apply and might be involved in negotiating the purchase of blocks of time or space for a particular client campaign.

The Assistant Media Buyer may review the data with the senior media buyer and/or the media planner and help decide what the most effective media buys would be. Low advertising rates do not mean that a particular medium is the right one. A low rate is only effective if the advertisement or commercial will be seen by the right people.

The individual may have writing duties, which would include reports on research findings, reports on price and effectiveness, comparisons between different media, memos, letters, and other correspondence.

In some agencies the Assistant Media Buyer may meet with the constant flow of salespeople and representatives who visit the agency in hopes of selling the media buyer on recommending his or her publication or television or radio station to account clients.

The Assistant Media Buyer may specialize in just one type of media, such as the purchase of broadcast time on radio or television, or may work with all types of media buys. The individual is responsible to either the senior media buyer to whom he or she has been assigned or to the media director, depending on the organization of the department. Assistant Media Buyers often have to work after normal business hours to meet deadlines or to finish up projects. Some people in this position feel they are working under stressful conditions because of deadlines and the general competitiveness of the industry.

Salaries

Annual earnings for Assistant Media Buyers working in agencies vary depending on the size and location of the agency and the experience and responsibilities of the individual. Salaries for this position can range from $28,000 annually for those with limited experience working in small agencies to $40,000 or more for those in larger agencies. In addition, most advertising agencies augment salaries with good benefit packages.

Employment Prospects

Since most agencies have at least one Assistant Media Buyer on staff and the larger agencies usually have several, individuals seeking this type of position have a fair chance of finding employment. Career opportunities are more plentiful in cities where the larger agencies are located. These include New York, Atlanta, Los Angeles, Chicago, Detroit, Minneapolis, Boston, Pittsburgh, Dallas, and Cleveland.

Advancement Prospects

Those who are aggressive and show an aptitude in the media field will have a fair chance of advancement. Career growth may, however, take time. Assistant Media Buyers move up the career ladder by becoming media buyers. Individuals can do this by being promoted in the agency where they are currently employed or by seeking a better position in another agency.

Education and Training

Those seeking careers in the media department of agencies should have a minimum of a bachelor's degree. Majors might include advertising, business, communications, economics, or marketing. Seminars and workshops in advertising, media, research, and marketing are also useful.

Experience, Skills, and Personality Traits

Assistant Media Buyers need to be good with numbers and should have both organizational and analytical skills. A general understanding of the advertising industry and a knowledge of media are necessary. Computer literacy is becoming a must in the field.

Individuals must know how to read advertising rate books and cards. They should have an aptitude for negotiating. Assistant Media Buyers should also have excellent oral skills as well as the ability to write well.

People in this field need to have an abundance of energy and must be enthusiastic and aggressive in order to succeed and move up the career ladder.

Unions and Associations

Individuals working in the media department of an agency may belong to a number of trade associations that will offer professional guidance and useful seminars and put them in touch with others in their field. Many of these associations also have student chapters and provide career advice. These organizations include the Advertising Club of New York (ACNY), the Advertising Research Foundation (ARF), Advertising Women of New York, Inc. (AWNY), American Advertising Federation (AAF), and the Business Marketing Association (BMA). Most agencies also belong to the American Association of Advertising Agencies (4A's). Employees of these member agencies can take advantage of a full spectrum of programs offered by the organization.

Tips for Entry

1. Try to find an agency that offers a media training program. You can locate these by writing to some of the

larger agencies and requesting information on these programs.

2. A summer job or internship in an agency will help you get your foot in the door as well as give you needed experience.

3. If you can't get a summer job or internship in an agency, consider a position in the advertising sales department of a television or radio station or a newspaper or magazine.

4. Send your résumé to advertising agencies and ask for an interview. If they have an opening, they might call you. Remember to ask that your résumé be kept on file for future openings.

5. Join trade associations and organizations. These will offer seminars, journals, workshops, career counseling, and an opportunity to make contacts.

6. Positions are often advertised in the classified section of the newspaper. Look under the headings of "Advertising," "Agency," or "Media."

7. Look for positions online. Check out some of the more popular employment Web sites such as www.monster.com and www.hotjobs.com.

MARKET RESEARCHER

CAREER PROFILE

Duties: Research market conditions in local, regional, and national areas to determine potential sales of products and services; compile surveys and questionnaires; tabulate results of research

Alternate Title(s): Market Analyst; Market Research Specialist

Salary Range: $25,000 to $58,000+

Employment Prospects: Fair

Advancement Prospects: Poor

Best Geographical Location(s): Most major agencies are located in large cities, including New York, Atlanta, Los Angeles, Chicago, Detroit, Minneapolis, Boston, Pittsburgh, Dallas, and Cleveland.

Prerequisites:

Education or Training—A bachelor's degree with a major or courses in advertising, business, statistics, social sciences, or marketing is required. Master's and Ph.D. are helpful for advancement.

Experience—Knowledge of questionnaire and survey techniques and tabulating necessary

Special Skills and Personality Traits—Analytical mind; ability to solve problems; mathematical competence; familiarity with statistics; ability to deal with stress; good writing and organizational skills; understanding of people; computer literacy

CAREER LADDER

```
┌─────────────────────────────────────┐
│   Research Supervisor or Director    │
└─────────────────────────────────────┘

┌─────────────────────────────────────┐
│          Market Researcher           │
└─────────────────────────────────────┘

┌─────────────────────────────────────┐
│          Research Assistant          │
└─────────────────────────────────────┘
```

Position Description

The Market Researcher is responsible for determining customers' needs, desires, interests, and willingness to pay for products and services. The Market Researcher working at an agency has an interesting job. He or she researches market conditions in local, regional, and national areas to determine potential sales of products and services.

Market Researchers are needed by the agency for many reasons. One is to help decide the kind of facts that should be stressed in advertisements. Another is to learn how effective a particular advertisement or commercial is. Other reasons include determining which media will most successfully sell a product, who is using specific products or services, and why people are purchasing other companies' or competitors' products.

In order to do market research the individual uses a number of research techniques. He or she might use a survey to find the answers to questions. The Market Researcher may be responsible for developing a survey questionnaire, or he or she may simply execute the survey. To do this, he or she would go out in public or phone a large number of people and ask them the questions on the survey. The survey might ask about a person's age, sex, and income level. It may ask about potential buyers' shopping habits and preferences. The respondents' answers would then be recorded and analyzed.

Market Researchers might use data that has already been recorded, such as information compiled by federal, state, and local agencies as well as private businesses. If this is the case, the Market Researcher would have to seek out the information and incorporate it into appropriate studies.

At times the Market Researcher might put together panels of consumers to test products in their home. Market Researchers may also conduct consumer buying surveys, audits, and new-product sales surveys. Many of the commercials currently reviewed on television are the result of market research. Most familiar are the blind taste tests. In this case a market researcher will set up a stand in a supermarket or mall and ask shoppers whether they prefer brand "A" peanut butter or brand "B". If the client's peanut butter wins the taste test, the commercial may be reenacted and used on the air.

While a lot of the time of a Market Researcher is spent writing surveys and analyzing them and writing reports on the findings, he or she often is out in the field executing interviews, supervising testing, and talking to people.

The Market Researcher must be comfortable speaking to groups of people, including the agency's clients, advertising executives, and marketing people to provide results of the research.

At times the Market Researcher will have to evaluate the effectiveness of advertising campaigns. To do this, the individual might bring in a group of people who have seen the commercials and ask them questions about their memory of the ad and if they plan to buy the product. If enough people fail to recall an ad or series of ads, the advertising campaign will probably be ruled ineffective and revised.

Market Researchers working in advertising agencies may also be responsible for doing the research to name or rename products. The individual may use questionnaires and surveys for a client's product and find that the public finds the name offensive, difficult to remember, or too much like that of another product. In these cases the Researcher would report to his or her supervisor, and a product name change would probably occur.

At certain agencies the Market Researcher works with the rest of the research department on all accounts. In other agencies the Market Researcher will be assigned specific client accounts for which he or she will do research. If the agency is very large, the Market Researcher may have supervisory functions, including training a field staff to perform interviews.

As so much of the research is dependent on people, the person in this type of position should be able to analyze not only numbers but people as well. For example, in a taste test many people will say they like anything, even if it is really distasteful. The Market Researcher must be aware of this and take it into account. The Market Researcher is, in effect, the liaison between the agency's client and the consumer who buys the product or service.

Depending on the structure of the agency for which the individual works, he or she will report directly to the V.P. of marketing or to the market research director or supervisor.

Salaries

Salaries for Market Researchers vary greatly depending on the size and location of the agency where the individual is working and the experience, duties, and education of the individual. Salaries can range from $25,000 annually for beginners to $58,000 plus for more experienced people at large agencies and with master's degrees or above. Compensation for most agency employees is supplemented by fringe benefit packages.

Employment Prospects

Employment prospects are fair for Market Researchers. To find employment, the individual will probably have to work in one of the major cities where advertising agencies are located, such as New York, Atlanta, Los Angeles, Chicago, Detroit, Minneapolis, Boston, Pittsburgh, Dallas, or Cleveland.

Advancement Prospects

Advancement prospects are poor for Market Researchers. While individuals can advance to supervisory positions such as market research supervisor or market research planner, advanced degrees are necessary.

Education and Training

Individuals interested in becoming Market Researchers should have at least a bachelor's degree with a major or courses in business, statistics, marketing, advertising, or behavioral sciences. An M.B.A. or Ph.D. will be useful in helping the Market Researcher advance his or her career.

Experience, Skills, and Personality Traits

Market Researchers must have good analytical minds and be problem solvers. Individuals in this type of work should have mathematical competence and be familiar with statistics. Good speaking, writing, and organizational skills are a must. The Market Researcher should like and have a good understanding of people and the way they act.

Additionally, it is almost essential now that the Market Researcher be computer literate. As with most jobs in advertising, the Market Researcher must be able to work under pressure in stressful situations.

Unions and Associations

Market Researchers do not usually belong to a union. They can, however, belong to trade associations such as the Advertising Club of New York, the Advertising Research

Foundation (ARF), Advertising Women of New York, Inc. (AWNY), the Council of American Survey Research Organizations (CASRO), the American Advertising Federation (AAF), Business Marketing Association (BMA), the American Marketing Association (AMA), or the Direct Marketing Association (DMA). These groups will put the individual in contact with others in the same field as well as offer guidance, support, and training.

Tips for Entry

1. This is a job in which a good education helps. If you can, earn a master's degree. If you can't, continue attending courses, seminars, and other programs.

2. Market Researcher positions are often advertised in the newspaper classified section under "Market Research," "Research," "Advertising," and "Marketing" categories.

3. If you can't locate position advertisements in the newspapers, write to an advertising agency's human resources department. Include a recent résumé.

4. If you are still in school, try to find a summer internship or trainee program. This will give you valuable experience as well as get your foot in the door of an agency.

RESEARCH ASSISTANT

CAREER PROFILE

Duties: Assist the market researcher in gathering, examining, and analyzing information

Alternate Title(s): Research Trainee

Salary Range: $23,000 to $30,000+

Employment Prospects: Good

Advancement Prospects: Fair

Best Geographical Location(s): Major cities such as New York, Los Angeles, Chicago, Atlanta, Pittsburgh, Dallas, Cleveland, and Washington offer the biggest agencies. Other cities may offer additional opportunities.

Prerequisites:

Education or Training—Bachelor's degree required; graduate degree helpful

Experience—Summer jobs or internships in marketing or research useful but not necessary

Special Skills and Personality Traits—Organization; accurate numerical and analytical skills; good verbal and written communication skills; computer knowledge

CAREER LADDER

```
┌─────────────────────────────┐
│      Market Researcher       │
└─────────────────────────────┘

┌─────────────────────────────┐
│      Research Assistant      │
└─────────────────────────────┘

┌─────────────────────────────┐
│         Entry Level          │
└─────────────────────────────┘
```

Position Description

The Research Assistant working in an agency helps the market researcher gather, examine, and analyze information. These data are used by the various departments in the agency to determine client advertising and marketing options.

Much of the job of the Research Assistant revolves around learning how and when to do things. The individual must determine how and where to research information and what to do with it once he or she has collected it.

The assistant has varied functions depending on the agency, his or her experience level, and the department's organization. Sometimes the Research Assistant works independently; at other times the individual works with the market researcher or others on the research team. The Research Assistant may take part in group meetings where members of the research department discuss different ways to test advertisements, commercials, and products and methods to analyze information that has been gathered.

With the current influx of electronic technology, much of the work of market researchers is done via computers. The Research Assistant may perform all varieties of computer work, from typing or inputting data that has been gathered to doing data searches and computer statistical analysis. The individual might be required to learn word processing programs as well as mathematical, statistical, and data-searching programs.

Depending on the individual's experience level, the assistant may help the research team develop surveys and questionnaires. The Research Assistant may do the legwork associated with formulating these type of tests. He or she may do research on similar and competitive products, media exposure, potential buyers, and demographics.

The Research Assistant is also involved in implementing the research strategies that have been developed. The individual might conduct surveys, interviews, taste tests, or telephone polls. After the testing is completed, the assistant is responsible for gathering the results and collating them in a form that can be analyzed.

The Research Assistant might be assigned to find and train a staff of workers to conduct the required tests. He or she would have to brief the workers by illustrating what questions to ask, how to ask them, and how to record results.

The Research Assistant is responsible for doing a lot of the grunt work associated with research. He or she frequently visits or contacts libraries, private businesses, and federal, state, and local agencies to seek out information for the market researcher, who then incorporates it into the appropriate study. The individual might make phone calls, take messages, compose letters, type surveys, and proofread results.

As he or she gains more experience, the Research Assistant will be required to clarify research problems and recommend solutions. He or she often has to locate research that has already been done by other industries and agencies as well as compile new data. The individual is also responsible for the analysis and evaluation of research results.

In some agencies the Research Assistant works wherever needed in the department. In others, the individual is assigned a market researcher to work with. Most work is supervised and/or checked until the assistant has gained proficiency in research methods and interpretation.

The Research Assistant may sit in on meetings with the client, account executive, copywriters, art directors, and media people. In time the Research Assistant will be delegated more and more responsibility. Eventually the individual will have the experience to develop all types of tests, questionnaires, and surveys as well as the capability to decide what type of test should be used in specific research.

Depending on the organization of the agency, the individual is responsible to either a market researcher or a research executive.

Salaries

Earnings for Research Assistants working in agencies vary greatly depending on a number of factors. These include the education, experience, and responsibilities of the individual as well as the size and location of the agency the person is working for.

Earnings can range from $23,000 to $30,000 or more annually. Those working in agencies may also have benefit plans to supplement their salary.

Employment Prospects

There are good employment prospects for those who are interested in entering the field of research. More and more companies are insisting on a full research program before they spend a fortune on advertising.

Individuals who want to work as Research Assistants in agencies will increase their employment prospects if they seek employment in a city where there are large numbers of agencies. These include New York, Atlanta, Los Angeles, Chicago, Detroit, Minneapolis, Boston, Pittsburgh, Dallas, and Cleveland.

Advancement Prospects

Research Assistants can advance their career by becoming market researchers. This may take from six months to two years, depending on the individual and the agency he or she is working for. Research Assistants who continue their education, obtaining a master's degree or possibly a Ph.D., have better advancement prospects. Individuals can also move up the career ladder by finding employment in private research firms, marketing companies, or the research departments of other businesses.

Education and Training

A good education is very important for people who want to get into market research. An undergraduate degree is the minimum educational requirement. Some positions may require graduate degrees. Courses in business, statistics, marketing, advertising, behavioral sciences, and research are useful.

Experience, Skills, and Personality Traits

Those interested in research should be highly organized. They should have accurate numerical and analytical skills. Individuals need communications skills, both written and verbal. Research Assistants should also be good with people and have the ability to talk to them and gain their confidence. Computer competence is a plus in some jobs and a requirement in others.

While some people obtain entry level jobs in this field with no experience at all, summer jobs or internships in marketing and/or research are useful.

Unions and Associations

Research Assistants have no bargaining union. They may belong to trade associations that will put them in touch with others in their field, help them make contacts, and provide useful information and seminars.

Some of these organizations include the Advertising Research Foundation (ARF), the Business Marketing Association (BMA), the Advertising Club of New York, Advertising Women of New York, Inc. (AWNY), the American Marketing Association (AMA), the Direct Marketing Association, Inc. (DMA), and the Council of American Survey Research Organizations (CASRO).

Tips for Entry

1. If you are still in school, you can often find a professor who is looking for an assistant in this field. This will provide you with the necessary experience.
2. You might also try to locate a summer job, internship, or trainee program in an agency or market research firm.
3. These types of positions are often advertised in the newspaper. Look in the classifieds under such category headings as "Market Research," "Research," "Advertising," or "Marketing."
4. Join appropriate trade organizations. Many of these offer valuable career assistance to students trying to enter the field.

ASSISTANT ART DIRECTOR

CAREER PROFILE

Duties: Assist art director in formulating advertisements and ad campaigns; create ads

Alternate Title(s): Junior Art Director; Art Director Assistant; Associate Art Director

Salary Range: $26,000 to $60,000+

Employment Prospects: Fair

Advancement Prospects: Fair

Best Geographical Location(s): Positions are located throughout the country. Jobs in major agencies are located in cities such as New York, Atlanta, Los Angeles, Chicago, Detroit, Minneapolis, Boston, Pittsburgh, Dallas, and Cleveland.

Prerequisites:

Education or Training—Art school training or college degree in fine art, commercial art, graphics, communications, or advertising preferred

Experience—Agency experience useful

Special Skills and Personality Traits—Creative; supervisory skills; artistic ability

CAREER LADDER

```
┌─────────────────────────────────────┐
│            Art Director             │
└─────────────────────────────────────┘

┌─────────────────────────────────────┐
│        Assistant Art Director       │
└─────────────────────────────────────┘

┌─────────────────────────────────────┐
│  Artist, Illustrator, Layout Person,│
│         or Graphic Designer         │
└─────────────────────────────────────┘
```

Position Description

The Assistant Art Director of an agency works with the art director, copywriter, and other members of the creative services department to formulate the visual appearance of advertisements. He or she might be totally responsible for an ad from the concept to the finished advertisement, or he or she may assist the art director with his or her ads. The individual may create print ads for any type of media including newspapers, magazines, billboards, direct mail, packaging, posters, books, or broadcast advertisements.

The Assistant Art Director is usually assigned one or more client accounts. Depending on the size and the organization of the agency, he or she may be assigned one or more client accounts or may assist the art director with his or her clients. Whatever the case, the individual works with the other agency people assigned to the same account to create advertisements for the client. For example, the individual might work with a graphic artist laying out a rough draft of an ad, or he or she might work with an artist or illustrator obtaining drawings and sketches for the advertisement. The Assistant Art Director also works extensively with the account executive, getting his or her feedback and ideas on advertisement concepts and needs.

One of the most important responsibilities of the Assistant Art Director is to work with the copywriter, trying to find the most effective way to put the words and graphics together. Ads must be effective or they won't sell the product or service that the client is trying to push. If ads don't work, the client may change advertising agencies in hopes of finding someone who can better express the company's product or service.

The Assistant Art Director often visits the client's plant or place of business to gain an insight into what the client wants and how they want it shown to the public. If, for example, a client wants to advertise a new computer line that is being marketed for schoolchildren, the Assistant Art Director might visit a school or homes that currently use the computers. In this way he or she can see the product in use and may come up with an advertising concept to sell the product to others.

Throughout the creative process the Assistant Art Director reviews and presents the final layouts to the art director, creative director, or account executive in charge of the client. It is also the responsibility of the Assistant Art Director to make sure that the advertising concept receives approval from the account executive, who gets it from the client. Even with this approval, after long periods of work to come up with, what the individual thinks is the perfect ad, the client may decide it is not what is wanted after all, and the Assistant Art Director must start all over again.

Depending on the size and the organization of the agency, another of the duties of the Assistant Art Director may be to supervise members of the creative services department. He or she may supervise artists, illustrators, cartoonists, and designers. If agencies are large, there could be a number of Assistant Art Directors working in the creative department. In smaller agencies there might be only one or two. If the agency the individual is working for is very small, he or she may also perform the duties of a graphic designer, illustrator, or artist. If the agency is larger, the Assistant Art Director may just create layout ideas for print media and storyboards for television.

Assistant Art Directors may work in both print media and broadcast media or might be assigned to just one. Individuals in this type of job may also specialize in particular fields, media, or types of layout.

Another responsibility of an Assistant Art Director is reviewing portfolios of freelance photographers, illustrators, artists, directors, and producers.

At certain agencies the Assistant Art Director, along with the art director, creative director, copywriter, and account executive, makes presentations of advertisements and advertising campaigns. It is therefore important that the Assistant Art Director be articulate, able to speak in public, and confident in his or her ideas.

This is a high-stress job in which work is often brought home. There is constant pressure to come up with creative ideas and advertisements. If the advertising campaign is successful, the Assistant Art Director will have the satisfaction of seeing his or her ads all over.

Depending on the organization of the agency, the Assistant Art Director is responsible to the art director, the creative director, or the account executive assigned to the client.

Salaries

Salaries for Assistant Art Directors working in agencies are dependent on the size, location, and prestige of the agency. Salaries will be higher for individuals working in larger, more prestigious agencies.

Salaries for Assistant Art Directors can range from $26,000 to $60,000 plus, depending on the agency. Compensation in most agency positions includes fringe benefit packages.

Employment Prospects

Employment prospects for Assistant Art Directors in agencies are fair. The individual will find more opportunities in a major city where there are many more agencies. These cities include New York, Atlanta, Los Angeles, Chicago, Detroit, Minneapolis, Boston, Pittsburgh, Dallas, and Cleveland.

Advancement Prospects

Chances of advancement as an Assistant Art Director are fair. If an individual is creative and good at what he or she does, there should be no problem moving up in a particular agency. Agencies like to promote from within. It should be noted that individuals in this position move around a lot. This gives ample opportunity to move to a bigger agency, to a better agency, or up the career ladder to become an art director or eventually a creative director.

Education and Training

An Assistant Art Director working in an agency usually has some sort of art training. This may come in the form of art school or a college degree in fine arts, commercial art, or graphics. The individual may also be hired with just some courses in drawing or graphics. Since much of this type of job is creative, many agencies will accept an applicant on the basis of a good portfolio. Assistant Art Directors may have degrees in communications with minors in art or in advertising.

Experience, Skills, and Personality Traits

One of the biggest qualifications for this job is creativity and the ability to display it to others. While it is not always necessary for the Assistant Art Director to create exact artwork for an advertisement, he or she must be able to explain to the artist what the concept should be. He or she must have the ability to visualize what an ad will look like when finished. The Assistant Art Director must also have supervisory skills and be a team member.

Assistant Art Directors must be articulate. An ability to write is helpful. A portfolio that illustrates commercial art ability and creativity is necessary, as is an understanding of the advertising business.

Unions and Associations

There are no bargaining unions for Assistant Art Directors working in agencies. Individuals may, however, belong to any number of trade associations, including the American Advertising Federation (AAF), the Art Directors Club, Inc. (ADC), the One Club, or the Society of Illustrators. These organizations will put the individual in contact with others in the same field and offer professional guidance and support.

Tips for Entry

1. Find an advertising agency and/or school with an internship program. Agencies are usually happy to keep you working after they have trained you.

2. This is not usually an entry level position. Start in the art department in any job you can obtain. You will move up quickly.

3. Put together a good portfolio. Try to show marketability, versatility, and creativity.

4. Before going to a job interview, find out something about the company and its client roster. Try to go in with a few creative ideas. This is a position where ideas can land you a job. Don't be afraid to communicate your creativity!

5. Take classes in advertising. You will not only improve your craft, you might make some important contacts.

COMMERCIAL ARTIST

CAREER PROFILE

Duties: Illustrate advertisements and commercials; prepare storyboards; lay out advertisements

Alternate Title(s): Artist; Graphic Artist; Illustrator

Salary Range: $24,000 to $50,000+

Employment Prospects: Fair

Advancement Prospects: Fair

Best Geographical Location(s): Positions are available throughout the country. Jobs in major agencies are located in cities such as New York, Atlanta, Los Angeles, Chicago, Detroit, Minneapolis, Boston, Pittsburgh, Dallas, and Cleveland.

Prerequisites:

Education or Training—Art school, art courses, or college degree with major in art helpful

Experience—Illustrating or advertisement layout useful

Special Skills and Personality Traits—Understanding of advertising; creative; artistic ability; knowledge of commercial art; drawing and illustration skills; computer skills

CAREER LADDER

```
┌─────────────────────────────────┐
│          Art Director           │
└─────────────────────────────────┘

┌─────────────────────────────────┐
│        Commercial Artist        │
└─────────────────────────────────┘

┌─────────────────────────────────┐
│     Illustrator or Entry Level   │
└─────────────────────────────────┘
```

Position Description

The Commercial Artist in an agency works in the creative department. The creative department is divided into the art division and the copywriting division. The individual in this position does with pictures what copywriters do with words. He or she comes up with creative ways of illustrating what the account executive and client want to show in an ad or commercial.

The Commercial Artist works with other staff members in the agency. He or she is responsible for creating the art that will be used in advertisements in the most appealing way possible. To do this, he or she must learn about the advertising campaign and the product from the account executive. The individual also needs to know what type of copy is being used in the ad. The Commercial Artist obtains this information from the copywriter. The two work hand in hand with the art director, who guides the artist on the ad concept.

In some agencies the Commercial Artist is responsible just for illustrating the ad. In others he or she is responsible for creating the layout of the ad. This is usually just a rough sketch of how the ad will look. He or she must consider such things as the type of art or pictures that will be used in the advertisement and where they should be placed in relation to the copy.

The individual is responsible for making a detailed drawing of the way the ad will look. If the Commercial Artist is working on a television commercial instead of a print ad or billboard, it will be his or her duty to put together a storyboard. The storyboard resembles a big comic strip and illustrates what will happen in a television commercial. These are often used to pitch a client on an ad idea or an advertising campaign.

The Commercial Artist must be adept at not only drawing and illustrating but other art forms as well. For example, he or she may be asked to do cartoons and should also be skilled in using computer graphics and layout programs.

In order for the Commercial Artist to make an advertisement eye-catching, he or she may do many drafts. These will include layouts and sketches.

When illustrating and laying out an ad the individual must select the correct size and typeface for lettering. He or she must also decide the style of type. For example, will the ad use bold lettering or italic? Nine-point type or thirty-six? The possibilities are endless, and the Commercial Artist must know what will be most effective.

At times the Commercial Artist may be asked to design a commercial logo or trademark for a client. The logo or trademark is the emblem or symbol that will assist consumers to remember the product every time they see it. To design a logo for a company, the artist may visit the company's plant. He or she will probably spend some time with the client as well as the advertising executive assigned to the account. The individual may have to design a dozen or more different logos until he or she finds one the client is happy with.

The Commercial Artist must determine what colors to use in the ad. He or she may try illustrating the same advertisement with a number of different colors. He or she may also lay out the ad in a number of different ways, hoping to come up with something that is both appealing and eye-catching.

Throughout the entire process of creating the finished advertisement the Commercial Artist must get approvals from his or her art director, the account executive, and the client. There will also be a great deal of input from the copywriter.

Depending on the size and the organization of the agency and the department, the Commercial Artist may specialize in working with one type of ad, such as print, outdoor billboards, or television; in many agencies, however, the Commercial Artist works on ads for all media.

Other duties of the Commercial Artist might include creating the artwork for new packages, merchandising and promotional materials, or booklets and manuals. At times he or she may be asked to revise an advertisement that has already been prepared by another individual. This is one of the hardest things to do, because most artists tend to see things differently.

The Commercial Artist is usually directly responsible to the art director. The commercial art position is not always a straight nine-to-five job. There may be times when ads must be finished in a day. The artist may find that days are not long enough to finish work and have to come up with creative ideas at home.

Salaries

Salaries for Commercial Artists working in agencies vary greatly depending on the experience and expertise of the individual as well as the size, location, and prestige of the agency. Annual earnings can range from $24,000 to $50,000 plus for artists working in agencies. Salaries are usually supplemented by fringe benefit packages.

Employment Prospects

Employment prospects for Commercial Artists are fair. Agencies are always on the lookout for creative people.

Those who have a good, diversified portfolio of commercial art will be snapped up quickly. Jobs in agencies are more plentiful in New York, Chicago, Los Angeles, Atlanta, Detroit, Minneapolis, Boston, Pittsburgh, Dallas, and Cleveland. It may be easier for beginners to land jobs in smaller agencies.

Advancement Prospects

Advancement prospects for Commercial Artists are fair. Much of the achievement of people in this position depends on their talent. A man or woman who consistently does good work, has creative ideas, and builds a good reputation should have no problem with career advancement.

Commercial Artists can move up by becoming art directors. Other individuals advance by finding employment at bigger, more prestigious agencies where salaries are notably higher. Others advance by becoming freelance people or by finding work in fields other than advertising.

Education and Training

While a formal education is not always necessary for this type of position, it sometimes helps. Individuals who seek Commercial Artist positions may have a bachelor's degree from a college with a major in art. Others may have art school training, while still others have taken just a few art courses.

Experience, Skills, and Personality Traits

Commercial Artists working in agencies should have a good knowledge and understanding of advertising. It goes without saying that the individual needs artistic ability. Just being artistic, however, is not everything. The individual needs to illustrate "commerciability." Drawing and illustration skills are a must, as are computer skills.

Commercial Artists should have knowledge of pasteup, mechanicals, typography, color, and photography. They should also have an innate sense of design.

The individual in this type of position must have a thick skin. Not every ad will get approval. He or she must be able to take constructive criticism and start over, if need be.

Unions and Associations

Commercial Artists working in agencies do not belong to bargaining unions. They may belong to trade associations such as the American Advertising Federation (AAF), the Art Directors Club, Inc. (ADC), the One Club, or the Society of Illustrators, among others. These associations provide support and guidance and often offer helpful seminars to members.

Tips for Entry

1. Put together a good portfolio. This is the one thing that can really help you get the position you want.

Make it neat and creative and diversified. Do not include mediocre work.

2. Write letters to agencies and ask if you can show them your portfolio. Knock on agency doors. The worst people can say is no. The best that can happen is that you will get a job you enjoy.

3. Join trade associations where you can meet other people in the field and make contacts.

4. Locate an agency internship or training program. This is a good way to get your foot in the door. Once there, dazzle them with your work. Do a little extra, learn as much as you can, and you will have a job.

COMPUTER GRAPHIC ARTIST

CAREER PROFILE

Duties: Design art, graphics, and type for advertisements, promotional material, and publications using a computer; lay out advertisements with the assistance of a computer

Alternate Title(s): Artist; Graphic Artist; Computer Artist; Computer Graphics Designer

Salary Range: $24,000 to $50,000+

Employment Prospects: Good

Advancement Prospects: Fair

Best Geographical Location(s): Positions available throughout the country.

Prerequisites:

Education or Training—College degree in commercial art or fine arts required in some positions; art school, art courses, computer graphics training, helpful in others

Experience—Computer graphics experience needed

Special Skills and Personality Traits—Total computer capability; working knowledge of one or more types of computers and computer programs; ability to produce computer graphics; understanding of advertising; creative; artistic ability; knowledge of commercial art

CAREER LADDER

```
┌─────────────────────────────┐
│   Assistant Art Director    │
└─────────────────────────────┘

┌─────────────────────────────┐
│  Computer Graphic Artist    │
└─────────────────────────────┘

┌─────────────────────────────┐
│   Entry Level, Pasteup      │
│   or Mechanical Artist,     │
│  or Freelance Computer      │
│      Graphic Artist         │
└─────────────────────────────┘
```

Position Description

Computer Graphic Artists working in the art department of an agency are responsible for creating art, graphics, and type for advertisements and other materials by computer. Individuals may be responsible for laying out advertisements and promotional materials with the computer.

Computer Graphic Artists have the ability to be creative with a keyboard, electric stylus, mouse, and scanner instead of using the standard pen, ink, pencil, paintbrush, or paint. The individual may use any number of different computers and computer programs to work with. One of the reasons that the Computer Graphic Artist is currently in demand is that he or she can often produce the same amount of work as a traditional artist more efficiently. Projects can be done in a shorter time period and often more accurately.

The Computer Graphic Artist has varied duties and responsibilities. He or she may function as a typesetter or typographer as well as an artist. The individual may be called upon to choose the type for headlines and body copy from the vast array of computer fonts available. Making headlines for advertisements with the use of a computer may take only seconds. The individual need only type in the words.

The Computer Graphic Artist may also be responsible for designing new or special fonts with the computer to meet the needs of a specific advertisement. While this still takes time, it can be done faster and reproduced more easily and more accurately.

The Computer Graphic Artist may be required to do cartooning, sketching, or even "painting" with the use of the computer. He or she works with a variety of different computer programs, depending on what type of project is required. These might include drawing, painting, graph, video presentation, cartooning, 3-D, font design, or page layout programs.

The individual often works with other departments in the agency. He or she may produce a variety of different computer-generated graphs, charts, and diagrams for presentations to the research department, or for executives working on bringing in new business. Data can constantly be changed and new charts generated with little or no trouble. The Computer Graphic Artist may also be responsible for using the computer to make overhead projector sheets for presentations. At times the Computer Graphic Artist may be required to develop the graphics for video presentations or slides for visuals.

Computer Graphic Artists may be responsible for designing original graphics or art for advertisements and other materials. The individual may also modify existing designs by making them larger or smaller, or changing colors or line weights. After the design is complete the artist gives it to his or her superior for approval. The Computer Graphic Artist stores work he or she has generated with the computer in the computer's memory, on a hard disk, electronic tape, or floppy disks, or by running it through a printer to obtain a hard copy.

The Computer Graphic Artist may be responsible for just the graphics of an ad, the headline type, the body type, or all three. He or she may also be required to do the layout with the help of the computer. When he or she obtains a graphically pleasing layout, it is saved, and a hard copy is printed for approval. Any changes can easily be made afterward with the cut-and-paste layout procedure.

The individual may use the same graphic design and layout procedure for other advertisements, logos, promotional and marketing material, sales pieces, and publications he or she is responsible for preparing.

The Computer Graphic Artist working in an agency is usually responsible to the art director or the assistant art director. He or she will work normal business hours. As in all other jobs in advertising, when an advertisement or other project must be finished or must meet a deadline, the individual must work overtime.

Salaries

Earnings vary greatly depending on the position and the individual's responsibilities and experience. Other factors include the size and location of the agency.

Earnings may start as low as $24,000 for an individual working in a small agency or one who has limited responsibilities and experience. Compensation may go up to $50,000 plus for individuals who are experienced in computer graphics, art, and advertising and are employed by major agencies.

Most of the larger and many of the smaller agencies also offer benefit packages to augment salaries.

Employment Prospects

Employment prospects are good for Computer Graphic Artists and are getting better. The field is getting larger and larger as technology gets more advanced. With new equipment and more computer art, layout, and design programs available, agencies are able to produce many advertisements and promotional materials faster, more accurately, and less expensively than with traditional artistic methods. Though not all art for advertisements and other materials can be produced by computer, a great deal of it can.

Positions can be found throughout the country. Small agencies as well as larger ones employ Computer Graphic Artists. Those interested in seeking employment at a larger agency may have to relocate to one of the cities where the major agencies are located, including New York, Atlanta, Los Angeles, Chicago, Detroit, Minneapolis, Boston, Pittsburgh, Dallas, and Cleveland.

Advancement Prospects

Advancement prospects are fair for Computer Graphic Artists. Much of the advancement in the art department of an agency revolves around how creative an individual is and how he or she can illustrate that creativity.

Computer Graphic Artists can climb the career ladder by becoming assistant art directors or art directors, depending on the agency they are working in. Individuals may advance their career by finding employment at bigger, more prestigious agencies where salaries are usually higher. Others in this field advance by building up their business and becoming freelance Computer Graphics Artists.

Education and Training

Educational requirements vary from agency to agency. The larger agencies usually require almost everyone to have a four-year college degree. Many individuals have degrees in either fine art or commercial art. While an art director might waive the degree if he or she sees a sensational portfolio, individuals must remember the competition at the larger agencies is fierce.

Smaller agencies may hire an applicant with art school training or art and computer graphics training.

Seminars and other courses in all facets of computer usage, graphics, layout, art, design, and advertising are advantageous.

Experience, Skills, and Personality Traits

Computer Graphic Artists need to be creative, artistic, talented individuals with an innate sense of style and design. Complete familiarity with the computer and various art, design, and layout programs is imperative. Experience with various types of computers and programs is a plus.

Individuals need the ability to work quickly. Art departments in agencies are busy places. Individuals should have a working knowledge of pasteups, mechanicals, typography, color, and photography.

Unions and Associations

Computer Graphic Artists working in agencies do not belong to any unions. Individuals may belong to a number of trade associations that will provide professional and educational guidance and put members together with others in their field.

These organizations include the American Advertising Federation (AAF), the Art Directors Club, Inc. (ADC), the One Club, the Society of Illustrators, the Graphic Artists Guild (GAG), and the American Institute of Graphic Arts (AIGA). Individuals might also belong to both general and specific computer clubs and user groups.

Tips for Entry

1. Join computer clubs in school and user groups in your local community. These offer you the opportunity to share knowledge of the subject and pick up pointers from others.

2. There are a host of computer-oriented magazines and other publications in the marketplace, with more coming out every day. (Check the appendix for names.) Reading these will keep you up on new machines, technology, tips, and techniques.

3. There are many seminars and courses offered throughout the country on desktop publishing, computer graphics, and other computer-oriented subjects. These will help you make professional contacts in addition to providing know-how and new skills.

4. Positions as Computer Graphic Artists in agencies are advertised frequently in trade publications and newspaper classified sections. Look under heading classifications of "Advertising," "Artist," "Computers," and "Graphics."

5. Put together a portfolio of your best work. It would be wise to include all types of graphics, art, and design with your computer graphics samples. This will illustrate to an art director that you are creative and flexible.

6. You might want to get some experience and samples for your portfolio by doing a few freelance assignments or by getting a part-time or summer job working with computer graphics.

LETTERING ARTIST

CAREER PROFILE

Duties: Produce and select the letters and type style for headlines and logos used in advertisements; design type; hand-letter type for advertisements

Alternate Title(s): Artist; Calligrapher; Hand-Lettering Artist; Engrosser

Salary Range: $24,000 to $50,000+

Employment Prospects: Fair

Advancement Prospects: Good

Best Geographical Location(s): More positions may be available in cities where large agencies are located, such as New York, Atlanta, Los Angeles, Chicago, Detroit, Minneapolis, Boston, Pittsburgh, Dallas, and Cleveland.

Prerequisites:

Education or Training—High school diploma, minimum requirement; art school, art courses, or college degree with major in art may be required or preferred.

Experience—Experience working with or knowledge of various type faces required

Special Skills and Personality Traits—Ability to work neatly and accurately; creative; artistic ability; knowledge of various type faces; computer capability; ability to hand letter and/or produce calligraphy; drawing and illustration skills

CAREER LADDER

```
┌─────────────────────────────────────────┐
│  Graphic, Commercial, or Sketch Artist   │
└─────────────────────────────────────────┘

┌─────────────────────────────────────────┐
│            Lettering Artist              │
└─────────────────────────────────────────┘

┌─────────────────────────────────────────┐
│       Mechanical or Pasteup Artist       │
└─────────────────────────────────────────┘
```

Position Description

The Lettering Artist working in an advertising agency is responsible for producing the letters on headlines and logos used in ad layouts. These layouts, or "comprehensives," as they might be called, are then submitted to the client complete with artwork for approval.

There are literally hundreds of different typefaces or fonts, styles, and sizes. The Lettering Artist works with the art director, assistant art director, and graphic, mechanical, and commercial artists developing an advertisement. Together they decide what typefaces to use in ads, what size and style should be selected, and how they should be reproduced. The individual must then be able to render or produce the type required.

In some agencies the Lettering Artist works with computers, electronics, and press type in order to produce lettering.

He or she will be responsible for choosing an appropriate type from the styles available. If the individual is working with a computer, for example, he or she decides which typeface or font is the best, types the words into the machine, and prints out the results. The artist may try a number of different styles to see which looks best in the proposed ad.

The Lettering Artist may also work with press-on type, which comes in sheets and is pressed onto lettering paper. This process must be handled with a great deal of care, since spacing and accuracy is extremely important in the finished product.

The Lettering Artists who are most valued in the agency are those who do hand lettering. This work demands a great deal of the artist's talent, patience, and creativity. These individuals work with varieties of ink, paint, pens, and brushes to design lettering that is original and not normally seen in ads.

Many clients prefer that the lettering in their advertisements be prepared in this manner. Their reason is simple. People often feel that ads that use creative, distinctive type styles will attract more attention than ads with ordinary, everyday type.

The Lettering Artist is responsible for designing the letters used in the various parts of an advertisement. He or she works with different types of strokes using a pen, brush, or pencil until the lettering is accomplished. The individual usually has to produce the type in various sizes. This is painstaking work. Each letter must be neat and exact. The Lettering Artist will work with tools such as rulers, T-squares, triangles, and arcs to help produce the finished letters.

The individual must know how to produce individual letters as well as script or connecting letters. The Lettering Artist must design in styles including bold, italicized, and slanted. A client often has an idea in his or her mind of exactly how they want the type to look. The Lettering Artist tries to convey this image on paper. The individual is responsible for spacing not only letters but lines of type as well. The Lettering Artist must be able to produce designed type in capitals as well as lowercase letters.

At times the Lettering Artist is required to produce the words for an advertisement in calligraphy. This is a style of lettering that produces a flowing, decorative type. There is no commercial type face available that compares. As in all other forms of hand lettering, calligraphy takes a great deal of patience and talent.

After approval of the type the Lettering Artist completes the process. He or she produces the final letters in ink or paint form if they are hand lettered. If the letters chosen are computer fonts, he or she types out the letters on the computer. Press type is pressed onto paper. The individual then pastes the letters and words on the advertisement in the correct place or gives the lettering to a pasteup artist.

The Lettering Artist usually works normal business hours. Like all other individuals working in the advertising agency, however, he or she may have to put in overtime if a project is not finished or a deadline must be met.

The Lettering Artist may be responsible to either the assistant art director or the art director of the department.

Salaries

Annual earnings for a Lettering Artist vary depending on the agency where he or she is working, its size, and its location. Earnings also depend on the skills and experience of the individual.

Salaries may start at $24,000 for an individual who is just entering the work force or for a Lettering Artist who is basically typing out letters and words on a computer or pressing type.

Earnings for individuals with more experience or for those with special hand-lettering, design, and calligraphy skills may go up to $50,000 or more annually. Most advertising agencies augment salaries with liberal fringe benefit packages.

Lettering Artists may additionally receive extra compensation for freelance or part-time work done for clients outside the agency.

Employment Prospects

Employment prospects are fair for Lettering Artists seeking work in advertising agencies. An individual with hand-lettering, design, and calligraphy skills may be more employable. Jobs in agencies are more plentiful in New York, Chicago, and Los Angeles, as well as Atlanta, Detroit, Minneapolis, Boston, Pittsburgh, Dallas, and Cleveland.

Almost every art department in every agency hires at least one Lettering Artist, if not more. While it may be easier for beginners to land jobs in smaller agencies, they may have to perform other artistic tasks within the department. Individuals may, however, feel that the experience is worth it.

In addition, Lettering Artists who are skilled in hand lettering and/or calligraphy will often be hired on a freelance or part-time basis by other agencies who don't have a hand letterer on staff or by clients who want hand work done on invitations, awards, certificates, plaques, and other special documents.

Advancement Prospects

Advancement prospects are good for Lettering Artists. Individuals may climb the career ladder by becoming sketch, graphic, or commercial artists, depending on their talents. Lettering Artists might also advance their careers by obtaining positions at larger, more prestigious agencies. The individuals who are highly skilled in hand lettering, design, and calligraphy will often be sought out by these larger agencies.

Education and Training

Educational requirements vary for positions like this. All require at least a high school diploma. Some agencies prefer for individuals to have four-year art degrees. Others will accept commercial art training.

Successful Lettering Artists usually have some type of training in the field, whether it be from high school, college, or art school. Useful classes to take in addition to regular art courses include drafting, drawing, design, lettering, printmaking, and calligraphy.

Many colleges, art societies, and craft co-ops offer extension courses and seminars in decorative lettering and calligraphy. Individuals might also find courses in computer capability and desktop publishing helpful.

Experience, Skills, and Personality Traits

Lettering Artists should be able to work neatly, accurately, and quickly. A knowledge of typefaces is essential. Individuals should be able to reproduce type in various sizes and styles. Lettering Artists need artistic ability and a sense of style, design, and color. They should be able to work in various media including pen, ink, paint, pencil, and paper.

The ability to produce hand lettering, decorative type, and calligraphy is especially useful.

Drawing and illustration skills are a must. In order to be more flexible and therefore more employable, individuals should also have knowledge of pasteup, mechanicals, and typography. Computer capability is necessary in almost every job of this kind.

Unions and Associations

Lettering Artists working in advertising agencies do not belong to any union. Individuals may belong to any of a number of trade associations that will put them together with other people in their field and offer opportunities for honing their skills. These might include the Society of Illustrators, the Art Directors Club, Inc. (ADC), the One Club, and the American Institute of Graphic Arts (AIGA), or the American Advertising Federation (AAF). Lettering Artists might also belong to local or statewide calligraphy societies.

Tips for Entry

1. If you are still in school, work on your school newspaper or yearbook. This will give you hands-on experience working with different kinds of type.
2. Consider a part-time or summer job working for a printer. This will give you even more experience with type and printing.
3. Put together a portfolio of your work. Almost every job in the art department of an advertising agency requires this presentation. Make it neat, creative, and diversified.
4. Join trade associations and attend their meetings, conferences, seminars, and courses. These will help you hone your skills and make professional contacts. Many of these trade associations also offer help putting your portfolio together as well as critiques on how to improve it.
5. Go to your local art store or print shop and find a catalog of the various type styles available.
6. There are many books in your local library and bookshops on hand lettering and calligraphy. These might prove useful in learning new skills.

MECHANICAL ARTIST

CAREER PROFILE

Duties: Pasteup; make mechanicals for advertisements

Alternate Title(s): Artist

Salary Range: $24,000 to $45,000+

Employment Prospects: Fair

Advancement Prospects: Good

Best Geographical Location(s)—Major cities such as New York, Los Angeles, Chicago, Atlanta, Pittsburgh, Dallas, Cleveland, and Washington, D.C., offer the biggest agencies. Other cities may offer additional opportunities.

Prerequisites:

Education or Training—Many companies require bachelor's degrees in fine arts or four-year degrees in commercial art; others prefer art school training.

Experience—Experience working in agency art department helpful, but not always necessary

Special Skills and Personality Traits—Neat; ability to work with hands; accuracy; ability to follow instructions and directions; knowledge of photography

CAREER LADDER

Sketch Artist or Graphic Artist

Mechanical Artist

Pasteup Artist or Entry Level

Position Description

The Mechanical Artist working in the art department of an advertising agency is responsible for pasting up a guide for the engraver of print advertisements the agency has created. These guides are called mechanicals. They are exact copies of the printed ads and are made in black and white. Mechanicals are used by printers or engravers to reproduce the ad on metal engravings or used in the photo offset production process.

The Mechanical Artist does not use any creative ability in this job. The individual will be given a sketch called a comprehensive. This sketch illustrates the way the ad is supposed to look. He or she pastes up all the different pieces of the ad on white illustration board. These components might include the artwork, photographs, type, logos, and borders.

The Mechanical Artist takes a photostat of the artwork and pictures and scales it to the correct size of the advertisement. A photostat, or "stat," for short, is a photographic reproduction used in making ad layouts. It is used to scale art, graphics, and type to the right size. The photostats are then used by the engraver to make the mechanical.

For example, if the agency were to run a full-page ad in a 9" by 12" magazine, the individual would have to make sure that the picture was scaled to fit the ad. He or she would also paste photostats of type proofs of the copy and headlines and any graphics or coupons to fit the page.

The Mechanical Artist must be sure that he or she puts everything exactly where the artist, creative director, or art director wants it placed. The individual must be precise and neat in his or her pasteup job.

In some agencies Mechanical Artists are also responsible for making stats. To do this, they must be familiar with stat cameras and their operation. In other agencies there are other people responsible for this task.

As Mechanical Artists become more proficient they may become involved in the preparation of color overlaying and separations. This is another step in the mechanical process and is done after the first mechanical is created and engraved. It is used when making advertisements that will eventually appear in color.

In smaller agencies the Mechanical Artist might also be responsible for performing the tasks of the pasteup artist.

These include cutting mats, mounting ads and storyboards, and collating promotional pieces.

The Mechanical Artist works normal business hours unless an advertisement must be finished to meet a deadline. He or she is then required to work overtime. The individual is responsible to the assistant art director, the art director, or the creative director, depending on the structure of the agency and the department.

Salaries

Mechanical Artists working in agencies may earn from $24,000 to $45,000 or more a year, depending on the agency location and size and the individual's responsibilities and experience.

Mechanical Artists with little or no agency experience average salaries in the low twenties. Individuals with more experience or those working in major metropolitan areas may earn more.

Agency employees may have their salaries augmented by benefit packages.

Employment Prospects

Employment prospects are fair for Mechanical Artists in agencies. While not all agencies do their own mechanicals, there are many that do. Large agencies often have a number of Mechanical Artists on staff. Jobs can be located in all geographical areas of the country. Those seeking work at a major agency should look in large cities, including New York, Los Angeles, Chicago, Atlanta, Pittsburgh, Dallas, Cleveland, and Washington, D.C.

Advancement Prospects

Advancement prospects are good for Mechanical Artists working in agencies. Individuals may take different paths in climbing the career ladder depending on what their skills are and where their talents lie. Some Mechanical Artists may become lettering artists, sketch artists, or graphic artists. Others may find employment as an assistant art director in an agency.

There are some Mechanical Artists who learn the skill and have an abundance of experience in producing mechanicals. These individuals may advance up the career ladder by locating a position in a design studio that does mechanicals for agencies. This will usually result in increased earnings.

Education and Training

Educational requirements for Mechanical Artists vary from job to job. Some agencies require that everyone working there have a college degree. Some prefer that employees working in the art department have a bachelor of fine arts or a four-year degree in commercial art. Others hire applicants who have art school training or who demonstrate creative skills.

Experience, Skills, and Personality Traits

The Mechanical Artist needs the ability to work neatly, accurately, and quickly. Every piece of artwork the Mechanical Artist pastes up must be in the precise place the art director wants it.

He or she should have a good sense of design and proportion. The individual in this position will not be required to have a lot of experience. In some agencies Mechanical Artists have worked their way up from being pasteup artists. In others, it might be an entry level job. Individuals need to be able to work well with their hands. Procedures for creating mechanicals will be illustrated for the individual, and he or she should be able to remember and follow instructions. An understanding of photography and the printing industry will be helpful in both obtaining and being successful at the job.

As most Mechanical Artists aspire to advance to doing creative designing work, it is important that they have artistic and creative talents.

Unions and Associations

Mechanical Artists working in agency art departments do not belong to any unions. They may belong to any of a number of trade associations that provide opportunities to get together with others in the field and make professional contacts. These associations also offer educational seminars, conferences, informational materials, and trade journals. These include the American Advertising Federation (AAF), the Society of Illustrators, the Graphic Artists Guild (GAG), and the American Institute of Graphic Arts (AIGA).

Tips for Entry

1. Put together your portfolio. Even though you may not be performing very creative work at this stage in your career, the book may help you land a job by showing the interviewers that you have talent.
2. Consider a summer or part-time job at a print shop. This will give you valuable experience that will be useful in your career.
3. Jobs as Mechanical Artists are often advertised in the classified sections of the newspaper. Look under heading classifications of "Artists," "Art," "Mechanical Artist," "Advertising," or "Advertising Agency."
4. Join some professional trade associations. Many have student memberships. Some of these organizations offer help in obtaining a job in the advertising field.

PASTEUP ARTIST

CAREER PROFILE

Duties: Mount artwork; cut mats; collate booklets

Alternate Title(s): Pasteup Man; Pasteup Woman; Pasteup Person

Salary Range: $20,000 to $26,000+

Employment Prospects: Fair

Advancement Prospects: Good

Best Geographical Location(s): Major cities such as New York, Los Angeles, Chicago, Atlanta, Pittsburgh, Dallas, Cleveland, and Washington, D.C., offer the biggest agencies. Other cities may offer additional opportunities.

Prerequisites:

Education or Training—Educational requirements vary; art school, art courses, or college degree with art major may be preferred or required.

Experience—No experience needed

Special Skills and Personality Traits—Neat; ability to work well with hands; accuracy; ability to follow instructions and directions

CAREER LADDER

```
┌─────────────────────────────┐
│  Sketch or Lettering Artist  │
└─────────────────────────────┘

┌─────────────────────────────┐
│       Pasteup Artist         │
└─────────────────────────────┘

┌─────────────────────────────┐
│        Entry Level           │
└─────────────────────────────┘
```

Position Description

The Pasteup Artist working in the art department of an agency works in the studio, or bullpen, as it is often called. The individual in this position starts at the bottom of the career ladder. The Pasteup Artist does most of the grunt work the others are too busy to do. The position can be compared to that of a secretary working in an office. The difference is, however, that instead of typing and filing the individual performs tasks useful to the art department of the agency.

The individual may work with mechanical artists, lettering artists, sketch artists, and art directors. Depending on the structure and size of the art department, he or she may work for just one person or may perform functions for everyone in the department.

He or she is responsible for pasting up art that other people in the department have put together. The Pasteup Artist cuts poster board mats for the various artwork pieces produced in the department. He or she must be comfortable with measurements and the use of cutting knives. The individual will also be expected to mount drawings, advertise-

ments, and storyboards. He or she learns how to properly size drawings and to perform the mounting procedures used in the studio.

At this stage of his or her career the Pasteup Artist is not required to use any creative skills. Everything that has to be done will be explained in detail. All the individual has to do is follow instructions.

It is important that the Pasteup Artist be able to work neatly, accurately, and quickly. In a large agency, the art department is a busy place. Work must be done when it is assigned and without mistakes. Another function of the Pasteup Artist is to copy and collate booklets, pamphlets, and leaflets that the art department has designed. The individual must make sure that the pages are all in the right order and that the number of copies is correct.

The Pasteup Artist may also function as a gofer. As he or she is the low person on the totem pole, the individual is often asked to bring finished artwork to other departments or to get preliminary sketches and idea sheets from others. The Pasteup Artist may do errands, make coffee, and even be asked to type a short memo. They may perform basic computer functions such as scanning and saving images or printing proofs.

Depending on the size and structure of the department, the Pasteup Artist may be responsible to either the assistant art director or the art director. While working hours are fairly normal in this position, the individual may be asked to stay late on occasion to help finish up a project or to meet an important deadline.

Salaries

Salaries for this position are very low. Annual earnings for Pasteup Artists can range from $20,000 to $26,000. In many agencies individuals start just above the minimum hourly wage. Salaries may be slightly higher in larger cities where the cost of living is greater. As individuals gain more experience earnings may go up.

Employment Prospects

Employment prospects are fair. Even though salaries are low for Pasteup Artists, there still is competition for these jobs. The reason is that people who are creative and want to get ahead move up from these positions.

Jobs in agencies are more plentiful in cities where larger agencies are located. These include New York, Chicago, and Los Angeles, as well as Atlanta, Detroit, Minneapolis, Boston, Pittsburgh, Dallas, and Cleveland.

Advancement Prospects

Advancement prospects are good. As indicated above, individuals who are creative and aggressive can move up. Depending on their skills, Pasteup Artists can become lettering artists, sketch artists, or commercial artists.

Pasteup Artists may move to another agency to locate a better position. However, individuals often find openings in the same agency where they are employed. Many Pasteup Artists do sketches, lettering, sample ad layouts, and show them to their art director. In this way, when an opening does occur the individual can be recommended.

Education and Training

While no formal education may be required for this position, a background in commercial art is helpful. Individuals may find that when interviewing for a job in an agency art department the person who has the better training will be the one who lands the job. Training may also be necessary in order to move up the career ladder.

Commercial art training or a college background with a major in art is helpful. Courses and seminars in art and advertising are also beneficial.

Experience, Skills, and Personality Traits

Experience is not usually required for this position. Individuals should, however, have the ability to work well with their hands. They should be able to work neatly and precisely. Knowledge of the use of cutting knives and mounting techniques helps but is not required. Procedures are usually demonstrated to the individual, and he or she should be able to remember and follow instructions.

As most people starting out in the job want to advance their careers, it is important that they have artistic and creative talents. Individuals who want to move up the ladder should also be articulate and possess good communications skills.

Unions and Associations

A Pasteup Artist working in an agency would not belong to any union. The individual may, however, belong to trade associations that provide support, guidance, education, and training. These include the American Advertising Federation (AAF), the Art Directors Club, Inc. (ADC), the One Club, and the Society of Illustrators, among others.

Tips for Entry

1. Locate an agency internship or training program. This is a good way to get your foot in the door. Do a little extra, learn as much as you can, and you will have a job.
2. Join trade associations where you can meet other people in the field and make contacts.
3. Find appropriate courses and seminars. By attending these you can make important contacts and learn something new.
4. Send your résumé and a cover letter to the art directors of larger agencies expressing your interest in a job.
5. Positions may be located in the classified sections of newspapers under the headings "Advertising" or "Artist."

BROADCAST PRODUCTION COORDINATOR

CAREER PROFILE	CAREER LADDER

Duties: Coordinate the production of radio and television commercials developed by an agency; develop budgets; oversee filming of commercials; locate film production studios or crews; negotiate fees for talent, locations, and production

Alternate Title(s): Production Coordinator; Production Manager; Broadcast Production Manager; T.V. & Radio Production Coordinator

Salary Range: $25,000 to $42,000+

Employment Prospects: Poor

Advancement Prospects: Fair

Best Geographical Location(s): More positions may be found in cities where major agencies are located, such as New York, Atlanta, Los Angeles, Chicago, Detroit, Minneapolis, Boston, Washington, D.C., Pittsburgh, Dallas, and Cleveland.

Prerequisites:

Education or Training—Four-year college degree required for most positions

Experience—Experience working in production department and/or broadcast industry

Special Skills and Personality Traits—Communication skills; detail-oriented; organizational skills; knowledge of broadcast industry; ability to work under pressure; computer capability; negotiation skills

```
┌─────────────────────────────────────┐
│   Production Director or Broadcast   │
│  Production Coordinator in Larger,   │
│      More Prestigious Agency         │
└─────────────────────────────────────┘

┌─────────────────────────────────────┐
│   Broadcast Production Coordinator   │
└─────────────────────────────────────┘

┌─────────────────────────────────────┐
│   Broadcast Production Assistant     │
│        or Traffic Assistant          │
└─────────────────────────────────────┘
```

Position Description

The Broadcast Production Coordinator working in an agency is responsible for making sure that the agency's radio and television commercials are produced. In smaller agencies a production manager or coordinator may be responsible for both print and broadcast production. In others, print and broadcast departments each have a manager. The individual in this position has varied responsibilities depending on the agency and the number of people working in the department.

The Broadcast Production Coordinator works with the copywriters and the creative director in coordinating the production of all broadcast advertisements and commercials prepared by the agency. The first thing the individual is responsible for is developing a budget for producing a particular commercial or advertising campaign. He or she must take all production costs into account when preparing this budget. These might include the cost of actors, actresses, and announcers, film or television production studios, producers, directors, props, location fees, and makeup people. The Broadcast Production Coordinator makes sure that the money paid to produce the commercial is within the proposed budget.

In certain agencies that do not have a casting director the Broadcast Production Coordinator may also be responsible for selecting actors, actresses, and announcers for commercials. The creative director may, for example, indicate that he or she is looking for a women with the "girl-next-door look" for an advertisement. The Broadcast Production Coordinator may hold auditions, put ads in papers or the trades, or call casting companies to find the perfect actress.

The individual may hire these people and perform the functions of a payment coordinator. It is imperative that the individual have a working knowledge of various talent unions, their contracts, and minimum payment scales. In this way the Broadcast Production Coordinator can estimate salaries. In some cases the individual may negotiate fees with actors or actresses who will be receiving salaries over the minimum scale or extra fees for the airing of a commercial over a certain number of times. He or she will deal with union members from SAG (Screen Actors Guild), SEG (Screen Extras Guild), AFTRA (American Federation of Television and Radio Artists), and AFM (American Federation of Musicians), among others.

The Broadcast Production Coordinator is required to handle contracts for the talent. Other responsibilities of the individual include dealing with contracts for production studios that will do the filming or taping of the commercials. The Broadcast Production Coordinator may have one or two studios he or she always works with or may investigate new studios. He or she may look into fees for the production, studio capabilities, and house directors or producers. At other times the individual may ask companies for bids as well as professional references. Since the Broadcast Production Coordinator will ultimately be responsible for having the commercial completed on time and within budget, he or she usually chooses production studios carefully.

The Broadcast Production Coordinator schedules dates for the filming of commercials. He or she is told at the outset of the project what the time frame is for producing the commercial. The individual must know the latest possible date for completing the commercial. If expensive broadcast time has been purchased by the media department of a client and a commercial is not ready for airing, the client will lose a great deal of money and the agency may lose the client.

The Broadcast Production Coordinator may be in charge of scouting locations for commercials that will not be filmed in a studio. The individual may perform this task or he or she may assign it to another person. The Broadcast Production Coordinator is responsible for checking the availability of dates for the location, negotiating fees, and dealing with contracts. If the location is out of the country, the individual may be responsible for checking into laws, rules, and regulations of the host country.

The Broadcast Production Coordinator is on location during the filming or taping of commercials. He or she oversees the production and makes sure that things go according to schedule. The individual tries to have the commercial done in as few takes as possible, and as quickly as possible. Extra time filming a commercial costs money.

If he or she has chosen a good film production crew, there are talented actors and actresses, and the script copy is right, the Broadcast Production Coordinator will have estimated correctly and be able to bring the commercial in on time and either at or under budget.

Once an advertisement or commercial is produced and finished, the Broadcast Production Coordinator is responsible for having it duplicated and distributed.

The work schedule of Broadcast Production Coordinators is often hectic. The individual works long hours. Depending on when and where the filming of commercials takes place, this could mean he or she will be working mornings, afternoons, evenings, or even weekends.

Depending on the agency, the Broadcast Production Coordinator might be responsible to either the broadcast director or the creative director.

Salaries

Earnings for Broadcast Production Coordinator vary from job to job. Individuals can expect to earn anywhere from $25,000 to $42,000 or more. Variables will include the size and location of the agency and the experience and responsibilities of the individual.

Broadcast Production Coordinators working in larger cities with a great deal of responsibility will have the highest earnings.

Most agencies also offer liberal benefit packages to augment incomes.

Employment Prospects

Employment prospects are poor for Broadcast Production Coordinators. While these are numerous agencies throughout the country, only the larger ones have this position. As noted previously, smaller agencies tend to have one person taking care of all production needs, both print and broadcast.

Those seeking Broadcast Production Coordinator positions should look to the cities where the major agencies are located, including New York, Atlanta, Los Angeles, Chicago, Detroit, Minneapolis, Boston, Washington D.C., Pittsburgh, Dallas, and Cleveland.

Advancement Prospects

Advancement prospects are fair for a Broadcast Production Coordinator working in an agency. The individuals can climb the career ladder in a couple of ways. The individual may find a similar position at a larger, more prestigious agency where he or she will receive increased earnings and responsibilities. The Broadcast Production Coordinator might also become a production director in an agency.

There are some individuals in this position who advance their careers by locating a job in a film or movie production house, becoming a producer or a casting director.

Education and Training

A college degree with a major in film, television, and radio and a minor in advertising would be ideal but is not always feasible. The Broadcast Production Coordinator should take classes in math, English, communications, advertising, liberal arts, and film, television, and radio broadcasting.

Experience, Skills, and Personality Traits

The Broadcast Production Coordinator must have the ability to deal with details. He or she will be working with contracts, fees, locations, and numbers. The individual may also be working on the production of more than one commercial at a time.

Communication skills are necessary. The Broadcast Production Coordinator should be articulate, have a pleasant phone manner, and be personable. He or she must work with a great many other people. Good interpersonal skills are necessary.

The Broadcast Production Coordinator should be good with numbers for the development of budgets, estimating payments and fees, and keeping commercial production within the proposed budget.

Negotiation skills are vital. This is important when the individual is negotiating with talent for commercials, for location fees, or for production expenses.

Much of the scheduling and budgeting in many agencies is done with the use of a computer. Many jobs of this type require that the individual be computer literate.

Unions and Associations

The Broadcast Production Coordinator working in an agency will not belong to a union but will work with many of the talent unions. These include SAG (Screen Actors Guild), SEG (Screen Extras Guild), AFTRA (American Federation of Television and Radio Artists), and AFM (American Federation of Musicians), among others. The individual must adhere to all union rules, regulations, and stipulations.

The Broadcast Production Coordinator may also be a member of the American Advertising Federation (AAF) or the Business Marketing Association (BMA). The agency may be a member of the American Association of Advertising Agencies (4A's). These organizations provide professional guidance, educational materials, internships, and training programs.

Tips for Entry

1. Try to locate an agency that offers a training program or internship in this department.
2. If you can't locate an agency training program or internship, contact advertising trade associations. They may be able to help you find one, or they may sponsor a program themselves.
3. If your school has a radio or television station, get involved.
4. Broadcast Production Coordinator positions are often advertised in trade journals or newspaper display and classified sections. Look under heading classifications of "Advertising," "Production," "Broadcast Production," "Commercial Production," or "Broadcasting."
5. There are employment agencies that deal specifically in advertising jobs. Before you get involved with the agency, find out who pays the fee when you get the job. In some agencies it will be the employer, while in others it is the employee.
6. Consider a summer or part-time job working for a professional film production company. It doesn't matter what you do while you're there as long as you get an overview of the industry.
7. You also might consider a job in a local radio or television station to get experience in the industry.

ASSISTANT PRODUCTION MANAGER, PRINT

CAREER PROFILE

Duties: Assist production manager in producing completed advertisements and marketing and promotional pieces; work with outside suppliers; obtain price quotes; check finished ads for accuracy

Alternate Title(s): Print Production Assistant; Associate Production Manager

Salary Range: $23,000 to $36,000+

Employment Prospects: Fair

Advancement Prospects: Poor

Best Geographical Location(s): More positions may be found in cities where major agencies are located, such as New York, Atlanta, Los Angeles, Chicago, Detroit, Minneapolis, Boston, Washington, Pittsburgh, Dallas, and Cleveland.

Prerequisites:

Education or Training—Four-year college degree required by most agencies

Experience—Production assistant, intern, or trainee or experience working in either advertising department of newspaper or print shop

Special Skills and Personality Traits—Detail-oriented; organizational skills; ability to proofread; knowledge of printing industry; ability to work under pressure; computer competency

CAREER LADDER

```
┌─────────────────────────────────────┐
│         Production Manager           │
└─────────────────────────────────────┘

┌─────────────────────────────────────┐
│  Assistant Production Manager, Print │
└─────────────────────────────────────┘

┌─────────────────────────────────────┐
│ Production Assistant, Intern, Trainee,│
│     or Position in Newspaper         │
│   Ad Department or Print Shop        │
└─────────────────────────────────────┘
```

Position Description

The Assistant Production Manager is responsible for helping the production manager with the actual mechanical production of printed material the agency develops and designs. These include advertisements, brochures, leaflets, flyers, sales pieces, billboard sheets, direct mail material, pamphlets, and all other advertising and promotional materials turned out by the agency. The individual has varied duties depending on the size of the agency, its structure, and the number of people working in the department.

The function of the production print department is to coordinate all the print ads and materials. This includes taking the ad sketches, photos, and other ideas and turning them into the actual advertisements that will be used in newspapers and magazines. The main goal is to make sure that the advertisements and other materials end up looking the way the copywriters and artists wanted them to look.

To do this the individual may assist in a number of ways. Depending on the agency once again, the assistant may begin by physically collecting the finished sketches and layouts for the advertisements from artists, copywriters, and account executives.

He or she may be responsible for searching out suppliers including typographers, photo-reproducers, airbrush artists, photostaters, photographers, engravers, electrotypers, art services, and paper suppliers. The individual may be required to assist the production manager not only by finding these companies but also by obtaining estimates on various projects from a number of different suppliers in any given category.

To do this he or she may call or write for proposals and estimates on the projects as they are assigned. He or she may also be responsible for asking various suppliers for bids on services or products. For example, the production department may need to have 100,000 copies of a booklet reproduced. The assistant is required to get estimates or bids on the paper required in addition to the printing.

It is as important to have work done on time as it is to get the best price. Paying a lower price on a service does not do much for the production of an ad if it is not ready when it is supposed to be. Newspapers and magazines do not hold up their production to wait for an advertisement that is late. It is therefore important that the department knows that the company they are dealing with usually meets their deadlines. The assistant may be required to check out references of the various suppliers who will be used to complete projects.

He or she may be responsible for bringing the sketch—or comprehensive, as it might be called—to the supply houses to turn it into the finished ad. He or she might also be responsible for explaining exactly what colors, types, and sizes, are required.

While the production manager is responsible for setting the timetables of when things should be finished, the Assistant Production Manager might be the individual responsible for making the various suppliers aware of the date and schedule. The individual must check in with the suppliers at periodic intervals to make sure that things are going according to schedule. He or she may have to follow up and constantly remind them of the deadline times and dates.

The Assistant Print Production Manager is responsible for checking finished type for accuracy. Every letter, punctuation mark, and space must be correct and placed where they are supposed to be. Colors, graphics, and sizes must also be checked. The grade of paper, ink, and finished sizes must all be accurate. The individual is also responsible for checking the quality. Messy, poorly printed advertisements and promotional materials are almost never useful. Everything on the finished piece of work should conform to the original comprehensive and mechanical the artist designed.

The Assistant Production Manager may be responsible for checking size requirements for advertisements with magazines, newspapers, or other publications. He or she may be required to obtain actual deadline times and dates from the advertising departments of these publications. The individual may or may not be required to deliver the finished ad to a publication.

The Assistant Production Manager may also be required to input data into computers. This information could include

information on suppliers, price quotes, estimates, and references. Data might also include specifics on advertisements such as deadlines, colors, and sizes. Billing information may also be required.

The Assistant Production Manager is responsible to the print production manager. The individual in this type of job comes to have a broad understanding of every part of the print production department. He or she usually works normal hours. As in other advertising positions, however, the individual may be required to work overtime to finish a project that needs to meet a deadline.

Salaries

Salaries differ from position to position in this job category. This is because in some agencies this is an entry level job, and in others the individual is required to have experience. Earnings will differ, too, depending on the duties and responsibilities of the individual and the size and location of the agency.

Annual earnings may range from $23,000 to $36,000 or more for Assistant Production Managers. The lower end of the salary range will be for those who have little or no experience. The higher end of the range will go to individuals who have more experience and more responsibilities, and who are working in larger agencies.

Employment Prospects

Employment prospects are fair for those seeking positions as Assistant Production Managers in agencies. Individuals with little or no experience usually find it easier to enter a smaller agency. Those with more experience or those who have been lucky enough to get some experience in an agency internship or training program may find employment in one of the larger agencies. These are in cities where the majority of the major agencies are located, including New York, Atlanta, Los Angeles, Chicago, Detroit, Minneapolis, Boston, Pittsburgh, Washington, Dallas, and Cleveland.

Advancement Prospects

Climbing the career ladder for Assistant Production Managers usually means that they will seek out positions as full-fledged print production managers. While there might be more than one assistant working in the agency, there will be only a single manager. There is not a lot of turnover in these positions, making advancement prospects poor.

Turnover is more frequent in smaller agencies. Individuals who are working in these types of situations improve their chances for advancement.

Education and Training

Most people seeking this position have some type of graphic or commercial art training. Almost every one of the major agencies requires a four-year college degree for this position. Some of the smaller agencies may just require a high school diploma or a two-year college degree. Individuals who will be trying to advance their career should have the four-year degree.

Experience, Skills, and Personality Traits

Assistant Production Managers need to be detail-oriented individuals with strong organizational skills. They must be able to handle a number of different projects at once.

The ability to interact well with those in all facets of the agency as well as printers, retouchers, typographers, and other people outside the agency is necessary. The individual should be personable yet firm when pushing people to finish promised projects.

An understanding of the printing industry is useful. The individual should have the ability to proofread accurately. He or she must be able to communicate the instructions of the art and copy people exactly.

Assistant Production Managers must be able to work under the constant pressure of deadlines. This is difficult, because often the individual has little control over getting the pieces of the advertisement together on time.

Many positions today require that individuals have the ability to work comfortably with computers.

Unions and Associations

Assistant Production Managers working in agencies do not belong to any union. Individuals may belong to a number of trade associations. These include the American Institute of Graphic Arts (AIGA), Printing Industries of America (PIOA), and the American Advertising Federation (AAF).

Tips for Entry

1. Consider getting a part-time or summer job working for a printer. This will give you hands-on experience in the printing industry.
2. You might also consider working in a newspaper, magazine, or other publication's advertising department. Through this experience you will learn how advertisements are put together and produced.
3. Try to locate an internship or training program at one of the large agencies. This helps you get your foot in the door of the agency world.
4. There are employment agencies that deal specifically with advertising agency jobs. Remember to check to see who bears the cost of the fee once you find a position. Sometimes it is the employee, sometimes the employer.

TRAFFIC COORDINATOR, PRINT

CAREER PROFILE

Duties: Schedule and oversee the work flow of print ads from inception to placement; make sure ads are completed on time

Alternate Title(s): Traffic Supervisor; Traffic Assistant Manager

Salary Range: $23,000 to $46,000+

Employment Prospects: Fair

Advancement Prospects: Fair

Best Geographical Location(s): Most large agencies are located in cities such as New York, Atlanta, Los Angeles, Chicago, Detroit, Minneapolis, Boston, Pittsburgh, Washington, Dallas, and Cleveland. Other opportunities exist throughout the country.

Prerequisites:

Education or Training—Four-year college degree required for most positions

Experience—Experience working in advertising, traffic, or production preferred but not always required

Special Skills and Personality Traits—Skill at dealing with details; personability; ability to deal with stress and pressure; computer literacy; communication skills

CAREER LADDER

```
┌─────────────────────────────────┐
│   Traffic Supervisor or Manager │
└─────────────────────────────────┘

┌─────────────────────────────────┐
│   Traffic Coordinator, Print    │
└─────────────────────────────────┘

┌─────────────────────────────────┐
│   Traffic, Advertising,         │
│   or Production Assistant       │
└─────────────────────────────────┘
```

Position Description

The Traffic Coordinator working in the print production department of an agency is responsible for making sure that the print advertisements the agency has created are completed on time and are placed on schedule. In most agencies the Traffic Coordinator works on a project basis. That means that he or she is responsible for certain accounts assigned to him or her by the traffic manager. This is initiated at the beginning of an advertisement campaign before an ad has been created.

The Traffic Coordinator is responsible for scheduling and overseeing the work flow of print ads and other print promotional materials. He or she interfaces with other members of the agency on a regular basis, checking the progress of projects and coordinating the placement of advertisements and printed materials.

The Traffic Coordinator is required to keep schedules of all advertisements for which he or she is responsible and to track their progress. The individual is responsible for the ads he or she is assigned from inception until completion and often placement.

Once an advertisement is assigned to the Traffic Coordinator, he or she will usually give it a work order number. This is done in order to keep track of the project. The Traffic Coordinator is responsible for knowing approximately how long the ad will take to complete. He or she is then required to follow the project from step to step to make sure that it is on schedule. For instance, the individual checks with the creative director to see what the estimated time frame is for a specific ad. The coordinator then checks with the copywriter to see if the copy is completed, and with the art director and/or artists to see if the graphics and design are done. If any of these individuals has not completed the project, the Traffic Coordinator must persuade and prod them to finish. In many agencies the Traffic Coordinator is referred to as a professional pest. He or she will not go away until the project is completed.

The Traffic Coordinator also works with the production department, account executives, and outside vendors such as printers and photographers. The individual must know how to time projects so that even in an emergency they will be on schedule. For example, the Traffic Coordinator must allow extra time in case clients are not pleased with the way an ad looks, or artwork gets lost, or the copywriter can't develop satisfactory copy. The most important part of the job is knowing how to plan and schedule time and projects effectively.

Depending on the agency and its structure, the Traffic Coordinator may be also responsible for reserving space in various media for ad placement. The individual is required to phone publications to find out when deadlines are for the specific issue. He or she is responsible for making sure that the assigned ad is completed in time to be placed. The Traffic Coordinator may personally deliver the ad or arrange to have it delivered.

Timing is everything in the Traffic Coordinator position. If he or she does not get an advertisement completed and moved to where it is scheduled to be placed on time, the ad will miss the publication deadline. This would mean that after everyone's hard work the ad will not be placed in the correct issue of the newspaper or magazine.

There is a tremendous amount of pressure and stress in this job. The individual is always in a position where he or she must keep tabs on other people's work and timetables. There will also be constant deadlines to meet.

The Traffic Coordinator is responsible directly to the traffic manager. The individual works normal business hours unless a project is near deadline and must be completed. He or she may then be required to stay late and work overtime.

Salaries

Earnings vary for Traffic Coordinators depending on their responsibilities and experience. Other variables include the size and location of the agency.

Salaries can range from $23,000 at a small agency to $46,000 or more at a larger one. Individuals working in major cities earn more than those in less metropolitan areas. The highest salaries usually go to individuals working in New York, Atlanta, Los Angeles, and Chicago.

Most employees at agencies are also offered benefit packages to augment their earnings.

Employment Prospects

Employment prospects are fair for Traffic Coordinators. There are many agencies located in major cities and a reasonable number of agencies even in smaller locations. Entry is often easier in smaller agencies. Those who seek work in a large agency should look in the cities where major agencies are located, including New York, Atlanta, Los Angeles, Chicago, Detroit, Minneapolis, Boston, Pittsburgh, Washington, Dallas, and Cleveland.

It is important to note that an individual may enter an agency at this level instead of starting as a traffic assistant. He or she must, however, have a college degree and a working knowledge of the department and its functions.

Advancement Prospects

Advancement prospects are fair for the Traffic Coordinator. Traffic Coordinators who climb the career ladder will become traffic managers. Jobs in the traffic department may lead to positions in other areas of the agency if the individual has talent, is aggressive, and lets supervisors know what his or her aspirations are.

Education and Training

Most jobs at agencies require that the individual has a minimum of a four-year college degree. As this position is often a stepping stone to other jobs in the agency, a well-rounded background is useful. Good choices for majors include advertising, marketing, communications, public relations, and liberal arts.

Experience, Skills, and Personality Traits

Much of the work of the Traffic Coordinator is done under pressure. The individual in this position must be able to deal with the pressure and stress associated with constantly having to meet deadlines. He or she must have a cool head and be able to handle emergencies that crop up.

The Traffic Coordinator should be organized and have the ability to handle many details at once. Today most agencies have their department computerized. As a result, it is imperative that the Traffic Coordinator have a working knowledge of computer usage.

The Traffic Coordinator needs to be personable and get along well with others. In order to get advertisements completed, traffic people often have to persuade the individuals in other departments to take care of important details.

Communications skills are a must for the individual. He or she will be getting instructions from other departments about what to do with advertisements and where to send them. The Traffic Coordinator needs to understand what is expected of him or her as well as the ability to communicate information to others.

Unions and Associations

There are no unions specific to Traffic Coordinators working in agencies. Individuals may belong to a number of professional trade associations, including the Advertising Club of New York or the Advertising Women of New York, Inc. (AWNY).

The agency the individual works for might also belong to the American Association of Advertising Agencies (4A's) or the Association of National Advertisers, Inc. (ANA).

These organizations provide educational and professional guidance as well as the opportunity to make contacts within the industry. Many offer literature, seminars, conferences, and trade journals that will be useful.

Tips for Entry

1. Try to locate an internship or training program in one of the larger agencies.
2. Consider a summer or part-time job working at a smaller radio or television station in their traffic department.
3. Job openings in traffic are advertised in newspaper classified sections. Look under the heading classifications of "Advertising" or "Traffic."
4. There are a number of employment agencies that specialize in locating jobs in the advertising industry. Before you get involved with one of these, check to see what the fee will be after they find you a job and who is responsible for paying it. In some agencies the job applicant is responsible, while in others the employer will pay.
5. Join trade associations, especially if they have student chapters. These organizations will be important in helping you network and make contacts that will prove useful when job hunting.

ASSISTANT CASTING AGENT

CAREER PROFILE

Duties: Assist casting director in locating and selecting models, actors, actresses, and announcers for television and radio commercials and print advertisements

Alternate Title(s): Casting Assistant; Assistant Talent Director; Talent Director Assistant; Talent Assistant; Casting Director Assistant; Assistant Casting Director

Salary Range: $24,000 to $45,000+

Employment Prospects: Poor

Advancement Prospects: Good

Best Geographical Location(s): Most positions are available in cities where major agencies are located, such as New York, Atlanta, Los Angeles, Chicago, Detroit, Minneapolis, Boston, Pittsburgh, Dallas, and Cleveland.

Prerequisites:

Education or Training—Four-year college degree required

Experience—Experience working with casting or production preferred, but not always required

Special Skills and Personality Traits—Energy; organization; ability to handle details; understanding of advertising industry; pleasant phone manner; communication skills; ability to type and/or use word processor or computer

CAREER LADDER

```
┌─────────────────────────────────┐
│         Casting Director         │
└─────────────────────────────────┘

┌─────────────────────────────────┐
│     Assistant Casting Agent      │
└─────────────────────────────────┘

┌─────────────────────────────────┐
│   Clerical or Secretarial Position│
│  in Casting Department, Intern,  │
│      Trainee, or Entry Level     │
└─────────────────────────────────┘
```

Position Description

The Assistant Casting Agent is responsible for helping the casting director select the proper talent for commercials. Actors, actresses, models, and announcers must be chosen for television commercials. Depending on the agency, the Assistant Casting Agent might be responsible for assisting in the selection of models for print media ads, too.

Duties vary for people in this position depending on the size of the casting department and the experience of the individual. In small agencies that have casting departments, the functions of the individual are broader. In larger agencies, responsibilities might be more specific.

Assistant Casting Agents with little experience are often responsible for a lot of the clerical duties in the department. They will be required to write and type memos and letters to talent agents and managers regarding casting for specific commercials. They also have to phone agents about casting calls and auditions or to have talent come back for additional interviews.

The assistant may be responsible for creating, mailing, or delivering display or classified advertisements to newspapers or the trades announcing casting requirements for specific commercials.

The Assistant Casting Agent is required to keep records on all talent who audition as well as actors, actresses, models, and announcers who send in résumés with photographs. He or she may keep information on file cards or may input the data into a computer. This information could include an actress's or actor's name, address, phone number, agent affiliation, and professional acting credits. It might also contain data about the individual's hair color, eyes, height, weight, age, personality type, and skills. If the talent had auditioned or been interviewed, the date would be indicated, along with any comments offered by the casting director. This information is used by the casting department when searching for a certain type of "face," look, or personality for a commercial.

The Assistant Casting Agent or casting assistant, as he or she might be known, may be responsible for arranging or running preliminary casting calls or auditions. Casting calls are events where many actors and actresses come in with a résumé and photograph (commonly known in the business as an 8 × 10 glossy).

During a preliminary casting call the Assistant Casting Agent will eliminate people who don't fit the look the casting director is seeking to play the specific role. People may be unsuitable for a particular commercial for any reason from being the wrong age to having the wrong hair color, body type, or accent.

The assistant takes résumés and photos from all applicants and file information for future casting of commercials. He or she gives the résumés and photos of the possible suitable applicants to the casting director. After the casting director reviews them and decides whom he or she wants to see, the assistant is responsible for calling the actors, actresses, or talent agents representing these people back for another audition or interview.

The Assistant Casting Agent may or may not participate in advanced auditions depending on the structure of the particular casting department and the duties of the individual. Being present at the auditions helps the individual learn more about choosing the correct personality, face, look, and voice for commercials.

He or she is responsible for calling or notifying the account executive responsible for the ad as well as the producer and any other necessary agency staff as to when the auditions are scheduled. He or she also sees to it that the actors and actresses receive scripts before auditions.

Once the talent is chosen, the Assistant Casting Agent may be responsible for seeing that it is booked through the proper talent agency. Other duties of the individual may include typing contracts with the correct dates, times, payments, and conditions. He or she is responsible for delivering the finished contracts and any other material to the talent or the talent agent and getting the contracts signed and returned. If the actor or actress is a union member, the individual may have to obtain a union membership number and take care of any other union-related business.

The Assistant Casting Agent is often on hand when the commercial is being filmed. The individual is responsible for checking many of the details involved in the casting procedure. Even after the commercial is cast, filmed, and finished, he or she may be required to check to be sure payments were made to talent, correct information was sent to the unions, and everything was handled correctly.

The Assistant Casting Agent is responsible to the casting director. He or she usually works long hours. The individual may go out after hours to actively search for new talent with the casting director. He or she may also work long into the night auditioning talent or at the filming of a commercial.

There is a lot of stress and pressure in this job. However, those in this particular field often get a great deal of gratification after a commercial is completed, broadcast on television or radio, and successful in the world of advertising.

Salaries

Salaries can range from only $24,000 for individuals who have limited experience and duties to $45,000 plus for those who have more extensive experience and responsibility. Assistant Casting Agents working in New York City and Los Angeles usually earn more than individuals employed in other cities.

Employment Prospects

Employment prospects are poor. Smaller agencies often delegate this duty to the commercial's producer. Larger agencies may have a number of casting directors on staff as well as a number of Assistant Casting Agents. Individuals can improve their chances of landing a position in this field by getting as much experience as possible before seeking a job.

Most positions for Assistant Casting Agents are available in cities where the larger agencies are located, such as New York, Atlanta, Los Angeles, Chicago, Detroit, Minneapolis, Boston, Pittsburgh, Dallas, and Cleveland.

Advancement Prospects

The hard part for Assistant Casting Agents is locating their first job. Advancement prospects are good once this occurs. Assistant Casting Agents move up the career ladder by becoming casting directors. Advertising agencies like to promote from within.

Once individuals have experience they can also move to a position in another agency or become a casting director for television or film.

It goes without saying that the Assistant Casting Agent must show promise to move up in the industry. He or she must either have or develop the ability to match faces with commercials.

Education and Training

Educational requirements vary for positions in this field. A four-year college degree is almost always necessary. Some individuals have liberal arts degree. Others have degrees in advertising, theater, acting, or broadcast communications.

Courses in graphic arts, photography, dramatics, video production, radio, and television will be useful to the individual in both seeking and advancing a career.

Experience, Skills, and Personality Traits

Individuals in these positions should be energetic, enthusiastic people with a great deal of personality.

Depending on their experience level and duties, Assistants Casting Agents may be required to perform a number of clerical tasks. They should, therefore, have the ability to type, use a word processor and/or a computer, do filing, and keep records. Individuals should be detail-minded and highly organized.

A pleasant phone manner is essential. The Assistant Casting Agent will be making and taking calls from agents, models, actors and actresses, and managers.

The ability to match the right face and personality with the right commercial is a plus. Some individuals have an innate ability to match faces with commercials. Others need a bit of experience selecting actors and actresses.

There are a number of ways individuals have landed jobs in this field. The individual may have worked in a clerical job in the casting department. He or she may have located a training program or internship offered by an agency in this department. Some Assistant Casting Agents have worked as an assistant or clerk with a commercial producer.

Unions and Associations

Assistant Casting Agents often work with talent from various unions including American Federation of Television and Radio Artists (AFTRA), the Screen Actors Guild (SAG), American Federation of Musicians (AFM), Actors Equity Association (Equity), American Guild of Musical Artists (AGMA), or the American Guild of Variety Artists (AGVA). Individuals may also belong to the Casting Society of America, a trade association for those working in the casting field.

These unions and trade associations may hold seminars or conferences and offer valuable information for talent buyers and casting directors as well as for the talent themselves. Many of the unions have minimum payments for their members to which casting departments must adhere. The unions also often have rules and regulations that must be met by the agency.

Tips for Entry

1. Participate in school plays and productions. If you can work in the casting, all the better.
2. If you are still choosing your college, try to find one with a theater arts or broadcast department. In addition to the courses, there will be a lot of extracurricular activities that will help prepare you for this type of job.
3. Volunteer your services to a nonprofit or local theater group. The hands-on experience is worth it.
4. You might consider trying out at a few casting calls yourself. This will give you experience with actors, actresses, models, and the casting experience in general.
5. See if you can land a part-time or summer job as a clerk, secretary, or assistant in a theatrical agent's office. You'll gain valuable experience and probably make some important professional contacts.
6. Read books on modeling, acting, advertising, and commercials. It will give you insight into the industry.
7. Try to locate an internship or training program at a larger agency in this department. This will help you get your foot in the door.

ADVERTISING ASSISTANT

CAREER PROFILE

Duties: Assist people in performing their work; type letters, memos, and proposals; do research; input information into computers; learn how to perform various jobs

Alternate Title(s): Assistant

Salary Range: $21,000 to $28,000+

Employment Prospects: Good

Advancement Prospects: Good

Best Geographical Location(s): Positions located throughout the country. Positions in major agencies are found in large cities, including New York, Atlanta, Los Angeles, Chicago, Washington, Detroit, Minneapolis, Boston, Pittsburgh, Dallas, and Cleveland.

Prerequisites:

Education or Training—Four-year college degree required

Experience—No experience necessary

Special Skills and Personality Traits—Self-motivation; aggressive; organization; computer literacy; ability to type; good phone manner; good communication skills; writing skills

CAREER LADDER

```
┌─────────────────────────────────┐
│      Position in Agency,         │
│   Depending on Qualifications    │
└─────────────────────────────────┘

┌─────────────────────────────────┐
│      Advertising Assistant       │
└─────────────────────────────────┘

┌─────────────────────────────────┐
│           Entry Level            │
└─────────────────────────────────┘
```

Position Description

An Advertising Assistant working in an agency can have many different duties and responsibilities depending on the department he or she is assigned to. Advertising Assistants may work in account services, media, research, creative areas, production, or promotion.

The main job of the individual in this position is to help people in the department perform their work while learning as much as possible about the functions of the department. In some agencies the Advertising Assistant floats from department to department learning different skills. This usually occurs in smaller agencies where fewer assistants are hired.

Generally, Advertising Assistants working in any department of the agency are responsible for doing a lot of clerical and secretarial work. This includes typing, inputting information into computers, answering phones, and filing. The assistant may make calls to obtain information on behalf of his or her supervisor. The individual also messengers memos, letters, and other materials to departments within the agency. While the job may sound like that of a glorified secretary, it must be remembered that the reason most people become Advertising Assistants is to break into the advertising business.

Duties are diversified, depending on the department in which the individual is working. For example, duties for an Advertising Assistant working in the account services department with account executives could entail any number of responsibilities. Depending on the individual's skills and qualifications, he or she may do anything from meeting clients and bringing them into the account executive's office to becoming involved with client proposals. This might include both writing and presentation. He or she interfaces with other departments, delivering proposals, memos, and components of advertisements. By watching the account executive the individual learns how to write proposals, prepare and give presentations, and make clients comfortable.

The assistant begins to understand how to develop advertising campaigns, how to deal with clients, and the responsibilities of other departments in the agency.

Assistants in the art department might do anything from scouring catalogs for a specific kind of type to helping develop concepts for ad designs. The individual learns how advertisements are prepared from beginning to completion.

The Advertising Assistant working in the copy department may write body copy, do research, or just take care of administrative tasks for the creative director. The individual should pick up more and more techniques as time goes by, learning through watching and doing.

It is important that the Advertising Assistant be self-motivated. The individual who does just what is asked of him or her will not make it in this business. There is a lot of competition, and agencies want the best people. The Advertising Assistant must watch for an opportunity to prove him- or herself and then grab it.

The Advertising Assistant is responsible to the director or coordinator of the department to which he or she has been assigned. While the individual is supposed to work normal business hours, the Advertising Assistant who comes in early and stays after hours is often the one who advances up the career ladder the most rapidly and is the most successful.

Salaries

Earnings are usually rather low for Advertising Assistants working in agencies. Salaries may range from $21,000 to $28,000 or more. Variables will include qualifications and responsibilities of the individual as well as the size and location of the agency.

Most agencies also offer benefit packages to augment annual earnings.

Employment Prospects

Employment prospects are good for Advertising Assistants at agencies. Every size agency, large and small, needs assistants. Smaller agencies may have only one or two on staff, while larger ones may have 25. The real giants in the agency world may have twice that.

Those who seek employment in one of the major agencies will have to look in the cities where most of the larger agencies are located. These include New York, Atlanta, Los Angeles, Chicago, Detroit, Minneapolis, Boston, Pittsburgh, Washington, Dallas, and Cleveland.

Advancement Prospects

Advancement prospects are good for Advertising Assistants. Individuals who are aggressive, enthusiastic, hard-working, creative, and talented will be promoted.

Advertising Assistants can take many paths when climbing the career ladder, depending on the area in which they have qualifications and the structure of the agency. An Advertising Assistant working in the creative department may be promoted to a junior copywriter position or an artist position. The Advertising Assistant may advance to be a junior account executive, researcher, assistant media buyer, estimator, or planner. Advancement avenues depend totally on the department in which one has been trained and where one's talents lie.

In agencies where Advertising Assistants float from department to department individuals will have more opportunities to decide which department they will best be suited for.

Education and Training

A four-year college degree is necessary for those looking for positions in agencies as Advertising Assistants. Majors may include advertising, marketing, journalism, communications, English, or liberal arts. Advertising Assistants who hope to work in the art department should have a degree in fine arts or commercial art or art training.

Any seminars on advertising, writing, or art skills will be helpful to the individual.

Experience, Skills, and Personality Traits

Advertising Assistants need to be bright, eager, aggressive, and self-motivated. They should be highly organized and have the ability to handle details. Individuals should have a yearning to learn everything they can about the advertising industry. They should be willing to do that little extra that wasn't expected of them.

Individuals who are entering the field should have a working knowledge of clerical skills. The ability to type, answer phones, and do filing is essential. Computer literacy is a plus. Administrative ability and dependability is necessary.

Good communication skills and writing skills will be useful to the Advertising Assistant who wants to climb the career ladder. Art skills will be helpful to the individual aspiring to work in the art department.

Unions and Associations

Advertising Assistants working in agencies do not belong to any unions. Individuals may join professional trade associations that make it possible to attend seminars, conferences, and educational lectures. Trade associations offer valuable written materials and trade journals to members.

Many of the organizations have student memberships and help those aspiring to be in the advertising industry to get a foot in the door.

Depending on what the individual is interested in, he or she may consider membership in the Young Professionals Division of the Advertising Club of New York, the Advertising Research Foundation (ARF), the Advertising Women of New York, Inc. (AWNY), the American Advertising Federation (AAF), the Society of Illustrators, the Graphic Artists Guild (GAG), or the American Institute of Graphic Arts (AIGA).

The agency for which the individual works might also belong to the American Association of Advertising Agencies (4A's) or the Association of National Advertisers, Inc. (ANA). These two organizations provide a wealth of information and help for those in the advertising industry.

Tips for Entry

1. Check to see if your college placement office knows of any openings in agencies. Recruiters often visit colleges looking for talented individuals.
2. Job openings are advertised in the classified section of newspapers. Look under the heading classifications of "Advertising," "Assistants," or "College Graduates."
3. Try to locate an internship or trainee program. These are usually found in larger agencies. Smaller agencies often create a position if you contact them. While there is little or no pay for these jobs, the experience will help get your foot in the door of the advertising field.
4. Put together a portfolio of art samples, writing samples, and ad concepts. The portfolio will be helpful when going job hunting.
5. Consider sending your résumé with a cover letter to the personnel or human resources office of agencies. There is a lot of turnover in entry level positions.
6. You might also consider either calling agencies and trying to set up interviews or knocking on doors with your résumé in hand.
7. If you know anyone who can help you get an interview, ask for assistance. You will have to prove yourself once you get the interview and the job. Remember to send a thank-you letter to the person who helped. He or she may have other contacts, in case you don't get a job on the first shot.

INTERN

CAREER PROFILE

Duties: Work in an advertising agency to learn skills, get experience, and make contacts

Alternate Title(s): Trainee

Salary Range: $0 to $400 a week; college credit often offered in lieu of earnings

Employment Prospects: Fair

Advancement Prospects: Good

Best Geographical Location(s): Internships are located through the country. Programs in major agencies are located in New York, Atlanta, Los Angeles, Chicago, Detroit, Washington, Minneapolis, Boston, Pittsburgh, Dallas, and Cleveland.

Prerequisites:

Education or Training—Undergraduate or graduate college student

Experience—College course work in advertising, research, or art, depending on the internship

Special Skills and Personality Traits—Eager; aggressive; desire to work in advertising industry; academic ability; writing skills; communication skills; creative; innovative

CAREER LADDER

```
┌─────────────────────────────────────┐
│         College Student             │
│  or Entry Level Position in Agency  │
└─────────────────────────────────────┘

┌─────────────────────────────────────┐
│             Intern                  │
└─────────────────────────────────────┘

┌─────────────────────────────────────┐
│             Student                 │
└─────────────────────────────────────┘
```

Position Description

An Intern works in an advertising agency learning the business by gaining hands-on experience. The individual obtains the necessary skills so that after graduation from college he or she will be ready to enter the advertising industry. The Intern is involved in actual work situations.

The Intern may work in just one specific area or may float from department to department in the agency. The individual may be assigned to account management, copywriting, media, research, art direction, or any department in the agency.

The Intern's responsibilities vary depending on the specific internship program, the agency, and the department he or she is working in. Most Interns work full-time at the agency for a specified period. This might vary from six weeks to 10 weeks.

In some programs the Interns are responsible for taking part in discussion groups, attending seminars, and complet-ing advertising projects as well as working in the agency. In others the individual is just required to fulfill his or her job-related functions. If the Intern is using the program to get school credit, he or she may be required to write a paper or do a project relating to the internship.

Interns learn how to perform agency tasks by actually doing them. The individual may work with creative and art directors developing concepts for advertising campaigns. He or she may write copy for television commercials and print advertisements or edit and change copy that has already been written.

The individual may work on storyboard ideas and copy for television commercials. If he or she has artistic qualifications, the Intern could be responsible for developing and creating print ads. The Intern in the art department might do sketches, lettering, or graphics for print ad presentations.

Interns working in the media department might help develop media plans, calculate the cost of media campaigns, learn how to buy media, and break down media spending for competitive clients.

An individual working in the research department may be responsible for developing questionnaires and executing research interviews and projects. He or she may research consumer trends in buying and spending. The Intern might also evaluate research that had been done previously.

Interns working in account services or management will work with account executives. The individual may attend and participate in client meetings and presentations. He or she might also write reports and proposals for client projects.

The Intern often meets with supervisors to discuss problems and solutions on the job. The Intern may review past and present advertising campaigns both to grasp the concept and to obtain ideas.

The whole idea of the internship program is to give the individual an overview of the advertising industry and agency experience. The Intern must grab every opportunity to learn as much as possible about advertising from experienced people who are on the job. This frequently means that the Intern will be working long hours at the agency and then going home and continuing to work on a project. It will all be worth it, however, when the Intern finishes school and obtains the job of his or her choice at an agency.

Salaries

Interns working in agencies are not always financially compensated and when they are, earnings are low. In some situations the Intern works in an agency for college credit or for the experience. In other situations the individual may earn a minimal salary.

In large agencies or in programs sponsored by major trade associations, compensation may be dependent upon education and experience. Interns who are still in undergraduate school may earn up to $250 a week. Those with a higher education may be paid up to $400 weekly.

Employment Prospects

Prospects are fair for individuals seeking internship programs. Many of these opportunities, however, will be in smaller agencies located throughout the country.

Individuals desiring to enter an internship with a major agency will have a more difficult time. Individuals will have to look for a position in a city where the larger agencies are located, such as New York, Atlanta, Los Angeles, Chicago, Detroit, Minneapolis, Washington, Boston, Pittsburgh, Dallas, and Cleveland.

Advancement Prospects

Individuals who have successfully gone through intern programs usually have an easier time finding employment after graduation. There are a number of reasons for this. The individual has had an opportunity for actual hands-on experi-

ence. The Intern has been trained in a specific aspect of the advertising industry. Finally, the individual usually has had the opportunity to make important professional contacts.

Interns who have completed internships at major agencies often find that the agencies want them back as employees after graduation.

Education and Training

Individuals usually become Interns while they are still in college. The Intern may work at an agency for a summer or may take some time during the school year for the internship.

Depending on what area of the industry the individual wants to focus on, he or she might consider majoring in advertising, marketing, liberal arts, English, journalism, or communications. Those interested in the creative side of the business may target courses in commercial or fine art.

Experience, Skills, and Personality Traits

Interns should be bright, aggressive individuals who are eager to learn more about the advertising industry. They usually hope to enter the field soon after graduation. The individual should be a good student who is either majoring in advertising or taking courses with an emphasis in the subject area.

The Intern should be articulate with good communication skills. He or she should be creative and innovative. Writing skills are important. A basic understanding of the advertising industry is necessary.

Individuals should have typing and word processing skills. Familiarity with and knowledge of computer usage is a plus.

Unions and Associations

Many trade associations for the advertising industry have student memberships. Others will supply educational literature and information for those aspiring to be in the advertising business.

Depending on the area the individual is planning on entering, he or she may want to contact the Young Professionals Division of the Advertising Club of New York, the Advertising Research Foundation (ARF), the Advertising Women of New York, Inc. (AWNY), the American Advertising Federation (AAF), the Art Directors Club, Inc. (ADC), the One Club, the Society of Illustrators, the Graphic Artists Guild (GAG), the American Institute of Graphic Arts (AIGA), the American Association of Advertising Agencies (4A's), or the Association of National Advertisers, Inc. (ANA).

Tips for Entry

1. Contact advertising trade associations. Many of these organizations sponsor intern programs.

2. Join student chapters of professional trade associations and attend their meetings. You will gain useful information as well as making important contacts.

3. Write to advertising agencies and inquire about internships. Many larger agencies have intern programs set up. In smaller agencies you may have to create a position.

4. Start putting together a portfolio of your work. This will show initiative and illustrate your talents.

5. Try to attend a college that has an advertising program. These are the ones frequently visited by recruiters and headhunters for agencies.

6. Obtain letters of recommendation from professors and employers. These are a good addition to your résumé.

7. Consider getting a short-term subscription to trade journals. These are good sources of information for possible internships.

8. There are internship programs available for minority students. If you are in this category, use them to your advantage.

RADIO AND TELEVISION

ADVERTISING DEPARTMENT COPYWRITER, TELEVISION/RADIO

CAREER PROFILE

Duties: Write copy and scripts for client and company advertisements to be aired on station

Alternate Title(s): None

Salary Range: $23,000 to $48,000+

Employment Prospects: Good

Advancement Prospects: Good

Best Geographical Location(s): All locations offer employment possibilities; major markets are located in larger cities around the country.

Prerequisites:

Education or Training—College degree in communications, journalism, English, public relations, advertising, or liberal arts

Experience—No experience required in many jobs; writing experience helpful

Special Skills and Personality Traits—Creative; good writing skills; aggressive; persuasive; understanding of advertising and the broadcast industry

CAREER LADDER

```
┌─────────────────────────────┐
│   Senior Station Copywriter  │
│    or Copywriter in Agency   │
└─────────────────────────────┘

┌─────────────────────────────┐
│ Advertising Department Copywriter, │
│       Television/Radio       │
└─────────────────────────────┘

┌─────────────────────────────┐
│    Entry Level or Writer     │
│      in Other Industry       │
└─────────────────────────────┘
```

Position Description

The copywriter in a radio or television station's advertising department writes the copy of words that are heard in the advertisements the station airs.

Most advertising copy aired nationally is written by the advertiser's agency. There are, however, many local, cable, or syndicated advertisements that must be prepared by the advertising department of television or radio stations.

The copywriter has varied responsibilities and duties, depending on the size and structure of the station and its advertising department. In smaller stations the copywriter might be responsible for everything from conceiving the ad idea to producing it and getting it on the air. In larger stations the individual may just be responsible for writing the copy. Whatever the responsibilities, the end result is basically the same: the copywriter must develop creative, effective, unique, and stimulating copy for ads.

Depending on the size and structure of the department, the copywriter may be responsible for developing an entire advertising campaign for an advertiser. At times he or she may just be required to write the copy for one ad. Advertisers usually have their own ideas of how the ad should sound and the information to be included. The copywriter must listen to the client's ideas and try to come up with something the advertiser likes that is effective.

The copywriter can work with either the salespeople or the advertisers themselves in order to obtain a feel for the points they want to get across in an ad and to learn about the audience they are trying to reach. If the product or service advertised is new to the copywriter, he or she may visit the advertiser's place of business to learn more about the product. The copywriter might also review copy from previous advertisements and from competing advertisements to develop ideas.

The copywriter may have to write a number of different drafts of copy for ads. The copy will then have to go to the advertiser for approval. The advertiser has the option of changing ad copy at any time. For example, he or she may hear or see the ad aired once and then decide that it won't do the job. The copywriter will then have to start all over.

The copywriter must be able to write in a variety of styles, from straight copy to dialogue. He or she must have the ability to write scripts for the actors and actresses who will be reading the lines. The dialogue must be crisp, clear, and believable. The individual may also have to write instructions for special sound effects, voiceovers, or stage directions if the ad is visual.

In larger stations the copywriter may work with producers, directors, and senior copywriters. The individual writing copy for a television advertisement as opposed to a radio ad also works with art directors, graphic designers, models, and camera people.

Successful copywriters have the ability to write advertising copy in such a way that the ad will stimulate enough interest in a product or service that a consumer will buy. Radio and television ads are often tested by advertisers through discount offerings or a special prize to a buyer indicating where he or she heard a particular ad.

The copywriter must be able to condense his or her words into the required time frame of the commercial. The individual may be asked to write copy for longer ads that can also be used for shorter spots. For example, the advertiser may want to run some 90-second commercials and some 30-second spots. Often the copywriter may put the "fluff" of the ad at the beginning and just delete it for the shorter time slots. The copywriter might also be asked to write copy that can be used jointly for both television and radio advertising.

Copywriters who are writing for televised ads may be asked to do their preliminary copy in storyboard fashion. In this way the advertiser can see from word to word what will be happening graphically when the words are spoken.

The copywriter has to work on many different projects at one time and finish them on tight deadlines. Advertisers usually want their ad written as soon as they decide that they want to advertise. The individual in this position must be able to handle the pressures of tight deadlines as well as the stress that can occur from having to constantly come up with creative copy for ads.

Depending on the structure of the advertising department at the station, the individual may be responsible to a senior copywriter or to the advertising manager.

This type of position usually has normal working hours. However, an individual may often bring work home or may be asked to stay late to finish needed copy for a project.

Salaries

Annual earnings for copywriters working in television or radio station advertising departments vary greatly depending on the size of the station, the location of the station, and the responsibilities and experience of the individual. Annual earnings for copywriters range from $23,000 to $48,000 plus.

Salaries are usually lower in small-market radio and television. These positions, however, are useful because they afford the individual with no experience a chance at employment.

Salaries go up for individuals with experience. Earnings are also higher in larger cities with middle- and large-market stations.

Employment Prospects

Employment prospects are good for individuals seeking employment as copywriters for radio or television station advertising departments. Those with no experience will, however, usually have to start out at a small-market station. As experience is gained employment opportunities open at larger markets.

Every city and even large towns now boast one or two radio stations. Many also have local or cable television stations. Employment possibilities may be found almost anywhere in the country. There is also a large turnover rate in many of the smaller market stations as people leave for bigger markets.

Advancement Prospects

Individuals can climb the career ladder by becoming copywriters at larger stations. Others advance by becoming senior copywriters at another station. Still other individuals move into copywriting positions in advertising agencies.

Advancement prospects are good for creative, aggressive copywriters working in radio or television station advertising departments. As noted previously, a little experience copywriting in a smaller station opens the door for employment opportunities in larger stations or other industries.

Education and Training

Individuals seeking careers in copywriting should have a college background. A degree is essential for most positions. Good choices for majors include journalism, communications, English, public relations, advertising and liberal arts.

Seminars and other courses in copywriting and advertising are useful for both the educational benefits and to make important contacts.

Experience, Skills, and Personality Traits

A copywriter looking for a position in a small-market radio or television station can often find a job with no experience at all. The individual should, however, have an understanding of advertising and the broadcast industry.

A good sense of style and flair for writing is important for copywriters. They should have a good command of the English language, including grammar and spelling skills. Individuals need to be creative in both their thinking and their writing skills.

Copywriters working in television and radio should also be articulate, persuasive, and aggressive in order to move up the career ladder.

Unions and Associations

A copywriter working in the advertising department of a radio or television station might belong to a number of trade associations. These organizations put the individual in touch with others in the field and often offer professional guidance and education. These organizations include the Writers Guild of America (WGA), the American Advertising Federation (AAF), the American Marketing Association (AMA), and the National Association of Broadcasters (NAB).

Tips for Entry

1. Write as much as you can. Offer to write promotional copy for nonprofit groups or civic groups.

2. If you are in school, work on your school newspaper or on the school television or radio station. Get to know as much as possible about writing and the broadcast industry.

3. These positions are often advertised in the classified section of newspapers under heading classifications of "Broadcasting," "Copywriting," "Radio," "Television," or "Advertising."

4. Positions are also advertised in trade journals. Check with your local library or radio or television station and ask if you can review copies.

5. Send your résumé and a cover letter to smaller-market stations and ask if a position is open. If not, request that your résumé be kept on file.

6. Many larger stations offer training programs and internships. Investigate these.

7. Check out station Web sites. Many list job openings.

PUBLIC RELATIONS ASSISTANT, TELEVISION/RADIO

CAREER PROFILE

Duties: Write press releases; assist PR director; handle media correspondence; take people on tours of station; coordinate promotions

Alternate Title(s): Publicity Assistant; Public Relations Trainee; PR Assistant; Publicity Trainee

Salary Range: $20,000 to $33,000+

Employment Prospects: Fair

Advancement Prospects: Good

Best Geographical Location(s): Positions in major markets may be located in large cities such as New York, Los Angeles, Boston, Philadelphia, Atlanta, and Chicago. Positions in smaller markets may be located in any city.

Prerequisites:

Education or Training—College degree in broadcasting, public relations, communications, journalism, or liberal arts

Experience—Experience in other public relations field or journalism helpful but not required

Special Skills and Personality Traits—Articulate; personable; outgoing nature; good writing skills; creative; typing skills

CAREER LADDER

```
┌─────────────────────────────────────┐
│     Public Relations Director        │
└─────────────────────────────────────┘

┌─────────────────────────────────────┐
│     Public Relations Assistant       │
└─────────────────────────────────────┘

┌─────────────────────────────────────┐
│  Intern, Entry Level, or Other Public│
│  Relations or Journalism Position    │
└─────────────────────────────────────┘
```

Position Description

A Public Relations Assistant working at a television and/or radio station can have an exciting job. If he or she is working at a major station, the individual will have the opportunity to work closely with celebrities. Even in a station in a small town people may consider D.J.'s, television anchor people, and talk show hosts as something special.

The assistant's main responsibility is to help the public relations director build the station's image and that of its on-air celebrities. During the course of carrying out his or her duties he or she will handle a lot of the grind work assigned by the PR director.

As a Public Relations Assistant an individual will often be asked to research and write press releases about events at the station. For example, the station may be hosting a telethon for a worthy cause. The assistant will have to research the event and write a news release about it. He or she might additionally be asked to arrange for a photograph of one of the stars of the extravaganza or might even have to personally take the picture. The press release will then be reviewed by the PR director. The PR assistant might be responsible for having copies made and sending them together with the photos to the appropriate media in the area.

Depending the size of the station, the PR assistant may act as a sort of secretary for the public relations director. He or she might have to type and copy memos, letters, envelopes, and press releases. He or she might also answer the phone in the public relations office.

The Public Relations Assistant will be expected to handle correspondence from the media as well as from fans of the station personalities. The individual must learn whom to let through on the phone to the public relations director and whom he or she can take care of.

Other responsibilities of a Public Relations Assistant might include taking people on tours of the station or introducing them to station celebrities. The assistant may write biographies of the station stars, compile press kits, and send out autographed copies of photos to fans.

If there is no promotion department, the Public Relations Assistant—or trainee, as he or she might be called—would also help in the promotion of the station. The individual might assist in coming up with and implementing contest ideas or other promotions to help boost station audiences. If the station is running contests, he or she might be responsible for finding companies interested in co-sponsoring promotions and/or donating prizes.

The Public Relations Assistant may be asked to work with nonprofit groups such as hospitals, health organizations, schools, museums, etc. in order to enhance the station's public image. For example, the individual may coordinate a health screening with an organization such as the American Cancer Society. The station would promote the event and possibly broadcast live from the scene at which the program is being conducted.

The Public Relations Assistant may be asked to represent the station and may have to make public appearances on behalf of the station. It is therefore imperative that the individual be articulate and personable. At other times the individual may be responsible for setting up public appearances for other station personnel such as disk jockeys, television stars, news anchors, and variety show hosts. The assistant may coordinate and attend, for example, a celebrity baseball game with on-air celebrities who make up the station's team.

Depending on the station that the assistant works for, its size, and the availability of other departments, he or she may have to update program schedules and distribute these to the media.

Everything that the public relations department does is geared toward letting people know what is happening at the station and having the station and its people look good in the public eye.

Salaries

Salaries for Public Relations Assistants working at radio or television stations vary greatly depending on a number of factors. These include the amount of experience the individual has and his or her responsibilities. Other variables include the size of the station and its geographic location.

Annual earnings for Public Relations Assistants working in small-market radio or television can range from $20,000 to $25,000. Earnings will be higher for individuals working in larger stations in major markets. Salaries for these individuals can go up to $33,000 or more annually.

Employment Prospects

Employment prospects for individuals seeking employment as Public Relations Assistants in major television or radio stations in major markets are not good. However, there are more positions available at smaller television and radio stations around the country. If an individual is willing to accept work at one of these smaller stations, he or she will have a fair chance at finding employment. Competition is keen at larger stations in major markets.

It must also be noted that there are now more opportunities than ever available with the influx of cable TV and independent stations around the country.

Advancement Prospects

Advancement for Public Relations Assistants working in television or radio stations can be obtained in a number of ways. He or she can become the station's public relations director. To do this, the individual must wait for the public relations director to leave or be promoted. Once the PR assistant has gained sufficient experience, he or she can also seek a position as PR director at other stations.

The assistant might also advance by working in the promotion department. Another option is for the assistant to seek work at larger stations where salaries are usually higher.

There is a lot of competition in all broadcasting jobs. The advancement potential in broadcasting PR is no exception.

Education and Training

A Public Relations Assistant working at a radio or television station is required to have a college degree. Majors could include communications, journalism, English, or liberal arts.

Courses or seminars in public relations or broadcasting are helpful for both their educational value and their networking value.

Experience, Skills, and Personality Traits

Public Relations Assistants working in broadcasting should be articulate, personable, and outgoing. They should like people. This is not a job for timid people who don't get along with others.

The PR assistant should have good writing skills, be creative, and not mind working overtime. Special promotions and public relations projects don't always happen during the traditional nine-to-five workday. They often occur at night or on weekends.

Typing is an important skill for the PR assistant. He or she may not have access to a secretary or may have to get a press release out on a deadline when the secretary is busy.

The PR assistant should also have the ability to work on several projects at once without becoming flustered. PR assistants may have had some experience in other public relations fields or in writing for newspapers.

Unions and Associations

Public Relations Assistants working in broadcasting do not usually have to belong to any unions. They may, however, belong to any number of trade organizations, including the Public Relations Society of America (PRSA), the National Academy of Television Arts and Sciences (NATAS), or the American Advertising Federation (AAF).

Tips for Entry

1. Join trade organizations and go to their seminars and conventions. Networking often leads to job interviews.
2. Job opportunities are often listed in trade journals. Read them and send résumés.
3. Résumés can also be sent to the personnel directors of radio and/or television stations. Ask to have your résumé kept on file if there is not a position open at the time.
4. See if there are any internship programs available at local radio or television stations. Internships often offer the experience needed to land a job.
5. Look in the classified section of a newspaper for job openings. Look under the "Broadcasting," "Television," "Radio," "Public Relations," "Advertising," and "Promotion" sections. There might also be opportunities in the display advertising section.
6. Don't forget to send résumés to public television stations and cable stations as well as local, regional, independent, and network stations.
7. Check out station Web sites. Many list employment opportunities.

ADVERTISING SALESPERSON, RADIO

CAREER PROFILE

Duties: Sell air time to advertisers; bring in new accounts and service current ones

Alternate Title(s): Salesman; Saleswoman; Salesperson; Account Executive

Salary Range: $18,000 to $95,000+

Employment Prospects: Excellent

Advancement Prospects: Excellent

Best Geographical Location(s): Most locations throughout the country offer job possibilities.

Prerequisites:

Education or Training—Four-year degree required for most positions

Experience—Experience in sales is helpful but not necessary in many positions

Special Skills and Personality Traits—Aggressive; sales skills; understanding of broadcasting industry; numerical skills; personable; articulate; self-motivation

CAREER LADDER

```
┌─────────────────────────────────┐
│        Sales Manager            │
│ or Salesperson at Larger Station│
└─────────────────────────────────┘

┌─────────────────────────────────┐
│  Advertising Salesperson, Radio │
└─────────────────────────────────┘

┌─────────────────────────────────┐
│        Entry Level              │
│  or Sales Job in Other Industry │
└─────────────────────────────────┘
```

Position Description

A Radio Advertising Salesperson is responsible for selling air time to people and businesses that want to advertise on the radio station. The salesperson works with the station's sales manager.

The Radio Advertising Salesperson also handles business the station already has. The stations sales manager usually assigns a number of accounts to each salesperson. The individual then services those accounts.

He or she is responsible for calling or visiting the advertiser on a regular basis to find out when they want to advertise, the number of spots they want to buy, how and if they want to change their commercials, etc. The salesperson will tell customers about new promotions the station is running and supply information about discounts and package rates. The individual might also offer suggestions for copy or content of the commercials.

The sales manager might also refer call-ins to the Advertising Salesperson. These are calls in which potential customers want more information about the station, its rates, demographics, etc. The individual will send out or deliver rate cards, informational sheets on the station and its demographics, comments from other advertisers, etc. He or she will then try to set up an appointment with the caller to discuss advertising on the station. The individual may offer special discounts for new advertisers in order to get them to try advertising on the station.

It is also the duty of the Radio Advertising Salesperson to bring in new business. To do this, the individual may make cold calls to potential advertisers. This means that the Advertising Salesperson calls businesses that have not expressed an interest in advertising on the station. The salesperson identifies him- or herself and the station affiliation and then requests an appointment to tell the potential advertiser more about the station. The individual must be able to accept rejection. He or she will not be able to make appointments on every call.

The salesperson might also bring in new business by increasing the number of spots current advertisers are buying. This can often happen when the client is running sales, specials, promotions, or contests. Additional spots might also be purchased by a client if the station is running discounts, promotions, or packages.

Depending on the structure of the station, the Advertising Salesperson may have a set sales territory or may be free to sell advertisements to any advertiser. In certain stations, one salesperson might be hired to sell advertising to specific types of clients, such as restaurants, retail shops and stores, entertainment, etc. In other situations the individual will be free to solicit any type of business in order to sell air time.

The Radio Advertising Salesperson must learn everything there is to know about the station in order to be able to sell advertising. He or she must know the type of audience it attracts, the programming, data about other types of businesses using the medium, how far the station reaches, and wattage. The individual must also know the same type of information about competing stations in the area. In this way, he or she will be able to discuss the competitive differences.

The salesperson must know about the various rates, discounts, and packages the station offers and be able to explain them to advertisers in a way they will easily understand. He or she must be knowledgeable about the length of advertisements and the time slots for which commercials may be sold.

The salesperson may be expected to attend training sessions and seminars the station or some outside training force offers. The individual may be required to attend weekly staff meetings during which sales techniques and suggestions are made.

The Advertising Salesperson may develop marketing or advertising ideas for current or potential customers. He or she might brainstorm with a client in order to help the individual come up with effective advertising ideas. He or she keeps up on current industry sales and advertising ideas and brings these to both current and potential clients.

The whole idea for the individual is to sell effective advertising to clients. If the ads are not effective, the customer will not purchase any more time. The individual may collect success stories or letters from clients on how advertising on the station helped increase business or draw people to a location. These will help prove to potential clients that advertising on the station works.

The Advertising Salesperson is expected to keep accurate records of advertising sold and billings. The individual writes orders and makes sure that they get to the appropriate people and departments at the station. He or she continuously checks with clients to make sure that they were happy with their commercials, to see that they were billed properly, and to inquire about the purchase of future advertising time.

The Advertising Salesperson often works in the field, making calls on businesses and others who are current or potential advertisers. At other times the individual works from his or her desk. The salesperson does not have anyone looking over his or her shoulder. In order to be good at this type of job, the individual has to know how to set priorities and organize the work day.

As many stations today have their own Web sites, Advertising Salespeople may also be responsible for selling advertising space on the station's site. In some cases, the radio station may hire salespeople specifically to sell Web site advertising.

The Advertising Salesperson working in a radio station is responsible to the station's advertising sales manager. While the individual can work normal business hours, he or she may arrange sales calls in the evening or on weekends. Successful salespeople are always trying to sell, even in social situations such as dinner parties or at meetings.

As individuals in this line of work are usually paid on a commission basis, they can experience a great deal of stress and pressure. The individual must realize that not every day will be a great selling day. Some days or weeks the person will sell more advertising, and sometimes he or she will sell less. If the person can't deal with this type of fluctuation and pressure, he or she might consider going into another type of work.

Salaries

Salaries vary greatly for individuals working as a Radio Advertising Salesperson. The great thing about being a salesperson is that the sky is the limit on earnings. Most Radio Advertising Salespeople are paid on a commission basis. This means that for every dollar of advertising space they sell they receive a percentage as a salary. Percentages vary from station to station, ranging from 10 percent to 20 percent, although the average commission is 15 percent. Salespeople who sell more earn more.

Annual earnings for Advertising Salespeople in radio can range from $18,000 to $95,000 plus, depending on a number of variables. These include the size and location of the station and the sales ability of the individual.

It is important to note that many stations offer a weekly or monthly draw against salary to salespeople. This is done for a couple of reasons. The first is to help beginning salespeople get into the swing of selling. The second is to adjust individuals' incomes in case they have a bad week or month.

Most radio stations also offer benefit packages to people working at the station in order to augment their income.

Employment Prospects

Employment prospects are excellent for salespeople who want to work in radio. There are many radio stations all over the country. Each of these stations hires at least one or two, if not more, salespeople. Individuals who are aggressive and hard-working and have a good selling track record will always be in demand.

Those who are just entering the job market in this field can find opportunities in small- or medium-market radio. As there is a high turnover in these jobs due to advancement, there are usually openings.

Advancement Prospects

Advancement prospects are excellent for a Radio Advertising Salesperson. People may advance in a number of ways. Many people feel that the best way to climb the career ladder is simply to increase their paycheck. The sky is the limit for salespeople. All they have to do is to continue to sell more and more spots.

Individuals may also advance by becoming station sales managers at either their station or another one. Many salespeople working in radio sales move up the career ladder by finding a position in a bigger market where they can obtain bigger and better selling territories.

Education and Training

Most radio stations prefer that their Radio Advertising Salespeople have a minimum of a four-year college degree. While it doesn't seem to matter what the individual majors in, he or she may find it useful to take courses in advertising, sales, business, English, sociology, psychology, writing, and communications.

There are also a variety of seminars offered through trade associations that may help the individual hone his or her skills.

Experience, Skills, and Personality Traits

A Radio Advertising Salesperson must really enjoy selling. Individuals cannot be timid. They must possess confidence in both themselves and their station. Good salespeople generally are individuals who can be aggressive without being offensive. In order to be successful in this profession, the individual must also be self-motivated and have the ability to work without constant supervision. He or she must be able to plan out a day of work, make appointments, make calls, etc. without someone sitting over his or her shoulder.

The Radio Advertising Salesperson should have a good sense of self and be articulate. Good verbal and written communication skills are a must.

A working knowledge of the broadcasting industry helps the individual understand more about what he or she is selling. The ability to work well with numbers is important in figuring costs and rates.

Unions and Associations

The radio station a salesperson works for may be a member of their state broadcasting association, the National Association of Broadcasters (NAB), Radio and Advertising Bureau (RAB), or the National Association of Broadcast Employees and Technicians (NABET). These organizations provide training, support, and materials. They also hold conferences and seminars during the year to bring together people in the field.

Tips for Entry

1. Look for these positions in the newspaper in either display ads or the classified section. Look under the headings of "Advertising," "Sales," "Salesperson," "Radio," or "Broadcasting."

2. Listen to area radio stations for job opportunities. They often advertise on their own station when openings occur.

3. Jobs may also be advertised in the broadcast trades. If your local library doesn't keep any of these on hand, you might want to ask a local radio station if you can look through their copies.

4. Any experience in sales may make you feel more comfortable about a selling position in radio. Consider working in a retail sales position on a summer vacation or as a part-time job.

5. Remember when you prepare your résumé to put down every sales job you have ever held. You might even want to include any special honors you had, such as being the highest-selling salesperson for your high school magazine subscription drive. Selling is selling. If you can sell magazines, you probably will be successful selling radio space.

6. Send your résumé and cover letter to small-market or middle-market radio stations. These stations experience a large turnover rate and may have openings. If they don't, ask that your résumé be kept on file. Address your letter to the station owner, manager, or personnel director. Try to get his or her name; don't just send your correspondence to a title.

7. Check out station Web sites. Many list employment opportunities.

TRAFFIC MANAGER, RADIO

CAREER PROFILE

Duties: Check daily logs; schedule commercials; supervise and coordinate traffic department; reorganize schedules to meet the needs of advertisers

Alternate Title(s): Traffic Supervisor; Traffic Coordinator

Salary Range: $22,000 to $49,000+

Employment Prospects: Fair

Advancement Prospects: Fair

Best Geographical Location(s): Positions located throughout the country.

Prerequisites:

Education or Training—Minimum requirements range from high school diploma to four-year college degree

Experience—Experience in broadcast traffic department

Special Skills and Personality Traits—Detail-oriented; organization; supervisory skills; typing or word processing skills; computer competency; communication skills; ability to work under pressure

CAREER LADDER

```
┌─────────────────────────────────────┐
│  Traffic Manager for Larger Station  │
│     or Advertising Salesperson       │
│    or Advertising Sales Manager      │
└─────────────────────────────────────┘

┌─────────────────────────────────────┐
│          Traffic Manager             │
└─────────────────────────────────────┘

┌─────────────────────────────────────┐
│         Traffic Assistant            │
└─────────────────────────────────────┘
```

Position Description

The Traffic Manager working in a radio station supervises and coordinates all employees in the traffic department. The individual is in charge of the entire department and everything that happens in it.

The traffic department in the radio station is very important. It is responsible for keeping a record of everything aired on the station. This includes advertising and commercial spots as well as programming information. The record that is kept is known as a log and is required by the FCC (Federal Communications Commission). The FCC is a government regulatory agency that licenses radio and television stations that broadcast to the public.

In a larger radio station the Traffic Manager may be responsible for 10 or more employees. In smaller stations, the Traffic Manager may be the only employee in the department. His or her responsibilities and duties vary depending on the size of the station.

The Traffic Manager is responsible for scheduling all commercials. He or she works with the station general manager, advertising sales manager, and possibly the station owner creating a sequence for the running of commercials. Together they decide how many commercials to put on the air each hour.

The Traffic Manager is responsible for making sure that advertisements and commercials are aired in the most effective way. For example, he or she must take care not to run two commercials for the same product directly after each other. The individual must also make sure that enough public service advertisements are aired. Public service announcements—or PSAs, as they are called—are advertisements made and aired by the station at no fee for nonprofit groups or community-service agencies. The FCC regulates how many PSAs must be aired in a specific time period. The Traffic Manager is responsible for training employees in the department. He or she must make sure that traffic assistants or representatives adhere to all FCC regulations and laws. To do this, the Traffic Manager may have group training sessions or work privately with each new assistant who comes in.

The Traffic Manager may assign the traffic assistants different duties. For example, one assistant may be assigned to work on programming while another may be required to do advertising and public service announcement traffic. The manager may assign one assistant to type logs while another may review them. The individual must make a determination as to what will be most effective for the department and what each individual is best at.

The Traffic Manager is responsible for getting daily logs typed or put into a computer. He or she usually has an assistant perform this task. However, if the individual is working in a smaller radio station, the Traffic Manager may do this him- or herself. All commercials, public service announcements, and programming must be listed on the log. The individual will go over all commercial orders and make sure that the information needed for the log is complete. If an assistant is doing this, the manager will be responsible for reviewing the completed daily log. Every advertisement must be listed with the exact time and date it is to be aired.

The Traffic Manager is required to check daily logs after the broadcast day. He or she must make sure that all commercials that were to be aired were done. The manager will see to it that on-air personalities and announcers either check off or initial each entry.

The Traffic Manager may authorize changes in the log sheet. This might occur if an announcer inadvertently forgets to air an advertisement and it must be placed on at a different time or if an advertiser calls up to change the date or time of the airing of a commercial. He or she must make sure when this is done that the daily log is changed and corrected. There is a no room for error in this position. The log sheets will eventually go to the FCC for review.

The Traffic Manager is frequently expected to review commercials for content. The individual must check each commercial and all ad copy for material that either the station or the FCC would find objectionable, sexist, or racist. If there is a problem, the Traffic Manager is responsible for giving the commercial to the advertising sales manager to handle.

The Traffic Manager may be called upon by salespeople to change the daily log in order to fit in an advertiser who wants to buy a lot of time. The manager will try to do this in as easy a way as possible without changing the entire day's scheduling.

The individual must understand the station, its programming, and its advertisers to be successful in this job. He or she may work overtime finishing logs and juggling schedules.

The Traffic Manager may be responsible to either the advertising sales manager, the general manager, or the station owner, depending on the structure of the station.

Salaries

Earnings for Traffic Managers working in radio depend heavily on the size, location, and prestige of the station as well as the experience and responsibilities of the individual.

Those working in small-market radio may have salaries of $22,000 to $30,000 annually. Those working in mid-market radio or in major markets may earn up to $49,000 a year or more.

Employment Prospects

Employment prospects are fair for Traffic Managers who want to work in radio. Radio stations are located throughout the country. Smaller stations often have only one person handling traffic duties. This means that an individual with even limited experience in traffic can frequently find a position as a Traffic Manager in small-market radio.

Those with more experience will find opportunities available in mid- and major-market radio. Major markets are located in cities such as New York, Los Angeles, Chicago, and Atlanta.

Advancement Prospects

Advancement prospects are fair for Traffic Managers. To climb the career ladder, most individuals who want to stay in the same industry look for positions in larger, more prestigious stations. This usually results in increased earnings.

Other Traffic Managers may advance their careers by becoming advertising salespeople at larger stations or advertising sales managers.

Education and Training

While there may be a limited number of positions requiring only a high school diploma or a two-year degree, the majority of radio stations want applicants who hold a four-year college degree.

Majors can be in almost any subject. Good choices for courses include broadcasting, radio, advertising, business, marketing, copywriting, and communications.

Experience, Skills, and Personality Traits

Traffic Managers need good supervisory skills. In larger stations they may be responsible for ten employees or more. They should have the ability to teach, explain, and instruct others in an easy-to-understand way. The individual should be personable and have good interpersonal skills.

The Traffic Manager working in a smaller station may be the only individual in the department. He or she would therefore need typing skills as well as the ability to work comfortably on a computer.

The individual must be articulate with good communication skills. He or she must be highly organized and accurate and have the ability to work with a lot of details. He or she should also be able to work well under pressure.

An understanding of radio and the advertising industry is extremely helpful.

Unions and Associations

Traffic Managers working in radio stations do not usually belong to any union. Individuals may join a number of trade associations relevant to the broadcast and radio industries. Some of the organizations offer individual membership while others offer membership to radio stations. These groups often have seminars, conferences, and training for people working in radio advertising. They also may provide trade journals, printed materials, and job guidance. These might include the state's broadcasting association, the National Association of Broadcasters (NAB), Radio and Advertising Bureau (RAB), or the National Association of Broadcast Employees and Technicians (NABET).

Tips for Entry

1. Look for seminars in radio, advertising, and traffic. These will give you an edge over other applicants and look good on your résumé when job hunting.
2. Become a member of your college radio or television station. This will give you an overview of what is entailed in working in broadcasting.
3. There are frequently part-time jobs in traffic open at smaller radio stations. These will give you hands-on experience in traffic.
4. If you can't find a summer or part-time job in the traffic department in radio, consider working in another department. The important thing is to get as much experience as possible.
5. Job openings for Traffic Managers are advertised in radio and broadcast trade journals. Look in your local library or magazine store to see if they get the trades. If not, consider a short-term subscription. You might also ask your local radio station if you can look through a few copies.
6. Job openings are also advertised in newspaper display and classified sections. Look under heading classifications of "Radio," "Broadcast," "Communications," and "Traffic."
7. Check out station Web sites. Many list employment opportunities.

TRAFFIC ASSISTANT, RADIO

CAREER PROFILE

Duties: Type daily commercial schedules; log commercials; keep track of advertising orders

Alternate Title(s): Radio Traffic Assistant; Traffic Representative; Traffic Clerk; Traffic Rep

Salary Range: $18,000 to $34,000+

Employment Prospects: Good

Advancement Prospects: Fair

Best Geographical Location(s): Positions located throughout the country.

Prerequisites:

Education or Training—Minimum requirements range from high school diploma to four-year college degree

Experience—Experience in broadcasting helpful, but not required

Special Skills and Personality Traits—Detail-oriented; organization; typing or word processing skills; computer competency; communication skills

CAREER LADDER

```
┌─────────────────────────────────┐
│  Traffic Manager or Coordinator │
└─────────────────────────────────┘

┌─────────────────────────────────┐
│       Traffic Assistant         │
└─────────────────────────────────┘

┌─────────────────────────────────┐
│      Entry Level, Intern,       │
│      or Clerical Position       │
└─────────────────────────────────┘
```

Position Description

The traffic department in a radio station is responsible for keeping track of everything that is announced and put on the air during the day on the station. This includes advertisements, commercials, public service announcements, and programming.

The Traffic Assistant is assigned an area to work in by the traffic manager or supervisor of the station. In many small stations the Traffic Assistant will be required to perform traffic responsibilities for all areas. In larger stations the individual will have specific duties dealing with advertisements, commercials, public service announcements (PSAs), or programming.

The Traffic Assistant has varied responsibilities depending on the size and structure of the station and the department. He or she may be responsible for typing the daily radio schedule. This schedule is called a log. It contains all the radio commercial and public service spot announcements.

In stations that have computerized traffic departments, the Traffic Assistant is responsible for typing information into the computer. Computerized logs are a lot easier to work on, as there are often mistakes or changes in advertising schedules. Without the generation of a computerized traffic log the Traffic Assistant must keep typing and retyping schedules as additions or deletions and corrections come in.

The Traffic Assistant is responsible for reviewing radio time sales orders and verifying the completeness of the data required for the log. This must be done for both local and national advertisements. For each commercial the Traffic Assistant must make sure he or she has the sponsor name, the date and time it is supposed to air, the length of the commercial, and whether it is to be live or recorded. If there is information missing, the individual will have to contact the salesperson involved to obtain it. The Traffic Assistant also includes the name of the announcer or disk jockey responsible for airing the commercial.

Another duty of the Traffic Assistant may be to keep records of the advertisements to make sure that commercials are run when they are scheduled. In many stations the on-air personalities and announcers are required to check off each item on the commercial log as they do it and to record the announcement time. The Traffic Assistant will deliver and pick up the completed log sheets daily. The individual may be responsible for reviewing the daily log sheets after use to check for authorized changes made during the broadcast day. In some situations the traffic manager or supervisor is responsible for performing this task.

The individual may deliver cassettes of commercial announcements or ad copy to the correct personnel. The Traffic Assistant may also be responsible for removing the commercial cassettes from the studio and storing them in the correct location.

The Traffic Assistant is expected to review advertisers' requests for specific dates and times at which they want their commercials to run. If the assistant finds that the date or time is not available, he or she may recommend other times or dates that are available.

In some stations the Traffic Assistant is required to preview advertisements before they are aired to make sure that they do not contain objectionable material. This is important because radio stations are governed by the FCC (Federal Communications Commission) and must adhere to its rules and regulations. The individual is responsible for keeping the daily commercial log up to FCC standards.

Depending on the station, the Traffic Assistant may also be responsible for performing clerical duties including billing, correspondence, filing, and answering phones. Other responsibilities might include writing copy for commercials, writing public service announcements, or timing commercials recorded on tape cartridges.

The Traffic Assistant usually works normal business hours. He or she is directly responsible to the traffic manager or coordinator, depending on the station.

Salaries

Salaries for Traffic Assistants working in radio range from approximately $18,000 to $34,000 depending on a number of variables. These include the size, location, and prestige of the station and the experience and responsibilities of the individual.

Individuals working in small-market radio or those who have little or no experience earn salaries in the low to mid-teens. Those with more experience or working in mid- or major-market radio may have earnings at the top end of the scale.

Employment Prospects

Employment prospects are good for Radio Traffic Assistants. There are a good number of radio stations located throughout the country. Many stations are owned by the same management and have both AM and FM divisions. Frequently the traffic duties of the AM and FM divisions are separate, creating a need for more traffic people. Individuals must be willing to relocate, if necessary, to find positions.

Those just entering the job market may find it easier to locate a job in a smaller market. These are usually found in less metropolitan areas. There are often openings because of a high turnover in this field as a result of career advancement.

Advancement Prospects

Advancement prospects are fair for Traffic Assistants. Individuals may climb the career ladder by becoming a traffic supervisor or traffic manager, depending on the structure of the station. Traffic Assistants may have to seek employment in larger, more prestigious stations in order to advance their career.

Education and Training

Educational requirements will vary from job to job. Depending on the station, minimum requirements can range from a high school diploma to a four-year college degree.

Courses in broadcasting, radio, advertising, marketing, copywriting, business, and communications will be useful to the individual in both obtaining a job and becoming successful at it.

Experience, Skills, and Personality Traits

The Traffic Assistant should be highly organized and have the ability to deal with many details. He or she needs good typing or word processing skills. With the current trend of computerizing the traffic department, it is extremely important that the individual be computer literate. He or she should be comfortable using computers and have a working knowledge of the equipment.

In order to be successful in his or her career, the individual should be personable and articulate and have good communications skills. The ability to remain calm and work under pressure is a plus.

Unions and Associations

Traffic Assistants working in radio stations may belong to a number of trade associations individually or may work for companies that are member stations. These organizations provide training, guidance, and written materials and usually hold seminars, conferences, and conventions throughout the year. These include state broadcasting associations, the National Association of Broadcasters (NAB), Radio and Advertising Bureau (RAB), and the National Association of Broadcast Employees and Technicians (NABET).

Tips for Entry

1. Become a member of your college radio station. This will give you hands-on experience in the industry.
2. You might also consider a part-time job or an internship at a local radio station. The experience value will prove useful.
3. Make sure that you take courses in computer technology. Today many stations are computerized, and you will be a step ahead with this knowledge.

4. Job openings are advertised in local newspapers in both the display and classified section. Look under heading classifications of "Radio," "Broadcast," "Communications," and "Traffic."

5. Openings are also advertised on local radio stations. Listen for opportunities.

6. Send your résumé and a cover letter to a number of radio stations. This is a high-turnover job. Openings occur frequently. Remember to ask that your résumé be kept on file if there are no current openings.

7. Large radio stations and trade associations often offer training programs and internships. Contact stations and associations and inquire about possibilities.

8. Check out station Web sites. Many list employment opportunities.

TELEVISION ADVERTISING REPRESENTATIVE

CAREER PROFILE

Duties: Sell advertising space to clients for television station; service accounts; bring in new business

Alternate Title(s): Salesman; Saleswoman; Salesperson; Sales Rep; Advertising Salesperson, Broadcast Salesperson; Account Executive

Salary Range: $22,000 to $100,000+

Employment Prospects: Good

Advancement Prospects: Good

Best Geographical Location(s): Larger cities may offer more possibilities; smaller markets may be easier to break into.

Prerequisites:

Education or Training—Four-year degree required

Experience—Selling experience is necessary in larger markets; entry level positions may not require experience

Special Skills and Personality Traits—Enjoyment of selling; ability to communicate; persuasive; self-motivation; knowledge of television industry

CAREER LADDER

```
┌─────────────────────────────────────────┐
│  Television Advertising Representative    │
│           for Larger Station              │
│  or Television Station Sales Manager      │
└─────────────────────────────────────────┘

┌─────────────────────────────────────────┐
│  Television Advertising Representative    │
└─────────────────────────────────────────┘

┌─────────────────────────────────────────┐
│  Sales Position in Different Industry,    │
│    Sales Assistant, or Entry Level        │
└─────────────────────────────────────────┘
```

Position Description

A Television Advertising Representative is responsible for selling advertising on the station to businesses and other individuals. Depending on the station, its size, and its structure, the TV Advertising Representative may sell to local, regional, or national accounts or may sell to all three.

Television Advertising Representatives, or sales reps, as they are often called, work under the direction of a sales manager who assigns accounts to them. The individual may also be assigned specific territories or areas in which he or she is permitted to sell.

The Television Advertising Representative services accounts currently advertising on the station. He or she may do this in a number of ways. The individual regularly calls or meets with the current advertisers to obtain future orders for insertion on the station. If the station is offering any special discounts or sales packages, the representative makes the advertiser aware of it. The representative also lets the advertiser know when station promotions are being planned or special programming will be aired.

In smaller, independent, and cable stations where the advertising department is limited in size, the Television Advertising Representative may work on commercial copy and content with the advertiser. He or she may also help the client develop an advertising campaign. In larger stations this is usually accomplished by the production staff, the copywriters, or the advertiser's ad agency.

The TV Advertising Representative must have a good working knowledge of the station and its programming. This information is valuable when offering suggestions to clients regarding the best time slot or period in which their ad should appear. If a commercial is shown in an inappropriate time period, even if the television station is number one in the ratings, the advertising won't draw the most effective results. For example, if an exclusive nightclub was advertising, it probably wouldn't want its commercial to air during the Saturday morning cartoon show. The individual must also know what time slots are available and how long commercials can be in the time slots.

In order to be successful in his or her job, the Television Advertising Representative must locate new advertisers. These might come from referrals from satisfied clients or from businesses calling the station to inquire about advertising rates. The majority of new business, however, will have to be produced by the advertising representative calling potential advertisers, visiting their places of business, sending information about the station, or a combination of all three. After making initial contact the individual will try to set up appointments to make presentations.

The Television Advertising Representative may put together sales packages including rate cards, discount cards, information sheets, station demographics, audience, and market share data. The individual sends or delivers this information when he or she visits potential clients or when advertisers call to get information on advertising space.

If the Television Advertising Representative is trying to sell space nationally, he or she may contact the advertising agencies that handle the potential national advertisers. Depending on the structure of the advertising sales department, the individual may make a sales presentation him- or herself to the agency account executive or may work with the sales manager.

He or she is required to write sales orders for commercial insertion and be responsible for getting them to the appropriate people at the station. These orders might go to production, traffic, continuity, and billing people.

The advertising representative is responsible for keeping records of when advertisements air, number of insertions, time of the commercial, billing names and addresses, people to contact for commercial content, rates charged, and discounts to be applied.

The individual may be required to attend advertising department sales meetings in which training techniques and sales problems are discussed along with new promotions, discounts, and packages the station is offering.

The advertising representative may work at his or her desk one day and be out in the field servicing accounts and trying to get new business the next. He or she must constantly keep motivated to keep selling. Many advertising representatives in the television industry work long hours. They begin working early in the morning and continue late into the night. They see every business as an opportunity to sell space.

As many stations today have their own Web sites, Television Advertising Representatives may also be responsible for selling advertising space on the station's site. In some cases, the station may additionally hire salespeople specifically to sell Web site advertising.

Advertising representatives are responsible directly to the sales manager of the department. The television industry in general is extremely competitive. Selling advertising space in the industry can add stress and pressure to the job.

Salaries

It is difficult to estimate earnings for Television Advertising Representatives. Earnings vary depending on the size, location, and prestige of the station as well as the experience and selling ability of the individual.

Compensation in jobs of this type can include a modest salary plus commissions on sales, straight commission, and draws against commissions.

A commission is a percentage of the money earned for the station that is paid to the sales rep who sells the advertising space. The percentage varies but is usually between 10 percent and 20 percent. For example, if an individual sold $2,500 worth of advertising for a week and was being paid 15 percent, he or she would earn $375.

If the individual earns a salary plus a commission, he or she would add the salary onto the $375 figure. Individuals who earn a draw against commission get a set amount of money each week or month that is taken out of their earned commission. If the person has a bad week, he or she still goes home with the draw. For example, the rep may have a $250 draw against commissions per week. If he or she sold the $2,500 worth of advertising space, he would not receive the draw. If he or she only sold $1,000 worth of space that week, and was receiving a 15 percent percentage, the individual would receive $150 from the commission and $100 from the draw.

Individuals who receive part of their salary in the form of a percentage of sales have the opportunity of earning as much as they want. TV Advertising Representatives may earn between $22,000 and $65,000 a year. Very successful sales reps can earn up to $100,000 plus annually.

Employment Prospects

Employment prospects are good for Television Advertising Representatives. Without salespeople, a television station would make very little money. A good sales representative is, therefore, always an asset to the station.

Television stations are located throughout the country. Local, independent, and cable stations are good choices for breaking into the field of television sales. These stations have a large turnover of employees and are usually in need of sales representatives.

Advancement Prospects

Advancement prospects are good for those in television advertising. An individual may advance in a number of ways. The advertising representative who is aggressive and sells well earns larger and larger commissions. To some, this is advancement enough. Other individuals may move up the career ladder by becoming a station's sales manager.

Other possibilities for advancement include the individual moving to a position in a larger, more prestigious station. The advertising rep might also stay at the same station and obtain a better territory.

Education and Training

Individuals working in television sales are usually required to hold a four-year degree. Good choices for majors include advertising, communications, business, marketing, and liberal arts. Courses in sales, psychology, public relations, writing, English, business, advertising, marketing, speech, math, and television broadcasting are useful.

Seminars in advertising and selling as well as the broadcast industry prove additionally helpful to the individual in order to help him or her hone skills and make contacts.

Experience, Skills, and Personality Traits

The most important skill a Television Advertising Representative can have is a love for selling. If the individual does not have this, he or she will usually not be good at the job. The TV Advertising Representative should be aggressive in a nonoffensive manner. Individuals should be persuasive and personable.

Good communication and phone skills are imperative. A good memory and organization skills are a must. The individual must keep records on many different clients, advertisements, insertion dates, etc. Getting things confused can be "the death of a salesman" (or woman).

The Television Advertising Representative must know how to read and interpret rate cards or discount sheets. He or she must be comfortable working with numbers, calculators, and adding machines. An understanding of the television industry and television advertising is necessary.

People working in television sales should be self-motivated and have the ability to work without a lot of supervision. They should also be able to deal with the rejection of not making a sale.

Unions and Associations

Depending on whether an individual is working for a network, syndicate, or cable station, he or she may belong to specific state, regional, or national broadcasting organizations.

Tips for Entry

1. If you are choosing a school, try to find one with its own television station. You will then be able to get hands-on experience working in a station.
2. Many local, small-market, and cable stations offer part-time, or summer employment in advertising sales.
3. Larger television stations often have internship programs in all areas of the station. Ask to work in the advertising department.
4. Positions may often be advertised on local or cable television stations.
5. Positions may also be advertised in display or classified ads in the newspaper. Look under heading classifications of "Advertising," "Sales," "Salesperson," "Broadcasting," "Cable," or "Television."
6. Jobs may be located in the television broadcast trades. If your local library doesn't keep these on hand, contact a local television station to ask if you can review a few issues. You might contact the trade journal itself and see if you can obtain a short-term subscription.
7. Send your résumé and a cover letter to the personnel director of every television and cable station you can find in the area in which you want to work. There is a high turnover in these jobs. You will probably be called in for an interview before you know it.
8. Check out television station Web sites for employment opportunities.

ADVERTISING SALES ASSISTANT, TELEVISION

CAREER PROFILE

Duties: Coordinate day-to-day activities in advertising sales office; assist in the creation of promotional packages for advertisers; write contracts and sales orders

Alternate Title(s): Sales Assistant; Advertising Sales Coordinator; Sales Coordinator

Salary Range: $18,000 to $28,000+

Employment Prospects: Good

Advancement Prospects: Good

Best Geographical Location(s): Positions may be found in areas where the smaller local markets are located as well as major markets such as New York, Los Angeles, Chicago, and Atlanta.

Prerequisites:

Education or Training—High school diploma required; college background or degree helpful

Experience—Experience in advertising, sales, or marketing useful but not required

Special Skills and Personality Traits—Good organizational skills; office skills; computer capability; numerical skills

CAREER LADDER

```
┌─────────────────────────────┐
│   Advertising Salesperson   │
└─────────────────────────────┘

┌─────────────────────────────┐
│ Advertising Sales Assistant │
└─────────────────────────────┘

┌─────────────────────────────┐
│         Entry Level         │
└─────────────────────────────┘
```

Position Description

An Advertising Sales Assistant working at a television station is responsible for coordinating the various day-to-day activities that occur in the station's advertising sales office. There is a considerable amount of organizational skills required to be successful in this job. The individual functions as a cross between the assistant to the advertising sales manager and the office manager.

The Advertising Sales Assistant, sales assistant, or advertising sales coordinator, as he or she might be called, has varied responsibilities depending on the organization of the station where the individual is employed.

Sales assistants work with many different people and departments in the television station. They may work with salespeople, account executives, programming executives, and people in the traffic and continuity, marketing, promo-

tion, public service, community relations, and public relations departments.

The sales assistant works directly with and is responsible to the advertising sales manager. Together they create promotional packages for potential advertisers to buy as well as develop attractive packaging options for those advertisers.

Clerically, the individual is responsible for all interoffice correspondence. This includes memos, letters, and information to all the salespeople about rates, packages, and station promotions. The sales assistant must stay up to date on all commercial time slots sold and those that are available. He or she is also responsible for checking and keeping on file all contracts, sales orders, and other pertinent information.

In many stations the sales assistant is also responsible for billing advertisers for commercial time that has been purchased. In other stations the individual will just be responsible for putting the numbers together and giving them to the billing or accounting department.

An important duty of the sales assistant is to direct potential advertisers who call the station to the correct salespeople. He or she also puts together and sends out rate cards and advertising information packages to those who call or write as well as to those who have talked to station salespeople.

When salespeople are not available the sales assistant may sell advertising space. It is therefore vital for the individual to understand how to read the station's rate card and keep on top of all promotions and advertising specials the station is running. The sales assistant must also have a complete knowledge of the programming of the station so as to schedule commercials for the most productive time slots for advertisers. The sales assistant writes advertising contracts and orders. The individual, however, does not receive a commission. He or she is paid strictly on a salary basis.

One of the main functions of the sales assistant is to keep in touch with the current advertisers and keep them abreast of new programming and packaging available. If an advertiser is interested in buying more time, the Sales Assistant will be responsible for getting them in touch with the correct salesperson.

Depending on the station, the individual may be responsible for locating per inquiry (PI) and direct response advertisers. Per inquiry and direct response ads are the advertisements often seen on cable and independent stations where potential buyers use a toll-free phone number to order records, cassettes, or novelty items. Instead of the TV station selling ad time for a specific amount per second, the station offers commercial time to advertisers for a flat fee based on a per response or inquiry call. The sales assistant must keep track of the number of responses or inquiries derived from each commercial and bill the advertiser accordingly. Additionally, the individual may view commercials to make sure that they are acceptable and meet station and FCC standards.

The sales assistant is responsible for scheduling the daily logs that show when commercials will be aired. The sales assistant must keep up with the times and dates advertisers' commercials are aired and what time slots are available for other commercials. The individual may also send information such as when ads were aired to the advertisers or agencies that purchased the time slots.

Hours for sales assistants are fairly regular. There may be some overtime during certain times of the year or when special advertising promotions are being run.

Salaries

Earnings for Advertising Sales Assistants vary greatly depending on a number of factors. These include the experience and responsibilities of the individual and the size and location of the station.

Those working in smaller independent or cable stations could earn from $18,000 to $22,000 annually. Advertising Sales Assistants working in larger stations in major markets may earn salaries of $19,000 to $28,000 or more per year.

Employment Prospects

Employment prospects are good for Advertising Sales Assistants seeking employment at television stations. Many stations hire more than one sales assistant for the department. Individuals may, however, have to relocate to areas where jobs are available.

There are currently more opportunities in this field than ever before. In addition to networks there are affiliates, locals, independents, and many cable stations available for employment possibilities.

Advancement Prospects

Prospects are good for advancement of Advertising Sales Assistants working in broadcasting. Depending on the organization of a station, individuals can advance their career by becoming salespeople or working in the promotion department.

Education and Training

While there are people who hold jobs as Advertising Sales Assistants who only hold a high school diploma, a college background is helpful. Useful courses include anything in the line of communications, advertising, sales, marketing, public relations, business math, television, or broadcasting.

Experience, Skills, and Personality Traits

Individuals working in this type of job in television sales should have good organizational skills. They should be able to deal with a multitude of people and projects at one time.

Advertising Sales Assistants should be good with numbers and articulate and should have good phone skills. Creativity and the ability to write are a plus. The ability to type and computer capability, as well as other office skills, are necessary.

Any type of experience in advertising, sales, marketing, or the broadcast industry is useful but not required.

Unions and Associations

Individuals may belong to state, regional, or national broadcasting organizations.

Tips for Entry

1. Any experience in advertising is a plus. Remember to put all advertising-related jobs and summer jobs on your résumé.

2. Positions may be easier to find in smaller markets. You may also consider looking for a position in radio until a television advertising sales position opens up.

3. These types of jobs are often advertised in the Sunday newspapers. Look under the heading classifications of "Television," "Radio," "Broadcasting," "Advertising," or "Sales."

4. Call or send résumés to the personnel director of any television stations that you are interested in working at. Remember to include cable stations and independents as well as networks and affiliates.

5. Television stations promote from within. You might consider taking a position as a secretary in the station until a job in this department opens up.

6. Check out television station Web sites for possible employment openings.

PROMOTION COORDINATOR, TELEVISION

CAREER PROFILE

Duties: Develop and implement special projects and promotions to enhance the station's image

Alternate Title(s): Special Projects Coordinator; Special Projects and Promotion Coordinator

Salary Range: $23,000 to $49,000+

Employment Prospects: Fair

Advancement Prospects: Fair

Best Geographical Location(s): Entry level positions may be found in areas where the smaller local markets are located; major markets such as New York, Los Angeles, Chicago, Atlanta, or any other large city offer positions to those with more experience.

Prerequisites:

Education or Training—Bachelor's degree required with major in communications, public relations, English, broadcasting, or journalism.

Experience—Publicity, promotion, journalism, or broadcast experience helpful

Special Skills and Personality Traits—Creative; good writing skills; communication skills

CAREER LADDER

```
┌─────────────────────────────────┐
│   Director of Public Relations  │
│   or Marketing or Promotion     │
│   Coordinator at Larger Station │
└─────────────────────────────────┘

┌─────────────────────────────────┐
│      Promotion Coordinator      │
└─────────────────────────────────┘

┌─────────────────────────────────┐
│   Entry Level (at small station)│
│   or Promotion Assistant        │
│   (at larger station)           │
└─────────────────────────────────┘
```

Position Description

A Promotion Coordinator working at a television station is responsible for developing and implementing special projects and promotions to enhance the station's image and make it more visible.

The Promotion Coordinator has varied duties depending on the size and organization of the station where he or she is working. At larger stations the individual has more specialized responsibilities, while the person working in a small station might be the only one in the department and have to do everything.

Many of the functions of the Promotion Coordinator revolve around writing. He or she is responsible for writing press releases and announcements about new programming, television specials, station personalities, promotions, and events in which the station is taking part. The individual may also be responsible for writing the little blurbs often seen in newspapers and TV guides about upcoming programs. The Promotion Coordinator may write newspaper ads to advertise television programs the station is airing or events in which the station is participating. He or she may also write brochures or booklets distributed by the station.

The individual is responsible for developing effective promotions and special projects as well as implementing them. He or she may come up with a variety of contests and sweepstakes to run on the station. The Promotion Coordinator must put the idea in writing and bring it to the station management. After the initial idea has been approved, the individual must find the appropriate time of the year to run the promotion, check into state and federal regulations, decide on a set of rules for participants, find sources for prizes, and implement the contest on the air. He or she is responsible for writing press releases on the event for other media as well as for on-air promotion. The individual is also responsible for advising members of the staff about the event.

Other projects the Promotion Coordinator may develop include the sponsorship of events for community organizations, such as marathons, sporting events, and other entertainment, and fund-raising telethons. Individuals working at cable stations also have to develop promotions that help attract new subscribers.

An important function of the Promotion Coordinator is to arrange appearances for station personalities at events and in other media. He or she may set up interviews with magazines and newspapers for feature stories on newscasters, or to interview show hosts or show stars.

In certain stations the Promotion Coordinator might also function as the public relations or community relations coordinator. In these cases, he or she could also be expected to write speeches for other members of the station, handle public relations problems, arrange press functions, and work with community groups.

The Promotion Coordinator works closely with the advertising department to find ways to increase the viewing audience, which will in turn increase advertising revenues. Together the two departments work on promoting and advertising new programs, new viewing seasons, and TV specials. The Promotion Coordinator may be asked to come up with attractive promotion packages for potential advertisers.

If the television station is a local network affiliate, the Promotion Coordinator might also work with the network on promotions and special projects. He or she may then be asked to travel to meet with network representatives. The individual must also travel on behalf of the station to any conventions, meetings, and seminars related to promotion or advertising.

The Promotion Coordinator works fairly normal hours. He or she may have to work late occasionally or work on a weekend if a special project is taking place. Depending on the organization of the station, the Promotion Coordinator may be responsible to the advertising director, the marketing director, or the general manager of the station.

Salaries

Salaries for a Promotion Coordinator depend greatly on the size and market of the television station for which he or she is working. Compensation is also dependent on the experience and responsibilities of the individual.

Smaller stations often offer annual earnings so low that they are close to minimum wage. Most individuals feel, however, that a low beginning salary is worth the experience value of the position. Earnings for those working in smaller markets can range from $23,000 to $28,000 annually. Income for those working in larger markets can range from $24,000 to $49,000 plus.

Employment Prospects

Employment prospects are fair for individuals seeking employment in promotion at television stations. Entry level positions in the promotion department may be open to individuals in smaller markets. It is not unusual to find a Promotion Coordinator at a small-market station who has just graduated from college. Smaller stations usually have a large employee turnover rate due to the fact that positions are often taken to gain experience and don't pay very high salaries. Chances of employment at larger television stations in major markets go up with experience. Stations in major markets may employ up to 10 people in the promotion department.

Advancement Prospects

Promotion Coordinators may advance their career by becoming director of public relations or marketing. Career advancement for Promotion Coordinators can also be attained by finding a position in a bigger city, a major market, at a network, etc. As noted above, there is a high turnover rate at television stations, especially in smaller ones. Television stations like to promote from within and often hire individuals working in local affiliates for positions at their networks. Advancement is easier for individuals working at smaller stations.

Education and Training

A college education and degree are necessary for those who want to work in almost any facet of television. While the college major can be in almost any field, courses should be taken in communications, public relations, English, broadcasting, journalism, television, or writing. Schools with broadcast facilities offer valuable hands-on experience. Seminars in publicity, promotion, and television are also very useful.

Experience, Skills, and Personality Traits

Those working in television promotion should have good communication skills. They should possess the ability to write well and to be creative, articulate, and persuasive. Individuals should have a basic knowledge of publicity, promotion, and public relations.

Experience working in television, even if it was only a summer job, an internship, or at a school station, is a plus. Journalistic experience on a community or school newspaper is helpful.

The ability to type and/or use a computer or word processor may be necessary.

Unions and Associations

Those working in promotion in television stations may belong to a number of different trade associations and organizations. These include the Public Relations Society of America (PRSA) and the National Academy of Television Arts and Sciences (NATAS). Stations may be members of the American Advertising Federation (AAF). Membership in these organizations offers individuals guidance and helps them make important contacts.

Tips for Entry

1. Try to find an internship or summer job at a station to gain some experience or help you get your foot in the door.
2. Look for a job in a small market. While positions such as this pay considerably less than those in major market stations, it is easier to break into the business this way.
3. Look in the classified section of a Sunday newspaper for job openings. Look under the "Broadcasting," "Television," "Public Relations," "Advertising," and "Promotion" sections. There might also be opportunities advertised in display advertising.
4. Don't forget to send résumés to public television and cable stations as well as locals, independents, and networks.
5. Many stations list employment opportunities on their Web site.

PROMOTION ASSISTANT, TELEVISION

CAREER PROFILE

Duties: Assist the promotion coordinator in the implementation of special projects and promotions at a television station

Alternate Title(s): Special Projects Assistant; Special Projects and Promotion Assistant

Salary Range: $18,000 to $35,000+

Employment Prospects: Fair

Advancement Prospects: Good

Best Geographical Location(s): Positions may be located in areas where smaller local markets are located; major markets such as New York, Los Angeles, Atlanta, Chicago, or any large city may also offer position possibilities.

Prerequisites:

Education or Training—Bachelor's degree with major in communications, public relations, English, broadcasting, or journalism required

Experience—Writing and/or publicity experience helpful but not required

Special Skills and Personality Traits—Good communication skills; good writing skills; creative; ability to type and/or computer capability

CAREER LADDER

```
┌─────────────────────────────────┐
│     Promotion Coordinator       │
└─────────────────────────────────┘

┌─────────────────────────────────┐
│     Promotion Assistant         │
└─────────────────────────────────┘

┌─────────────────────────────────┐
│  Student or Entry Level Position │
└─────────────────────────────────┘
```

Position Description

A Promotion Assistant working in a television station is responsible for helping the promotion coordinator implement special projects and promotions that enhance the station's image and make it more visible.

The Promotion Assistant has varied duties depending on the size and organization of the station where he or she is working. Part of the responsibility of the individual centers on "grunt work." At smaller stations, where there is not a large staff, the assistant may carry out many of the functions of a secretary, including typing, answering the phones, or writing letters and memos. He or she may also check details of the various promotions and special events on which the coordinator is working.

Even though the station for which the Promotion Assistant works will help publicize a promotion, other media are needed to help spread the word. The assistant usually has a good business relationship with most of the media in the area. One of the main functions of the Promotion Assistant is to call editors, newspeople, etc. to discuss promotions, programming, and special events put on by the station.

As the Promotion Assistant gains more experience he or she may help the coordinator with writing responsibilities. The individual might begin by writing press releases or announcements about new programming, television specials, station personalities, promotions, and events in which the station is participating. The assistant may also be responsible for writing the little blurbs often seen in newspapers and TV guides about upcoming programs. Most, if not all, writing is usually checked by the coordinator at this point in the individual's career. The Promotion Assistant may also learn to write copy for newspaper ads that advertise television programs the station is airing or events in which the station is taking part.

While the individual is not responsible for developing promotions and special projects, he or she assists in their implementation. The assistant may be asked to take the ideas of the promotion coordinator and put them on paper or may be asked to come up with ideas about implementation.

To do this, the Promotion Assistant might be involved in research on former station promotions and special events as well as those of competing stations. The assistant may be responsible for checking federal rules and regulations for contests and sweepstakes, preparing rules for participants, locating sources of contest prizes, and keeping station personnel aware of internal promotions.

Depending on his or her experience, the Promotion Assistant may act as the station liaison when the station is sponsoring events for community organizations, such as marathons, sports events, or other entertainment, and fund-raising telethons. The individual should be on hand at the event to assist the promotion coordinator in making sure that all programs go smoothly.

At times the Promotion Assistant may work with station personalities, accompanying them to personal appearances and other events. The individual is often responsible for checking the details, times, etc. of these personal appearances. The Promotion Assistant may also accompany station personalities to interviews for stories with magazines and newspapers the promotion coordinator has arranged.

If the station is relatively small, the Promotion Assistant could also function as the public relations or community relations assistant. In these cases, he or she could also be expected to help coordinate press functions and work with community groups.

The Promotion Assistant works fairly normal hours. He or she may have to work late occasionally or work on a weekend if a special project is taking place. The Promotion Assistant is responsible to the promotion coordinator of the station.

Salaries

Salaries for Promotion Assistants vary greatly based on the size and market of the television station for which the assistants work. Compensation also depends on the experience and responsibilities of the individual.

Smaller stations often offer annual earnings so low that they are slightly above minimum wage. Most individuals feel, however, that a low beginning salary is worth the experience value of the position. Earnings for those working in smaller markets or on local cable stations can range from $18,000 to $21,000 annually. Income for those working in larger markets can range from $19,000 to $35,000 plus.

Employment Prospects

Employment prospects are fair for individuals seeking employment as Promotion Assistants at television stations.

Entry level positions in the promotion department may be open to individuals in smaller markets and cable. Smaller stations usually have a high employee turnover rate because positions are often taken to gain experience and do not pay very high salaries. Chances of employment at larger television stations in major markets go up with experience. Stations in major markets may employ a number of Promotion Assistants.

Advancement Prospects

Promotion Assistants may advance their careers by finding positions as promotion coordinators. Other individuals move up the career ladder by becoming public relations or community relations directors or coordinators.

Career advancement for Promotion Assistants might also be attained by finding a position in a bigger city, in a major market, at a network, etc. As noted above, there is a high turnover rate at television stations, especially in smaller ones. Advancement is easier for individuals working at smaller stations.

Education and Training

A college education and degree is necessary for those who want to work in television. Helpful majors include communications, public relations, English, broadcasting, and journalism.

Seminars in publicity, promotion, and television are also very useful.

Experience, Skills, and Personality Traits

Those working in television promotion should be articulate with good communication skills. Individuals should be eager to learn. The ability to write well is important, as is creativity.

Experience working in television, even if it was only a summer job, an internship, or while working at a school station, is a plus. Journalistic experience on a community or school newspaper is also helpful.

Good phone skills are necessary. The ability to type and/or use a computer is a plus.

Unions and Associations

Promotion Assistants or the station for which they work may be members of the Public Relations Society of America (PRSA), the National Academy of Television Arts and Sciences (NATAS), and the American Advertising Federation (AAF). These organizations are useful for making contacts and for professional support.

Tips for Entry

1. Try to find an internship or summer job at a station to gain some experience or help you get your foot in the door.

2. Look for a job in a small market or in cable. While positions such as this pay considerably less than those in major-market stations, it is easier to break into the business this way.

3. Look in the classified section of a Sunday newspaper for job openings. Look under the "Broadcasting," "Television," "Public Relations," "Advertising," and "Promotion" sections. There might additionally be opportunities advertised in display advertising.

4. Don't forget to send résumés to public television and cable stations as well as locals, independents, and networks.

TELEVISION ADVERTISING GRAPHIC ARTIST

CAREER PROFILE

Duties: Create and design artwork, graphics, and sets for commercials produced for advertisers buying time from a television station; design graphics for advertisements and material the station uses to promote itself

Alternate Title(s): Artist; TV Advertising Artist; Television Graphic Designer; Graphic Designer

Salary Range: $23,000 to $48,000+

Employment Prospects: Fair

Advancement Prospects: Fair

Best Geographical Location(s): Positions may be available in any area in which television stations are located.

Prerequisites:

Education or Training—High school diploma the minimum requirement; art school, art courses, or college degree with major in art required for many positions

Experience—Commercial or graphic art experience helpful; portfolio necessary for most positions

Special Skills and Personality Traits—Creative; artistic ability; sense of color, design, and layout; knowledge of commercial art; drawing and illustrating skills; computer capabilities; ability to work in broadcast studios; understanding of both broadcast and advertising industries

CAREER LADDER

```
┌─────────────────────────────────────┐
│        Assistant Art Director        │
└─────────────────────────────────────┘

┌─────────────────────────────────────┐
│ Television Advertising Graphic Artist│
└─────────────────────────────────────┘

┌─────────────────────────────────────┐
│  Entry Level, College or Art School  │
│  Student, or Freelance Commercial    │
│        or Graphic Artist             │
└─────────────────────────────────────┘
```

Position Description

The graphic artist working in the advertising department of a television station is responsible for all artwork and design required in a commercial. The individual is required to work with businesses that advertise on the station as well as station personnel, including copywriters, producers, directors, and salespeople.

The Television Advertising Graphic Artist performs a variety of duties. He or she is required to design commercial sets. Depending on the station and the number of people working in the department, the individual may just sketch out the set or may design it, paint it, and actually build or construct it. The graphic artist might be called in to decide what color the set will be, what color clothes actresses, actors, and models should wear, and lighting.

The Television Advertising Graphic Artist is also responsible for designing and creating the graphics used in the commercial. These might include things such as the art or title cards for the ad. The individual may paint, draw, or use press type, computer type, and graphics to do the words, logos, and other art for commercials.

Graphic artists are responsible for deciding what kind, size, and color of type should be used in commercials and what color the background should be if and when words and graphics are shown on the screen. For example, if the graphic artist is preparing a piece for the conclusion of a commercial, such as the kind that sells old records via a toll-free phone number and accepting credit cards, he or she will have to make certain decisions. The color of the last screen with the call-in information must be selected. Type style and size for the phone number, address, and other information as well as the position and size of the logos for the credit cards must also be chosen.

The graphic artist works with a commercial project from the inception of the idea to the final taping. During this time the individual may change color schemes, type sizes, graphics, or set design if he or she feels it improves the commercial.

The graphic artist needs to be proficient in all types of artistic design. Depending on the project and the situation, he or she may have to design, sketch, paint, draw, hand letter, or cartoon to achieve the necessary effects. Today a great deal of the design in television advertising graphics is accomplished with the use of computers. At times the individual may also use still photos or slides, working that medium into the finished ad.

The graphic artist may be responsible for developing and designing suitable logos for station advertisers. Creating an outstanding logo for a television advertiser is important for the graphic artist. If the advertiser likes the logo, he will use it in all his advertising—on other stations as well as in print ads. This will be helpful to the individual when attempting to climb the career ladder.

The graphic artist working in the advertising department also does graphics for ads the station uses to promote itself. For example, he or she might design and do the artwork for newspaper, magazine, and billboard ads. He or she may be required to do typesetting or headlines, work with color separations, and prepare mechanicals.

The individual may also be required to do graphics and design for the promotional materials the station uses, including brochures, newsletters, and signs.

In some stations the graphic artist may have additional duties working with other departments, including programming, news, marketing, or public relations. In these situations the individual would perform the same type of functions for the other departments—developing set designs, graphics, or art for print ads, brochures, or billboards.

In small stations there might be one or two graphic artists on staff. In large stations there will be a number of graphic artists working. These individuals usually work on art and graphics in either the programming and news departments or the advertising and sales departments.

The graphic artist working in the advertising department of a television station usually works normal hours. If an advertisement or commercial is on a deadline, however, the individual may have to work overtime.

Depending on the structure of the station and the advertising department, the graphic artist may be responsible to either an art director, if the station has one, or the director of advertising.

Salaries

Annual earnings for graphic artists working in the advertising department of television stations vary greatly depending on the size, location, and prestige of the station and the responsibilities and experience of the individual.

Individuals working in smaller stations or those with less experience may earn $23,0000 annually. Graphic artists with more experience or those working in larger, more prestigious stations may earn up to $48,000 or more a year.

Most television stations augment salaries with fringe benefit packages.

Employment Prospects

Employment prospects are fair for individuals seeking employment as graphic artists working in the advertising department of television stations. There are numerous local, independent, network, and cable stations located throughout the country, and more are springing up.

It is important to note that individuals may have to work as graphic artists for the entire station and not just in the advertising department. Individuals might also have to relocate to find an opening.

A little experience goes a long way in this field. Individuals who have hands-on experience working in school stations and local stations may be chosen over applicants who have no experience.

A good portfolio of the individual's best work is also usually necessary in obtaining these type of positions. Superiors who see talent or the potential for talent often hire individuals even without experience.

Advancement Prospects

Advancement prospects are fair for Television Advertising Graphic Artists. In order to climb the career ladder, the individual must become the art director or assistant art director or will have to locate a position in a larger, more prestigious station. This move usually means that the individual will receive a higher salary.

Individuals may advance their career by eventually moving into the producing or directing of televised commercials or programming. They might also leave advertising and become a graphic artist in another industry.

Education and Training

Educational requirements differ from station to station in this job. Some require four-year degrees with a major in fine art or commercial art. Others require a high school diploma and art school training. Some stations may require classes in television broadcasting. Still others aren't interested in the type of education an individual has as long as he or she is creative, can perform the job, and is willing to learn.

Since a great deal of television graphics is done on computer today, it is important to have computer training. Courses or seminars in computer graphics are imperative.

Seminars and other courses in various facets of art techniques, commercial art, television, and broadcasting are additionally useful.

Experience, Skills, and Personality Traits

Graphic artists working in television advertising need to be creative both on paper and conceptually. They must have a good sense of color, design, and layout and the ability to illustrate this talent. The graphic artist must be competent in all forms of artwork, including sketching, lettering, painting, and cartooning. The more media the individual can master and the more flexible he or she is, the better his or her opportunity to obtain a job and move up the career ladder.

Individuals should be comfortable working around television cameras and have a working knowledge of the commercial studio. As indicated above, individuals should also be computer capable. Knowledge of color separation, mechanicals, photography, and cinematography are necessary. An understanding of the advertising industry as well as the broadcast industry is helpful.

Graphic artists working in TV advertising departments must be able to work quickly and accurately and meet deadlines without putting themselves into stressful, pressured situations.

Unions and Associations

Graphic Artists working in the television industry may belong to the National Association of Broadcast Employees and Technicians (NABET), a union representing people working in broadcasting.

Individuals might also belong to any of a variety of trade associations, including the Broadcast Designers Association (BDA), the American Advertising Federation (AAF), the Art Directors Club, Inc. (ADC), the One Club, the Graphic Artists Guild (GAG), the American Institute of Graphic Arts (AIGA), or the Society of Illustrators. These associations provide support and guidance and often offer helpful seminars and training to members.

Tips for Entry

1. Try to locate an internship program in the advertising department of one of the larger television stations.
2. Consider a summer or part-time job working in any capacity at your local TV station.
3. If your school has a television station, try to get some experience at it. Hands-on experience is always useful.
4. Put together a portfolio of your best work. Make it creative, neat, and diversified. You will probably be required to show your work before you get a job. A good portfolio can get you the position you are after.
5. Join appropriate trade associations. Some of these can help you hone your skills. Attending meetings and conferences can help you make important contacts.
6. Check out station Web sites for possible employment opening.

ADVERTISING PRODUCTION ASSISTANT, TELEVISION

CAREER PROFILE

Duties: Assist in the production of advertisements for television; put up props; adjust lighting and microphones; take care of paperwork; coordinate scheduling for shooting commercials

Alternate Title(s): Floor Assistant; Staging Assistant; Production Apprentice

Salary Range: $24,000 to $33,000+

Employment Prospects: Fair

Advancement Prospects: Good

Best Geographical Location(s): Larger cities offer more employment prospects; smaller-market cities may provide easier access to entry level employment.

Prerequisites:

Education or Training—Two-year degree required for most positions; four-year degree preferred

Experience—Experience in television or cable preferred but not required

Special Skills and Personality Traits—Detail-oriented; typing, word processing, or computer skills; ability to lift heavy objects; understanding of advertising industry

CAREER LADDER

```
┌─────────────────────────────────┐
│       Associate Producer        │
└─────────────────────────────────┘

┌─────────────────────────────────┐
│ Advertising Production Assistant │
└─────────────────────────────────┘

┌─────────────────────────────────┐
│   Entry level or Administrative  │
│     Assistant in Department      │
└─────────────────────────────────┘
```

Position Description

The Advertising Production Assistant working in the studio of a television station is responsible for assisting the producer and other members of the production staff in filming or taping advertisements and commercials that are to be aired on the station.

The individual works with copywriters, actresses, actors, models, hairdressers, makeup people, directors, advertising salespeople, secretaries, cue card people, lighting people, and electricians. Together they assemble and produce effective advertisements for the station's clients.

The Advertising Production Assistant may have varied duties depending on the structure and size of the advertising department and his or her experience. In smaller stations the individual may have more diversified duties. This, however, gives the assistant a more rounded education in the craft of producing commercials.

For example, in a smaller station the Advertising Production Assistant may be asked to help with the copywriting of scripts for commercials. In larger stations the individual would not usually perform that task. He or she may, however, provide input on whether dialogue sounds strained and be asked to make suggestions for improvements.

The assistant is responsible for taking down the changes made in advertising scripts and making the necessary corrections. He or she may physically do the retyping of the script or may give the corrections to a production secretary. The individual is then responsible for circulating the new commercial script to the proper people.

If the studio does not have cue card people, the Advertising Production Assistant may be asked to write the dialogue on cards. He or she may then be required to hold up the cards during the filming of the commercial for the actors and actresses.

The individual might also be responsible for actually setting up the lighting or for instructing the lighting people where the lights should be placed. The production assistant may be responsible for setting up microphones, cameras, or other electrical equipment or may just instruct other members of the crew where to put things at the suggestion of the producer and director of the commercial.

Depending on the situation, the Advertising Production Assistant may help the producer and director cast the models, actors, actresses, and announcer. The individual may call agents looking for a specific type of face, look, or personality. He or she may schedule casting appointments for both the producer and director as well as the casting manager, if there is one on staff at the station.

In most cases, the individuals responsible for assisting the producer and director of the advertisement in making sure that the correct props are available and in setting them up where needed. The individual may also be required to handle such tasks as marking the set floor where the actors an actresses are supposed to stand.

The production assistant is responsible for scheduling studio time for the shooting of the commercials. The individual must notify everyone involved in the commercial when to be available and where to be. This includes camera people, assistant directors, directors, associate producers, producers, floor managers, actors, actresses, models, and announcers. The advertising client usually wants to be notified when the taping is taking place so that he or she can be there.

It is the responsibility of the production assistant to make sure all legal papers are in order and releases are signed by the models and announcers. The individual is responsible for keeping records of studio time, costs, and visuals.

After the commercial is completed the Advertising Production Assistant may be required to take down the set and return props. He or she may also have to run off copies of the commercial for the director, producer, or advertiser to review.

It is important to note that in smaller stations the production assistant often works not only as part of the advertising department but also as part of the programming department.

Hours for this job are fairly normal. Things can get quite hectic, however, when there are a large number of commercials to make in a limited time period.

Depending on the structure of the station and its advertising department, the production assistant may be responsible to either the producer or director of commercials or the advertising director.

Salaries

Salaries for Advertising Production Assistants can range from $24,000 to $33,000 or more per year. Variables include the size of the station, its location, and the experience and responsibilities of the individual. At certain stations the Advertising Production Assistant may be represented by a union. In these cases the union sets minimum earnings for individuals.

Stations in smaller markets usually have the lowest salaries because individuals in these positions are just entering the job market.

Employment Prospects

Employment prospects are fair for individuals seeking employment as production assistants in television station advertising departments. With the current surge of new local, syndicated, and cable television stations around the country there will be more and more opportunities for employment in the coming years.

It is probably easier for individuals with little or no experience to enter the job market in smaller stations. They may, however, act as production assistants for the entire station as opposed to just the advertising department.

Advancement Prospects

Advancement prospects are good for Advertising Production Assistants working in television. Those individuals who move up the ladder fastest usually are talented, aggressive, and assertive and have gone beyond the call of duty in their work.

Advertising Production Assistants can become associate producers or producers for the advertising department of the station. They might also become associate producers for programming. Individuals might also climb the career ladder by locating a position in a bigger station, an advertising agency, or a private production company.

Education and Training

Most positions as Advertising Production Assistants in television require at least a two-year degree. Many TV station managers prefer that their new employees have four-year bachelor's degrees.

When thinking about choosing a school, try to locate one that has broadcast facilities as well as classes in broadcast and video production and techniques. This will give you experience that another job applicant might not have. Classes in advertising are also important.

Individuals who have finished school or are taking other majors may find outside courses and seminars in broadcast techniques, advertising, and television useful.

Experience, Skills, and Personality Traits

Advertising Production Assistants should be eager to learn all that they can about the trade. They should also be willing to do more than the job calls for. Nonthreatening aggressiveness and assertiveness help the individual move up the career ladder.

An understanding of the television and advertising industries is useful. Knowledge of camera angles, direction, and lighting is helpful but may not be necessary for an entry level position.

The ability to work on many details at one time and a good memory are essential. Typing, word processing, or computer skills may be necessary, depending on the job. As the individual may be called on to move props, he or she must be able to lift and carry heavy objects.

The individual in this position should be a "people person." He or she will work with large numbers of people, including directors, script writers, copywriters, models, actresses, actors, agents, lighting people, and electricians. The ability to get along with others is imperative.

Unions and Associations

Depending on the station and the responsibilities of the individual, Advertising Production Assistants may be represented by the National Association of Broadcast Employees and Technicians AFL-CIO (NABET), the International Brotherhood of Electrical Workers (IBEW), or even the Writers Guild of America (WGA) (if the individual is doing copywriting). The individual might also belong to any of a number of trade associations, including the American Advertising Federation (AAF) or the Association of Independent Commercial Producers (AICP).

Tips for Entry

1. If you have no experience at all, you might try to dazzle the person interviewing you with a great desire to learn the craft of producing. Once you get the job, be willing to work hard and do more than the next person.

2. You might put together a portfolio of storyboards for commercials. These don't have to be for actual products (although they can be). The portfolio will illustrate that you have a concept of putting together an advertisement. You might put in some of your writing samples. The more diversified your talents (especially in a small station), the more useful you will be to the advertising department.

3. If you are still in school and there is a college television station, get some experience. If your school doesn't have a station, consider working as an intern or a secretary at a local station for the summer.

4. Positions in this field may be located in the classified section of newspapers under heading classifications of "Broadcast," "Advertising," "Production," or "Television."

5. Larger stations often offer training programs or internships. Try to locate these opportunities.

6. You might also consider sending your résumé with a cover letter to the personnel director asking if there are positions open. Remember to request that your résumé be kept on file if there are no current openings.

7. Television stations often advertise their employment openings on their Web site.

SPORTS AND ENTERTAINMENT

UNIT PUBLICIST

CAREER PROFILE

Duties: Publicize new and upcoming movies, films, and television shows

Alternate Title(s): Movie Publicist; Movie Press Agent; Television Publicist; Television Press Agent

Salary Range: $25,000 to $125,000+

Employment Prospects: Poor

Advancement Prospects: Good

Best Geographical Location(s): Los Angeles and New York offer most opportunities.

Prerequisites:

Education or Training—College degree required for most positions

Experience—Some experience in publicity or entertainment necessary

Special Skills and Personality Traits—Creative; ability to write; good phone manner; aggressive; personable; articulate; self-motivation; ability to handle stress and pressure

CAREER LADDER

```
┌─────────────────────────────────┐
│ Unit Publicist with More Prestigious │
│     Projects or Press Agent     │
└─────────────────────────────────┘
              ▲
┌─────────────────────────────────┐
│         Unit Publicist          │
└─────────────────────────────────┘
              ▲
┌─────────────────────────────────┐
│ Assistant Unit Publicist, Intern, │
│ or Publicity or Press Agent Assistant │
└─────────────────────────────────┘
```

Position Description

A Unit Publicist for a television show or movie is responsible for publicizing new and upcoming movies, films, and television shows. While part of this job encompasses the glamour of TV and movies, there is another part filled with routine tasks and details.

The Unit Publicist is in charge of making sure that both the general public and the media know that a new movie or television show is being released. The Unit Publicist must create sufficient excitement about the project so that everyone wants to see it.

This is accomplished in a number of ways. The individual may set up media interviews with local television, radio, newspaper, and magazine editors around the country. He or she may set up the same type of interview with network, cable, and syndicated television and radio shows. The individual also tries to set up interviews with national magazine and newspaper editors.

The Unit Publicist is responsible for writing press releases and biographies of stars, compiling press kits, putting together fact sheets, and making sure that photographs and video clips are available. The individual must also make sure that the right people get this information. The Unit Publicist may send press packages to reviewers, critics, print editors, news editors, or talent coordinators. He or she might also distribute this information at press parties or conferences. Many movies and television shows now rely on provocative Web sites to generate audience interest.

The Unit Publicist is responsible for arranging both local and national press conferences and parties. If the individual is creative, he or she may develop a unique idea or "hook" in order to gain attention for the television show or movie. The purpose of all the interviews and press coverage is to attain as much exposure in the media as possible.

The individual may be responsible for clipping press releases from magazines and newspapers and getting audio and video clips of interviews, reports, and television shows. If the Unit Publicist does not perform this duty, he or she may be responsible for having an intern or assistant take care of the task or may retain a clipping service to handle the job.

The Unit Publicist often travels to other cities with stars of the television show or movie. During these travels he or she makes sure that the star gets to and from each interview on time. The individual provides press releases, biographies, press kits, photos, video clips of the movie or television show, etc. to the reporter, editor, or producer of the interview. The Unit Publicist might also spend a few minutes with the individual interviewer trying to point the interview in a positive direction. If, for some reason, the Unit Publicist does not accompany stars to these interviews, he or she arranges for another escort to meet, greet, and accompany the star to the interview.

The individual works with the studio, producer, or network producing the show. He or she helps arrange screenings for both critics and reviewers. If reviews are good, the Unit Publicist sees that copies are made or takes a quote and uses the piece to get more publicity for the project.

While Unit Publicists may freelance, most work with publicity and public relations firms hired specifically for the project. The Unit Publicist is then assigned an individual project to work on. After the movie or television show comes out the individual is reassigned to another project. If the individual is freelancing, he or she is responsible to the production company, studio, or network that hired him or her. If the Unit Publicist works for a publicity or public relations firm, he or she is responsible to a senior publicist, press agent, or one of the V.P.s of the company.

There is a lot of stress in this type of job. The individual must constantly come up with creative ways to publicize the movie or television show. The Unit Publicist might also deal with the pressure of tight deadlines, stars who don't really want to participate in interviews, and interviewers who really don't want to be doing the story. If the people in charge are not satisfied with the kind of publicity received, the amount of exposure, or the success of the project, the Unit Publicist often is blamed.

On the other hand, Unit Publicists who end up with a hit television show or film rarely get any personal recognition. The individual in this type of position must have a thick skin and a lot of stamina to survive.

Salaries

Earnings for Unit Publicists can vary greatly. An individual who is working independently or freelancing or one with little experience may be hired for a low-budget film and make $350 to $500 a week. Another person working for a large public relations firm or an independent Unit Publicist who has proven him- or herself can earn up to $2,500 a week plus.

Generally speaking, salary ranges depend on the experience the individual has, his or her track record, and the specific project.

Employment Prospects

Employment prospects are poor for Unit Publicists. These jobs are available, but only on a limited basis. It may seem that many television shows and movies are being released, but there are really only a limited number. In order to get a freelance job or work independently you almost have to know someone in the business.

There are slightly better prospects for individuals who want to work in public relations offices as Unit Publicists. This is one of those jobs for which you have to have a lot of good luck and be in the right place at the right time.

Advancement Prospects

Those who are lucky enough to find employment as Unit Publicists have good advancement prospects. Climbing the career ladder in this profession depends on how creative the individual is and how much exposure he or she can get for a project. Advancement is also dependent on the same things that helped the individual get the job in the first place: a lot of good luck and the proper timing.

Unit Publicists move up the career ladder by obtaining more prestigious projects or finding positions in larger public relations or press agent firms.

Education and Training

Unit Publicists who work for public relations firms, press agents, or production companies are usually expected to have at least a college background. Many positions require a college degree. Good choices for majors include public relations, communications, journalism, English, and liberal arts.

There is no educational requirement for those who work as independent or freelance Unit Publicists. However, all individuals in this line of work benefit from seminars and courses on publicity, public relations, or entertainment marketing.

Experience, Skills, and Personality Traits

The Unit Publicist needs some sort of experience in either publicity or entertainment. He or she should be creative and have the ability to come up with unique ideas and angles for publicity.

The individual in this position should be articulate, aggressive, and personable. The ability to write well with an interesting, factual style is necessary.

A good phone manner is needed to arrange interviews and pitch stories to editors and talent coordinators. The individual should also be able to handle many projects at once without getting flustered. The ability to deal with stress and pressure is needed.

Unions and Associations

Unit Publicists may belong to any of a number of trade associations that can help them professionally and put them together with others in their field. These include the Public Relations Society of America (PRSA) and the National Entertainment Journalists Association (NEJA).

Tips for Entry

1. Some of the larger entertainment public relations firms offer summer intern programs. Send your résumé and a cover letter to the personnel department to inquire. You might want to follow up with a phone call a few days after your letter arrives. In this way, if there isn't a position, you might be able to create one.

2. Get some experience actually doing publicity. Volunteer to do publicity for school or local concerts, plays, or theater groups.

3. Write reviews for local or school newspapers. This will give you valuable writing experience.

4. Work as an intern at a local television or radio station.

5. Join trade associations and attend their meetings, seminars, and conferences. This will help you make much-needed contacts.

6. If you know people in the business, talk to them. Don't be shy. See if they can help you set up an interview. This is not the time to see if you can get a job without help. You'll have to prove yourself once you get the interview.

PRESS AGENT

CAREER PROFILE

Duties: Make the name of an entertainer, singer, musical act, movie star, television star, or actor better known; compile press kits; write press releases; arrange press conferences; plot publicity campaigns

Alternate Title(s): Publicist

Salary Range: $23,000 to $150,000+

Employment Prospects: Fair

Advancement Prospects: Fair

Best Geographical Location(s): New York, Los Angeles, Hollywood, Chicago, Atlanta, Philadelphia, Washington, and other large and culturally active cities offer the most opportunities.

Prerequisites:

Education or Training—College degree in communications, journalism, English, advertising, marketing, or public relations preferred

Experience—Newspaper or magazine reporter, journalist, or critic experience helpful; experience in publicity or public relations a plus

Special Skills and Personality Traits—Creative; good writing skills; persuasive; ability to work under pressure; knowledge of entertainment industry; aggressive

CAREER LADDER

```
┌─────────────────────────────────┐
│    Independent Press Agent       │
└─────────────────────────────────┘

┌─────────────────────────────────┐
│          Press Agent             │
└─────────────────────────────────┘

┌─────────────────────────────────┐
│       Press Agent Trainee        │
└─────────────────────────────────┘
```

Position Description

The basic duty of a Press Agent or publicist is to create methods to make an entertainer's name or an entertainment project better known. The best way to do this is to keep the entertainer or the project in the public eye as much as possible. The more popular and well known people and projects are in show business, the better.

Press Agents may work with any type of entertainer, including movie stars, television stars, actors, disc jockeys, radio commentators, models, comedians, singers, musicians, or magicians. A Press Agent might also work with book authors, TV news people, sports figures, politicians, and public speakers or with television shows, sports events, movies, or almost any type of special event.

The Press Agent should not have a big ego. Agents must be willing to accept the fact that if a client is successful, the client will take and get the credit. If he or she fails, the Press Agent will often get the blame.

The Press Agent must be able to come up with creative campaigns for placing their clients in the public eye. This might be done in any number of ways, including inducing magazine and newspaper editors to do feature stories and articles on their clients or scheduling television and/or radio appearances. The Press Agent might or might not use some type of advertising campaign that features their client. Press Agents often create hype to gain notoriety for their client. Hype is a supersaturation of publicity in the media used to promote people and projects in the entertainment business. While publicity should technically always be true, hype sometimes exaggerate facts.

Press Agents must write creative press releases that the press will use. The successful Press Agent has the ability to come up with a good hook or angle for a press release. The hook is what will draw attention to that particular press release while it sits on a desk with dozens of others. Press kits consisting of press releases, biographies, pictures, reprints, reviews, and articles must also be compiled by the agent. He or she is responsible for sending the press kits—or media kits, as they are sometimes known—to editors, TV and radio producers and talent coordinators, or column planters. The individual must know how to get through to these people in order to place a client on television or radio, or to have feature articles written. The Press Agent must also have the ability to work under the constant pressure of deadlines.

Press Agents are responsible for calling and arranging press conferences for their clients. The agent must know what type of event is important enough to call a press conference, how to put one together, and how to have the right people attend.

Often the media isn't really interested in a client until he or she is so well known that publicity will be self-generating.

Some acts are so well known that every editor, television and radio show, journalist, and reporter wants an interview or an appearance. In these cases the Press Agent must be selective and decide which opportunities are in the best interest of the client. For example, a well-known entertainer would gain more media attention from an appearance on *The Tonight Show* than from a local morning talk show.

The Press Agent might also have to act as the "bad guy" to keep the press away from a client if he or she feels it would harm a client's image to give interviews. The Press Agent might also turn down an interview if he or she feels it would overexpose the client in the media.

Press Agents often attend press parties, dinners, luncheons, and other social events on a client's behalf or to make contacts. These contacts are important to the individual in promoting the client and in building a client list for the individual Press Agent or his or her company.

A Press Agent is usually responsible directly to the client. He or she may also be responsible to the client's management representative. If the Press Agent works for a company, he or she answers to his or her supervisor or to the owner or president of the company.

Salaries

Salaries for Press Agents depend on a number of different variables, including experience, type of client, and whether the Agent is working for him- or herself, a radio station, a television station, or an agency. The individual may also work part-time for one or more clients.

A Press Agent may earn anywhere from $23,000 to $100,000. Press Agents working with major stars might make $150,000 or more.

Employment Prospects

Press Agents may work for public relations firms, television stations, radio stations, record companies, film companies, publicity firms, or other press agents. There are a fair number of jobs available for qualified individuals at PR firms and publicity organizations. Positions at major television and radio stations, film companies, and record companies are harder to come by. A Press Agent can also work as an independent, which means that he or she has to get his or her own clients. Press Agents working as independents usually have a proven track record with clients in order to get other clients and be successful.

Advancement Prospects

A Press Agent can advance his or her career by seeking opportunities to work with better, more famous clients. The interesting thing about advancement in this field is that it can happen at any time. For example, a Press Agent might move up the ladder of success by working with a relatively unknown client, such as a new actor on a TV pilot, that hits it big; or he or she might work with a client who lands a role in an Emmy-winning movie. Anything can happen.

Education and Training

Although there are exceptions, the most qualified person applying for the job will usually get it. While a Press Agent does not really need a college degree, it helps. Courses in communications, journalism, public relations, advertising, marketing, English, and business are helpful in honing the skills necessary for the job. Seminars and courses in publicity and promotion are also useful.

Experience, Skills, and Personality Traits

A Press Agent needs to be creative. The individual must be able to come up with angles for clients' press releases, media events, and feature stories. He or she must be articulate and a good writer in order to write press releases and to persuade the media to use his or her ideas for articles and appearances. The Press Agent must also be able to work under the constant pressure not only of deadlines but also of clients who feel that they are not getting the exposure that they deserve.

In order for Press Agents to gain a good reputation with reporters, journalists, producers, TV and radio people, they must be credible. Otherwise they will lose their contacts.

Press Agents often have prior experience as journalists, producers, reviewers, or talent coordinators.

Unions and Associations

Press Agents may belong to the Association of Theatrical Press Agents and Managers (ATPAM), the National Entertainment Journalists Association (NEJA), or the Public Relations Society of America (PRSA). These organizations offer seminars, booklets, periodicals, and other helpful information to those in the industry.

Tips for Entry

1. Some of the larger entertainment public relations firms, record labels, and television stations have internship programs. Most internships are low-paying or unpaid.

2. Prepare your résumé and samples of your writing (any published articles from school or local newspapers or magazines, etc.). Send them to entertainment-oriented public relations companies in areas in which you are interested in working.

3. Work with a local television station, theater, or entertainer as an independent publicist to get some experience for yourself and for your résumé. At this level you probably will have to work for a nominal fee.

4. Work as a reviewer for your local newspaper or magazine entertainment section. This will help you build contacts.

5. Volunteer to handle the publicity for a not-for-profit entertainment event. This will give you important experience for your résumé.

PRESS AGENT TRAINEE

CAREER PROFILE

Duties: Assist a senior press agent in making an entertainer, singer, musical act, movie star, television star, or actor better known; compile press kits; write press releases; arrange press conferences; do grind work for press agent

Alternate Title(s): Junior Publicist; Junior Press Agent; Assistant Publicist; Assistant Press Agent

Salary Range: $20,000 to $33,000+

Employment Prospects: Fair

Advancement Prospects: Fair

Best Geographical Location(s): New York, Los Angeles, Hollywood, Chicago, Atlanta, Philadelphia, Washington, or any large and culturally active city offer the greatest number of opportunities.

Prerequisites:

Education or Training—College degree in communications, journalism, English, advertising, marketing, or public relations preferred

Experience—Writing experience helpful; knowledge of entertainment business useful not always necessary; experience in publicity or public relations a plus

Special Skills and Personality Traits—Creative; good writing skills; articulate; ability to work under pressure; aggressive

CAREER LADDER

```
┌─────────────────────────────────┐
│       Senior Press Agent        │
└─────────────────────────────────┘

┌─────────────────────────────────┐
│      Press Agent Trainee        │
└─────────────────────────────────┘

┌─────────────────────────────────┐
│   Intern or Entry Level Position │
└─────────────────────────────────┘
```

Position Description

The Press Agent Trainee (or junior publicist, as he or she might be known) assists the senior press agent in making an entertainer's name or an entertainment project better known. The entry level position is a good way to break into the entertainment business.

The Press Agent Trainee may work with any type of entertainer, including movie stars, television stars, actors, disc jockeys, radio commentators, models, comedians, singers, musicians, and magicians, depending on whom the senior press agent is representing. He or she might also work with book authors, TV news people, sports figures, politicians, public speakers, television shows, sports events, movies, and other special programs.

He or she might sit in on a creative meeting with a client but will not usually contribute any campaign idea to the client directly. If he or she does come up with a concept, it is usually discussed with the senior press agent in a private meeting.

The Press Agent Trainee does a lot of the grind work for the press agent. He or she might type press releases, calendar event sheets, and envelopes. The trainee is the one who puts together the various parts of the press kits, stapling, compiling, and placing information in press kit folders.

The Press Agent Trainee spends a lot of time on the phone calling important press people on behalf of the senior press agent and answering routine calls from the media.

As the individual gets more experience he or she might begin writing press releases or a bio sheet on the client. At this point most of the writing will have to be checked by the senior press agent before it goes out to the media.

With more experience the Press Agent Trainee will begin to find hooks or angles for press releases. These are the ideas that make a press release exciting and capture the attention of editors and talent coordinators.

The Press Agent Trainee learns how to plan press conferences. He or she addresses envelopes for invitations, makes calls, learns who is to be invited and the correct time to hold a conference, etc. During the press conference he or she gives press or media kits to the people attending, mingles, and makes sure everything is going according to schedule.

At times the Press Agent Trainee will act as a buffer for the press agent. For example, when the press agent is preparing to break a big story that he or she isn't ready to let the media in on yet, the trainee might answer the phones and keep the media at bay.

The Press Agent Trainee usually has opportunities to attend press parties, dinners, luncheons, and other social events with the press agent. These events help the trainee make important contacts that will help him or her meet people in the media and in the industry. This is especially important at this time in a trainee's career. Contacts not only help the individual do a better job at this stage but also assist him or her in finding better jobs and/or potential clients.

The Press Agent Trainee at this point often seems like a glorified secretary. There is a lot of typing, envelope stuffing, phone answering, keeping track of bills, and running around involved. Eventually he or she begins writing releases, talking to clients, and doing more and more work without supervision.

The Press Agent Trainee gets little recognition. He or she must accept this fact, much as a senior press agent does. The Press Agent Trainee is getting paid to keep someone else's name, image, or product in the public eye. When and if a press or publicity campaign works, the press agent won't get much credit; the Press Agent Trainee will get even less. Worse than that, if the trainee does come up with a good campaign idea, the senior press agent may take full credit. Ego cannot play a big part in the Press Agent Trainee's life.

Salaries

Salaries for Press Agent Trainees are relatively low. It is important to remember, though, that as the individual gains experience salaries go up. Press Agent Trainees may begin their career earning $20,000 and might go up to $33,000 or more annually.

Employment Prospects

Press Agent Trainees may work in public relations firms, television stations, radio stations, record companies, film companies, or publicity firms or for independent press agents. While there are not unlimited numbers of jobs in this field, an individual who is willing to work in any of the above media and is also willing to work in a major city will have a fair chance at finding employment.

Advancement Prospects

As mentioned previously, a Press Agent Trainee's position at times seems like that of a glorified secretary. Fortunately, though, the trainee phase does not last forever. If the individual is lucky, he or she will soon have the experience necessary to become a full-fledged publicist.

Advancement can move in many directions for the Press Agent Trainee. He or she can become a senior press agent for a company or go out and locate clients on his or her own, working on a freelance basis. Advancement usually means a dramatic rise in salary.

Press Agent Trainees who show a flair for publicizing people and who are aggressive will move up the ladder of success.

Education and Training

Although there are some successful press agents who haven't even finished high school, a college degree in business, marketing, advertising, English, journalism, liberal arts, etc. is usually required to get a job as a trainee. Any course or seminar in public relations, publicity, or marketing is also useful.

Experience, Skills, and Personality Traits

A Press Agent Trainee needs creativity. He or she must be articulate and a good writer in order to develop press releases and to persuade the media to use his or her ideas for articles.

The Press Agent Trainee must work well under the constant pressure not only of deadlines but also from the senior press agent who is being put under pressure by his or her clients.

The Press Agent Trainee must be credible or the individual will not build a list of contacts. In order to advance his or her career, it is important for the Press Agent Trainee to be aggressive in a nonthreatening way. Press agents are often concerned that the trainee will become too "capable" and take their job.

Unions and Associations

Press Agent Trainees do not have to belong to any union. They may belong to trade associations that can put them in contact with others in their field as well as providing professional guidance and support. These include the Association of Theatrical Press Agents and Managers (ATPAM), the Public Relations Society of American (PRSA) or its student chapter, or the National Entertainment Journalists Association (NEJA).

Tips for Entry

1. Try to find an internship program. While most internships are low-paying or even nonpaying positions,

getting involved in one is a good idea. Once someone invests time in training, you are likely to remain with his or her company. Internships can be found at many of the larger entertainment public relations firms, record labels, and television stations.

2. Work at a local television station, theater, or radio station during the summer to gain some experience in the entertainment industry.

3. Work as a reviewer for a local or school newspaper or magazine entertainment section. This gives you needed experience and helps you build contacts.

THEATRICAL PRESS AGENT

CAREER PROFILE

Duties: Publicize Broadway and off-Broadway shows, regional theater groups, etc.; compile press kits; write press releases; arrange press conferences; develop publicity and promotional campaigns

Alternate Title(s): Press Agent

Salary Range: Minimum $1,801.44 per week plus benefits for a Broadway production.

Employment Prospects: Poor

Advancement Prospects: Fair

Best Geographical Location(s): New York, Hollywood, and Los Angeles offer most opportunities; Chicago, Atlanta, Philadelphia, Washington, or any large and culturally active city may hold additional possibilities.

Prerequisites:

Education or Training—Three-year apprentice program required

Experience—Experience in publicity or public relations a plus

Special Skills and Personality Traits—Creative; innovative; good writing skills; good communications skills; ability to work under pressure; knowledge of entertainment industry

CAREER LADDER

Theatrical Press Agent Working with More Prestigious Projects

Theatrical Press Agent

Theatrical Press Agent Apprentice

Position Description

A Theatrical Press Agent works with theater productions such as Broadway plays, off-Broadway shows, and regional theater groups. His or her main function is to publicize a production in order to get it as much exposure as possible. This in turn makes people aware of the show and generates audiences. The individual develops various forms of publicity and promotion to put and keep the production in the public eye as often as possible.

Much of the work of the Theatrical Press Agent is done even before a show has opened. During this time period the individual works on creating ideas, putting programs and concepts together, and developing preopening publicity.

The Theatrical Press Agent has many responsibilities. Once he or she is hired to work on a production, the individual is required to develop a publicity and promotional campaign. This might include putting together a press kit about the show, its actors and actresses, etc. The individual is responsible for getting information about the talent for biographies and fact sheets and arranging for photographs. He or she must talk to the talent, producer, and director to try to come up with unique details for press releases, interviews, and feature articles.

The individual is responsible for dealing with media. He or she might arrange press conferences, press parties, opening-night parties, and media events. The Theatrical Press Agent may set up television and radio interviews with the stars on talk, variety, and news shows to help publicize the production. This exposure might include local, regional, and national programs.

The Theatrical Press Agent calls editors and reporters with feature stories and article ideas. With luck and a good idea the individual can obtain press coverage in print media as well as on television and radio.

A successful Theatrical Press Agent uses every avenue possible to obtain press coverage for his or her project. The individual calls theater critics and reporters from newspapers, magazines, radio, and television. He or she may also contact cooking editors, fashion editors, or financial editors, offering interesting tie-in possibilities with the show and its stars. For example, the individual may place an actress on a television talk show cooking segment. The Theatrical Press Agent may arrange for a financial reporter to interview the financial backer of a successful play. The idea is to get as much publicity reaching as many different people as possible.

If the show features well-known stars, the Theatrical Press Agent may take photos or arrange for a photographer to take pictures of the star attending a media event, party, or fundraiser. He or she may also pass information along to a television, radio, or publication columnist about the celebrity.

He or she may develop and set up media events and promotions to attract attention. The more creative and innovative the promotion, the more publicity it will receive from the media.

The Theatrical Press Agent is responsible for supervising the advertising of the show. He or she may or may not work with advertising agencies on this task.

It is the responsibility of the Theatrical Press Agent to contact critics and other members of the media to invite them to show openings. The individual must find out who is coming ahead of time, arrange for tickets, assign seats, and have the appropriate press material on hand for distribution.

The Theatrical Press Agent puts in long hours. He or she often starts early in the morning contacting media people, writing press releases, or developing and implementing publicity and promotional strategies. Late at night the individual may still be hard at work.

Theatrical Press Agents work under a lot of pressure and stress. There are constant deadlines to meet. They must continually come up with new, clever, creative, and innovative ideas to obtain publicity and promotion. There can be a lot of glamour working in the theatrical world. There is also a lot of hard work that must be done by a Theatrical Press Agent.

Salaries

Theatrical Press Agents belong to the Association of Theatrical Press Agents and Managers, AFL-CIO (ATPAM), a bargaining union that negotiates salaries and working conditions.

As of November 2004, the minimum salaries allowed for Theatrical Press Agents working on Broadway productions were $1,801.44 per week plus 8.5 percent vacation pay. In addition, individuals receive an 8 percent pension for a welfare fund.

It is difficult to estimate earnings of Theatrical Press Agents because these individuals may not work every week

of the year. They are usually hired for a specific theatrical project, and there is no way to tell how long each will last.

It is important to note that these figures are minimums. Individuals who are in demand can command weekly salaries that are much higher.

Employment Prospects

Employment prospects are poor for Theatrical Press Agents. To get into this profession, the individual must first apprentice with a press agent who is a member of the Association of Theatrical Press Agents and Managers (ATPAM). This apprenticeship takes three years to complete. During this time the Theatrical Press Agent must show talent, creativity, and an aptitude for the profession.

After becoming a member of ATPAM the individual will have to build a good reputation for him- or herself in order to be hired to do the job.

Advancement Prospects

Advancement prospects are fair for individuals who are good at their jobs, create a lot of excitement for theatrical productions in the media, and have built up their professional reputations.

Theatrical Press Agents move up the career ladder by obtaining more prestigious projects to work on. These include shows that are produced, directed, or written by famous producers, well-known directors, and established authors, as well as shows that spotlight major stars.

Individuals who have placed their productions positively in the eye of the public and have developed innovative promotions, creative publicity campaigns, and a good working relationship with the media will be in demand.

Education and Training

There are no educational requirements for the position of Theatrical Press Agent. Individuals must, however, go through a three-year apprenticeship working with an ATPAM member.

Those who are considering college should take courses in writing, communications, journalism, public relations, advertising, marketing, English, theater arts, and business. Seminars and courses in publicity and promotion are also useful in honing skills.

Experience, Skills, and Personality Traits

Theatrical Press Agents need to be creative, innovative people. They should possess the ability to write well. A good command of the English language, word usage, and spelling is necessary. Individuals should be able to produce factual, accurate press releases, feature stories, and other materials with unique angles or hooks to catch the editor's eye.

Theatrical Press Agents should be articulate and possess excellent communication skills. A good phone manner is essential. Much of the press agent's work will be done via the telephone.

The ability to create excitement through unique publicity and promotional campaigns is imperative to the individual's success as a Theatrical Press Agent. A good working relationship with the press and media is helpful.

The individual should be able to handle many details at once without getting flustered. He or she must also be able to deal with the stress and pressure that often come with the job.

The Theatrical Press Agent will be working a lot of long, hard hours. It is important that the individual have a real love of his or her job.

Unions and Associations

As noted previously, the bargaining union of Theatrical Press Agents is the Association of Theatrical Press Agents and Managers, AFL-CIO (ATPAM). This organization negotiates and sets the minimum salary that can be paid to Theatrical Press Agents. It also sets standards for the profession and provides a welfare fund for members.

Theatrical Press Agents might also belong to trade associations, including the Public Relations Society of America (PRSA). This organization offers seminars, booklets, periodicals, and other helpful information to those in the industry.

Tips for Entry

1. Get experience doing publicity and promotion for school productions or local theater groups.
2. Take courses in all facets of writing. Honing your skills now will help in the future.
3. Become a member of Public Relations Society of America (PRSA). The organization offers student membership. You will have the opportunity to attend seminars and conferences that will be helpful in learning skills.
4. You must go through a three-year apprentice program to become a Theatrical Press Agent. To do this, it is necessary to find an ATPAM member who will sponsor you. Contact the union if you have any questions or to locate the closest branch office.

THEATRICAL PRESS AGENT APPRENTICE

Duties: Assist senior press agent in publicizing and promoting theatrical productions; learn techniques of the trade

Alternate Title(s): Press Agent Apprentice

Salary Range: Minimum of $350 per week for first year of apprenticeship

Employment Prospects: Poor

Advancement Prospects: Good

Best Geographical Location(s): New York, Hollywood, and Los Angeles offer most opportunities; Chicago, Atlanta, Philadelphia, Washington, or any large and culturally active city may hold additional possibilities.

Prerequisites:

Education or Training—No educational requirement

Experience—Experience with publicity helpful

Special Skills and Personality Traits—Good verbal communication skills; good writing skills; ability to handle details; innovative; creative; aggressive; personable

```
┌─────────────────────────────────┐
│    Theatrical Press Agent       │
└─────────────────────────────────┘

┌─────────────────────────────────┐
│ Theatrical Press Agent Apprentice│
└─────────────────────────────────┘

┌─────────────────────────────────┐
│  Entry Level or Publicity Assistant │
│        in Other Industry        │
└─────────────────────────────────┘
```

Position Description

The Theatrical Press Agent Apprentice is a full-time paid assistant who works in the office of a senior theatrical press agent. The individual helps the senior press agent to publicize and promote theatrical productions in order to obtain as much exposure as possible.

The individual works as an assistant for a three-year period. During this time the individual works with one specific press agent at a time. He or she may change employers during the time of the apprenticeship; the employer, however, must be a certified union member of the Association of Theatrical Press Agents and Managers (ATPAM).

When an individual decides to become a theatrical press agent, he or she applies to work with a senior theatrical press agent who is a member of ATPAM. If the senior press agent feels that the applicant is dedicated to the profession, he or she will sponsor the individual, who can then become an Apprentice.

The individual is a Theatrical Press Agent Apprentice for the next few years. He or she takes this time to learn everything possible from the senior press agent about publicizing

and promoting theatrical productions such as Broadway and off-Broadway shows and regional theater.

The Theatrical Press Agent Apprentice learns the techniques of the profession. Everything he or she does is under the strict supervision of the senior press agent. It is important for the apprentice to work with an individual he or she both likes and respects professionally. The two will be spending many hours together. Much future success of the apprentice is the result of the training received from his or her superior.

A great amount of the apprentice's time is spent watching the senior press agent do his or her job. As the apprentice monitors the mentor's techniques, he or she finds that many of the techniques used in publicity are similar. For example, every time the press agent arranges and runs a press conference he or she follows the same basic steps. The press agent may create new promotions, but a location must always be chosen for the program, the media must be invited, and there has to be a reason to hold an event.

The Theatrical Press Agent Apprentice learns how to write a press release, put together a press or media kit, and prepare biographies. At this point in the educational process the individual will just be learning. He or she might gather information for the senior press agent or check the accuracy of facts but probably won't do much actual writing. As time goes by in the apprenticeship the individual begins to write simple press releases or bio copy.

The individual also learns how to stage media events. This might include the development of ideas to attract media attention as well as the implementation of actual events. The apprentice assists with many of the details involved in the running of these events. He or she may do a lot of the legwork, including reviewing the media guest list, checking to make sure that press kits are compiled and brought to the event location, or helping to greet media people.

The Theatrical Press Agent Apprentice learns to put press lists together and may be responsible for making sure that names, addresses, and phone numbers are kept accurate. He or she may make calls on behalf of the senior press agent to the media and others. The individual learns what types of advertisements are most effective and when and where ads should be placed.

The Theatrical Press Agent Apprentice does a lot of running around. He or she may deliver press kits, press releases, photographs, etc. The individual might accompany one of the stars of the production to a press interview or television appearance.

On opening nights the Theatrical Press Agent Apprentice helps the senior press agent with his or her duties. The individual may call critics or reviewers to make sure that they will attend, put names on seats so that the reviewers will know where to sit, or pass out press kits and media information.

The Theatrical Press Agent Apprentice's main function is to assist the senior press agent in every way while learning everything the individual knows about publicizing and promoting theatrical productions.

The Theatrical Press Agent Apprentice is responsible directly to the senior press agent. He or she works long hours. This is not a nine-to-five job. After the apprenticeship the individual will be ready to strike out on his or her own and become a full-fledged theatrical press agent.

Salaries

Minimum salaries for Theatrical Press Agent Apprentices are set by the bargaining union, the Association of Theatrical Press Agents and Managers, AFL-CIO (ATPAM).

Currently, individuals receive a minimum of $350 per week for the first year of their apprenticeship.

Employment Prospects

Employment prospects are extremely limited for a Theatrical Press Agent Apprentice. To obtain this position an individual must first locate an Association of Theatrical Press Agents and Managers union member who is willing to

sponsor him or her. He or she then works with the senior Theatrical Press Agent learning the ropes.

While the union is recognized across the country and through Canada, it is difficult to find jobs.

Advancement Prospects

Advancement prospects are good for individuals who become Theatrical Press Agent Apprentices. He or she goes through a three-year program and learns as much as possible about performing the functions of the job. Those who make it through the program and are creative, innovative, and aggressive will become full-fledged Theatrical Press Agents.

Education and Training

There is no educational requirement for a Theatrical Press Agent Apprentice. The individual must go through a three-year apprentice program learning the skills of the trade.

Those who are considering college first, may want to take courses in public relations, writing, communications, journalism, advertising, marketing, English, theater arts, and business.

Experience, Skills, and Personality Traits

Individuals must have good communications skills to excel in this position. They should be able to verbalize clearly, intelligently, and articulately. The ability to make and take phone calls and obtain correct information is essential.

The Theatrical Press Agent Apprentice must have excellent writing skills. He or she should be good at spelling, word usage, and grammar. The ability to write clearly, accurately, and factually is important.

In order for the individual to succeed in the world of theatrical press agentry, he or she should be an innovative, creative person, someone who can brainstorm and come up with unique ideas and concepts for publicity and promotion.

Individuals should be aggressive, persuasive, and able to get along well with others.

Unions and Associations

Theatrical Press Agent Apprentices are members of the Association of Theatrical Press Agents and Managers, AFL-CIO (ATPAM). This is a bargaining union that negotiates and sets minimum salaries for members, sets standards for the profession, and provides a welfare fund for members.

Individuals may also belong to trade associations that offer professional and educational guidance and other information. The most prominent trade association for those working in publicity is the Public Relations Society of America (PRSA). This organization also offers a student membership.

Tips for Entry

1. Contact the Association of Theatrical Press Agents and Managers (ATPAM) to get information regarding

the union, branch offices, members who might sponsor you, and specifics about apprentice applications.

2. Get as much experience as you can ahead of time doing publicity and promotion. If you're in school, work on your school theater productions. If you are not, you might consider doing publicity for a local theater group.

3. You might also want to take seminars in publicity, promotion, and writing. These will help you learn the basics.

4. Join the Public Relations Society of America (PRSA) or their student chapter to take advantage of their seminars, courses, literature, and professional guidance. Look in the appendix for their address and phone number.

5. You might consider getting a summer or part-time job working in the administrative end of local theater groups, summer stock, etc. This will give you a partial understanding of the theater industry.

6. You might also consider applying for a part-time or summer job as a journalist, critic, or reviewer for a local publication. This will help you hone your writing skills as well as giving you valuable experience.

PROFESSIONAL SPORTS TEAM PUBLICIST

CAREER PROFILE

Duties: Create public interest in team and players; create publicity; prepare and write press releases, press kits, informational sheets, and yearbooks; deal with media

Alternate Title(s): Sports Publicist; Team Publicist; Publicist

Salary Range: $23,000 to $100,000+

Employment Prospects: Poor

Advancement Prospects: Good

Best Geographical Location(s): Cities hosting professional sports teams.

Prerequisites:

Education or Training—Four-year college degree required

Experience—Sports writer or reporter or experience in college sports information preferred

Special Skills and Personality Traits—Understanding of the specific sport; public relations skills; good writing skills; articulateness; ability to deal with media; energy; ability to deal with many projects

CAREER LADDER

```
┌─────────────────────────────────┐
│   Professional Sports Publicist  │
│   for More Prestigious Team       │
│   or for Individual Athlete       │
└─────────────────────────────────┘

┌─────────────────────────────────┐
│   Professional Sports Publicist  │
└─────────────────────────────────┘

┌─────────────────────────────────┐
│   Sports Information Director     │
│   or Sports Writer or Reporter    │
└─────────────────────────────────┘
```

Position Description

A Professional Sports Team Publicist has an interesting job. The individual's main function is to publicize a professional team and its players. This creates public interest, which in turn makes people want to attend games and fill up stadiums and arenas. With the current interest in televised sports, increased popularity of a team or an athlete means that the owner can get more money and better deals for televised events.

The publicist in this field might work with professional teams in any sport, including hockey, baseball, basketball, jai alai, soccer, football, etc. He or she might work with either major leagues or minor leagues. It is important that the individual have an understanding of the sport with which he or she works in order to be effective in the job.

The professional sports industry is a major force in the entertainment world. The Professional Sports Team Publicist works with the sports news media daily. The individual deals with newspapers, magazines, and television, cable, and radio stations. On the professional level, the sports team publicist works with local, regional, and national media.

He or she must know sports editors and call to inform them of new deals being made by the team, new players, coaches, owners, and managers. The Professional Sports Team Publicist frequently receives calls from the sports media asking specific questions or requesting interviews with players, coaches, trainers, or management.

The Professional Sports Team Publicist (or team publicist, as he or she might be called) is responsible for setting up schedules of appearances for team members, coaches, management, and owners. This could be for paid appearances or for appearances for nonprofit groups and charities. For example, a popular team member might be the national chairperson for an organization fighting teenage alcohol and drug abuse.

Professional teams receive a lot of requests for public appearances by either individual athletes or the entire team. The publicist must decide which appearances to accept and which to decline. He or she must then write courteous letters of regret with explanations for those requests that were not accepted.

The team publicist arranges guest appearances on television and radio talk, variety, news, and sports shows for team members, as well as print interviews. He or she also develops feature story ideas for both sports editors and the general media.

The publicist must know everything that is happening, including dates of games, scores, and players' injuries. The individual prepares press releases on a regular basis. During times when major events are occurring within the team, he or she may write releases more frequently. These releases are sent to sports media from a prepared media list.

The individual also prepares statistical information sheets, injury data, etc. regularly. He or she is responsible for interviewing players, managers, coaches, and owners to obtain information for biographies, team yearbooks, press kits, and game programs.

The sports publicist arranges and conducts press conferences. Major leagues usually hold more conferences than minor leagues. The individual may present press conferences weekly, or even more frequently if there is a major event taking place (such as a major trade or the signing of a popular athlete).

The sports publicist is available to the media at games as well as at practice sessions. He or she must arrange for press passes, press credentials, and seating for members of the media. The individual also arranges locker-room interviews. He or she is responsible for passing out press kits, biographies, and releases to press people.

If the team is traveling to another city, the sports publicist gets on the phone calling media in that city, arranging interviews, appearances, and press conferences. The Sports Publicist might travel to the city ahead of time and take care of these tasks in person. In this manner he or she gets to know the sports press in other cities.

The individual in this job frequently socializes with sports writers and reporters. He or she attends sports-related functions as well as social functions on behalf of the team. The sports publicist is always looking for a way to publicize his or her team and its members.

The sports publicist works long hours and many weekends. Activities sometimes slow down slightly during the off-season for the sport. The individual in this position is responsible to the team owners.

Salaries

Salaries vary from job to job depending on the team the individual works for. Salaries can range from $23,000 to $100,000 plus.

Variables include the sport, the type of league the individual works with, and the team's popularity and success.

Earnings also depend on the individual's experience level and responsibilities.

Employment Prospects

Employment prospects are poor for Professional Sports Team Publicists. There are a limited number of sports teams to promote in the country, and competition for these jobs is fierce.

There are some teams that have a Professional Sports Team Publicist and an assistant publicist or a number of assistants. Individuals may have more luck finding jobs in the minor leagues and with less well-known teams.

Advancement Prospects

Advancement prospects for Professional Sports Team Publicists are good once an individual has held a job in this profession. The team publicist may go on to work for another team in the sports industry or an individual athlete or may go into sports marketing and endorsements. The individual might also start his or her own public relations or publicity company or find a job in a top agency. He or she might become a press agent for people in other facets of the entertainment industry.

An individual may work for a team that isn't very well known or doesn't have a lot of prestige, and overnight things can change. A team's popularity in sports is often measured by its ratings. A team can win unexpectedly and all of a sudden it becomes popular, making the publicist position even more valuable.

Education and Training

The team publicist is usually required to hold a four-year college degree. The exception to this is a former professional athlete who has an understanding of sports, public relations, and publicity from working in the industry.

The Professional Sports Team Publicist may find courses and seminars in public relations, publicity, marketing, journalism, English, writing, media exposure, sports studies, and physical education useful.

Experience, Skills, and Personality Traits

Professional Sports Team Publicists usually have had previous experience with the media. They often were sports writers or reporters themselves. Some individuals in this position worked as college sports information directors before holding down a job in professional sports.

The team publicist must have a total understanding of the sport, the players, and the industry. He or she must also have a full working knowledge of how to use public relations and publicity tactics to promote the team. The individual should be a good writer with the ability to turn out factual, concise, and interesting press releases, biographies, and yearbooks.

The ability to communicate well and speak articulately is essential. The individual must be comfortable speaking to large groups. He or she may often conduct press conferences.

The team publicist should be personable. Sports writers and reporters must like the individual and feel, comfortable talking to him or her. A good working relationship between the team publicist and the sports media is necessary.

The individual must be energetic. He or she must be able to work long hours, handle many details, and work on a lot of different projects at one time.

Unions and Associations

The Professional Sports Team Publicist does not belong to any union. However, he or she may belong to any of a number of trade associations, including the National Sportscasters and Sportswriters Association (NSSA), the Public Relations Society of America (PRSA), and the National Federation of Press Women (NFPW).

Tips for Entry

1. Consider a summer or part-time job as a sports reporter for a local newspaper.

2. Work on your school newspaper. It is important to gain as much experience as possible writing.

3. Work in a college sports information office as an assistant, aide, etc. This will give you a good overview of the job on an amateur level.

4. The Professional Sports Team Publicist often has a number of assistants or trainees working with him or her doing the legwork and clerical work. Try to locate one of these positions.

5. An internship or summer job in the sports department of a local television station would also prove helpful. You could learn how sports reporters work and make some valuable contacts.

6. Make sure you look on the Web sites of professional sport teams. Many list employment opportunities.

HOSPITALITY AND TOURISM

HOTEL PUBLICIST

CAREER PROFILE

Duties: Publicize hotel; write press releases and compile press kits; deal with guest problems

Alternate Title(s): Hotel Public Relations Specialist; Hotel PR Rep, Public Relations Director

Salary Range: $24,000 to $65,000+

Employment Prospects: Fair

Advancement Prospects: Fair

Best Geographical Location(s): Any location may have opportunities; New York, Los Angeles, Chicago, Atlanta, the Catskills, Poconos, Adirondacks, and any other vacation or resort area may hold additional opportunities.

Prerequisites:

Education or Training—A bachelor's degree with major in communications, journalism, public relations, English, or liberal arts is required. A master's degree is helpful; seminars and workshops in publicity and PR are useful.

Experience—Experience in public relations, publicity, sales, travel, or the hospitality industry needed

Special Skills and Personality Traits—Ability to write and communicate well; outgoing; assertive; creative; ability to deal with stress

CAREER LADDER

```
┌─────────────────────────────────────────┐
│  Marketing Director or Sales Director    │
└─────────────────────────────────────────┘

┌─────────────────────────────────────────┐
│             Hotel Publicist              │
└─────────────────────────────────────────┘

┌─────────────────────────────────────────┐
│  Guest Relations Representative,         │
│  Hotel Salesperson, or PR                │
│  or Journalism Position in Other Field   │
└─────────────────────────────────────────┘
```

Position Description

A Hotel Publicist can work in an independent hotel or for a hotel in a major chain. Individuals might work in resorts, health spas, meeting complexes, or convention hotels. The individual working in this situation has varied duties. The major responsibility, however, is to publicize the facility.

One of the duties of the Hotel Publicist is to develop and write stock press releases on the hotel. He or she must also write press or news releases on special events and promotions of the facility. For example, the hotel might host a beauty contest or a nationally televised golf tournament. In order to get the most publicity from the event, the publicist writes press releases and distributes them to the media. The individual is also responsible for putting together fact sheets about the facility.

The publicist working in a hotel setting may be responsible for taking photographs or arranging for photos of the hotel and any special events and promotions that take place there. One of the main duties of the publicist is to develop and put together press kits on the facility. He or she is responsible for sending press kits and press releases to various media. The individual must compile media lists for the general trade as well as for those specific to the type of facility. For instance, if the hotel is a health spa, the publicist sends information to health publications, travel publications, or women's magazines as well as to the general press.

The Hotel Publicist should have a good working relationship with news editors for print, television, cable, and radio. It is also beneficial for him or her to develop a relationship with television and radio producers, guest coordinators, and print feature editors. He or she will then be in a better position to have stories placed in print, guests placed on talk and variety shows, and feature stories published.

The Hotel Publicist also works extensively with travel agents. He or she may set up "FAM" or familiarization programs so that travel agents can visit the hotel, use its facilities, and, it is hoped, recommend the hotel to their clients. A lot of work for the FAM program is preparatory. The Publicist must contact agents and find people who are willing to come during the specific time period of the program. He or she must work with other departments in the hotel securing a block of good rooms and planning activities, parties, dinners, etc. During these FAM programs the publicist is busy paying full attention to the agents. He or she may conduct tours or on-site inspections, answer questions, and attend cocktail parties or dinners with the agents.

The Hotel Publicist may work with chairpeople of convention groups, helping them publicize their meetings.

Depending on the size and location of the hotel, the publicist may work with a "column planter" or gossip columnist. Through this person he or she can often place the name of the hotel in newspaper or magazine articles. Often the column planter works with the Hotel Publicist because celebrities frequently vacation there.

While the Hotel Publicist may publicize the fact that celebrities are vacationing at the hotel, he or she must often try to keep the fact quiet. In certain instances the Hotel Publicist works with the celebrity's own publicist to keep vacation plans secret.

Often hotels have celebrity entertainers in their showrooms or nightclubs. The Hotel Publicist may be asked to publicize an event to help bring in bookings or just to get some publicity for the hotel. The Hotel PR person may also work in conjunction with a celebrity's PR people, helping them to do their job.

The publicist working in a hotel deals with a good number of travel editors. He or she may be asked to entertain such individuals, taking them to dinner or on tours and discussing the hotel's high points. The individual may be responsible for the development of special events and promotions to help promote the property. He or she may also be in charge of implementing events, including supervising people who help put the idea into action.

Hotel Publicists may also handle public relations problems that occur in the hotel. This might include anything from problems guests have at the hotel to dealing with the press in case of an emergency at the hotel.

There is a fair amount of stress that goes with this job as a result of deadlines, items out of the individual's control, and hotel management who believe they should be getting more and better publicity. Work hours can be long for the Hotel Publicist. On the other hand, many individuals feel that in this position they get a lot of experience in different aspects of publicity and public relations that they might not get in other PR work. They also enjoy meeting and mixing with people and can deal with unexpected problems that arise in the course of a day.

Salaries

Salaries for Hotel Publicists vary greatly depending on the experience and duties of the individual. Salaries also depend on the size, location, and prestige of the facility.

Salaries can start out at $24,000 to $30,000 for beginners. With more experience earnings can go to $65,000 or more.

Employment Prospects

Employment prospects for publicists in hotels are fair. Individuals may find employment at large hotels, hotel chains, resorts, health spas, meeting complexes, or convention hotels. While there are considerable numbers of facilities, not all employ on-staff publicists. Many use the services of independent public relations firms instead.

Advancement Prospects

Advancement prospects for Hotel Publicists are fair. Individuals can advance by moving to a position in a bigger or more prestigious facility. Others move up the career ladder by becoming hotel marketing or sales directors. Still others join public relations firms or strike out on their own as independent publicists and public relations professionals.

Education and Training

Hotel Publicists should have a college degree. Majors might include journalism, communications, public relations, English, or liberal arts. A master's degree may be helpful in obtaining a position or moving up the career ladder.

Seminars and workshops in publicity and public relations might also be helpful.

Experience, Skills, and Personality Traits

Publicists working at hotels should enjoy working with the public. Individuals should be outgoing, aggressive, articulate, and personable. The publicist should be creative enough to come up with angles for press releases, media events, and feature stories. A good writing style is a must.

Publicists must also have the ability to deal well with the pressure and stress of deadlines.

Many publicists working in hotels began their careers in the hotels' sales departments. Others worked in guest relations. Still others worked in public relations or journalism in an unrelated field.

Unions and Associations

Publicists working for hotels may belong to any of a number of trade associations. One of the major organizations is the Hotel Sales and Marketing Association International (HSMA). Another is the Public Relations Society of America (PRSA). This organization offers seminars, periodicals, and other information to those in the industry.

Tips for Entry

1. Contact the head offices of major hotel chains. They can tell you where to send résumés. They also may have training programs available.
2. Openings can often be located in the classified section of Sunday newspapers. Look under the heading classifications of "Public Relations" or "Hotels."
3. Public relations journals and periodicals often have openings advertised in their job mart sections.
4. There are employment agencies that deal specifically in either the public relations field or the hotel field.
5. Stop by human resources departments of hotels to inquire about job openings.
6. Check out hotel Web sites. Many list employment openings.
7. You might also look for openings on some of the more popular employment Web sites such as www.hotjobs.com and www.monster.com.

DIRECTOR OF PUBLIC INFORMATION, TOURISM AND DEVELOPMENT

CAREER PROFILE

Duties: Create and direct promotional and public relations efforts of county, city, state, or other regional area; direct "FAM" programs; coordinate efforts of business and community groups trying to promote their products and services

Alternate Title(s): Publicity Director; Public Information Specialist

Salary Range: $25,000 to $125,000+

Employment Prospects: Fair

Advancement Prospects: Fair

Best Geographical Location(s): All locations may offer employment possibilities.

Prerequisites:

Education or Training—Four-year college degree required

Experience—Experience in publicity, public relations, or journalism

Special Skills and Personality Traits—Enthusiasm; good writing skills; understanding of tourism industry; flexibility; communication skills; public speaking ability

CAREER LADDER

```
┌─────────────────────────────────────┐
│   Director of Public Information     │
│   in Larger, More Prestigious Area   │
└─────────────────────────────────────┘

┌─────────────────────────────────────┐
│   Director of Public Information,    │
│   Tourism and Development            │
└─────────────────────────────────────┘

┌─────────────────────────────────────┐
│   Public Information Assistant       │
│   or Publicity, Public Relations,    │
│   or Journalism Position             │
└─────────────────────────────────────┘
```

Position Description

Most counties, cities, and states in the country constantly strive to bring in more residents, tourists, visitors, vacationers, businesses, conventions, and events. To do this, local government, chambers of commerce, or other organizations create departments or offices of tourism or economic development. Within these offices or departments the Director of Public Information is responsible for creating and directing promotional and public relations efforts.

The Director of Public Information must design and develop public relations campaigns and programs to enhance the public image of the specific area. The individual may work with an advertising or public relations agency in order to accomplish this.

The director is responsible for coordinating the efforts of community groups, organizations, and local businesses that are attempting to promote their products and services to those in and outside of the immediate area.

A portion of the job involves writing press releases and feature stories that feature the area and its resources. The Director might also arrange for editors, reporters, and producers from print and broadcast media to visit the area to write articles or produce televised features.

The Director of Public Information develops familiarization programs and tours for media people. Editors, reporters, photographers, and television producers are invited to an area for a short period of time. During this period they are guests of the tourism department. The transportation, accommodations, meals, and entertainment are generally paid for by the area's tourism or development department. The program might be cosponsored by area attractions and businesses that will pay a share of the costs. These programs bring media people into the area, showing them the attractions available. The desired end result of familiarization programs is for the editors to write positive articles about the area and its attractions.

The same types of programs are often conducted for business leaders interested in learning about the opportunities available in a specific area or for travel agents who want to know more about the area's tourism attractions, hotels, and restaurants.

The director often leads the tours, meeting with people, telling them about the area, and making them feel comfortable. The individual may design and offer token gifts with the area name or logo emblazoned on them for souvenirs.

One of the responsibilities of the Director of Public Information in tourism and development is to represent the area at trade fairs and business and tourism shows. The individual may be required to develop an appropriate booth, set it up, and be on hand to talk to show participants and visitors.

The Director of Public Information in tourism and development must develop and create brochures, advertisements, and sales pieces to be used to lure business and tourism to the area. The individual may work with a graphic designer, artist, and copywriter or may perform these tasks alone, depending on his or her abilities and qualifications.

The position requires that the individual represent the area and the specific department at special functions, events, and programs. These activities could include dinners, fundraising events, political functions, or area special events.

He or she will be expected to respond to requests for information by phone or to make sure that brochures, pamphlets, leaflets, and other promotional and marketing materials are sent.

Depending on the size and structure of the department, the individual may be required to train employees and administer the entire public information office.

The Director of Public Information works long hours. He or she is frequently expected to attend functions, events, and trade shows after hours or on weekends. There may be extensive travel required.

The individual in this position may be responsible to the director of economic development of the area or to the chairperson or president of the board that did the hiring.

Salaries

Annual earnings for this position vary greatly from job to job. There are individuals earning $25,000 annually in this position and those earning $125,000 plus. Variables include the size and location of the area being promoted, its budget, and the qualifications, experience, and responsibilities of the individual.

Generally, the smaller the area, the lower the salary. Individuals working for villages may earn between $25,000 and $35,000. Those working for large counties, cities, or vacation spots may earn between $40,000 and $100,000. There are some individuals in this industry who are earning over $125,000 annually.

Employment Prospects

Employment prospects are fair and growing for those aspiring to be in this field. Possibilities exist throughout the country. Jobs may be located in the tourism or economic development departments of villages, cities, counties, regions, or states.

Individuals may have to relocate if a position is open in a specific area. A good point to note about this type of job is that if the individual does have to relocate for any reason, he or she can usually find a similar position anyplace in the country.

Advancement Prospects

Advancement prospects are fair for Directors of Public Information working in tourism and development. There are many paths for the individual to take to advance his or her career. He or she may become a director of economic development or may find a position as a Director of Public Information in a larger, more prestigious area.

The individual might also advance his or her career by locating a position in a public relations agency or by working as the director of public relations or marketing in a larger corporation.

Education and Training

The Director of Public Information working in tourism and economic development is required to hold a four-year college degree. Good choices for majors include public relations, travel and tourism, marketing, communications, English, and liberal arts.

Seminars on various facets of tourism, writing, public relations, and publicity will be useful for both making professional contacts and honing skills.

Experience, Skills, and Personality Traits

The Director of Public Information must be a confident, articulate individual with good communication skills. He or she should be comfortable speaking in front of large groups of people.

The individual should be capable of writing a variety of different types of materials, from speeches and press releases to promotional literature. He or she must write clearly, factually, and creatively, with a sense of style. The director should have a good command of the English language, word usage, spelling, and grammar.

The Director of Public Information must have an understanding of the tourism industry and know the area in which he or she is functioning. This is necessary in order to create and develop effective publicity, public relations, and promotions to draw people to the area.

The individual should have a complete working knowledge of the skills of public relations. He or she must know how to prepare press releases, reach the media, arrange press conferences, and create and develop promotions and public relations campaigns. The individual should be flexible so that if something unexpected occurs in an area, he or she can deal with it.

The director should be persuasive and aggressive while being personable. Depending on the size of the department and the situation, the individual may need supervisory skills.

Unions and Associations

The Director of Public Information working in tourism and development may belong to the American Federation of State, County & Municipal Employees (AFSCME) or a similar union. The individual may be a member of any of a number of different trade associations, including the Public Relations Society of America (PRSA), International Association of Business Communications (IABC), the Association for Women In Communications (AWC), and the National Federation of Press Women (NFPW).

Individuals might also belong to the National Association of Counties Information Officers (NACIO), the National Tour Association (NTA), or the Association of Travel Marketing Executives (ATME).

Tips for Entry

1. You should consider working as an assistant or in a clerical position in the publicity or public information office of a city, state, county, or other region.
2. Larger areas may offer training programs or internships in the public information office. Write or call and ask. If an area does not offer this type of program, see if you can create such a position. The hands-on learning experience will be valuable to you when trying to land a job.
3. Publicity or journalism experience is important in this field. Look for summer or part-time jobs working at newspapers or publications or in publicity or public relations positions.
4. Jobs for public information directors in tourism and development are usually advertised in the newspaper. Look in the classified sections under heading classifications of "Tourism," "Public Information," "Public Relations," "Publicity," or "Economic Development." Jobs might also be under the name of the area, village, county, city, or state where you are looking for opportunities; for example, "Orange County" or "New York State."
5. Job openings are also advertised in trade journals. Get a short-term subscription to keep up on trends and learn about job possibilities.
6. Don't forget to check out employment opportunities online.

HOTEL ADVERTISING ASSISTANT

CAREER PROFILE

Duties: Assist in the development of advertising campaigns and individual promotional ads for hotel; develop annual advertising budget; create advertisements

Alternate Title(s): Ad Assistant

Salary Range: $23,000 to $35,000+

Employment Prospects: Fair

Advancement Prospects: Fair

Best Geographical Location(s): Any location may have opportunities; New York, Los Angeles, Chicago, Atlanta, the Catskills, Poconos, Adirondacks, and any vacation or resort area may hold additional opportunities.

Prerequisites:

Education or Training—Bachelor's degree with major in advertising, communications, public relations, or liberal arts preferred

Experience—Experience in advertising helpful but not always required

Special Skills and Personality Traits—Knowledge of copywriting and graphics; understanding of hospitality industry; creative; aggressive; ability to deal with stress

CAREER LADDER

```
┌─────────────────────────────────┐
│    Hotel Advertising Manager    │
└─────────────────────────────────┘

┌─────────────────────────────────┐
│   Hotel Advertising Assistant   │
└─────────────────────────────────┘

┌─────────────────────────────────┐
│           Entry Level           │
└─────────────────────────────────┘
```

Position Description

An advertising assistant works in a hotel or motel setting with the facility's advertising manager or advertising agency. Individuals might work in an independent hotel or in a specific hotel of a major chain, or at a resort, health spa, meeting complex, or convention hotel.

Duties of the individual vary depending on the size of the facility and the number of people in the advertising department. Responsibilities also differ if the hotel is using the services of an outside advertising agency. In either situation the Hotel Advertising Assistant's main function is to assist either the advertising manager or the advertising agency in developing effective advertising for the markets the hotel must reach.

One of the more important responsibilities of the Hotel Advertising Assistant is to help develop the advertising budget for the following year. To do this, he or she will have to do extensive research on advertising rates in the various media. Research must also be conducted on the demographics, audience, and effectiveness of the media. The advertising assistant may develop a questionnaire to help determine which of the hotel's current advertising programs are most effective.

The advertising assistant is responsible for calling or writing to the media in order to obtain their current rate cards, discount cards, and demographic information sheets. He or she must become familiar with reading, deciphering, and remembering this information in order to write a budget projection.

If the hotel is working with an advertising agency, the assistant acts as a liaison between the hotel management and the agency about the type of business they want to attract consumers, salespeople, or conventions. If no ad agency is involved, the individual helps lay out and develop advertising programs for the facility that will attract the desired type of business.

If the hotel is not using an advertising agency, and depending on the size and structure of the facility's advertising department, the individual may be involved in the copywriting, graphics, and audiovisual components of the actual advertising. In other situations the advertising assistant may farm out these duties to freelance copywriters, graphic artists, or producers.

The advertising assistant may be responsible for creating any or all of the advertising themes for the hotel. In doing this, he or she tries to incorporate information about the facilities and services found at the location, such as swimming pools, ice skating rinks, health clubs, tennis courts, convention centers, and concierge floors.

Depending on the size and structure of the facility, the individual may be responsible for taking photos or supervising the photography for hotel advertising pieces, brochures, and sales and promotional pieces. In this capacity the individual may also be responsible for having releases signed by guests or models who are used in advertising photos. Even if the hotel is using an ad agency the Assistant is usually on hand to make sure things go smoothly.

The advertising assistant is responsible for developing or assisting in the development of advertising campaigns for the consumer market and the media. He or she may come up with the concept or may just do the research on the type of ad that will attract consumers. The individual also helps decide where to place advertisements. He or she helps determine if local, regional, or national advertising will be used. Decisions must also be made on whether to use magazines, newspapers, billboards, television, or radio. If the hotel is part of a national chain, the individual may work with the corporate headquarters when local specials, restaurant packages, or entertainment are advertised.

The assistant must make sure that ads are prepared properly and delivered on time to the correct media. He or she may also be responsible for keeping track of billing and other records. The individual may audit advertisements by tracking tear sheets as well as copies of audio and video advertisements.

Another important function of the advertising assistant working in a hotel setting is to assist in the development of travel agency sales pieces. In order to continue to build business it is necessary for the individual to come up with interesting, innovative sales pieces for travel agents to show to their clients. The assistant also works on the development of advertising campaigns for the travel agency market and its media. He or she might write sales letters directed to travel agencies, trying to pique their interest in selling the hotel's rooms.

The Hotel Advertising Assistant may help develop convention and group market advertising campaigns and write sales letters directed to convention groups.

The Hotel Advertising Assistant works with and supports all of the hotel's public relations and marketing efforts. If one of these departments is working on a special campaign, the Advertising Assistant may be asked to come up with the appropriate advertising to supplement the public relations and marketing project.

An advertising assistant working in a hotel setting usually works normal business hours. There can be a fair amount of stress in this position due to tight deadlines, advertising campaigns that might not reach the expectations of hotel management, and the strain of having to continually come up with creative ideas.

Depending on the structure of the hotel, the advertising assistant could be responsible to the hotel management or owner, the advertising director (if there is one), or the director of marketing or public relations.

Salaries

Salaries for this position can range from $23,000 to $35,000 or more yearly plus fringe benefit packages. Annual earnings will vary depending on a number of factors. These include the size and location of the hotel and the responsibilities of the individual. If the Assistant is working in a situation where there is an out-of-house advertising agency, he or she usually earns considerably less than an individual working with an in-house advertising department.

Employment Prospects

Employment prospects are fair for those seeking employment as advertising assistants in the hospitality field. While there are considerable numbers of facilities, not all use in-house advertising departments. Many use the services of independent advertising agencies instead.

Individuals may find positions in independent motels or hotels, major chains, resorts, health spas, meeting complexes, convention hotels, etc.

Opportunities may be located in major cities as well as in vacation and resort areas such as Aspen, Key West, or the Adirondacks.

Advancement Prospects

Advancement prospects are fair for advertising assistants working in the hotel field. Individuals may climb the career ladder by becoming hotel advertising directors or managers. Other possibilities for advancement include becoming the director of public relations, marketing, or sales at a hotel or locating a position as an account executive in an advertising agency specializing in accounts in the hospitality industry.

Education and Training

A college degree is almost always required for a position as an advertising assistant working in a hotel. Good choices for majors include advertising, public relations, communications, business, hospitality, or liberal arts.

Experience, Skills, and Personality Traits

People working as advertising assistants need to be creative. They will have to come up with ideas for ad campaigns and individual advertisements. The individual should have knowledge of how an ad is put together, graphics, and copywriting. The ability to read and understand rate cards is necessary.

Individuals also need to be aggressive and articulate. Everyone working in every sector of the hospitality field should be personable and like people.

Unions and Associations

There are a variety of trade associations to which advertising assistants working in the hotel field might belong. These include the Hotel Sales and Marketing Association (HSMA), the Public Relations Society of America (PRSA), the American Advertising Federation (AAF), and the Direct Marketing Association (DMA). These organizations offer helpful seminars, conferences, and publications to those in the field.

Tips for Entry

1. Choose an area in which you would like to live and work and write to the county publicity or tourism office asking for a list of hotels and resorts. Send your résumé and a cover letter to the personnel director of the facility. Try to obtain his or her name by calling the hotel before sending the letter.
2. These positions are often advertised in the classified section of newspapers. Look under the heading classifications of "Advertising," "Hotels," "Motels," "Hospitality," "Spas," or "Convention Center."
3. Many larger hotels and hotel chains offer internship programs. Write to their corporate headquarters to inquire. You can find corporate headquarter phone numbers and addresses by calling the toll-free reservation phone number and asking.
4. There are employment agencies that deal specifically with the hotel and hospitality field. Keep in mind that if you use one of these agencies to help you find a job, there may be a fee.
5. Don't forget to check out hotel Web sites to see if they have employment opportunities listed.

NIGHTCLUB OR RESTAURANT PUBLICIST

CAREER PROFILE

Duties: Publicize and promote nightclub or restaurant; write press releases, feature stories, and articles; deal with public relations problems

Alternate Title(s): Publicist; PR Person; PR Specialist; PR Rep; PR Representative; Public Relations Director

Salary Range: $24,000 to $65,000+

Employment Prospects: Fair

Advancement Prospects: Fair

Best Geographical Location(s): Large cities will offer more opportunities.

Prerequisites:

Education or Training—Bachelor's degree in communications, public relations, journalism, English, or liberal arts

Experience—Experience in public relations, publicity, journalism, the entertainment industry, and/or the food industry helpful

Special Skills and Personality Traits—Outgoing; aggressive; creative; good writing skills

CAREER LADDER

```
┌─────────────────────────────┐
│  Nightclub or Restaurant    │
│     Marketing Director      │
└─────────────────────────────┘

┌─────────────────────────────┐
│ Nightclub or Restaurant Publicist │
└─────────────────────────────┘

┌─────────────────────────────┐
│     Public Relations        │
│  or Journalism Position     │
│ in Other Field or Entry Level │
└─────────────────────────────┘
```

Position Description

Publicists interested in working in an area close to the entertainment field can go into nightclubs and restaurants. People working in these environments are on the fringe of the entertainment industry. Depending on the place, the Publicist may work directly with entertainers or may just work in facilities that entertain others.

The individual working in this situation has varied duties. The person is responsible for publicizing and promoting the restaurant or club in every conceivable way.

Whether the publicist is working for a nightclub or restaurant, he or she is responsible for developing and writing press releases. He or she must know how to write stock releases for press kits as well as releases about special events and promotions of the facility. Other writing duties may include the writing of fact sheets about the club or restaurant, weekly or monthly "event" memos, calendars, reports to owners and/or managers on the success of programs, feature stories and articles, and so on.

The publicist compiles press kits on the club or restaurant. He or she sends these press kits and press releases to various media. The individual must put together the media lists for the general trade as well as for those specific to the facility. For example, if the publicist is working in a nightclub, he or she would need to have music and entertainment columnists, editors, and radio personnel on his or her list. If the publicist is working for a gourmet restaurant, he or she would need food and wine editors and critics on the media list. The individual should also have a good working relationship with news editors for the print trade as well as television, cable, and radio. It is also beneficial to the publicist to develop good working relationships with television and radio producers, guest coordinators, and print feature editors. He or she will then be in a better position to have stories placed.

The publicist working in a club or restaurant may be responsible for the advertising campaign of the venue. Depending on the size and organization of the facility, the individual might write ad copy, design ads, decide where to place advertisements, and/or put together advertising budgets.

Publicists might also be responsible for developing promotional ideas to bring the facility additional business. For instance, a publicist working in a club might designate non-alcoholic nights for those too young to drink or may come up with wine-tasting evenings in conjunction with local wineries. Those working for restaurants may design monthly gourmet dinner extravaganzas or coupon specials.

Another of the duties of the publicist is to deal with day-to-day public relations problems. If a patron is not happy because of bad food, bad service, or any other unpleasant occurrence, it is up to the publicist to try to smooth things over. He or she may write an apology note on behalf of the facility or might offer the patron a free meal or a bottle of wine.

The publicist may also have marketing duties. He or she could additionally be responsible for getting groups or private parties to use the facility.

The publicist may work with gossip columnists in order to get the name of the club or restaurant in newspaper or magazine articles and entertainment pieces on television in conjunction with celebrities who frequent the facility.

If the individual is working in a nightclub setting where there is live entertainment, he or she may publicize the various entertainers who will be appearing through press releases. The publicist may also set up guest spots on television and/or radio programs in the area to publicize an act's appearance at the venue. Publicists may also work with a celebrity's PR people, helping them to promote their act while doing the same for the club or restaurant.

The publicist working in a nightclub or restaurant might be responsible to the general manager, owner, or marketing director, depending on the organization of the facility. People in this position often begin work later in the day than publicists working in other fields. They also tend to work later into the evening.

Salaries

Salaries for publicists working in nightclubs and restaurants vary greatly depending on the experience and duties of the individual. Salaries also depend on the size, location, and prestige of the facility.

Salaries can start at $24,000 to $28,000 for those beginning in the field. Annual earnings can go up to $65,000 or more for those with more experience or working in larger, more prestigious restaurants and clubs.

Employment Prospects

Employment prospects for publicists seeking employment in nightclubs or restaurants are fair. Individuals may find employment at large restaurants and clubs as well as in the chains. It should be noted, however, that while there are considerable numbers of restaurants and clubs in this country, not all employ on-staff publicists. Many use the services of private public relations firms instead.

Advancement Prospects

Advancement prospects for individuals working in nightclubs and restaurants are fair. Individuals can advance by moving to a position in a bigger or more prestigious facility. Some individuals move into the position of marketing director. Others move up the career ladder by joining public relations firms or striking out on their own as independent publicists or public relations professionals.

Education and Training

Nightclub or Restaurant Publicists should have a college degree. Majors might include journalism, communications, public relations, English, or liberal arts.

Seminars and workshops in publicity and public relations might also be helpful.

Experience, Skills, and Personality Traits

Publicists working in nightclubs or restaurants should enjoy working with the public. Individuals should be outgoing, aggressive, and personable. The publicist should be creative and well-spoken and have good writing skills. Publicists working in this field should also have a basic knowledge of the entertainment industry and/or the food industry.

Unions and Associations

Publicists working for nightclubs and restaurants may belong to any of a number of different trade associations. These include the Public Relations Society of America (PRSA) and the National Federation of Press Women (NFPW).

Tips for Entry

1. Contact the head offices of major restaurants. They will tell you where to send résumés. They also may have training programs available.
2. Openings can often be located in the classified section of Sunday newspapers. Look under the heading classifications of "Public Relations" or "Entertainment."
3. Public relations journals and periodicals often have openings advertised in their job mart sections.
4. There are employment agencies that deal specifically in the public relations field, the restaurant field, and the entertainment field. Don't forget to check into the agency fee you might have to pay if they find you a job.
5. There are a number of services throughout the country that have phone numbers you can call to listen to lists of public relations job openings and descriptions. For example, the Public Relations Society of America (PRSA) has such a job service.
6. Check out job opportunities online. Start by looking on the major employment Web sites such as www.monster.com and www.hotjobs.com.

RESTAURANT/CLUB ADVERTISING MANAGER

CAREER PROFILE

Duties: Develop advertising campaigns and individual promotional ads for a restaurant and/or club; create advertisements; develop advertising budget

Alternate Title(s): Ad Manager

Salary Range: $24,000 to $55,000+

Employment Prospects: Fair

Advancement Prospects: Fair

Best Geographical Location(s): Larger cities offer more opportunities.

Prerequisites:

Education or Training—Minimum of a two-year degree required for most positions; four-year degree preferred

Experience—Experience in some form of advertising or marketing useful

Special Skills and Personality Traits—Knowledge of copywriting, graphics, and layout; creative; detail-oriented; knowledge of club or restaurant industry

CAREER LADDER

```
┌─────────────────────────────────────────┐
│   Advertising Manager in Larger,         │
│   More Prestigious Club or Restaurant;   │
│   Restaurant or Club Marketing Manager   │
└─────────────────────────────────────────┘

┌─────────────────────────────────────────┐
│   Restaurant/Club Advertising Manager    │
└─────────────────────────────────────────┘

┌─────────────────────────────────────────┐
│        Advertising Assistant             │
│    or Assistant Working in Club          │
│      or Restaurant Management            │
└─────────────────────────────────────────┘
```

Position Description

The advertising manager working in a restaurant or nightclub is responsible for developing effective advertising campaigns as well as single ads for the location. The function of this advertising is to make the public aware of the existence of the restaurant or club, to attract more people, and to let customers know of special attractions, discounts, and entertainment.

The responsibilities of the advertising manager begin with the development of an advertising budget. The individual must research the various media available. He or she calls or writes for rate cards, fact sheets, and demographics of the media in the area. At times salespeople from various media might meet with the advertising manager to let him or her know of upcoming special issues or discounts. The individual is then responsible for choosing the best media for the lowest prices.

The advertising manager also looks into the types of audience or customers the business wants to attract. For example, an elegant, expensive, four-star gourmet restaurant would not gear its advertising toward teenagers. A moder-ately priced, family-oriented restaurant might try to bring in families with young children with their advertising.

Clubs may want to advertise to hard rockers, people over 21, or teens. The type of audience that the club or restaurant is trying to attract will make a difference in the type of ad created as well as the location where the advertising is placed. It is important that the ad manager learn as much as possible about the media, the intended audience, and the restaurant or club in order to plan effective advertising campaigns.

The advertising manager must make decisions on whether to use print media such as newspapers and magazines to place ads or to use broadcast media such as radio and television. At times the individual may choose both types of media. While television advertising used to be extremely costly, today, with the surge of new local and cable stations, it can now be quite cost effective.

The advertising manager may work with the restaurant or club owners, managers, public relations people, and marketing staff to develop promotions that will help attract customers to the location. These might include discount coupons, early-bird specials, the saluting of a specific country through meals and drinks, contests, or two-for-the-price-of-one drinks. The ad manager uses the promotion or special as the main advertising theme. In certain clubs or restaurants the advertising manager might also perform the duties and functions of public relations, marketing, and/or promotion.

If the restaurant or club hosts entertainment, the ad manager is expected to advertise events in a timely fashion. In this way, tickets can be sold and seats can be filled. The individual may work with radio stations or other media on giveaway promotions in which the station offers free meals or tickets to entertainment events as station contest prizes. These are in exchange for free or discounted advertising rates. Such arrangements help advertise a club or restaurant and are less costly than regular advertising rates.

The advertising manager may be responsible for creating and laying out actual ads. He or she may do the copywriting, graphics, and audiovisual components of ads or may farm out these duties to graphic artists, copywriters, or producers. In many newspapers and magazines across the country the advertising department will work with ad managers on developing, designing, and laying out ads.

If the individual is using radio or television as a medium, he or she will work with the station's ad department in creating effective commercials.

Depending on the structure and organization of the restaurant or club, the advertising manager may also be responsible for putting together other advertising and promotional pieces, brochures, and sales pieces.

The advertising manager is responsible for developing the entire thrust of the restaurant's or club's advertising campaign. He or she comes up with a variety of ideas and then discusses their feasibility with managers, owners, or the marketing people, depending on the organizational structure of the facility.

It is the responsibility of the advertising manager to make sure that all ads are prepared properly, checked for accuracy, and delivered on time to the correct media for insertion. The individual is responsible for keeping track of all advertising billings and records. He or she also audits and keeps files of all advertisements placed by tracking tear sheets from print media and either audio or video dubs of broadcast commercials.

The advertising manager working in a restaurant or club may not always work normal business hours. He or she may come in early one morning and have to stay late at night to audit the effectiveness of the advertising for a specific event or special.

There is quite a bit of pressure and stress in this job. If the restaurant or club isn't busy enough, even if the cause is mediocre food or bad service, it is often blamed on a poor advertising campaign. The individual must constantly come up with innovative, creative ways to advertise the facility even if nothing new is really happening.

The advertising manager working in a club or restaurant may be responsible to the marketing director, the restaurant or club manager, or the owners.

Salaries

Annual earnings for advertising managers working in restaurants and clubs can range from $24,000 to $55,000 plus. Salaries vary depending on the size and location of the facility and the experience and responsibilities of the individual.

Advertising managers just entering the field earn salaries on the lower end of the scale. Those with more experience and added responsibilities who are employed by good-sized clubs or restaurants in metropolitan areas earn considerably more.

Employment Prospects

Employment prospects are fair for those seeking employment as advertising managers in restaurants or clubs. While there are countless restaurants and clubs throughout the country, usually only the larger facilities hire someone for this position. Often the duties of the advertising manager are taken over by a manager, owner, or public relations or marketing person.

Individuals might find a good source of employment in clubs or restaurants owned by major hotel chains. These facilities often offer training programs that place the person in a job after completion.

Depending on the structure of the restaurant or club and the size of its staff, the individual may enter this position directly from college or may become an assistant to the advertising manager, public relations or marketing director, or manager of the facility.

Advancement Prospects

Advancement can take many routes for the advertising manager in this field. He or she might become the advertising manager for a larger, more prestigious club or restaurant, or the individual might climb the career ladder by becoming an ad manager in a different industry.

If the individual wants to stay in the restaurant or club field, he or she might become the director of public relations or marketing for a facility. He or she may go into management or eventually ownership of a club or restaurant.

Education and Training

Many jobs as advertising manager for clubs or restaurants require only a two-year degree. There are others, however, in which a four-year degree is necessary. Most of the positions in major chain hotel- or motel-owned restaurants and clubs insist on a four-year degree before putting you through their company's training program.

Good major choices include advertising, marketing, public relations, journalism, and liberal arts.

There are a number of seminars available for individuals who would like to know more about various aspects of advertising, copywriting, and restaurant and club promotion. These would be beneficial for their educational value as well as to help build a contact list.

Experience, Skills, and Personality Traits

Advertising managers need the ability to handle a lot of projects at one time without getting flustered. They should be creative people capable of copywriting and with a knowledge of advertising graphics and layout. The ability to read and understand advertising rate and discount cards is essential. The ability to develop a projected budget and work well with numbers is necessary.

An understanding of the club and restaurant industry is helpful. Individuals should be personable and articulate.

There are those who enter this field with little or no actual experience. Others have gone through training programs. Some people have worked as assistants in clubs or restaurants and have moved up into the position.

Unions and Associations

Advertising managers working in clubs or restaurants may belong to any of a number of trade associations, including the American Advertising Federation (AAF) and the Direct Marketing Association (DMA). Individuals might also represent their clubs in the National Federation of Music Clubs.

Tips for Entry

1. Think about trying to obtain a job as an Advertising Manager in the restaurant or club of a hotel/motel. These clubs can be found throughout the country. You can send your résumé and a cover letter directly to the hotel office or, if it is part of a chain, to the main headquarters.
2. Try to obtain some experience working in a club or restaurant. If possible, see if you can work as an assistant to someone in advertising, public relations, or marketing. If not, a position in any capacity will help you understand the club and restaurant industry a little better.
3. Get experience with advertising. It doesn't have to be in the club or restaurant field. Offer to sell some advertising for a nonprofit journal. Work for a school or local newspaper in the advertising department.
4. Take seminars in advertising. These will give you added confidence and more knowledge of the field and build up contacts.
5. Look in the classified section of the newspaper under heading classifications of "Advertising," "Nightclubs," "Clubs," "Restaurants," or "Marketing."

NONPROFIT AGENCIES

ADVERTISING ASSISTANT, NONPROFIT ORGANIZATION

CAREER PROFILE

Duties: Initiate or assist in the creation and development of the ad concept; budget advertising dollars; produce advertisements

Alternate Title(s): Ad Assistant

Salary Range: $22,000 to $30,000+

Employment Prospects: Fair

Advancement Prospects: Fair

Best Geographical Location(s): Positions may be obtained throughout the country; larger cities may offer more opportunities.

Prerequisites:

Education or Training—College degree required with major in advertising, public relations, marketing, business, communications, or liberal arts

Experience—Internship or volunteer experience working in advertising departments useful but not required

Special Skills and Personality Traits—Knowledge of copywriting, layout, and graphics; ability to deal with stress; ability to read rate cards

CAREER LADDER

```
┌─────────────────────────────────┐
│  Director of Advertising,        │
│  Marketing, or Public Relations  │
│  in Nonprofit Organizations      │
└─────────────────────────────────┘

┌─────────────────────────────────┐
│  Advertising Assistant,          │
│  Nonprofit Organization          │
└─────────────────────────────────┘

┌─────────────────────────────────┐
│  Internship or Entry Level       │
│  Position                        │
└─────────────────────────────────┘
```

Position Description

An Advertising Assistant in a nonprofit organization may work in any of a variety of different settings. The individual may work for a health care facility, school, zoo, cultural center, library, trade association, foundation, or charitable agency. The common thread for all these organizations is that they are set up in a category called not-for-profit or nonprofit. What this means is that the organization is not structured for a corporate individual or business to make a profit. Instead, all profits are used for perpetuating the mission of the organization.

The Advertising Assistant working in an organization such as this has varied duties and responsibilities depending on the size and structure of the department in which he or she works.

The Advertising Assistant may be responsible for everything, including initiating the ad concept to implementing it, budgeting for it, producing it, and getting it in the mail or otherwise delivering it to the media; tracking tear sheets or clippings, visual cuts, and audio tapes; and checking bills for placement.

Specifically, the individual may be called upon to assist in the planning of advertising campaigns or single ads. The Advertising Assistant may be responsible for doing the research necessary to find out what is needed to make people aware of the organization and its causes.

The Advertising Assistant may also be required to help develop budgetary projections for the various media that will be utilized by a specific campaign or on an ongoing basis. To do this the assistant might write letters and make phone calls to get prices, rates, and other pertinent advertising information on the various media. As many different publications and broadcast stations have special rates and discounts for nonprofit organizations, the individual may also have to supply proof of the agency's nonprofit status.

Planning advertising budgets is not always easy for individuals working in nonprofit organizations. Agencies are constantly subjected to fluctuations in budgetary allotments, changes in administrative or board leadership, governmental regulations, and societal pressures.

Once again depending on the size and structure of the organization and the advertising department, the individual may be involved in the development of copy, graphics, and audiovisual components of the actual advertising. In other organizations the Advertising Assistant may farm out these duties to freelance copywriters, graphic artists, or producers.

Another responsibility of the Advertising Assistant may be to place, track, and audit the advertising. To do this it is necessary for the assistant to know how to read advertising rate cards and other demographic material in order to know what ads will cost, what kind of discounts can be expected, what section of the paper or other publication the ad can appear in, and what time slot will be most effective for specific advertisements.

The Advertising Assistant must have a working knowledge of postal regulations for not-for-profit agencies, as well as the application of Internal Revenue Service regulations as they affect not-for-profit advertising and direct mail. Without this, he or she may not meet the standards of advertisements for these types of groups.

Advertising Assistants, like many others working in nonprofit settings, are subject to high stress because of the pressures of absolute deadlines in the media and the personalities of creative people with whom they may work. Individuals must also deal with the indecision of superiors who do not always make clear their goals, objectives, and specific requirements.

The Advertising Assistant is responsible to the advertising director of the organization, if there is one. If not, the individual could be responsible to the director of marketing or public relations. In very small organizations the Advertising Assistant may be responsible directly to the chief executive officer of the agency.

Salaries

Earnings for Advertising Assistants working in nonprofit organizations begin low. Salaries can range from $22,000 to $30,000 or more annually.

The higher salaries are for those working in larger, more prestigious organizations located in major cities. Liberal fringe benefit packages are often offered to individuals to augment income.

Employment Prospects

Employment prospects are only fair for Advertising Assistants seeking work in nonprofit settings. While there are numerous nonprofit organizations, many delegate the responsibilities of this job to an individual in public relations or marketing. Others use the services of advertising agencies. Still others use freelance or part-time employees to handle the duties of this job.

Individuals may look for potential employment in hospitals and other health care facilities, museums, nonprofit theater groups, cultural centers, zoos, libraries, nonprofit foundations, trade associations, or charitable organizations located throughout the country.

Advancement Prospects

Most nonprofit organizations experience a high rate of employee turnover. As a result, advancement prospects for the Advertising Assistant are fair. Individuals may move up the career ladder by finding a position in a larger, more prestigious nonprofit or may become the organization's director of either public relations or marketing.

Other individuals find advancement by obtaining advertising positions in the corporate, for-profit world.

Education and Training

Advertising Assistants working in nonprofit settings usually are required to have a college degree. Good majors for this position include advertising, public relations, marketing, business, communications, and liberal arts.

Seminars in the workings of nonprofit organizations, advertising, copywriting, and graphics are useful to the individual not only for the educational background, but in order to help make contacts as well.

Experience, Skills, and Personality Traits

Advertising Assistants should have both knowledge and skills in copywriting, editing, graphics, ad layout, and budget preparation. An understanding of the workings of the nonprofit world are helpful.

Individuals need to be articulate verbally as well as on paper. The ability to work on more than one project at once is necessary, as is the ability to deal with the stress of meeting deadlines.

Advertising Assistants working in nonprofit organizations often land their first jobs immediately after college graduation. Others have held internships or similar positions in other industries.

Unions and Associations

Individuals working in nonprofit organizations usually belong to trade associations specific to their organization. Advertising Assistants might also belong to other associations that provide guidance, support, and seminars to individuals. These include the American Advertising Federation (AAF), the Direct Marketing Association, Inc. (DMA), the National Society of Fund Raising Executives (NSFRE), and the Council for the Advancement and Support of Education (CASE), among others.

Tips for Entry

1. Volunteer to do the advertising for civic or nonprofit groups in your community. This will give you the experience you will need when you are ready to look for a job.
2. Look for internships or summer employment offered by many nonprofit organizations throughout the country.
3. Send your résumé with a covering letter to the executive directors of nonprofit organizations. Ask that your résumé be kept on file if there are no positions open.
4. These positions may be advertised in the classified section of newspapers under the headings of "Advertising," "Marketing," "Public Relations," or "Nonprofit."

COPYWRITER, NONPROFIT ORGANIZATION

CAREER PROFILE

Duties: Develop and write copy for both internal and external written and visual publications, including press releases, brochures, annual reports, newsletters, and leaflets

Alternate Title(s): Writer

Salary Range: $22,000 to $40,000+

Employment Prospects: Fair

Advancement Prospects: Fair

Best Geographical Location(s): Opportunities located throughout country.

Prerequisites:

Education or Training—College degree with major in English, public relations, communications, or liberal arts

Experience—Writing experience helpful

Special Skills and Personality Traits—Excellent writing skills; good command of the English language; creative

CAREER LADDER

```
┌─────────────────────────────┐
│    Publication Assistant    │
└─────────────────────────────┘

┌─────────────────────────────┐
│         Copywriter          │
└─────────────────────────────┘

┌─────────────────────────────┐
│         Entry Level         │
└─────────────────────────────┘
```

Position Description

A Copywriter working with a nonprofit organization may work for foundations, trade associations, charitable organizations, health care facilities, cultural centers, museums, zoos, libraries, or any other organization classified as "not-for-profit." While settings for these organizations vary, duties are fairly consistent.

The individual in this job is required to write copy for all publications the organization issues. These could include both internal and external publications, such as newsletters, brochures, leaflets, annual reports, letters, press releases, and other materials helpful to the fund-raising, marketing, or promotional objectives of the organization. The Copywriter may also be required to write copy and/or scripts for audio and visual projects the organization may prepare.

Depending on the situation, the Copywriter may work directly with the publication assistant or the director of public relations, marketing, fund-raising, or development. In some cases the Copywriter may work with all of the individuals on various projects. For example, the Copywriter may be required to develop a fund-raising letter for the director of fund-raising, copy for a brochure for the public relations department, newsletters for the publication assistant, and a leaflet for the marketing or development department.

In very large organizations there may be up to half a dozen Copywriters working on various projects. In other organizations there could be just one Copywriter for the entire agency.

In smaller organizations the Copywriter could also be responsible for putting together entire publications, functioning as a publication assistant might. In these cases the Copywriter would also have duties such as developing outlines, proposals, preliminary sketches, and budget estimates for the publications. He or she might also have to coordinate the activities of other individuals needed to complete a publication, such as graphic people, artists, printers, etc. Once again depending on the size of the organization and the number of people working in the department, the Copywriter may function as a layout artist, laying out brochures, newsletters, and leaflets in a graphically pleasing manner. The individual might also give suggestions to a printer on layout and oversee the project.

In many nonprofit organizations today Copywriters are expected to input material directly into computers. If the organization is using desktop publishing, the individual might also be expected to develop the layout for the project and put the copy into a form that is camera-ready for a printer.

The Copywriter is expected to research all his or her projects. The individual may not only be required to obtain information but at times must also verify that information obtained from others is 100 percent accurate. Names, numbers, and dates must be checked, and spelling needs to be verified.

After the Copywriter has finished writing the copy he or she will give it to either the publication assistant or the director of the department who requested the project. The information, style, and general content will then generally have to be approved by a superior. If everything is satisfactory, the copy will be set up as a press release, brochure, leaflet, or newsletter, depending on the project.

The Copywriter must understand which projects should be short and to the point and which publications are to be longer and more in-depth. For example, a calendar of events for a newsletter or newspaper column would probably be short, just naming the events with dates and times and possibly a short explanation of each. A press release describing a major event that the nonprofit organization is holding, however, would probably be longer and developed in more depth.

The Copywriter needs to know the different styles accepted by various newspapers, magazines, and other media. While some publications accept flowery press releases, others just want the facts. The Copywriter who doesn't know the difference will not have his or her press releases placed in the publication.

Copywriters working in nonprofit organizations must get to know the lingo of the particular organization and must know when to use it. For example, a Copywriter working in a health care facility might be writing a brochure for distribution internally to hospital staff. In that case it would be acceptable to use health care facility lingo known to health care practitioners. The same words, however, might not be understood by the general public reading a health care article in a newspaper or magazine.

Copywriters working in nonprofit organizations might be asked to attend meetings, dinners, or events in order to obtain information for press releases or articles.

Individuals may also work closely with the volunteer portion of the organization, the people who are the backbone of many nonprofit organizations.

Copywriters may be responsible directly to the publication assistant; the public relations, marketing, fund-raising, or development director; or a senior copywriter, depending on the size and structure of the organization.

Hours for Copywriters are fairly normal. There will be times, however, when the individual must attend functions, affairs, and meetings after the normal working day ends. The Copywriter might also have to work overtime when there is a deadline to meet or a special project that requires completion.

Salaries

The salary for a Copywriter working in a nonprofit organization depends on the size and location of the agency as well as the experience and responsibilities of the individual.

Those working in smaller settings usually receive lower salaries. Individuals working in larger organizations or in facilities in urban areas can usually command higher annual earnings.

The Copywriter can expect to earn between $22,000 and $40,000 or more annually. Salaries are augmented by fringe benefit packages in many nonprofit organizations.

Employment Prospects

Employment prospects are fair for those seeking employment as Copywriters in nonprofit organizations. There are nonprofit groups in most urban areas as well as a good number in smaller regions. Hospitals and other health care facilities, museums, nonprofit theater groups, cultural centers, zoos, libraries, nonprofit foundations, trade associations, and charitable organizations all offer potential employment.

While there are numerous nonprofit organizations throughout the country, there are some who delegate the responsibilities of the Copywriter to either the public relations department or the publication assistant.

For those seeking part-time employment there are also many smaller nonprofit organizations that use the services of freelance and part-time Copywriters.

Advancement Prospects

Advancement for Copywriters is attained by obtaining a position in a larger organization. The individual might also become a publication assistant or a director or assistant director of public relations or marketing.

As most nonprofit organizations experience a big employee turnover, opportunities for advancement are fair.

Many Copywriters who want to move up the career ladder look for a position writing copy for an advertising or public relations agency.

Education and Training

Individuals aspiring to be Copywriters should have a college education. A degree in English, public relations, communications, or liberal arts is usually required.

Seminars and additional courses in all facets of writing are useful.

Experience, Skills, and Personality Traits

Copywriters need to have a good command of the English language. A sense of writing style is necessary. The individual should also enjoy writing.

Those working in nonprofit organizations should have a knowledge of the type of group they are working with and a general understanding of and belief in the organization. For example, working in a health care facility and writing about it is hard if a person is uncomfortable being around people who are ill.

Those working as Copywriters often have experience writing for their school papers or volunteering to prepare reports, press releases, etc. for community or civic groups.

Unions and Associations

Those working for nonprofit groups usually belong to a number of local civic and community organizations. Copywriters might also belong to trade associations that offer seminars, courses, and other professional guidance and put the individuals in touch with others in their field. These groups include the Public Relations Society of America (PRSA), the National Society of Fund Raising Executives (NSFRE), and Council for the Advancement and Support of Education (CASE), to name a few.

Tips for Entry

1. Volunteer to write press releases or do the publicity for local community or civic groups. This gives you valuable experience as well as helping you to make necessary contacts.

2. If you are still in school, write for your school newspaper. If not, try to write a column for a local newspaper or other publication.

3. Positions as Copywriters are often advertised in the classified section of newspapers. Job possibilities might be found under the heading classifications of "Public Relations," "Marketing," "Copywriter," or "Writer."

4. Try to find all the nonprofit organizations in the area in which you want to find employment. You can often find lists of these at the local chamber of commerce. Send your résumé and some writing samples to the organization's executive director. Ask that your résumé be kept on file if there isn't a position available.

COMMUNITY RELATIONS/PUBLIC RELATIONS COORDINATOR, POLICE DEPARTMENT

CAREER PROFILE

Duties: Develop and implement community relations programs; write press releases; act as spokesperson; deal with media

Alternate Title(s): Public Relations Coordinator; Community Relations Coordinator; Public Information Specialist; Public Relations Director; Community Relations Director; Community Relations/Public Information Director; Community Relations/Public Information Representative

Salary Range: $24,000 to $56,000+

Employment Prospects: Fair

Advancement Prospects: Good

Best Geographical Location(s): All locations offer possibilities; larger cities may offer more positions.

Prerequisites:

Education or Training—Minimum requirement in some positions is a two-year degree. Other positions require a four-year college degree

Experience—Experience working with community groups is helpful; publicity, public relations, or community relations experience is preferred

Special Skills and Personality Traits—Communication skills; writing skills; ability to work well with people; ability to deal with media

CAREER LADDER

```
┌─────────────────────────────────────────┐
│  Community Relations/Public Relations    │
│             Coordinator in               │
│         Larger Police Department         │
│    or Public Relations or Community      │
│   Relations Director in Other Industry   │
└─────────────────────────────────────────┘

┌─────────────────────────────────────────┐
│  Community Relations/Public Relations    │
│               Coordinator                │
└─────────────────────────────────────────┘

┌─────────────────────────────────────────┐
│       Publicity, Public Relations,       │
│     or Community Relations Assistant     │
└─────────────────────────────────────────┘
```

Position Description

The Community Relations/Public Relations Coordinator working in a police department is responsible for a number of different functions. Depending on the size of the police department and its annual budget, there may be one person working in this department or a number of people. The individual must develop and implement community relations programs, fulfill public relations duties, and act as a spokesperson for the department. In very large police departments there is one person responsible for each of the different functions.

The Community Relations/Public Relations Coordinator is expected to work with the department to create programs to meet the needs of the local community. For example, the individual may put together a self-defense program for senior citizens, a drug and alcohol abuse program, and a youth program. The individual may also work out the details of sponsorship of various events and programs. In many communities local police departments sponsor youth clubs, boxing teams, and baseball teams.

The Community Relations/Public Relations Coordinator works with the local community, its problems, and its needs when creating these programs. If, for instance, there is a rash of burglaries in the area, the individual may develop a program showing citizens how to protect and safeguard their homes. These programs are usually offered free of charge and may be given through local civic groups or nonprofit organizations.

The Community Relations/Public Relations Coordinator is responsible for developing and writing press releases and feature articles. He or she must write releases regarding all community relations programs as well as police department activities. These might include honors and awards for police officers or major accomplishments of the department.

Other writing functions might include informational booklets, pamphlets, or other literature about the department and its programs. The individual may develop leaflets for citizens on a variety of subjects, such as how to spot drug or alcohol abuse in teenagers or what to do in the case of a mugging.

The Community Relations/Public Relations Coordinator is responsible for sending representatives of the department to speak at schools, community groups, and civic organizations. The individual may receive requests for these appearances or may seek out opportunities for exposure. He or she may also arrange to have representatives appear on local television or radio talk and news shows or to be interviewed in the print media.

The Community Relations/Public Relations Coordinator responds to informational requests from the media and the community. He or she may act as the department spokesperson either informally or formally. The individual often speaks on camera for television, on radio, or to reporters and editors of print media answering questions or offering statements about police situations. He or she often helps police officers work out statements to give to the press to make sure that they are clear and factual.

If there is a major development in a big case that the police are working on, the individual might also schedule and arrange press conferences or press briefings.

The Community Relations/Public Relations Coordinator may work long hours. He or she frequently works at night and on weekends implementing programs or speaking to the media about a major development. Depending on the specific police department and the organizational structure of the local government, the individual may be responsible to the mayor, the department's chief of police, or the police commissioner.

Salaries

Salaries for Community Relations/Public Relations Coordinators vary greatly. The size, location, and budget of the police department and the experience level and responsibilities of the individual are factors. Generally, the smaller the area, the lower the salary.

Earnings can range from $24,000 to $56,000 or more annually for those in this position. Individuals working in larger communities and cities are compensated with salaries at the higher end of the scale.

Employment Prospects

Employment prospects are fair for Community Relations/Public Relations Coordinators working in police departments. Opportunities are available throughout the country in small towns as well as large cities.

Almost every police department has a Community Relations/Public Relations Coordinator, although in very small communities the position may be part time, or the individual may be required to fill other functions.

Advancement Prospects

Advancement prospects are good for the Community Relations/Public Relations Coordinator working in a police department. Individuals may climb the ladder by locating a position in a larger law enforcement agency, which will result in increased earnings and responsibilities.

The Community Relations/Public Relations Coordinator might also advance his or her career by finding a similar position in another nonprofit field, a newspaper or magazine, or in the corporate world. The individual may also become a public relations director or coordinator.

Education and Training

Educational requirements vary from job to job. Some positions may have a minimum requirement of a two-year college degree, while others require a four-year degree. In some positions the individual can substitute experience for the degree. Those seeking career advancement need at least a bachelor's degree.

Good choices for majors include public relations, marketing, English, liberal arts, and communications. Seminars in publicity, public relations, public speaking, and those dealing with nonprofit groups will be useful to the individual.

Experience, Skills, and Personality Traits

The Community Relations/Public Relations Coordinator working for a police department must be imaginative, creative, and innovative. The individual is often working on a limited budget and has to develop unique programs.

The Community Relations/Public Relations Coordinator should be a people person. He or she should be personable and able to work well with people from all age groups and all socioeconomic backgrounds. The Community Relations/Public Relations Coordinator should have the ability to relate to young children as well as to senior citizens.

The individual requires good communication skills. He or she should be articulate and comfortable speaking to groups. Good writing skills are important for developing program proposals, press releases, and informational sheets. The individual should have a good grasp of the English language, word usage, spelling, and grammar. Organizational and planning skills are imperative.

The ability to deal with the media is essential. The individual must develop a good working relationship with reporters, editors, and newscasters as well as their community service directors.

In many communities the ability to speak more than one language is a plus.

Unions and Associations

Unless the Community Relations/Public Relations Coordinator is also a police officer he or she would not belong to any union. Individuals who are police officers belong to state police officers' unions, the Police Benevolent Association (PBA), or other bargaining unions.

The individual in this position usually belongs to many of the nonprofit, civic, and community groups in the local area. He or she may also be a member of any of the communications or public relations trade associations, including the Public Relations Society of America (PRSA) and National Federation of Press Women (NFPW).

Tips for Entry

1. Get hands-on experience working in the community by joining a number of nonprofit organizations.
2. A part-time or summer job writing for a newspaper will give you experience writing as well as working with the media.
3. These positions are often advertised in newspaper display and classified sections. Look under heading classifications of "Law Enforcement," "Police," "Public Relations," "Public Information," or "Community Relations."
4. Talk to your local police department to find out if they have a community relations program. Volunteer your assistance in running some events or doing publicity.
5. Take seminars and courses. These will be useful for both educational value and making professional contacts.

GRAPHIC ARTIST, NONPROFIT ORGANIZATION

CAREER PROFILE

Duties: Create the art, illustrations, and other graphics necessary for a nonprofit organization's publications, visuals, flyers, and advertisements

Alternate Title(s): Graphic Designer; Artist

Salary Range: $24,000 to $48,000+

Employment Prospects: Fair

Advancement Prospects: Fair

Best Geographical Location(s): Positions may be located throughout the country.

Prerequisites:

Education or Training—Art school training or college degree with major in commercial art useful

Experience—Graphic art experience in school, publication, advertising agency, or industry helpful, but not required

Special Skills and Personality Traits—Artistic ability; creative; ability to draw, sketch, letter, and design; sense of style; understanding of advertising; knowledge of workings of nonprofit organizations; computer skills

CAREER LADDER

```
┌─────────────────────────────────┐
│   Graphic Artist in Larger,     │
│  More Prestigious Nonprofit     │
│ Organization, Advertising Agency,│
│  or Corporation or Art Director │
└─────────────────────────────────┘

┌─────────────────────────────────┐
│       Graphic Artist,           │
│     Nonprofit Organization      │
└─────────────────────────────────┘

┌─────────────────────────────────┐
│   Freelance Artist or Student   │
└─────────────────────────────────┘
```

Position Description

The Graphic Artist working in a nonprofit organization is responsible for creating the art, illustrations, and other graphics necessary for the organization's publications, visuals, flyers, and advertisements.

The individual may work in a school, health care facility, museum, zoo, cultural center, library, nonprofit foundation, trade association, or charitable organization. He or she may work with one or more departments, including art, advertising, public relations, marketing, fund-raising, or publications.

Depending on the size and structure of the organization, the Graphic Artist may just execute actual art suggested by someone else or may develop the whole graphic concept of an advertisement, flyer, brochure, or design.

The Graphic Artist must be artistically talented in many areas. The individual may be required to draw, sketch, and do lettering. He or she must have a good sense of color and style. The artist is responsible for the artistic or graphic layout of projects.

The Graphic Artist—or designer, as he or she might be called—sketches and draws ideas for graphics in pencil, ink, and/or paints, depending upon the project. Many graphic artists now also create artwork and other graphics with computers using special software.

If the organization does not use the services of an advertising agency, the Graphic Artist may function as an ad designer. He or she may be responsible for choosing the graphics, type, and position of copy in ads.

Depending on the size of the organization, there may be one or more Graphic Artists working in a department along with an art director, or the individual may function as the art director as well.

In certain agencies the individual is responsible primarily for the graphics and design of the nonprofit's advertisements. He or she must become familiar with various sizes of ads, column widths, color usage, type faces, etc. that are to be used. In other organizations the Graphic Artist is responsible for preparing artwork for brochures, leaflets, posters, flyers, newsletters, annual reports, and any other publication or material the organization uses.

The Graphic Artist may be required to design a logo or trademark for the organization. He or she may also have to design stationery, envelopes, and fund-raising material. In order to do this the individual will often have to prepare several sketches to be reviewed and accepted by the organization's executive director. As many nonprofit organizations are governed by boards of directors, the individual may have to have designs and other work reviewed and accepted by the chairperson of the board or possibly by the entire board of directors. Once designs are approved, final versions may be laid out using desktop publishing software.

Services in nonprofit groups are often augmented by the help of volunteer organizations and auxiliaries. At times the Graphic Artist may be required to work with these groups, designing program covers or posters for their events.

Depending on the size of the organization with which the artist is working, he or she may be responsible for preparing and pasting up master mechanicals for printers. In other organizations the individual may work with printers choosing colors, type sizes, paper, and so on. In some they may prepare electronic files for printing.

Another function of the Graphic Artist working for a nonprofit organization may be to design packaging for giveaways, merchandise, gift shop bags, T-shirts, or balloons. Many organizations use these type of materials as well as other promotional merchandise to raise funds and to promote the cause of the organization.

The Graphic Artist working in this setting usually works normal business hours. The individual may be required to work late on occasion to meet the deadline for a project.

Depending on the structure of the organization, the Graphic Artist may be responsible to an art director, advertising director, publication assistant, or the director of public relations, marketing, or fund-raising.

Salaries

Annual earnings for Graphic Artists working in nonprofit organizations may be lower than those for individuals in the same type of job in an advertising agency or industry. Salaries depend on a number of variables, including the size, type, and location of the organization and the experience, expertise, and responsibilities of the individual.

Salaries for this position can range from $24,000 to $48,000 or more annually, with the larger earnings going to individuals in very large nonprofit organizations. Many positions also offer fringe benefit packages.

Employment Prospects

Employment prospects for Graphic Artists in nonprofit situations are only fair. While there are numerous nonprofit organizations throughout the country, many do not employ people in this position. Some use the services of part-timers or freelancers.

Those interested in working in this type of setting may have more luck finding employment in larger cities where there are more opportunities available. Others feel that they can break into the field with less trouble in smaller areas where there is less competition.

Advancement Prospects

Graphic Artists can climb the career ladder by finding a position in a larger, more prestigious organization. Individuals may advance their careers by becoming art directors. Still others advance by locating a position in the art department of an advertising agency or the art department of a large corporation.

Advancement prospects depend on ability, talent, a good amount of luck, and being at the right place at the right time.

Education and Training

A college education is not always necessary for this position. Training, however, is useful. Those who plan on attending college should look for a school that has a major in commercial art. There are also many art schools that offer training.

Any additional courses in art, advertising, design, desktop publishing, etc. are also helpful.

Experience, Skills, and Personality Traits

First and foremost, the Graphic Artist needs to be talented, creative, and artistic. He or she should have a good sense of style and design. An understanding of advertising is helpful.

The individual should be able to draw, sketch, letter, and design. The artist also needs a working knowledge of pasteup, mechanicals, and typography. They will also need computer software skills using programs such as Photoshop and Illustrator, as well as a knowledge of desktop publishing.

Those working in nonprofit fields should also have a knowledge of the type of organization for which they are working and an understanding of the structure and workings of nonprofit organizations in general.

Unions and Associations

Graphic Artists can belong to any of a number of trade associations that provide support, guidance, and seminars for members. These include the Art Directors Club, Inc. (ADC), the One Club, and the Society of Illustrators.

Individuals working in nonprofit organizations usually also belong to trade associations directly related to the nonprofit field in which they work (health care, cultural, education, etc.).

Tips for Entry

1. Put together a portfolio of your best work. Most jobs in this field require samples. If this is your first job, put together a portfolio of work from school. Make sure it is both creative and neat.

2. Write letters to larger nonprofits and ask if you can show them your portfolio. Knock on doors.

3. Join trade associations where you can meet other people in the field and make contacts.

4. Many larger nonprofit organizations have internships available. This is a good way to get your foot in the door. Once there, dazzle them with your talent. Do a little extra, learn as much as you can, and you will have a job.

5. Positions may be located in the classified section of newspapers under the heading classifications of "Artist," "Graphic Artist," or "Commercial Artist." Other positions may be found under specific nonprofit categories such as health care, cultural organizations, museums, and education.

6. Check out openings online at employment Web sites such as Monster.com and Hotjobs.com.

ASSISTANT DIRECTOR
OF HOSPITAL PUBLIC RELATIONS

CAREER PROFILE

Duties: Assist director of department in fulfilling responsibilities for patient and public information; help with internal and external communications for facility; promote the hospital's image

Alternate Title(s): PR Assistant; Assistant PR Director

Salary Range: $24,000 to $50,000+

Employment Prospects: Good

Advancement Prospects: Good

Best Geographical Location(s): Positions available throughout the country.

Prerequisites:

Education or Training—Bachelor's degree in public relations, communications, journalism, advertising, business, or English required

Experience—Writing experience necessary; graphic experience helpful

Special Skills and Personality Traits—Ability to tolerate hospital atmosphere; good writing and communication skills; knowledge of graphics, typography, photography, and layout; computer skills

CAREER LADDER

```
┌─────────────────────────────────────────┐
│  Director of Hospital Public Relations   │
└─────────────────────────────────────────┘

┌─────────────────────────────────────────┐
│           Assistant Director             │
│      of Hospital Public Relations        │
└─────────────────────────────────────────┘

┌─────────────────────────────────────────┐
│          Public Relations Trainee        │
│           or Entry Level Position         │
└─────────────────────────────────────────┘
```

Position Description

The Assistant Director of Hospital Public Relations assists the director of the department in fulfilling the responsibilities for patient and public information. He or she is also responsible for helping with internal and external communications for the hospital or health care facility. The Assistant Director of Hospital Public Relations—or PR assistant, as he or she might be called—promotes the hospital's image and enhances its reputation as a health care center.

The PR assistant must understand hospital policies and procedures and be able to carry them out. For example, the facility might have a policy that no patient's condition can be given out. The individual must follow this policy when media calls come in. He or she must be able to relay this information to the press without their thinking that they are being snubbed.

It is vital for the PR assistant to maintain a professional, honest relationship with the media. When he or she sends out press releases or calendar events a friendly business relationship can mean the difference between getting the story in the paper or on the air and not obtaining any exposure. It is also important for the individual to maintain accurate media lists so he or she knows whom to call or send information to.

The Assistant Director of Hospital Public Relations is often asked by the PR director to produce news releases, feature stories, and special-request articles for the news and other media sources. He or she must have the ability to write in a clear, concise, and interesting manner. The assistant may obtain material for these releases by doing research or interviewing hospital staff, patients, volunteers, or others in order to develop the story. At times he or she may be required to take photographs of events or people in order to enhance a news story. At other times he or she may just arrange to have a photographer on hand to take pictures.

Another duty of the Assistant Director of Hospital Public Relations may be to assist in the preparation of internal hospital communications such as staff newspapers, program and promotional materials, letters, and internal memos.

He or she may additionally be asked to design and/or write the copy for brochures, graphic materials, and special reports. The assistant may also develop patient information kits or questionnaires for quality assessment. The public relations assistant must have the ability to tabulate, review, and report responses.

Another writing responsibility the assistant PR director may be asked to handle is preparing an annual report. The individual may gather information and statistics and may write, edit, and lay out graphic concepts. He or she may also assist in the development, preparation, and placement of advertising.

Hospitals often hold special events to raise money, to increase the utilization of hospital services, and to enhance the image of the hospital. The Assistant Director of Hospital Public Relations may be responsible for helping to develop and execute such events.

Depending on the size of the public relations department, the assistant PR director may also assist with hospital fundraising, development, and marketing programs. The individual might be asked to serve as the management representative for the hospital's auxiliary or may assist with any promotion of the hospital, such as hospital tours and other in-hospital or community events.

The assistant director of public relations in a hospital or other health care facility generally works regular hours. He or she may work overtime to attend hospital meetings, functions, or special events or to finish a timely project. The individual reports directly to the public relations director of the hospital.

Salaries

Salaries for the Assistant Director of Hospital Public Relations vary greatly depending on experience of the individual and size and location of the health care facility.

Salaries can start at approximately $24,000 and go to $50,000 or more. Those with more experience or those working at larger facilities in metropolitan areas can expect earnings at the higher end of the scale.

Employment Prospects

Employment prospects for individuals interested in becoming an assistant director of public relations in a hospital or health care facility are good. There are countless hospitals, mental health facilities, clinics, and senior citizen homes located throughout the country. Most of these places have public relations departments. Individuals seeking this type of position might have to relocate to find a job.

Advancement Prospects

Advancement prospects are good for assistant directors of public relations in hospitals. Individuals can move up to the position of director of public relations, director of public information, or director of fund-raising. An Assistant Director of Hospital Public Relations might obtain a position in a larger hospital where salaries would be higher.

Education and Training

Individuals seeking a position in the public relations department of a hospital or other health care facility are usually required to have at least a bachelor's degree. Emphasis might be in public relations, communications, journalism, advertising, business, psychology, or English.

Experience, Skills, and Personality Traits

People working in hospital and health care public relations should have the ability to define a problem logically, clearly, and concisely and to analyze it from all points of view. They should be capable and comfortable talking to the media.

Assistant Directors of Hospital Public Relations should also have a knowledge of graphics, typography, photography, and layout. The ability to type and to use word processors and computer equipment is essential.

A good writing style is necessary. Public speaking ability is required in most positions, as is the ability to communicate on the telephone in a polite, friendly, and effective manner.

People in this position should be able to accept constructive criticism, demonstrate good judgment, and have common sense.

One of the most important traits a person working in hospital public relations must have is the ability to tolerate a hospital/health care atmosphere.

Unions and Associations

The Assistant Director of Hospital Public Relations is not required to belong to any bargaining union. He or she may, however, belong to the Public Relations Society of America (PRSA), the Academy of Hospital Public Relations (AHPR), International Public Relations Association (IPRA), Association for Healthcare Philanthropy, or the American Society for Hospital Marketing and Public Relations (ASHMPR).

Tips for Entry

1. Look for an internship in a hospital public relations, marketing, or fund-raising department. This will give you valuable experience.
2. Join a hospital or health care facility auxiliary and volunteer to do their publicity. This will help you become familiar with people and policies in hospitals.
3. There are employment agencies that deal specifically with public relations positions. You might want to consider using one to help you find a job.
4. Public relations positions in health care are advertised in both the classified section of newspapers. Look under "Health Care," "Public Relations," or "Marketing" headings.
5. Join trade associations and get their monthly periodicals. Positions are often advertised in the trade journals.
6. Look for openings online. Many health care facilities have web sites advertising employment opportunities.
7. You can also check out employment Web sites such as www.hotjobs.com and www.monster.com.

PUBLICATION ASSISTANT, NONPROFIT ORGANIZATION

CAREER PROFILE

Duties: Develop or assist in the development of written publications for nonprofit organizations in order to promote the agency's objectives

Alternate Title(s): Assistant Director of Publications

Salary Range: $22,000 to $37,000+

Employment Prospects: Good

Advancement Prospects: Fair

Best Geographical Location(s): Larger cities offer more opportunities.

Prerequisites:

Education or Training—College degree with major in English, public relations, communications, or liberal arts

Experience—Writing skills acquired either in college or in a prior job

Special Skills and Personality Traits—Excellent writing skills; communication skills; understanding of layout and graphics; good command of the English language; computer competency

CAREER LADDER

```
┌─────────────────────────────┐
│   Director of Public Relations  │
│        or Marketing             │
│    or Publication Director      │
└─────────────────────────────┘

┌─────────────────────────────┐
│     Publication Assistant       │
└─────────────────────────────┘

┌─────────────────────────────┐
│         Copywriter              │
└─────────────────────────────┘
```

Position Description

A Publication Assistant working in a nonprofit organization may work in any of a variety of different settings. He or she may work in a health care facility such as a hospital or nursing home, or in a museum, cultural center, zoo, or library. The individual might also work for a nonprofit foundation, a trade association, or a charitable organization.

Whatever the setting, the Publication Assistant performs a variety of duties. Depending on the size of the organization, the individual's responsibilities range from ancillary functions to full responsibility for the development of publications required by the organization.

The Publication Assistant works with the director of public relations, marketing, fund-raising, or development or with the chief executive officer of the organization or agency to develop or assist in the development of the written materials used to promote the agency's objectives. These publications include internal and external newsletters, brochures, leaflets, annual reports, press releases, and other materials collateral to the fund-raising, marketing, or promotional objectives of the organization.

To fulfill these responsibilities the Publication Assistant might be required to develop outlines, proposals, preliminary sketches, and budget estimates for the publications. He or she works with both superiors and subordinates in implementing whatever publication decisions are made.

The individual may also coordinate timetables and projection schedules for printers, graphic artists, copywriters, photographers, and any others who might be involved in the preparation of the publication.

In smaller nonprofit organizations the Publication Assistant may be required to perform many functions that might be delegated or farmed out in larger organizations. Therefore, the individual must be qualified to work with a variety of different people and businesses. For example, the Publication Assistant may have to recommend paper stock, type styles, and graphic formats for a certain project. He or she may also be asked to secure bids from a range of printing suppliers.

In many nonprofit organizations computerized desktop publishing is now utilized to save money as well as time. In these situations the Publication Assistant may be required to input copy for a project into the computer and to develop the layout and create a master mechanical that can go directly to a printer.

Depending on the size of the nonprofit organization with which the individual is working and the number of employees in the department, he or she may be responsible for writing the actual copy for publications. The individual may also be required to do research on facts for copy used in publications in order to obtain correct information.

In other organizations the Publication Assistant may just look over copy submitted by copywriters or other agency people, checking on information as well as performing editing duties.

Once again depending on the size of the organization and the number of people working in the department, the Publication Assistant may function as a layout artist, laying out brochures, newsletters, leaflets, etc. in a graphically pleasing manner. The individual might also give suggestions to a printer on his or her ideas for layout and may oversee the project.

At times the individual may be involved in the mailing or distribution of materials. In other situations the Publication Assistant is responsible for publications only up to the time when they are completed and printed.

In certain nonprofit organizations the Publication Assistant is expected to cover newsworthy events and promotions put together by the organization. He or she might write press releases on the event or take photographs to be used in the internal or external publications of the group.

Since most nonprofit organizations depend heavily on volunteers for special events and other fund-raising activities, the Publication Assistant assigned to prepare volunteer activity enhancement material may also have to attend planning sessions and events. The individual may additionally develop publications such as instruction sheets, manuals, and/or newsletters specifically dedicated to the volunteer network that promotes the purpose of the group.

The Publication Assistant working in a nonprofit organization can be responsible to the group's director of public relations, director of marketing, director of fund-raising, or director of development or to the agency's chief executive officer. While most of the work of the Publication Assistant is done during normal working hours, the individual may, on occasion, have to work at night or on weekends attending meetings, functions, or special events or may have to stay late to meet a publication deadline.

Salaries

Earnings for Publication Assistants working in nonprofit settings vary greatly depending on the size of the organiza-

tion, its location, and the experience and responsibilities of the individual.

Annual earnings for Publication Assistants can range from $22,000 to $37,000 or more. Fringe benefit packages are often offered to individuals working in these settings.

Employment Prospects

Employment prospects are good for those seeking positions as Publication Assistants in nonprofit organizations. There is an abundance of nonprofit groups in most urban areas as well as a good number even in smaller regions. Hospitals and other health care facilities, museums, nonprofit foundations, trade associations, and other charitable organizations offer potential employment.

Advancement Prospects

As most nonprofit organizations experience a big employee turnover, opportunities for advancement for a Publication Assistant are fair. An individual seeking to climb the career ladder may become the director of public relations, fundraising, marketing, or development. The individual might also find employment as a Publication Assistant or director at a larger, more prestigious organization where the salary will generally be higher.

Education and Training

A college degree is usually required in order to attain a position as a Publication Assistant. Good choices for majors include public relations, communications, English, and liberal arts.

Seminars and courses in writing, graphics, and layout are extremely helpful.

Experience, Skills, and Personality Traits

Excellent writing skills are necessary for the Publication Assistant. He or she should have a working knowledge of grammar, spelling, and word usage. A good writing style is a must. An understanding of graphics, layout, and the printing industry is usually required. Individuals in this position should also know how to edit other people's writing. Publication Assistants need to be able to communicate verbally as well as on paper. Computer skills are required for most positions.

Unions and Associations

A Publication Assistant working in a nonprofit organization does not usually belong to any union. He or she may, however, belong to any of a number of trade associations that can provide the individual with professional guidance and support as well as putting him or her in touch with others in the same field. These include the Public Relations Society of America (PRSA), National Society of Fund Raising Executives (NSFRE), and the Council for the Advancement and Support of Education (CASE). Individuals might also belong to trade associations specifically related to their individual field in the nonprofit area.

Tips for Entry

1. Volunteer to write and develop press releases, brochures, and flyers for local nonprofit or civic organizations.
2. Summer jobs or internships are often available in nonprofit organizations' fund-raising and development or public relations departments. Write to the director of the organization and inquire about the availability of these programs.
3. Positions such as this are often advertised in the classified section of newspapers under the heading classification of "Public Relations," "Fund-raising," "Writer," or "Publications." Positions might also be located in employment display advertisements in the newspaper.
4. Check out the Web sites of not-for-profit organizations. Many post employment opportunities.
5. Career employment Web sites such as Monster.com and Hotjobs.com also may offer opportunities.

ASSISTANT DIRECTOR OF FUND-RAISING AND DEVELOPMENT, NONPROFIT ORGANIZATION

CAREER PROFILE

Duties: Assist director of department with fund-raising programs

Alternate Title(s): Assistant Director of Development; Assistant Director of Fund-raising; Fund-raising Assistant Director

Salary Range: $23,000 to $50,000+

Employment Prospects: Fair

Advancement Prospects: Fair

Best Geographical Location(s): Positions may be located throughout country.

Prerequisites:

Education or Training—Bachelor's degree in marketing, advertising, communications, journalism, or liberal arts required; MBA helpful in advancement

Experience—Publicity, public relations, and fund-raising experience useful

Special Skills and Personality Traits—Aggressive; organization; good writing, communication, and interpersonal skills; knowledge of computers

CAREER LADDER

```
┌─────────────────────────────────┐
│   Director of Fund-raising       │
│   and Development or Director    │
│   of Public Relations or Marketing│
└─────────────────────────────────┘

┌─────────────────────────────────┐
│   Assistant Director of Fund-raising │
│   and Development                │
└─────────────────────────────────┘

┌─────────────────────────────────┐
│   Trainee Position, Entry Level, │
│   or Fund-raising Staff Member   │
└─────────────────────────────────┘
```

Position Description

The Assistant Director of Fund-raising and Development working in a nonprofit setting can be employed in many different types of organizations. He or she might work in a hospital, health care organization, museum, cultural center, or library. The individual may also work for other types of charitable organizations, nonprofit foundations, or trade associations.

The main duty of someone in this position is to assist the director of the fund-raising and development program raise moneys for the organization or facility. This is not an easy job because there are so many organizations vying for the funds donated by the public.

Responsibilities in this type of job vary from position to position. However, there are a number of duties that remain the same no matter the setting.

The Assistant Director of Fund-raising and Development is responsible for assisting the head of the department with developing programs to raise funds for the institution. The individual helps raise the money not only for large capital campaigns but also for some of the smaller programs of the organization. After the creation or development of these programs he or she assists in their implementation. Programs to raise money can differ and run from weekly bingo games and special-event shows to huge annual fund-raising dinners, auctions, dances, telethons, and entertainment events. Other types of programs the assistant might help develop and implement include century clubs and other annual giving or sustaining campaigns.

The individual's duties might involve working with or supervising other staff members in the department. He or she might also work with the public relations or marketing departments. Depending on the structure of the organization, the assistant may act as the assistant to the public relations, publicity, or marketing director.

Much of the fund-raising accomplished in nonprofit organizations is made possible by volunteers who do a lot of legwork. The assistant is responsible for working with the volunteers who help implement many of the programs. The individual must have the ability to make people feel wanted, needed, and useful in order to get things done. He or she might also be responsible for helping to locate volunteers to assist on projects.

The Assistant Director of Fund-raising and Development may be asked by the director to cultivate potential donors. To do this the individual might attend luncheons, dinners, meetings, parties, and other affairs on behalf of the organization. At times the assistant will be asked to speak to groups of people about fund-raising functions. At other times he or she may lead tours in order to show visitors the building or facility and the people being helped by the organization to illustrate how programs are working.

The assistant might seek out grants offered by the government and private foundations. Depending on the circumstances, he or she may just locate these grants or may be responsible for writing proposals for them. The Assistant Director could also be responsible for seeking annual gifts from individuals and corporations and for locating sponsorship for various projects the organization has undertaken.

The assistant is responsible for writing reports for the director of the department as well as describing the progress of varied fund-raising projects to the board of directors. He or she might write press releases or do other publicity to promote fund-raising and development programs.

Other writing responsibilities include direct-mail pieces, advertising copy, flyer copy, fund-raising letters, invitations, speeches, and brochures.

Part of the job of the Assistant Director of Fund-raising and Development is to help the director run special events to raise money. Responsibilities encompass doing anything that needs to be done in order to run a successful and effective program. This might include finding locations for dinner dances, planning menus, making phone calls to assure good attendance at an event, locating individuals and businesses to donate door prizes, conducting phonathons, locating guest speakers and chairpeople, keeping records of moneys, soliciting donations, etc. The individual may help run one special event a year or one a week, depending on the organization.

Some Assistant Directors of Fund-raising and Development are also responsible for keeping records of donor management and resource development. Individuals might send out acknowledgments and thank-you letters to donors.

The Assistant Director of Fund-raising and Development working in a nonprofit setting is responsible to the director of the department. The individual also works closely with the board of directors and the executive director of the organization.

Salaries

Salaries for Assistant Director of Fund-raising and Development who work for nonprofit organizations vary greatly depending on many factors, including the experience of the individual and the organization's type, size, location, and prestige.

Salaries for this position can range from $23,000 to $50,000 or more annually. Individuals might also receive fringe benefit packages.

Employment Prospects

Employment prospects are fair for those seeking the position of Assistant Director of Fund-raising and Development in nonprofit organizations. There are numerous possibilities for work, such as hospitals, schools, colleges, universities, health care organizations, museums, cultural centers, libraries, charitable organizations, nonprofit foundations, and trade associations.

Individuals can usually find employment in any location in the country. Larger cities offer more job possibilities. There are also a fair number of part-time positions available in this field.

Advancement Prospects

Advancement prospects for the Assistant Director of Fund-raising and Development working in a nonprofit organization are fair. The individual can advance by becoming the director of fund-raising and development or the director of public relations or marketing in the same organization. He or she might advance by moving to a position in a larger nonprofit group, which would mean a salary increase.

Education and Training

The educational requirement for this position is a college degree. Important majors include marketing, public relations, English, journalism, liberal arts, and communications. A master's degree will help in career advancement.

Any seminar on fund-raising, development, marketing, or grant writing will be useful.

Experience, Skills, and Personality Traits

The Assistant Director of Fund-raising and Development working for a nonprofit organization should be fairly aggressive and have good organizational skills. He or she should have excellent writing and communication skills. Computer capability is helpful. The individual must also have good interpersonal skills and the ability to deal well with volunteers.

Any experience in public relations, publicity, the running of special events, and fund-raising is a plus.

Unions and Associations

The Assistant Director of Fund-raising and Development does not have a bargaining union. He or she may belong to trade associations that provide useful contacts as well as offering seminars and courses to hone skills in this field. Associations include National Society of Fund Raising Executives (NSFRE), Direct Mail/Marketing Association, Inc. (DM/MA), The Association for Healthcare Philanthropy, and the Council for the Advancement and Support of Education (CASE), to name a few.

Tips for Entry

1. Join one or two nonprofit organizations you are interested in. Volunteer to be on the fund-raising commit-tee. This will provide useful experience as well as being good for your résumé.

2. Look in the classified sections of Sunday newspapers under "Fund-raising," "Public Relations," "Health Care," and "Grant Writing" headings. This type of position may also be located in the display advertising section of Sunday newspapers.

3. Join trade associations. Subscribe to their journals and attend their seminars and conventions.

4. Many colleges and nonprofit organizations offer internship and trainee programs in this field.

5. Look for positions online. Check out the Web sites of not-for-profit organizations. Many post employment opportunities.

6. You might also look on some of the more popular employment Web sites such as www.hotjobs.com and www.monster.com.

GUEST SERVICES COORDINATOR, NONPROFIT ORGANIZATION

CAREER PROFILE

Duties: Provide a hospitable, comfortable atmosphere for guests (clients, members, patients, visitors, etc.) of nonprofit organization; take people on tours of institution; make guests or clients feel important and special; prepare literature and materials about services of the organization

Alternate Title(s): Guest Relations Coordinator; Guest Services Representative; Patient Relations Coordinator

Salary Range: $23,000 to $48,000+

Employment Prospects: Fair

Advancement Prospects: Fair

Best Geographical Location(s): Positions may be located throughout the country.

Prerequisites:

Education or Training—Four-year college degree required

Experience—Experience in hospitality industry and public relations helpful, but not always required

Special Skills and Personality Traits—Interpersonal skills; good communications skills; writing skills; ability to handle details; sensitivity; empathy

CAREER LADDER

```
┌─────────────────────────────────┐
│   Guest Services Coordinator    │
│    in Larger Organization,      │
│   Guest Services Director,      │
│      or Public Relations        │
│     or Marketing Director       │
└─────────────────────────────────┘

┌─────────────────────────────────┐
│   Guest Services Coordinator    │
└─────────────────────────────────┘

┌─────────────────────────────────┐
│   Public Relations Assistant,   │
│   Guest Services Assistant,     │
│   or Administrative Assistant   │
└─────────────────────────────────┘
```

Position Description

The Guest Services Coordinator provides, develops, coordinates, and supports all of the amenities and other hospitality aspects of a nonprofit organization. The purpose of guest services is to offer a hospitable, comfortable atmosphere, assistance with routine or special activities, and special VIP services. The individual in this position works as part of the public relations department.

He or she may work for any of a variety of different types of organizations, including museums, hospitals and health care institutions, zoos, cultural centers, or libraries. The individual may also work for other types of charitable organizations, nonprofit foundations, or trade associations.

In some organizations there is only one person in this position. In others there are a number of Guest Services Coordinators. Functions vary depending on the specific institution or organization.

The Guest Services Coordinator is responsible for creating a comfortable atmosphere. The individual must make sure that the customer, guest, client, or patient is made to feel that he or she is regarded as a very important person.

The individual may be responsible for training staff members to understand guest relations concepts. He or she explains to staff how to treat the organization's guests when they are in the institution. The Guest Services Coordinator also trains employees with phone-answering responsibilities to do that task so that people calling in feel that they are important and special and are being well taken care of.

To perform his or her job the Guest Services Coordinator may be expected to develop and implement surveys and questionnaires regarding guests' attitudes. The individual may, for example, work in a hospital. He or she might find through a survey that nurses are not responding to calls from patients' families in a timely fashion, or that food is being brought to patients cold. The Guest Services Coordinator can take these problems and work with administration to solve them.

The Guest Services Coordinator may take people on tours of the organization's facilities and provide them with literature and souvenirs. He or she may develop or create special "nicety" packages for guests. In a hospital it may be a cosmetic basket of soap, toothpaste, toothbrush, comb, etc. In a zoo the individual may create a package with postcards, bumper stickers, and a small stuffed animal. Cultural centers may give bottles of wine or champagne. These packages usually have the name of the organization emblazoned on them. They may be given to all guests or they may be offered only to special guests.

The Guest Services Coordinator is expected to handle any problems that arise with guests so the patron is made to feel that he or she is right. This could mean that the Guest Services Coordinator has an employee apologize to a patron. In situations where the coordinator learns about a problem by phone or mail, he or she may have to write a letter of apology. The individual might also take charges off a bill or send a free pass.

In many nonprofit situations the Guest Services Coordinator is also responsible for a number of marketing and administrative duties. Museums, cultural centers, and zoos, for example, may raise funds for the institution by renting out the property to the public for special functions, parties, or even filming events. The individual may be in charge of planning, coordinating, and supervising these functions. When an event is taking place the Guest Services Coordinator will be expected to be on site to assist with any problems that may arise.

The Guest Services Coordinator may also be required to market the institution. He or she may be responsible for preparing and distributing general information materials on the organization, the services, and any programs available.

The individual usually works normal business hours. If there is an unexpected problem or if the individual is supervising an event at the organization, he or she will be required to work overtime.

The Guest Services Coordinator may be responsible to either the guest services director or the public relations director, depending on the size and structure of the organization.

Salaries

Earnings for Guest Services Coordinators vary depending on the size and budget of the nonprofit organization and the experience and responsibilities of the individual. Salaries can range from $23,000 to $48,000 or more annually.

Individuals who have few or no administrative functions and those working in small organizations have salaries ranging from the high teens to the low twenties. Individuals working in larger organizations or those with a great deal of responsibility average earnings between $35,000 and $48,000.

Employment Prospects

Employment prospects are fair for Guest Services Coordinators in the nonprofit world. Individuals must look toward the mid-size and larger nonprofit groups. Many smaller organizations may not have Guest Services Coordinator positions. Instead the responsibilities are often delegated to the public relations department.

Jobs may be located throughout the country. Individuals have a variety of different types of organizations to choose from, including zoos, museums, health care facilities and hospitals, charitable organizations, trade associations, and other nonprofit organizations.

Advancement Prospects

Advancement prospects for Guest Services Coordinators in the nonprofit sector are fair. Individuals may find similar positions in larger nonprofit organizations, resulting in increased earnings and responsibilities. One might also become a guest services director, if the organization has such a position.

Guest Services Coordinators may also climb the career ladder by becoming the assistant director or director of public relations or the assistant director or director of marketing.

Education and Training

The Guest Services Coordinator working in a nonprofit organization is usually required to hold a four-year college degree. Good choices for majors include public relations, communications, English, liberal arts, marketing, and journalism.

Seminars on public relations, writing, and working with nonprofit groups will be useful to the individual for both the educational value and making professional contacts.

Experience, Skills, and Personality Traits

The Guest Services Coordinator needs good interpersonal skills. He or she should be personable and genuinely like people. The individual should have the ability to put others at ease and make them comfortable.

Good communication skills are necessary. The Guest Services Coordinator should be articulate, have the ability to speak comfortably in front of groups, and be able to deal with antagonistic, irate, or dissatisfied clients. A pleasant telephone manner is also required.

The individual often works on many different projects at one time. He or she should have the ability to handle details without becoming flustered.

The Guest Services Coordinator should be able to write well. He or she may be expected to prepare letters, proposals, and other written materials. A variety of public relations and publicity skills are often needed. The ability to type or use a computer or word processor may be necessary.

Experience working in the hospitality industry is helpful.

Unions and Associations

The Guest Services Coordinator working in a nonprofit situation does not belong to a union. While there are no specific trade associations for the individual to belong to, he or she may be a member of the Public Relations Society of America (PRSA).

Tips for Entry

1. Consider a part-time or summer job in a hotel or resort as a guest relations clerk or assistant.

2. Many nonprofit organizations hire assistants to work with their Guest Services Coordinator. This will get your foot in the door of the field.

3. Get experience in publicity or public relations by volunteering your efforts to a nonprofit organization.

4. Attend seminars and classes. This will help you hone skills as well as giving you the opportunity to make professional contacts.

5. Send your résumé and a cover letter to nonprofit organizations and ask for an interview.

6. Positions for Guest Services Coordinators are advertised in both trade journals and newspaper classified sections. Look under heading classifications of "Guest Services," "Public Relations," or "Guest Relations."

PUBLISHING

PROMOTION COORDINATOR, NEWSPAPERS

CAREER PROFILE

Duties: Develop promotions for newspaper to enlarge circulation, obtain greater advertising space sales, and create community goodwill; develop special-edition supplements; design projects that create advertising tie-ins

Alternate Title(s): Promotion Manager

Salary Range: $23,000 to $60,000+

Employment Prospects: Fair

Advancement Prospects: Good

Best Geographical Location(s): Positions may be located throughout the country.

Prerequisites:

Education or Training—Four-year college degree required

Experience—Journalism, public relations, promotion, or advertising experience required

Special Skills and Personality Traits—Imagination; innovative; creative; good writing skills; knowledge of advertising and the newspaper industry; articulate

CAREER LADDER

```
┌─────────────────────────────────────┐
│     Advertising Sales Director,      │
│  Promotion Coordinator at Larger     │
│ Publication or Promotion Director    │
└─────────────────────────────────────┘

┌─────────────────────────────────────┐
│       Promotion Coordinator          │
└─────────────────────────────────────┘

┌─────────────────────────────────────┐
│     Public Relations, Advertising,   │
│      or Promotion Assistant          │
└─────────────────────────────────────┘
```

Position Description

A Promotion Coordinator working in a newspaper is responsible for developing promotions for the publication. The promotions assist in obtaining a large circulation for the paper. The larger the circulation, the more the newspaper can charge for space to advertisers who want to place ads. The promotions are also used to develop advertising tie-ins for advertisers. Many of the promotions created help to develop goodwill within the community.

For example, the Promotion Coordinator may develop a program in which the newspaper sponsors special events such as golf, bowling, tennis, baseball, softball, and other sports tournaments for a local charity or group of charities. While they may develop, organize, and implement the program to raise funds and awareness for the charity, the Promotion Coordinator may also find ways to sell space to local businesspeople who want to get involved in the project.

The Promotion Coordinator is responsible for developing ideas for special-edition supplements of the paper to attract advertisers. These are used for promotional tie-ins. The individual may develop a number of these supplements every year. Examples include special sections on vacation and travel; food and dining; health and fitness; back-to-school; men's, women's, and children's fashions; and real estate.

The Promotion Coordinator may design contests to stimulate circulation as well as bring in new advertisers. He or she may, for instance, start an annual newspaper cooking contest. In addition to the contest promotion itself, the individual may develop a cookbook section in which businesses can advertise.

The Promotion Coordinator has a number of responsibilities when developing and implementing projects. He or she might begin by writing a proposal that would be given to the advertising manager, publisher, or management for approval. Once it is approved, the individual is responsible for creating and writing advertising pieces to inform readers of the program. In some cases the individual may advertise various promotions in other publications or via local radio or television commercials. He or she may also be responsible for writing press releases about the promotions.

The Promotion Coordinator may be expected to plan and design the publication's public service advertisements, activities, and promotions. He or she might also work with schools, teachers, and administrators to develop educational uses for the newspaper. The individual may come up with an annual promotion in which children learn about advertising and the newspaper industry by designing advertisements for local businesses in school. The business people will then have the opportunity to buy space to have the children's advertisements appear in a special supplement.

The Promotion Coordinator works normal business hours. He or she may, however, be required to work overtime to complete projects, meet deadlines, be on hand for promotions, or attend public events on behalf of the newspaper.

The individual works with the advertising sales department, keeping them abreast of all future promotions. He or she may be responsible to the advertising sales manager or director or to the publisher, depending on the structure of the newspaper.

Salaries

Annual earnings vary greatly for Promotion Coordinators working in newspapers, depending on a number of variables. These include the size, location, and circulation of the paper and the experience level and responsibilities of the individual.

Salaries can range from $23,000 to $60,000 a year. A Promotion Coordinator with limited experience working in a small newspaper would earn an average of $23,000 to $27,000 annually. Those working for large metropolitan daily newspapers may earn between $40,000 to $50,000. Individuals who work for newspapers with extremely large circulations and high advertising rates may earn $60,000 or more.

Employment Prospects

Employment prospects are fair for Promotion Coordinators working in newspapers. Newspapers of all sizes are located throughout the country and usually have this position. However, some of the smaller newspapers may combine the functions of the Promotion Coordinator with that of the sales manager.

Individuals may have to relocate or take a position in a smaller paper in order to find employment.

Advancement Prospects

Advancement prospects are good for a Promotion Coordinator. There are a number of different ways the individual can climb the career ladder. He or she may locate a similar position in a larger, more prestigious newspaper. This would result in increased earnings and responsibilities. There is a

fairly good chance of this occurring after the individual obtains some experience. There is a great deal of turnover in this field due to advancement and mobility of people in the newspaper field.

The Promotion Coordinator might be promoted to the newspaper's advertising director position. In some situations the Promotion Coordinator moves out of the newspaper industry and into promotion in magazines, book publishing, radio, television, advertising.

Education and Training

Most positions as Promotion Coordinators in newspapers have a minimum requirement of a four-year college degree. Good choices for majors include advertising, marketing, business, public relations, communications, liberal arts, journalism, and English.

Experience, Skills, and Personality Traits

The Promotion Coordinator should have a basic understanding of the newspaper industry. He or she should know about circulation, advertising, and the audience of the particular paper. The Promotion Coordinator should have a working knowledge of public relations, advertising, and marketing.

The individual needs good communication skills. He or she must be able to speak before groups of people comfortably and articulately.

Writing skills are necessary, too. The Promotion Coordinator needs to be able to write simple press releases, proposals, and reports. The individual may also need to write advertising copy. In certain situations, the ability to lay out ads will also be needed.

He or she should be creative, innovative, and imaginative. This will be important when developing both promotional and advertising ideas and concepts.

Unions and Associations

The Promotion Coordinator does not usually belong to any bargaining union. He or she may belong to any of a number of trade associations and groups that provide educational materials and professional guidance, plus conferences, conventions, meetings, and seminars for bringing people in the same field together. These include the International Newspaper Promotion Association (INPA), the International Circulation Managers Association (ICMA), the American Newspaper Publishers Association (ANPA), The Newspaper Guild (TNG), the Public Relations Society of America (PRSA), the American Advertising Federation (AAF), and the National Federation of Press Women, Inc.

Tips for Entry

1. Join trade associations and organizations. Many of these offer student memberships. These groups will give you advice on obtaining a job, helpful literature,

and seminars that will help hone your skills as well as assisting in making professional contacts.

2. Try to locate an internship or training program in a newspaper. These are often available through trade associations or the newspapers themselves. Write and inquire. Remember to indicate the department that you're interested in.

3. Promotion Coordinator positions are often advertised in classified section of the newspaper. Look under heading classifications of "Promotion Coordinator," "Promotion," "Advertising," or "Sales."

4. If you are just getting into the job market, you might have an easier time locating employment in a smaller area or on a smaller newspaper. The pay will be less than at a major paper, but you will get valuable experience that will help you move up the career ladder.

5. Consider sending your résumé with a cover letter to a number of newspapers indicating your interest in working in the promotion department. Ask that your résumé be kept on file. When a position opens up, they might call you for an interview.

6. Look for a job online. Many newspapers have Web sites listing their employment opportunities.

7. Don't forget to check some of the career employment Web sites such as Monster.com and Hotjobs.com.

PUBLIC RELATIONS ASSISTANT, MAGAZINES

CAREER PROFILE

Duties: Assist the public relations director with public relations duties; write press releases; help develop public relations and publicity strategies for the magazine

Alternate Title(s): PR Assistant; Publicity Assistant

Salary Range: $23,000 to $36,000+

Employment Prospects: Fair

Advancement Prospects: Fair

Best Geographical Location(s): New York City, as well as other major cities, may offer more job possibilities.

Prerequisites:

Education or Training—Four-year degree required

Experience—Writing, publicity, or public relations experience preferred but not required in all positions

Special Skills and Personality Traits—Good writing skills; creative; articulate; ability to work under pressure; good phone skills

CAREER LADDER

```
┌─────────────────────────────────┐
│     Public Relations Director   │
└─────────────────────────────────┘

┌─────────────────────────────────┐
│    Public Relations Assistant   │
└─────────────────────────────────┘

┌─────────────────────────────────┐
│  Intern, Trainee, or Entry Level │
└─────────────────────────────────┘
```

Position Description

The Public Relations Assistant working for a magazine or other publication assists the director of the department with the public relations functions. The main responsibility of the public relations department is to publicize the magazine to consumers and advertisers as well as the media.

While magazines make money on subscriptions and single-issue sales, most of their income comes from selling advertising space. Selling more copies of a magazine means that the publication can raise advertising rates. It is therefore important for the magazine to be in the public eye as much as possible. This is accomplished through public relations, publicity, marketing, and advertising.

The Public Relations Assistant may have varied duties depending on the type and size of the magazine and the number of people working in the public relations department.

One of the main duties of the Public Relations Assistant is to write press releases that are distributed to other media, such as magazines, newspapers, news services, and television and radio stations. The PR assistant may write releases about special issues being prepared or interesting articles that will be in forthcoming issues.

The individual might also be required to develop press releases on staff promotions, special awards and honors to be presented to the magazine or its staff, or any other event considered newsworthy.

The PR assistant may also be required to develop and write feature stories and special-interest articles on the magazine and members of its staff. These, too, will be sent to the media.

Depending on the experience of the Public Relations Assistant, his or her writing and other work may have to be reviewed by the public relations director. The individual may have to type press releases and articles, putting them directly into a computer, or may have a secretary responsible for this task.

The Public Relations Assistant may be asked to develop, write, and design promotional materials and internal publications such as brochures, newsletters, memos, flyers, and posters.

The individual may also be required to prepare media lists, make sure that they are up to date, and keep in contact with various editors, reporters, producers, and talent coordinators.

The Public Relations Assistant may write or call talent coordinators and producers of talk, variety, and news shows on radio and television to set up interviews for magazine personnel. For example, the public relations director may decide that the publication's health and beauty editor would be a good weekly guest on a midday news show. The PR assistant might be responsible for making the calls to find a show that also considers this a good idea.

The individual must also assist in arranging interviews with news people to help promote the magazine and must respond to media questions when called.

At times the Public Relations Assistant acts as a buffer for the public relations director. He or she may be required to field phone calls, talk to people, and take care of minor problems directed to the PR director.

The Public Relations Assistant may work with the PR director developing new promotions or contests that the magazine might hold to increase readership. The individual might also assist with the marketing or advertising department, publicizing promotions and projects.

Developing, preparing, compiling, and distributing press kits is another important function of the Public Relations Assistant. To do this, the individual must handle a number of areas. He or she writes general press releases focusing on the publication, as well as using specific releases from the past. The individual also chooses photos that have appeared in the magazine or on covers of the publication and articles or stories that have appeared in other publications; demographics sheets; fact and bio sheets; brochures; and rate cards. He or she compiles these into a folder and distributes them to the media (and possibly to the advertising department).

The PR assistant may, at the director's discretion, handle any other public relations duties or functions. He or she may, for example, be the publication's speaker at local or civic groups or may represent the magazine at dinners, fund-raising functions, seminars, or industry conferences.

The individual in this job is directly responsible to the publication's public relations director or manager. He or she is required to work normal business hours. When the department or magazine is working on special projects or promotions, the individual may have to work late or on weekends.

Salaries

Public Relations Assistants working for magazines earn salaries ranging from $23,000 to $36,000 or more annually. Variables that affect earnings include the size, prestige, and location of the publication as well as the responsibilities and experience level of the individual.

Individuals working in major cities, where most of the larger publications are headquartered, usually earn more than those working in suburban areas.

Employment Prospects

Employment prospects are fair for those seeking employment as Public Relations Assistants in the world of magazines and publications. While there are thousands of magazines published throughout the country, not all of them have public relations departments. This is especially true for many smaller publications and specialized trade magazines. Most of the larger publications, especially consumer magazines, do hire people for this position.

As many publications are located in New York City or other major cities, individuals may have to relocate if they want to work in these positions.

Advancement Prospects

Advancement prospects for a magazine Public Relations Assistant are fair. There is a lot of competition in the publication field. Individuals who move up the career ladder must be aggressive and outgoing. They must demonstrate to their supervisors that they are capable of doing the job.

The next rung on the career ladder for a PR assistant working at a magazine is to become the public relations director. The individual may have to seek this type of position at another publication if the current PR director is not promoted or leaving for another position. Individuals might also advance to become marketing director or manager at the publication.

Some individuals advance their careers by locating public relations jobs in television, radio, or another industry.

Education and Training

Almost every magazine hiring Public Relations Assistants requires the individuals to have a minimum of a four-year college degree. Good choices for majors include public relations, communications, English, marketing, journalism, and liberal arts.

Additional seminars and courses in public relations, writing, and publicity are helpful, as are specialty seminars in publicity for publications. These courses help the individual learn new skills and make important contacts.

Experience, Skills, and Personality Traits

The PR assistant should have excellent writing skills. A good command of the English language, grammar, and spelling is necessary. The ability to write interesting, informative, and factual press releases is imperative.

The individual also needs to have a creative mind. He or she helps develop ideas, press releases, and promotions. Artistic creativity, or at least a sense of graphic style, is a necessity for the Public Relations Assistant. He or she may be required to do publication layouts, decorations for parties, or any of a number of other functions in which creativity and style are needed.

Typing, word processing, and/or computer skills are usually required in these positions. A good phone manner is necessary. The individual is often requested to take incoming calls and make outgoing calls. He or she must also be extremely articulate and comfortable speaking in public.

The Public Relations Assistant who is to be successful in his or her job must be enthusiastic, friendly, outgoing, and willing to do the little extras without being asked or expected.

Unions and Associations

The most prominent trade association for people working in any facet of public relations is the Public Relations Society of America (PRSA). This group also offers student membership to those who are interested in getting into the field. The PRSA holds workshops, seminars, courses, and conferences throughout the year. They also offer trade journals and books helpful to those in the industry.

Tips for Entry

1. Join the student chapter of the Public Relations Society of America. This organization provides training and materials helpful in obtaining jobs in public relations. They also have a job-location program for members.

2. There are employment agencies that deal specifically with finding public relations positions. Before you work with one of these, however, check to find out who will pay the fee if they find you a job. In some agencies, the job applicant pays. In others, the employer bears the cost.

3. Many larger magazines offer intern programs. Write to the publication headquarters to inquire.

4. Positions may be listed in the newspaper classified section. Look under the heading classifications of "Public Relations," "College," "Publicity," "Magazines," or "Publications."

5. Positions may also be located in the help-wanted section of trade journals.

6. Consider sending your résumé and a cover letter to the personnel directors of magazines. Remember to ask that your résumé be kept on file if there are no jobs currently available.

7. Check out various magazine Web sites. Many list employment opportunities.

ADVERTISING SALES REPRESENTATIVE, NEWSPAPERS AND MAGAZINES

CAREER PROFILE

Duties: Sell advertising space in magazine and/or newspapers to clients; give advice on ad design and budget

Alternate Title(s): Sales Rep; Salesperson; Salesman; Saleswoman; Account Executive

Salary Range: $19,000 to $100,000+

Employment Prospects: Excellent

Advancement Prospects: Good

Best Geographical Location(s): All locations are good for obtaining jobs; larger cities offer bigger publication possibilities.

Prerequisites:

Education or Training—High school diploma, minimum requirement; college degree or background may be preferred or required.

Experience—Selling experience helpful, but not necessary

Special Skills and Personality Traits—Personable aggressive; strong desire to succeed; organization; ability to work without constant supervision; ability to deal with discouragement

CAREER LADDER

```
┌─────────────────────────────────────┐
│     Advertising Sales Manager        │
└─────────────────────────────────────┘

┌─────────────────────────────────────┐
│   Advertising Sales Representative   │
└─────────────────────────────────────┘

┌─────────────────────────────────────┐
│  Advertising Sales Rep Assistant,    │
│  Advertising Sales Rep Trainee,      │
│     or Entry-Level Position          │
└─────────────────────────────────────┘
```

Position Description

Whether an Advertising Sales Representative works for a newspaper or a magazine, his or her main function is to sell advertising space. If the rep (or salesperson, as they are sometimes called) works for a local newspaper or magazine, he or she often works directly with local businesses to sell advertisements. Advertising Sales Representatives working with national newspapers or magazines also work with advertising agencies whose clients have purchased ads.

The sales rep calls on businesses that buy space. These clients might include restaurants, department stores, chain stores, doctors, dentists, lawyers, shops of all kinds, movie theaters, concert halls, nonprofit organizations, etc. Local or regional clients are those who sell products or services in a local or regional area. National clients include companies that produce products or services sold on a national or international level.

An Advertising Sales Representative is usually assigned a sales territory in which to work. This means that he or she has a certain locality or area to sell ads in. The rep usually sells only in his or her territory. Territories can be large or small. If a rep is working for a national publication, for example, he or she might cover either the Southwest region, the East Coast region, or the Upper Midwest. A rep working for a local daily newspaper might have the entire city in which he or she is located to sell ads.

Depending on the size of a newspaper or magazine, the Advertising Sales Representative might write ads, acting as a copywriter. At other small publications the sales representative might also design and lay out advertisements.

Clients often want to advertise their products or services and call the sales representative to get information and rates on the publication. After the call the salesperson usually makes an appointment to meet with the potential client to offer this information as well as to give a sales spiel.

At times the Advertising Sales Representative must go out and find customers. At this point he or she may make "cold calls." These are phone calls or visits made to a potential client without advance warning and without the client having called the publication to buy ad space. The rep may call a client to talk about a special promotion that the publication is running. For example, a newspaper might have an issue dedicated to health services. The Advertising Sales Representative would then contact all the hospitals, doctors, dentists, and labs, to see if they would like to participate in the issue and buy advertising space.

An Advertising Sales Representative often works on his or her own. It is up to the individual to sell as many ads as possible. Often the job is not nine to five. The sales rep may find that he or she has to make a sales call to a client at eight in the morning or eight at night. No one watches what a sales rep does all day. It is up to him or her to organize his or her time and efforts effectively.

Much of the work of an Advertising Sales Representative is done in the field. That means that the rep is often on the road trying to sell space. He or she might set up appointments one day and visit the clients the next. At other times the Advertising Sales Representative might be in the office helping clients decide where, when, and how their advertising dollar would be best spent. The rep also spends a great deal of his or her time on the phone locating potential clients or telling current customers about the status of their ads.

The Advertising Sales Representative must be able to set goals for him- or herself and not get discouraged when he or she doesn't sell every client. Salespeople often have dry times when ads don't sell as well as expected. Individuals must be able to keep a positive attitude during these periods.

The Advertising Sales Representative works under the supervision of a retail advertising manager. Under this direction the rep learns of all special sales campaigns or promotions for the publication. The individual works closely with his or her ad manager. Through this individual the sales rep obtains leads, gets pointers on effective selling techniques, and obtains territories.

Salaries

Salaries may be paid to Advertising Sales Representatives in a number of ways. The person might receive a straight salary; the individual may receive a small salary and commissions; or the sales rep might be paid by commissions alone. As most sales reps receive part of their income by commission, it is difficult to estimate income. In most cases, one of the great things about being an Advertising Sales Representative is that earning potential can be limitless. An Advertising Sales Representative working for a newspaper or magazine may have annual earnings ranging from approximately $19,000 to $100,000 or more.

Employment Prospects

Employment prospects for Advertising Sales Representatives are excellent. There is usually an abundance of opportunities in almost any town, city, or state where an individual might want to live. As advertising is the way a publication makes its money, publications are constantly looking for good sales reps. Advertising sales jobs are one of the best ways of breaking into any type of advertising career.

Advancement Prospects

Advancement for Advertising Sales Representatives can be obtained in many ways. An Advertising Sales Representative might advance his or her career by becoming an advertising manager or director. The rep might also advance his or her career by obtaining bigger and better territories in which to sell. The advertising rep may climb the ladder of success by getting bigger accounts, which would lead to higher earnings.

Education and Training

A high school diploma may be all that is required of an Advertising Sales Representative in some situations. Other positions may require or prefer a college degree or college background. Courses or seminars in selling and advertising can be useful to the individual seeking this type of position.

Experience, Skills, and Personality Traits

An Advertising Sales Representative must be personable and aggressive and have the ability to deal with the discouragement of not selling every ad. He or she must enjoy selling and have a genuine liking for the public. The rep cannot be timid. He or she must seek opportunities to sell advertising space and then sell them to clients. As reps are often paid a commission, they must also have a strong desire to succeed. Sales reps must be organized and have the ability to work without constant supervision. An understanding of math is useful for figuring out costs.

Unions and Associations

Advertising Sales Representatives often belong to a number of business and civic groups. Through these organizations individuals begin to build a good list of contacts to call in order to sell advertising. Sales reps working for publications might also belong to the International Newspaper Advertising and Marketing Executives (INAME) and the Newspaper Advertising Bureau (NAB).

Tips for Entry

1. A letter and résumé to newspaper and magazine personnel offices will often land you an interview.
2. There are many seminars that can help you become a better salesperson. Look for these in the newspaper or at your local community college.
3. Advertising Sales Rep positions are regularly advertised in newspapers in the classified section. If you don't find job openings under "Advertising," look under "Salesperson," "Sales," or "Account Executive."

COMMUNITY RELATIONS COORDINATOR, NEWSPAPERS AND MAGAZINES

CAREER PROFILE

Duties: Act as liaison between a publication and the community; plan, organize, and develop programs to meet publication and community needs

Alternate Title(s): Community Affairs Coordinator; Community Relations Director; Community Affairs Director

Salary Range: $23,000 to $45,000+

Employment Prospects: Fair

Advancement Prospects: Good

Best Geographical Location(s): Large cities offer more opportunities.

Prerequisites:

Education or Training—College degree in public relations, journalism, English, liberal arts, or communications

Experience—Previous work with community groups is useful. Writing and publicity experience is helpful.

Special Skills and Personality Traits—Ability to work well with people; writing skills; communication skills; organizational skills; creative

CAREER LADDER

```
┌─────────────────────────────────────┐
│       Public Relations Director      │
└─────────────────────────────────────┘

┌─────────────────────────────────────┐
│   Community Relations Coordinator    │
└─────────────────────────────────────┘

┌─────────────────────────────────────┐
│      Other Position in Journalism,   │
│      Publicity, or Public Relations  │
└─────────────────────────────────────┘
```

Position Description

An individual working as a Community Relations Coordinator for a newspaper or magazine acts as a liaison between the publication for which he or she works and the community. His or her main function is to assess the needs of the community and find ways to meet them. People in this position have to organize, develop, and plan programs to satisfy local community requirements.

The Community Relations Coordinator has varied duties. He or she may look for specific problems in the community or may respond to local nonprofit organizations or individuals who need assistance. Part of the responsibility of the Community Relations Coordinator is meeting with various members of nonprofit groups and service organizations. Through these meetings the individual determines what, if anything, can be accomplished for each organization.

The Community Relations Coordinator must decide if causes are worthwhile, develop specific projects and ideas to help, locate volunteers to put the event together, and handle publicity and promotion to insure a successful program. The Community Relations Coordinator also works with local businesses, business associations, and business leaders to help increase business and commerce in the area.

The individual may learn about a family in the area who has no health insurance with a child who needs an expensive, life-saving operation. In this instance the coordinator might organize and advertise fund-raising programs through the publication in order to help raise money. The newspaper or magazine might sponsor auctions, fairs, dinners, baseball games, car washes, entertainment, etc. for the purpose of raising money for the cause. Alternatively, the coordinator might work with another organization to cosponsor events or run advertisements free of charge in the publication to help promote a program. In addition to working with local community groups, the coordinator may work with national nonprofit organizations.

Community Relations Coordinators (or community affairs coordinators, as they might be known) may design and implement annual events for the benefit of the entire community. They may, for example, sponsor, coordinate, and advertise a program such as a town block party, a health fair in conjunction with local hospitals, or cooking classes in conjunction with health associations. Whenever there is a crisis in the local area the Community Relations Coordinator is called upon to lend a hand through programs, publicity, or advertising support.

The person in this job is usually a community-minded individual. As the Community Relations Coordinator he or she represents the publication at many organization meetings. He or she may also belong to civic and/or service organizations such as the American Cancer Society, the American Heart Association, youth associations, hospital auxiliaries, Rotary, Kiwanis, 4-H, Girl Scouts, Boy Scouts, or educational boards.

As a Community Relations Coordinator the individual may oversee the design and ad copy for public service announcements (PSAs). He or she may also be responsible for the actual designing and/or writing of ads for the publication.

The Community Relations Coordinator may have to do quite a bit of creative, promotional writing. He or she spends a good portion of time writing press releases and publicity for events that will be sponsored by the publications, as well as composing business letters. Community Relations Coordinators might be responsible for making and updating lists of nonprofit groups in the area with names, addresses, and phone numbers to contact. They may also write booklets or leaflets about how to prepare organizational publicity for the publication and will often be called upon to write reports on the success of a community relations project.

Community Relations Coordinators should be outgoing. A lot of the work is done outside of the office. There are meetings to attend and business associates to visit. One may have to speak at organization meetings or at dinners and luncheons.

Depending on the size of the publication for which the individual works, he or she may act as the promotion coordinator or public relations director. While much of this job is done in a normal nine-to-five time slot, meetings and special projects and promotions may keep the individual out some evenings and weekends. The Community Relations Coordinator may be directly responsible to the director of publicity, general manager, or publisher, depending on the organization of the publication.

Salaries

Salaries for Community Relations Coordinators vary depending on the size of the publication, the location, and the experience of the individual. Someone working in this position at a daily newspaper or a small weekly magazine might start at $23,000 to $28,000. At larger publications or those in more metropolitan areas the Community Relations Coordinator might earn $45,000 or more.

Employment Prospects

Employment prospects are fair for Community Relations Coordinators working for publications. While there are numerous publications that relegate the duties of this position to the public relations, publicity, or promotion staff, many are beginning to see the importance and necessity of having a Community Relations Coordinator on staff.

Advancement Prospects

Advancement prospects for Community Relations Coordinators are good. Individuals can obtain positions in bigger, better-known publications. They might also become public relations directors at newspapers or go into public relations or community relations work for nonprofit groups, trade organizations, or corporations.

Education and Training

A college degree in public relations, journalism, English, liberal arts, or communications is useful to those aspiring to be Community Relations Coordinators. Seminars on public relations and publicity are also helpful.

Experience, Skills, and Personality Traits

Community Relations Coordinators should be community-minded and like to help people. People in these positions usually belong to civic and nonprofit groups and are the first to volunteer to help. Individuals should also be outgoing, aggressive, and articulate and have the ability to work well with people. Good writing, organizational, and planning skills are a must.

Community Relations Coordinators may have held a job in other newspaper or magazine positions previously or may have worked in publicity or public relations.

Unions and Associations

There are no unions to which Community Relations Coordinators must belong. Individuals in this field, however, may belong to various civic groups, service organizations, and/or nonprofit groups.

Tips for Entry

1. Become a member of various civic organizations and nonprofit groups such as the American Red Cross, the American Heart Association, the American Cancer Society, a hospital auxiliary, or school PTAs. Volunteer to do their publicity. This way you will start making

contacts in the field as well as getting to know the various media people in a community.

2. Visit editors, publishers, and personnel officers of newspapers and magazines and see if you can create a position even if one does not currently exist. If you can't talk them into a full-time position, see about a part-time job.

3. Internships are a great way to get your foot in the door. Many newspapers and magazines throughout the country offer internships and trainee positions.

4. Many newspapers and magazines have Web sites listing their employment opportunities.

5. Just because a position does not currently exist does not mean you cannot create one. If you see a need in a newspaper or magazine and they do not have a position, send a letter with your résumé suggesting the possibility. You just might get a call.

ADVERTISING ASSISTANT, BOOK PUBLISHING

CAREER PROFILE

Duties: Help advertising manager advertise books; write copy for book jackets, advertisements, sales letters, circulars, and catalogs; act as a buffer for the advertising manager

Alternate Title(s): Ad Assistant; Advertising Trainee

Salary Range: $23,000 to $29,000+

Employment Prospects: Fair

Advancement Prospects: Good

Best Geographical Location(s): New York, Chicago, Boston, and other large cities may offer opportunities.

Prerequisites:

Education or Training—College background in business, liberal arts, journalism, art, or advertising needed

Experience—Writing and advertising experience helpful, but not always necessary

Special Skills and Personality Traits—Good writing skills; creative; artistic ability; ability to type and use computer

CAREER LADDER

```
┌─────────────────────────────────┐
│      Advertising Manager         │
└─────────────────────────────────┘

┌─────────────────────────────────┐
│      Advertising Assistant       │
└─────────────────────────────────┘

┌─────────────────────────────────┐
│  Entry Level Position, Intern,   │
│     or Secretarial Position      │
└─────────────────────────────────┘
```

Position Description

An Advertising Assistant working for a book publishing house assists the advertising manager and other members of the advertising department in selling books. Duties of an Advertising Assistant vary depending on the size of the publishing house and the number of people working in the advertising department.

If the house is small, and the only other employee in the department is an advertising manager, the Advertising Assistant might be expected to fulfill administrative duties such as typing letters, updating the returns from mail or ad campaigns, returning phone calls, keeping records of the cost of ads, and checking prices.

In a larger house where there is an advertising manager, receptionists, and administrative assistants, the Advertising Assistant would have many more diversified duties. In this case the individual would assist in more creative ways.

For example, an Advertising Assistant might be responsible for writing copy for book jackets. This could include the blurbs describing the book's contents or information about the author. To do this the individual may have to call and interview the author to gather information.

He or she might also be asked to write copy for sales letters, circulars, direct-mail pieces, and book catalogs. It is, therefore, important that the Assistant be able to write clearly, concisely, accurately, and with style.

The Advertising Assistant works with the advertising manager, learning how to budget the amount of money to be spent on each new book. For example, a book written by an author who has already written three best-sellers will have a bigger advertising budget than a book by a new author. Advertising is expensive, and publishers can't afford to spend a great deal of money on a book subject or author not proven to be in the best-seller class.

As advertising is so costly, the advertising manager might decide to do something called list advertising. This is a type of ad in which many different books from the publisher are listed, with a short description of each. If this type of advertising is used, the Assistant will be called upon to write the descriptions of the books.

At other times the Advertising Assistant writes copy for display ads for different types of publications. For example, he or she might have to write an ad for a book to go into a consumer publication, a specialty publication, and a trade journal. While the ads would be for the same book, the advertisement might be different because the periodicals are geared toward different audiences.

He or she learns how to read and use *Advertising Rate and Data,* the book that lists advertising rates for television, radio, magazines, and newspapers throughout the country. He or she also becomes familiar with rate cards, which tell all about prices of ads in a certain medium. At this time the individual learns the lingo of advertising—terms like *ad frequency* and *audience size.*

It is important that an Advertising Assistant know how to use a calculator and/or adding machine to check numbers and prices when working on advertising costs.

In certain positions the Advertising Assistant might also be responsible for laying out ads for which he or she has written copy or those created by the advertising manager.

Working in the advertising department, the Assistant may devise and/or design promotional material that will be used to advertise or sell books. Copy for materials such as the posters you see in bookstore windows, display racks, and flyers that can be given to customers must all be created and written.

At times the Advertising Assistant acts as a buffer for the advertising manager. For example, irate authors may call the advertising department demanding to know why their book wasn't advertised properly or wasn't advertised sufficiently.

The Advertising Assistant works closely with people in the sales, promotion, and publicity departments. Together they work toward the common goal of selling as many books as possible. The job can be quite stressful due to deadlines that must be met, ads that have to be designed, or budgets that must be maintained. Hours are not always the traditional nine to five. When work has to be finished, the Advertising Assistant must usually stay late with the rest of the department.

Salaries

Annual earnings for Advertising Assistants depend upon the size and location of the publishing house and the experience and responsibilities of the individual.

Salaries for Advertising Assistants can range from $23,000 for a beginner in a small company to $29,000 or more for an individual in a larger publishing house.

Employment Prospects

Employment prospects for Advertising Assistants are fair. Most of the jobs are in New York City, where the majority of book publishing houses are. Jobs can also be located in Chicago, Boston, and other large cities.

Advancement Prospects

Advancement prospects are good for Advertising Assistants. After a reasonable amount of experience an individual can often find a job as an advertising manager. Other Advertising Assistants advance their career by working in advertising agencies or other advertising fields.

Education and Training

Advertising Assistants should have some college background. Majors might include business, liberal arts, journalism, art, or advertising. Seminars and courses on advertising and the book field would be useful both for knowledge and for making contacts.

Experience, Skills, and Personality Traits

The Advertising Assistant should have good writing skills. Creativity with ad copy and/or layout is helpful. Typing skills and the ability to use a calculator and/or adding machine are useful. Math skills to estimate and keep to budget are additionally beneficial.

A person in this position must deal with the stress of meeting deadlines and writing and designing ads. Knowledge of the book business is helpful for the individual's career advancement as well as in the job at hand.

Unions and Associations

Advertising Assistants working in book publishing houses may belong to any of a number of trade associations that can help the individual get together with others in the same field and that offer professional guidance and training. Organizations include the Publisher's Ad Club (PAC), the American Advertising Federation (AAF), and the Direct Marketing Association, Inc. (DMA), among others.

Tips for Entry

1. Jobs in this field can sometimes be found in the classified section of newspapers in areas where there are publishing houses. The *New York Times* Sunday classified section is a good place to start. Look under "Advertising" or "Publishing."

2. Send your résumé to various publishing houses. You can find their names and addresses by looking in *Writers' Digest or Literary Marketplace.*

3. *Publishers Weekly,* a trade publication, lists job openings.

4. Attend a seminar or convention put on by an organization that deals with the book trade, such as the American Booksellers Association or the American Library Association to make contacts.

PUBLICITY ASSISTANT, BOOK PUBLISHING

CAREER PROFILE

Duties: Assist publicity director in getting publicity for newly released books; compile press kits; write press releases; send out review books; book authors on talk shows

Alternate Title(s): Press Assistant; Publicity Trainee

Salary Range: $23,000 to $30,000+

Employment Prospects: Fair

Advancement Prospects: Fair

Best Geographical Location(s): New York, Boston, Chicago.

Prerequisites:

Education or Training—College degree in liberal arts, English, journalism, or public relations

Experience—Writing experience helpful

Special Skills and Personality Traits—Creative; persuasive; articulate; ability to write well; computer skills

CAREER LADDER

```
┌─────────────────────────────┐
│     Publicity Director      │
└─────────────────────────────┘

┌─────────────────────────────┐
│     Publicity Assistant     │
└─────────────────────────────┘

┌─────────────────────────────┐
│     Intern or Entry Level   │
└─────────────────────────────┘
```

Position Description

A Publicity Assistant working at a book publishing company has an interesting, active job. The main responsibility of the individual is to work with the publicity director, helping him or her publicize new books as they come off the press.

The Publicity Assistant works with the director doing a variety of jobs. One important area in which the assistant becomes involved is making sure that press and media lists are in order. Names and addresses of people who write book reviews, magazine and newspaper editors, television and radio producers, and other important individuals must be put on this list. As people that work in the different media change jobs frequently, the list must constantly be updated. The individual must also update lists of specialty reviewers, such as music reviewers, food editors, and craft editors.

Sending out review copies of books is another important duty. The Publicity Assistant must check with the publicity director to make sure which people on the list are to receive review copies. Those on the list who don't receive a review copy usually receive either a press kit or a press release.

Publicity Assistants must also make sure that review copies and press kits are sent to publications in the book trade. These copies must get to the publications in a timely fashion, as most magazines have tight deadlines. If the review copy is received too late, the review might not get into the current issue of the publication—or, even worse, might not get in at all.

When the Publicity Assistant sends review copies, he or she includes a release slip that indicates the release date of the book. A note requesting copies of the review if and when it appears is also usually included.

In certain publishing companies the Publicity Assistant might develop a questionnaire for authors to answer. At other companies the assistant just sends the questionnaire or talks to and interviews authors who have written books for the company. In this way he or she can gather material for press releases. He or she usually asks the author about the availability of local publications, radio stations, and television stations. A press release with a local slant can then be prepared and sent out. Many assistants compile complete biographies on their authors, including all reviews of the book.

At times the Publicity Assistant may put together press kits for a new book. He or she includes a review copy, adds a news release about the book and some information on the author, and puts in a photograph of the writer or a picture of the book jacket.

The Publicity Assistant may write press releases for new books or may just gather information and give it to the publicity director to write. The individual may also fill requests from media for information on authors.

As a Publicity Assistant, an individual works with the publicity director, trying to come up with interesting, unique ways to publicize the book. This might include anything from having interesting photos taken for newspaper placement to developing an angle that will help gain required publicity. The art of finding a hook or good angle for a press release is in locating some fact, or in some way presenting the material, such that an editor or talent coordinator is moved not merely to mention the book, but to develop an entire column. If an article about the book or an interview with the author gets national exposure, it will usually sell many thousands (if not tens of thousands) of additional books.

In certain book publishing houses Publicity Assistants submit books to organizations for awards or other prizes. The Pulitzer Prize is probably the most prestigious, but there are others. Obtaining an award or prize gains additional publicity and boosts book sales dramatically.

Booking appearances on radio and television talk, variety, and news shows is yet another duty of the Publicity Assistant. While much of the contact work is done by the publicity director, the Publicity Assistant often sends out the press kits and review copies and makes call backs to talent coordinators in an effort to obtain talk show appearances that will plug the book. It is essential for the assistant to get to know as many talk show producers, executives, and talent coordinators as possible. A publicity person with these contacts will always be employable.

The Publicity Assistant is expected to accompany the author on a personal appearance tour to various cities. The Publicity Assistant helps arrange press conferences for authors. He or she might be required to book the room, arrange for the refreshments, send out invitations, call people to make sure that they are attending, and set up the room. The assistant might also help set up bookstore autograph sessions (at which the author meets with bookstore patrons and signs their copies of his or her book).

The Publicity Assistant works closely with almost every department in the company. At one time or another he or she will probably deal with editors and people in the advertising, marketing, promotion, and sales departments. The assistant usually keeps the other departments informed about what the publicity department is planning for a new book release. In this way, all departments will supplement and bolster each other.

Salaries

Annual earnings for Publicity Assistants working in publishing houses depend upon the size and location of the company. Salaries can start at $23,000 a year and may, in some positions in larger companies, reach $30,000 or more.

Employment Prospects

Employment prospects are fair for Publicity Assistants who want to live in New York City, where the majority of book publishing houses are located. Other cities such as Boston and Chicago also have a number of book publishing houses. There are a number of publicity firms that offer freelance jobs for entry level positions assisting independent publicists who augment the publicity departments in book companies.

Advancement Prospects

Advancement prospects are good for Publicity Assistants. As people leave jobs the Assistant is often moved into the publicity director's position. Once a Publicity Assistant has gained the necessary experience and made valuable media contacts, he or she can usually locate a better position.

Education and Training

A college degree in liberal arts, public relations, English, or journalism is preferred. Look for seminars put on by book associations or public relations groups in order to make contacts and get additional training.

Experience, Skills, and Personality Traits

It is necessary for a Publicity Assistant to know how to type accurately. While there might be a secretary to help out, often much of the office work is typed by the assistant. Computer skills are imperative. The individual must also be creative, persuasive, and write well. Much contact with media people is over the phone, so an articulate approach and a good telephone manner are essential.

Unions and Associations

A Publicity Assistant may belong to any of a number of publicity or public relations organizations. The most widely recognized is the Public Relations Society of America (PRSA).

Tips for Entry

1. Buy the Sunday edition of the *New York Times.* Jobs in this field are listed under "Publishing."
2. Look in *Writer's Market or Literary Marketplace* for names and addresses of publishers to whom you can send résumés.
3. There are employment agencies that deal specifically in jobs in the publishing industry. If you decide to try this, make sure you check out who pays the fee if you get the job—you or the company that hires you.
4. Check out opportunities online at career employment Web sites such as Monster.com and Hotjobs.com.

FREELANCE AND CONSULTING

PUBLIC RELATIONS GENERALIST

CAREER PROFILE

Duties: Develop public relations and publicity campaigns; write press releases, annual reports, and speeches; design promotions; place clients on television and radio

Alternate Title(s): PR Rep; Public Relations Representative; Public Relations Specialist; Publicity Man or Woman; PR Freelancer

Salary Range: $22,000 to $200,000+

Employment Prospects: Good

Advancement Prospects: Good

Best Geographical Location(s): Positions may be located throughout the country.

Prerequisites:

Education or Training—College degree in public relations, communications, English, journalism, or liberal arts, useful; seminars on public relations, publicity, and marketing helpful

Experience—Journalism, publicity, and/or public relations experience necessary

Special Skills and Personality Traits—Excellent writing, communication, and organizational skills; aggressive; articulate; good graphic sense; ability to deal with stress; computer skills

CAREER LADDER

```
┌─────────────────────────────────┐
│   Public Relations Generalist   │
│   with More and Bigger Clients   │
│      or V.P. or Partner          │
│   in Public Relations Agency    │
└─────────────────────────────────┘

┌─────────────────────────────────┐
│   Public Relations Generalist   │
└─────────────────────────────────┘

┌─────────────────────────────────┐
│  Public Relations Representative │
│      or Journalism Position      │
└─────────────────────────────────┘
```

Position Description

Public Relations Generalists may work for any type of client. Individuals freelancing in this field may work for political candidates, health care facilities, corporations, trade associations, retail businesses, schools, nonprofit groups, and other organizations. They also might work for a public relations consulting firm. They can have one client or many.

The Public Relations Generalist has varied responsibilities depending on the type of client or clients he or she has. The individual may be retained to develop promotions for a client. He or she may also implement them and/or design campaign budgets.

The Public Relations Generalist might be hired to write copy for brochures, leaflets, booklets, instructional manuals, or advertisements. Other types of writing responsibilities include press releases, biographies, annual reports, and speeches. Public Relations people may be retained to put together press kits or to write feature articles or case histories.

A Public Relations Generalist could be hired by a major corporation or other business to handle one or all of its public relations responsibilities. He or she might serve as a spokesperson for the client or may just advise the client on how to respond to the press or other media.

Some Public Relations Generalists may be responsible for placing clients on television and radio talk, variety, and news shows. They must come up with unique angles on clients, contact show producers or talent coordinators, send media kits, call and recall contact people, and finally book clients on interview shows. The individual might be responsible for escorting clients to and from shows or working with the client beforehand preparing for the media exposure.

Public Relations Generalists must be adept at all facets of public relations. In one day an individual may plan an entire public relations campaign for one client, write press releases for a different client, field media questions for still another client, and design a brochure for yet another. Another day may find the individual busy implementing an important promotion, going to a client meeting with the vice president of a corporation, and setting up a press conference. Work days are rarely dull.

Freelance Public Relations Generalists may work in their own office, from their home, or in a client's office or plant. Depending on the setup, worked out at the beginning of the client contact, the individual may pay for his or her office supplies and equipment, may be reimbursed for these expenses, or may have the equipment supplied. The individual might also be reimbursed for such expenses as paper, stamps, envelopes, and toll calls.

One of the drawbacks of freelancing is that the individual does not usually receive any type of personal fringe benefits. He or she must pay for his or her own health insurance or dental and medical bills.

The individual in this position must be able to deal with the stress of keeping clients, finding projects, and organizing everything that must be accomplished. While the freelance Public Relations Generalist is his or her own boss, so to speak, he or she is ultimately responsible to the people who hired him or her for various projects.

Salaries

Earnings can vary greatly for freelance Public Relations Generalists. Individuals may get paid a set fee on a per project basis or may get paid by the hour. They might also be paid a monthly retainer. It is impossible to estimate rates. Hourly rates can vary between $25 and $500 plus an hour, depending on the individual's experience and reputation in the field. Monthly retainers can run between $250 a month and $10,000 a month, depending on the client, the individual, and his or her responsibilities. Those who have a number of good clients can earn from $40,000 to $200,000 or more annually.

Employment Prospects

Employment prospects are good for the individual who is aggressive and has built up a good reputation for him- or herself. The freelance Public Relations Generalist must go out and look for clients, have clients come to him or her, and be recommended by others in order to earn money and stay employed. For some, this is easier in a large city. Other people feel that they can more easily build a good reputation in a smaller community.

Advancement Prospects

Advancement prospects for freelance Public Relations Generalists are good. Individuals must constantly seek out new clients. This may be done through word of mouth or advertising. If the individual is good at what he or she does, he or she will move up the career ladder by getting more and more clients and by obtaining clients who pay bigger and better fees.

Individuals might also advance by joining a public relations firm or agency in a top position or as a partner.

Education and Training

Individuals who plan on freelancing in this field should have a college degree. Majors might include public relations, English, journalism, communications, or liberal arts. Potential freelancers might also take a number of business courses.

Seminars and other courses relevant to public relations, publicity, and marketing will also be useful.

Experience, Skills, and Personality Traits

The freelance Public Relations Generalist should have a knowledge of public relations and of business. The more skills he or she has, the more employable he or she will be. All types of writing and communications skills are needed. This includes the ability to write not only press releases and feature stories, but newsletters, speeches, ad copy, brochures, and direct-mail pieces. Public Relations Generalists should have good media contacts or the ability to make them.

The individual needs to be aggressive, articulate, well-groomed, and well-spoken. He or she must sell him- or herself to potential clients. A good phone manner is essential.

The freelance Public Relations Generalist should be organized and able to deal with many different projects at once. Knowledge of research is useful. An ability to work under stress is necessary.

Office skills may be needed if the individual does not have access to a secretary. Computer skills are essential.

Unions and Associations

Freelance Public Relations Generalists do not belong to any union. Individuals in this type of work usually belong to a number of trade associations. These organizations help the individual make contacts needed to attract clients, hone his or her skills through seminars and conferences, and keep him or her up to date on industry happenings through trade journals.

One of the biggest professional organizations for PR people is the Public Relations Society of America (PRSA). Individuals might belong to any of a number of other organizations, including specialized PR groups (see Appendix under "Trade Associations and Unions" for specialized organizations).

Tips for Entry

1. Try to get some type of public relations experience before you strike out on your own.

2. Potential clients will want to know your track record. If you don't have one yet, try volunteering your services to a nonprofit or community group. When people see how effective you are, you will begin to attract clients.

3. Have professional business cards made up and pass them out to everyone.

4. You might consider taking a small ad in a local newspaper advertising your specialty.

5. You may want to take a part-time job in public relations to get some experience before you jump right into freelancing.

6. Offer to speak about public relations and publicity at meetings and events. This will help people in the area to know about you. Good places to start include Kiwanis, Rotary, business and professional groups, and other civic organizations.

FREELANCE SPEECHWRITER

CAREER PROFILE

Duties: Write speeches for executives or other individuals in business, industry, nonprofit groups, or politics

Alternate Title(s): Writer

Salary Range: $23,000 to $150,000+

Employment Prospects: Poor

Advancement Prospects: Fair

Best Geographical Location(s): Positions may be located throughout the country.

Prerequisites:

Education or Training—College background or bachelor's degree useful

Experience—Speechwriting while in school helpful

Special Skills and Personality Traits—Excellent writing skills; good style; knowledge of public speaking; sense of humor

CAREER LADDER

```
┌─────────────────────────────────────┐
│        Staff Speechwriter            │
│    or Freelance Speechwriter         │
│   with More Prestigious Clients      │
└─────────────────────────────────────┘

┌─────────────────────────────────────┐
│        Freelance Speechwriter        │
└─────────────────────────────────────┘

┌─────────────────────────────────────┐
│      Public Relations Position       │
│         or Entry Level               │
└─────────────────────────────────────┘
```

Position Description

A Freelance Speechwriter prepares speeches for individuals in business, industry, politics, and trade and nonprofit organizations. The speechwriter may be retained by the chief executive officer (CEO) of a corporation, the board president of a hospital or university, or any other individual who might be required to give speeches. The Freelance Speechwriter may write speeches for individuals who must appear in public or give presentations or news conferences.

Freelance Speechwriters are hired by other individuals for a number of reasons. An executive might look to a speechwriter because time and work demands placed on him or her don't allow the time to prepare a speech. Another individual might not have the ability to put thoughts down on paper for a presentation in an interesting, clear, flowing order. Still another might serve as spokesperson for a company but might not be responsible for the preparation of a speech or its content.

In order for the speechwriter to prepare a speech for an individual, he or she has to do some background work. The individual must do some research to select an appropriate subject and direction. To do this, the speechwriter might talk directly with the speaker or visit libraries, trade sources, or people in the business itself.

The speechwriter must become familiar with the speech giver's style by looking over previous speeches of the individual and discussing style and nuances with the speaker. The speechwriter must also get to know the personality of the speaker so that when he or she writes the speech it can be tailored to the individual.

The speechwriter must learn the main presentation points that the speaker wants to get across. The individual must also know to what type of audience the speech will be geared. An in-house speech, for example, would be written differently than a speech for the general public.

The writer will have to know how to format the speech. The individual must take into account the length and timing of the presentation and the contents. The writer must also keep in mind that the body of the speech should sound like the speaker in its words and style.

After the speechwriter has completed a rough draft of the speech it must be reviewed with the speaker. At this time changes, additions, deletions, etc. can be put into the copy. The speechwriter may also work with the speaker, rehearsing the preliminary presentation to locate any rough spots or difficult words and passages. If the speaker is not comfortable saying the words, they must be changed.

The speechwriter must give the speech to the speaker in an easy-to-read style. This might mean typing the entire speech on index cards or on paper using large type. The writer might just type key points on cards so the speaker can speak "off the cuff." The individual might provide the speech to another party who will type it into a Teleprompter.

Depending on the type of speech the writer is retained to prepare, he or she might also be responsible for preparing the speaker to handle questions and answers that might be asked of the speaker in response to the speech. The individual may develop a list of potential questions and answers so that the speaker is comfortable with the situation.

Freelance Speechwriters may work on one speech at a time or may be involved in a number of different projects. Individuals must relate well to the executives who are the majority of speakers and understand their thought patterns.

Individuals in this type of position do not have normal work hours. They might meet with executives or other potential speakers at any time of the day or after regular business hours. Freelance Speechwriters can work on speeches during the day or may work long into the night to develop the perfect speech.

Freelance Speechwriters are responsible directly to the person who hired them to write the presentation. This could be the speaker or may be the speaker's superior.

Salaries

Earnings for Freelance Speechwriters are hard to estimate. Compensation is usually paid on a per project basis. There are also individuals who are hired to write a number of speeches for a company or who are retained on a monthly basis.

Annual earnings for individuals depend on the number of speeches they write, the number of clients they have, and their prestige. More prestigious, better-known clients usually pay more to have their speeches prepared.

Individuals might earn between $23,000 and $150,000 or more. A fairly successful Freelance Speechwriter can earn between $35,000 and $50,000 yearly. Those who work with well-known clients, such as politicians, might earn $60,000 to $150,000 plus annually.

Employment Prospects

Individuals who have a flair for speechwriting are always in demand. In order for Freelance Speechwriters to find employment, however, they must find clients to write speeches for. Individuals just starting out as speechwriters may have a better chance of obtaining clients if they are in a less populous area where they are better known. Those with experience find more success in larger cities where there are more corporations, businesses, industries, and associations.

Those who are adept at writing may find clients while they are still in school or after graduation.

Advancement Prospects

Freelance Speechwriters can advance their careers in a number of ways. Good speechwriters are always sought out by others in need of the service. Individuals might obtain more prestigious clients, such as well-known political candidates, or may climb the career ladder by becoming a staff speech-

writer for a major corporation. Others may move up by becoming public relations directors in industry and business.

Education and Training

While a Freelance Speechwriter is not required to have a college background, it certainly helps. A bachelor's degree with a major in public relations, English, journalism, communications, or liberal arts will be useful. Individuals might also be interested in taking classes and seminars in public speaking and speechwriting to help hone their skills.

Experience, Skills, and Personality Traits

Freelance Speechwriters need excellent writing skills. Individuals should possess an ability to write with style and humor. No one wants to hear or present a boring speech. An understanding of public speaking is necessary.

Professionals in this field should keep up on current events and other happenings. A knowledge of research methods is also essential for the speechwriter to fully understand a subject that is not totally familiar.

Individuals should be articulate and good at dealing with people. The ability to work on several projects at once is necessary, as is the ability to set and keep to time frames.

Many who begin careers in speechwriting prepared speeches in high school, college, and after graduation for nonprofit groups.

Unions and Associations

There are no particular bargaining unions or trade associations for Freelance Speechwriters to belong to. Depending on the type of clients an individual works with, he or she might join specific trade associations. Individuals might also belong to public relations groups such as the Public Relations Society of America (PRSA), which offers professional support and guidance.

Tips for Entry

1. Read as much as you can on all subjects, especially current affairs. This will help you gain insight into what is happening in the world.
2. Write as much as you can. Hone your skills in all facets of writing.
3. Attend writing seminars. This will give you added confidence as well as building a contact list.
4. Send brochures or tasteful flyers to major corporations, industries, and associations advising them of your service.
5. Volunteer to write a speech for a local political candidate or a community leader. The best way to increase your business in this field is by word of mouth.
6. Join community groups and volunteer organizations as well as any trade associations you can. Other members of these groups will need your service and feel they know you better if you belong to their organization.

FREELANCE COPYWRITER

CAREER PROFILE

Duties: Write copy for advertisements, articles, sales letters, speeches, booklets, manuals, training films, press releases, etc.

Alternate Title(s): Writer

Salary Range: $23,000 to $150,000+

Employment Prospects: Good

Advancement Prospects: Fair

Best Geographical Location(s): Client possibilities may be located throughout the country.

Prerequisites:

Education or Training—College degree with major in English, liberal arts, communications, journalism, advertising, public relations, or marketing useful

Experience—Writing experience helpful

Special Skills and Personality Traits—Creative; excellent writing skills; articulate; organizational skills, ability to work alone

CAREER LADDER

```
┌─────────────────────────────────┐
│   Freelance Copywriter with     │
│  Larger Clients or Copywriter   │
│     in Advertising or Public    │
│        Relations Agency         │
└─────────────────────────────────┘

┌─────────────────────────────────┐
│      Freelance Copywriter       │
└─────────────────────────────────┘

┌─────────────────────────────────┐
│     Journalism Position         │
│    or Copywriter Trainee        │
└─────────────────────────────────┘
```

Position Description

A Freelance Copywriter may be hired to write copy for almost any product, service, idea, or event. He or she may work with advertising agencies, public relations agencies, newspapers, television stations, magazines, manufacturing companies, corporations, stores, shops, printers, publishing companies, nonprofit organizations, and municipalities, as well as with individuals.

The Freelance Copywriter may work from his or her home or office or in the office of a client. Once retained or hired by a client, he or she is responsible for developing creative ways to say what the client wants to say. The copywriter must be able to understand the concept the client is trying to convey and be able to put the concept clearly into words.

Freelance Copywriters have a lot of meetings with potential clients. During these meetings the individual finds out as much information as possible. The client may have a rough draft of what he or she wants to say. Or the client might have samples of styles of work that should be followed. The copywriter must also determine if the client wants as many or as few words as possible in the piece of copy. Other things he or she might want to find out are what the deadline is, who should be contacted for approval, and how long a commercial will be (if the copy is for a television or radio ad).

During this meeting the copywriter and the client should agree on a fee for the work completed. In some situations the individual is paid up front. In most instances, however, he or she is paid after final approval.

The Freelance Copywriter hired to write copy for advertisements may be responsible for all the ad copy or for just the headline, text, or body of the ad. The individual may be hired to write copy for print ads as well as scripts for broadcast commercials. Depending on his or her ability and skills, the copywriter may also be asked to lay out the way the words should appear in relation to the graphics of the project.

He or she must constantly develop and create words that will catch the eye of the public. In cases where the individual is working on copy for advertisements, his or her main function is to make the copy so appealing that it attracts attention, thus attracting customers.

The individual must often obtain additional background information on writing assignments and secure current development information through research and interviews. He or she must continually review advertising trends, consumer surveys, and other data to formulate the way he or she should write the copy.

Freelance Copywriters may also be hired to write the copy for articles, bulletins, sales letters, direct-mail pieces, speeches, booklets, informational leaflets, or instructional manuals. They might also be retained to write slogans for a product or a company. Individuals could be hired to write scripts for training films, instructional movies, press releases, blurbs for book jackets, or virtually anything else.

After the individual completes a rough draft he or she usually gives it to the client for approval before moving on. In this way the copywriter is sure he or she is moving along on the same track as the client. If the client is not happy with the work at this point, the copywriter must correct and revise the copy until the client is satisfied.

The individual must be able to work on several projects at once or he or she will not be able to make a good living freelancing. The Freelance Copywriter must be flexible and creative. He or she must be able to write the dialogue for a radio commercial as well as he or she can write the copy for a brochure or leaflet. While the Freelance Copywriter is, in essence, his or her own boss, he or she is ultimately responsible to the individual who did the hiring. This might be anyone from an account executive to a small store owner who has retained the individual to write an ad.

Salaries

Income for Freelance Copywriters is dependent on a number of factors. Earnings vary depending on the number and type of clients an individual has and how successful he or she is.

Copywriters may be compensated by working on a per project basis or may work on an hourly rate. Individuals may also be retained to do a certain amount of work each month.

Earnings for Freelance Copywriters can average between $23,000 and $150,000 or more annually.

Employment Prospects

Employment prospects for Freelance Copywriters are good. There is an abundance of opportunities for individuals with a flair for writing. Freelancers may work with almost any kind of corporate client as well as nonprofit organizations. Often newspapers, magazines, and radio and television stations need someone on an irregular basis. Potential clients may need someone to work on a per project basis instead of on staff and therefore use freelancers.

Advancement Prospects

Advancement for a Freelance Copywriter can come in a couple of ways. Prospects are fair. The individual may start getting more and bigger clients. This will lead to a constant flow of work and higher earnings. Another method of advancement might be for the Freelance Copywriter to obtain a full-time position at a corporation, organization, or agency.

Education and Training

Educational requirements for Freelance Copywriters include a college degree. Possible majors are communications, journalism, English, advertising, public relations, and marketing.

Since the success of a Freelance Copywriter is dependent on his or her flexibility to do all types of projects, the individual might also take courses or seminars in all facets of writing from advertising copywriting to press releases; from script writing to developing speeches.

Experience, Skills, and Personality Traits

An individual in this position needs an excellent, creative style of writing. He or she should also be persuasive and articulate. The Freelance Copywriter needs the ability to deal with stress and pressure. Individuals should have the ability to work on their own for long periods of time and be extremely organized.

Freelance Copywriters should have a good knowledge of the advertising industry as well as an understanding of business in general. Experience in any facet of writing is useful.

Unions and Associations

Freelance Copywriters who write scripts for television or radio may belong to the Writers Guild of America (WGA), a bargaining union for television, radio, and film scriptwriters. Individuals may belong to any of a number of different trade associations, including the American Advertising Federation (AAF), Direct Marketing Creative Guild, the American Marketing Association (AMA), the Advertising Club of New York, the Advertising Research Foundation (ARF), Advertising Women of New York, Inc. (AWNY), the One Club, and the Public Relations Society of America (PRSA).

Tips for Entry

1. Get as much experience writing as you can. Write for your school newspaper if you still are in school. If you're not, try to get experience writing for your local community newspaper.
2. You might want to get some experience writing copy in an advertising or public relations agency. If you can find a trainee or intern position, go for it.
3. Put together a portfolio of work you have done. Include anything that has received exposure. If you are just starting out, do samples for your portfolio book.
4. Make up professional business cards and give them to everyone you know. Leave them in businesses if you can. Tack them up in supermarkets and department stores.
5. Join some trade associations. These will help give you moral support as well as making important contacts.
6. You might consider taking a small ad in your local paper announcing your new business venture. Remember to make it creative. If you can't catch people's eye with your own ad, you won't be able to do it for anyone else.

FREELANCE GRAPHIC ARTIST

CAREER PROFILE

Duties: Design art and copy layouts for businesses, industries, and agencies

Alternate Title(s): Freelance Commercial Artist; Graphic Artist; Commercial Artist; Artist

Salary Range: $23,000 to $150,000+

Employment Prospects: Good

Advancement Prospects: Fair

Best Geographical Location(s): Opportunities may be located throughout the country.

Prerequisites:

Education or Training—Art school training or college education with major in art helpful

Experience—Experience in advertising or commercial art useful

Special Skills and Personality Traits—Creative; artistic ability; good sense of design; commercial art skills; aggressiveness; computer skills

CAREER LADDER

```
┌─────────────────────────────────────────┐
│      Freelance Graphic Artist            │
│   with More Clients and Bigger,          │
│  Better Projects and Fees or Full-time   │
│   Position as Artist or Art Direction    │
│     in Agency, Business, or Industry     │
└─────────────────────────────────────────┘

┌─────────────────────────────────────────┐
│        Freelance Graphic Artist          │
└─────────────────────────────────────────┘

┌─────────────────────────────────────────┐
│     Illustrator or Artist in Agency      │
│              or Student                  │
└─────────────────────────────────────────┘
```

Position Description

A Freelance Graphic Artist designs art and copy layouts on an independent basis for businesses, industries, and agencies. Among the clients the artist may serve are publications, book companies, printers, record companies, department stores, advertising agencies, public relations agencies, hospitals, municipalities, schools, museums, trade associations, hotels, entertainment complexes, and corporations.

A successful Freelance Graphic Artist is talented in many artistic areas. The artist who is creative and can draw, sketch, do lettering, and cartoon has more opportunities to obtain clients then one who specializes in just one facet of art.

The artist should have a good understanding of advertising and business. Many freelancers in this field find a large portion of their clients require advertising design. The individual should be able to develop a creative design for an ad and have a working knowledge of layout. He or she should be able to choose and coordinate the best graphics for the copy.

Freelance Graphic Artists are often hired to design logos and trademarks for businesses or other industries. The logo or trademark is the symbol that identifies a product or company. The artist may draw rough sketches of a number of different symbols until he or she finds one the client likes. After the client approves one of the rough drafts of the logo the artist finishes the project, adding just the right color, type size, and style.

It is important for the Freelance Graphic Artist to know a considerable amount about type faces, sizes, and styles. While the possibilities are endless, the individual must know what will look the most effective on paper.

Other types of work the Freelance Graphic Artist might become involved with include illustrating fashions; designing packaging; hand lettering; painting or drawing graphic materials; designing book jackets; and designing, laying out, and preparing for printing booklets, pamphlets, brochures, and posters.

People who work freelance must continually seek out new clients and projects. Sometimes there is an abundance of work, while at other times there is almost nothing coming in. The up-and-down income flow is something that must be considered. Individuals must be able to deal with this and should have the ability to deal with stress and pressure when there are tight deadlines to be met.

Salaries

It is almost impossible to estimate the annual income of a Freelance Graphic Artist. Earnings depend on a number of factors. These include the number of clients the individual has and the number, size, and prestige of the projects he or she does for those clients.

Earnings also depend on the amount or fee the artist charges for work completed. Graphic artists may work on an hourly basis, per project, or on a monthly retainer.

Graphic artists who are just beginning their freelancing career can have annual earnings of $23,000 to $30,000. Individuals who are successful can have yearly incomes of $45,000 to $150,000 or more.

Employment Prospects

A creative, aggressive individual should have no trouble building up a freelance business. There are unlimited opportunities for Freelance Graphic Artists in most communities and cities. It is important to note that being in the right place at the right time also helps. A plan to secure clients is very important, too.

Advancement Prospects

There are a number of ways a Freelance Graphic Artist can advance his or her career.

If the individual wants to remain a freelancer, advancement means obtaining more clients and bigger, better-paying projects. Many graphic artists freelance until they can find a full-time position. Advancement for these individuals would mean a full-time job as an artist or art director in an agency or in the advertising department of a newspaper, corporation, or department store.

Education and Training

While a Freelance Graphic Artist is not required to have a college degree or a formal education, it sometimes helps. One reason is that the individual may desire to seek a job at some time during his or her career that would require a degree. Another reason is that a bachelor's degree from a college with a major in art, art school training, and/or art classes help the individual hone skills and become a more well-rounded artist. The person will also have an opportunity to make professional contacts.

Experience, Skills, and Personality Traits

Freelance Graphic Artists need the ability to work on their own. They set their own time frames to get projects done. A knowledge of running a business is essential.

Individuals in this field should be very creative and have a great deal of artistic ability and a good sense of design. Graphic artists need the ability to demonstrate "commerciability" in their work.

The artist should know how to do pasteups, layouts, mechanicals, typography, photography, and color. Drawing and illustration skills are a must. An understanding of advertising is necessary. A background in advertising or some form of commercial art is needed in order to build up a good freelance business. This might come from working in an advertising agency or in the advertising department of a newspaper, department store, or corporation. Computer skills are also required.

Freelance people need to be aggressive and have confidence in themselves and their work.

Unions and Associations

Freelance Graphic Artists do not belong to any type of bargaining union. They may join trade associations to learn more about their craft, make contacts, or attend seminars and courses offered by the organizations. These include the American Advertising Federation (AAF), the Art Directors Club, Inc. (ADC), the One Club, and the Society of Illustrators, among others.

Tips for Entry

1. Join trade associations and other organizations where you can meet others in your field and get support and guidance. Attending professional seminars will help you make useful contacts.
2. Potential clients will want to see samples of your work. Put together a good portfolio. Make it neat, creative, and diversified.
3. When you complete a project for a client, ask for a written reference. Many people are wary of using freelancers because they're not sure the project will get finished on time or be completed satisfactorily. The best way to get new clients is by word of mouth from other satisfied customers.
4. Make up professional business cards and give them to everyone. You might also print up flyers or brochures and send them to local businesses. Be sure they are creative and well done.
5. If you are just starting your freelance business, you might consider placing a display ad in your local newspaper on a regular basis. Make sure it is creative.

PLACEMENT SPECIALIST

CAREER PROFILE

Duties: Place clients on radio and television shows; schedule media tours; prepare clients for interviews; arrange for clients to be interviewed for print media

Alternate Title(s): Placement Professional

Salary Range: $23,000 to $200,000+

Employment Prospects: Fair

Advancement Prospects: Fair

Best Geographical Location(s): Positions may be located throughout the country.

Prerequisites:

Education or Training—A college background is useful, but not always necessary.

Experience—Experience in publicity, public relations, advertising, or selling is helpful.

Special Skills and Personality Traits—Good phone manner; persuasive; articulate; good communication skills; excellent writing skills

CAREER LADDER

```
┌─────────────────────────────────────┐
│  Placement Specialist for Prestigious│
│       Clients or Press Agent         │
│      or Publicist in Large Agency    │
└─────────────────────────────────────┘

┌─────────────────────────────────────┐
│       Placement Specialist           │
└─────────────────────────────────────┘

┌─────────────────────────────────────┐
│        Publicity Assistant           │
│       or Press Agent Trainee         │
└─────────────────────────────────────┘
```

Position Description

A Placement Specialist is an individual whose main function is to place people as guests on television and radio shows. The individual might also arrange for clients to be interviewed for print media. There are television talk shows throughout the country. There are television talk, news, and variety programs. There is also an abundance of radio news and talk shows on the airwaves today, with more being scheduled every month. These shows must have guests booked on a constant basis.

The Placement Specialist (or placement professional, as he or she is frequently called) may work for any of a variety of different types of clients. He or she may work for celebrities such as movie stars, television actors and actresses, singers, recording acts, dancers, musicians, or other show business personalities. The individual might place book authors, magazine writers, political figures, and speakers.

The placement professional may arrange interviews for people who are not well known. The individual might place doctors, lawyers, health care professionals, trade association directors, etc. He or she might also place spokespeople for corporate clients. If a Placement Specialist is good at the job, the individual can place almost anyone or anything on a broadcast interview show.

The individual must decide whether the client should be placed on a local, syndicated, national, or cable show. While most clients want to get on Jay Leno, David Letterman, or *Good Morning America,* this is not always feasible. The Placement Specialist must look at the client objectively and make a decision about what kind of shows he or she can book the client on.

Local shows are television or radio shows that have a local listening or viewing audience. There is a difference, however, between small-market local and major-market local. New York City is an example of a major local broadcast market. Kingston, N.Y., is an example of a small local broadcast market. The individual usually finds it easier to place guests on shows in small local markets than in larger local markets.

Placement Specialists often find that syndicated shows are good places to place clients. These are shows bought by local stations that may be shown in a number of different locations. There can be small syndicated shows that go to only two or three areas and large ones, such as *Oprah,* which are bought by local stations throughout the country.

The Placement Specialist frequently uses cable shows when arranging interviews for clients. More and more of these are springing up. They are useful to the individual because they are so plentiful, usually in need of guests, and have specialized audiences.

As noted previously, most clients aspire to be on national shows. These are programs shown throughout the country on the affiliate stations of the networks. Placing guests on these shows is more difficult because, unless the individual is placing a very well-known celebrity, national exposure is hard to achieve.

Once a Placement Specialist obtains a client, he or she usually meets with the person to discuss goals and to obtain information needed in order to place him or her. The individual finds out why the client seeks exposure. It may be to bring attention to a cause, to publicize an event, to attain fame, or to help sell a product or service.

The Placement Specialist must obtain a biography of the client, press kits, news releases, photographs, and any other pertinent information. In some cases the Placement Specialist puts together bios, press kits, and news releases for an additional fee. In other instances the information is supplied to the individual.

The Placement Specialist must find out if the client wants to do a media tour or just one or two placement shots. He or she must also know the geographic locations to which the individual will travel.

The Placement Specialist then goes to work. He or she takes the specific city or cities and begins making a list of potential shows. The individual must know what radio and television stations are in the area as well as what type of programming is available. He or she then writes a cover letter and sends it with press information to either the program producer or the guest coordinator. If the Placement Specialist does not hear from a program within a reasonable amount of time, he or she may call the producer or guest coordinator to ask about the possibilities of an interview for the client. The Placement Specialist may often call or write a producer just at the time another guest has cancelled or when a specific show is in the planning stages.

The Placement Specialist who is successful is persuasive without being offensive. The individual must be persistent and keep trying to get clients booked on shows.

If the individual is not handling a well-known celebrity, he or she may have to come up with an angle in order to make the client seem interesting enough to be a guest. The Placement Specialist often seeks out programs specific to the individual client's needs in order to make placement easier. For example, someone trying to place a financial speaker might look for business programs. An individual placing the owner of a catering company might look to morning or afternoon information shows.

If the individual is booking a media tour, he or she must make sure that the scheduling is both cost and time efficient. A client cannot easily be in Los Angeles in the morning, New York City in the afternoon, and San Francisco in the evening. With new technology the client can, however, do phone interviews for radio without even leaving the house. In this manner he or she may do up to 10 interviews in a day and spend no time traveling.

In some instances the Placement Specialist may accompany clients to shows or arrange for someone else to accompany them. In other situations the Placement Specialist prepares a list of shows, the dates and times of appearances, contact names at the stations, and phone numbers and addresses. This is given to the client. The Placement Specialist may also send confirmation letters to program personnel.

In some instances the specialist may work with clients, preparing them for interviews. He or she performs mock interviews to make sure that the individual can answer questions easily and feels comfortable in front of a microphone or television camera. It is important that the Placement Specialist make sure that clients arrive when they are supposed to, dressed appropriately, and are adequately prepared. Even one guest who doesn't show up, or one who clams up in front of a television camera, can hurt the reputation of the Placement Specialist, making it impossible for him or her to book another guest on that show.

Placement Specialists work long hours. If they have a lot of clients or they are placing people in different time zones, they may stay on the phone for hours. The Placement Specialist who is doing consulting or freelancing is usually responsible to the client who has done the hiring.

Salaries

Earnings are almost impossible to estimate for Placement Specialists. The individual may work on a per project or freelance basis. He or she may also be retained for weeks, months, or longer by clients.

Placement professionals may earn from $25 to $7,500 plus per placement on a show, depending on the specific program and whether it is local, cable, syndicated, or national. Individuals might be compensated by a flat fee per week, month, or city. Once again, there are many variables.

Earnings may be increased by performing other services such as writing press releases, compiling press kits, preparing clients for interviews, or accompanying them to shows.

Successful Placement Specialists may earn up to $200,000 plus annually.

Employment Prospects

Individuals who are interested in becoming a Placement Specialist on a consulting or freelance level will have to find clients. There are people all over the country in every field who want media exposure. Individuals may have to advertise and do publicity and promotion in order to make people aware of their business, but they can usually find clients to get started.

This job can be accomplished successfully by seasoned pros or by those just entering the field. It all depends on the individual's persistence, perseverance, persuasiveness, and personality.

Advancement Prospects

Anyone can become a Placement Specialist, but not everyone is successful. Individuals who obtain clients and get them booked on shows have no problem finding additional clients. The Specialist may have to advertise and promote his or her business or may obtain new clients via satisfied existing clients.

Placement Specialists who climb the career ladder advance by obtaining a larger client list and more prestigious clients.

Education and Training

While there are no educational requirements for Placement Specialists working on a freelance or consulting level, some training will help. If the individual is in college, a major in public relations, communications, journalism, English, liberal arts, marketing, or advertising will prove useful.

Seminars and courses in publicity and media placement are helpful in honing skills and making contacts.

Experience, Skills, and Personality Traits

The Placement Specialist must be persuasive and persistent. He or she needs to be articulate, with good communication skills and an excellent phone personality. The individual constantly calls and writes to producers and talent coordinators and must have the ability to talk them into using his or her clients as guests.

The Placement Specialist should know how to write press releases, compile press kits, and prepare effective letters. The individual must be creative and innovative. He or she must frequently come up with unique angles to get clients booked on shows.

As time goes on the Placement Specialist begins to build a list of producers and talent coordinators at stations across the country. A good working relationship with these people is important to the Placement Specialist's success.

Unions and Associations

There are no unions to which the Placement Specialist must belong. He or she may become a member of the Public Relations Society of American (PRSA). This organization provides useful seminars, educational materials, and guidance to people working in publicity or public relations.

Tips for Entry

1. You may want to begin your career by volunteering to place people from a local nonprofit group on television or radio shows to publicize an event that the group is holding. This will give you hands-on experience.
2. Place a small display ad in a local publication. Keep it running regularly as long as you can. When people need your service they will remember seeing your advertisement.
3. Use your skills to get yourself on television or radio to publicize your own business.
4. Send out a brochure or letter to corporations and trade associations in your area letting them know about your service. You should receive some responses.

VIP COORDINATOR

CAREER PROFILE

Duties: Meet important visitors, clients, or business associates; arrange hotel accommodations, meals, and tours; accompany people to interviews

Alternate Title(s): VIP Specialist; VIP Representative; VIP Rep; VIP Escort; Arrangement Representative

Salary Range: $75 per day to $75,000+ per year

Employment Prospects: Fair

Advancement Prospects: Fair

Best Geographical Location(s): Large cities offer the greatest number of possibilities.

Prerequisites:

Education or Training—Minimum, high school diploma

Experience—No experience necessary

Special Skills and Personality Traits—Friendly; articulate; ability to deal with details; organizational skills; neat appearance

CAREER LADDER

```
┌─────────────────────────────────┐
│   VIP Coordinator with Many     │
│ Prestigious Clients or Press Agent │
│ Clients or Press Agent or Publicist │
└─────────────────────────────────┘

┌─────────────────────────────────┐
│        VIP Coordinator          │
└─────────────────────────────────┘

┌─────────────────────────────────┐
│  Entry Level, Public Relations, │
│     or Publicity Assistant      │
└─────────────────────────────────┘
```

Position Description

A VIP Coordinator is hired to meet important people who are coming into a city and to make them feel comfortable. The term *VIP* means "very important person." The job is in the public relations area but may also spill over into the advertising field.

Individuals may be hired by advertising agencies, corporations, public relations agencies, press agents, publicists, television and radio stations, placement specialists, book and magazine publishers, entertainment agencies, or government agencies.

The VIP Coordinator usually meets a variety of different types of people in his or her job. The individual may be responsible for meeting an advertising agency client from a foreign country, a book author, an entertainer, a radio personality, a movie star, or clients from public relations agencies.

Depending on the situation, the VIP Coordinator has varied responsibilities. He or she may be responsible for making travel arrangements for people to and from their destination. Once a client arrives in the specific city, the individual meets him or her at the airport or train station. The VIP Coordinator may meet the client with a limousine or may perform the driving tasks.

In some instances the VIP Coordinator is responsible for arranging transportation for the client while he or she is in town. Once again, this might be a limo, a car with a driver, or a rented car.

The VIP Coordinator may accompany clients to interviews at radio and television stations, to print publication interviews, to venues where they will be presenting speeches, or to meetings. The individual may also implement VIP public relations programs of press agents, publicists, or placement specialists.

The VIP Coordinator is often responsible for meeting agency clients from foreign countries. After greeting the clients at the airport and taking them to their hotel the individual may be responsible for changing foreign currency into American money or arranging for translators. He or she may also handle arrangements for shopping tours, shows, entertainment, sightseeing tours, and restaurants.

The VIP Coordinator is often asked to make special arrangements for spouses and children of clients accompanying them on business trips. The individual may seek out baby-sitters, physicians, and special food.

At times the VIP Coordinator must locate and hire secretarial or business services or any other service the client might need during his or her stay.

VIP Coordinators are responsible for arranging for the safety and comfort of their clients. When they are coordinating the visit of a VIP they may be on 24-hour call. If the client has an emergency or requires anything, it is the job of the Coordinator to take care of it.

Most VIP Coordinators find this type of job exciting, glamorous, and fun. They often meet and mingle with interesting people from all over the country and the world.

Salaries

It is almost impossible to estimate annual salaries for VIP Coordinators. Earnings vary depending on the type of arrangement they have. Coordinators may be compensated on a per project, daily, or weekly basis. Fees can range form $75 to $350 per day or up to $1,500 per week or more. Those paid on a per project basis charge fees based on time and responsibilities involved in a project.

There are VIP Coordinators who work part time. Successful VIP Coordinators who work full time may earn $75,000 plus per year.

Employment Prospects

Employment prospects are fair for individuals seeking this type of work. The VIP Coordinator may have to relocate to a large city where there are more opportunities. Clients could include corporations, advertising agencies, public relations agencies, press agents, publicists, television and radio stations, placement specialists, book and magazine publishers, entertainment agencies, and government agencies.

Individuals may have to advertise their service, market their business, or look into advertising sources for possible leads. Other individuals may find employment through help wanted ads.

Advancement Prospects

VIP Coordinators who want to move up the career ladder may take a number of different paths depending on their aspirations. The individual might build a large list of prestigious clients. The coordinator may build up a business to the point where he or she must hire additional coordinators to handle jobs.

Other VIP Coordinators advance by becoming press agents, publicists, public relations specialists, or placement specialists.

Education and Training

Other than a high school diploma, there are really no stringent educational requirements for a VIP Coordinator working on a freelance basis. However, some corporations or agencies prefer an individual who has a four-year college degree.

The VIP Coordinator should have training in or a knowledge of English, writing, public relations, marketing, and possibly a foreign language.

Experience, Skills, and Personality Traits

The VIP Coordinator should be an outgoing individual with a lot of personality. He or she should be personable, likable, and friendly with a neat, well-groomed appearance. The individual meets with important people and must look like he or she fits in.

The VIP Coordinator should be articulate and well-spoken and have good communication skills. He or she needs to be well-organized and able to deal with a lot of details at once without getting confused. The ability to work under pressure is imperative. The function of the VIP Coordinator is to make people feel comfortable. If he or she gets flustered, it can be contagious.

VIP Coordinators who are fluent in another language are more marketable and useful to clients who have foreign visitors coming into the country.

Unions and Associations

VIP Coordinators don't have a specific trade association devoted especially to their job classification. Many individuals belong to public relations, marketing, or advertising associations, depending on their affiliations with different companies and their responsibilities. Attending meetings and seminars presented by these organizations provides individuals with a good source of contacts for potential business as well as an opportunity to gain valuable skills.

Individuals might belong to the Public Relations Society of America (PRSA), the American Advertising Federation (AAF), The Direct Marketing Association, Inc. (DMA), the Advertising Club of New York, and Advertising Women of New York, Inc. (AWNY).

Tips for Entry

1. The ability to speak a foreign language will make you more valuable. Consider taking some classes or brushing up on this skill.
2. You might send letters, brochures, or business cards with your business name, address, and phone number to corporations, agencies, and publishers. Ask that your information be kept on file. It might be wise to send mailings on a regular basis. Eventually someone will need your service and remember you.
3. On occasion there are positions like this advertised in the newspaper classified section. Look under heading classifications of "VIP Rep," "VIP Coordinator," "Client Coordinator," "Arrangement Rep," "Public Relations," or "Advertising."
4. You might want to get hands-on experience by working for a short time as a travel coordinator or travel escort for a bus or travel company.

CRISIS MANAGEMENT CONSULTANT

CAREER PROFILE

Duties: Prepare corporate executives and other clients to effectively deal with crises; handle crisis management; prepare statements

Alternate Title(s): Crisis Management Specialist

Salary Range: $30,000 to $250,000+

Employment Prospects: Fair

Advancement Prospects: Good

Best Geographical Location(s): Positions may be located throughout the country; greatest number of opportunities will exist in cities with many large corporations.

Prerequisites:

Education or Training—Minimum of bachelor's degree in public relations, communications, liberal arts, or marketing

Experience—Public relations; crisis management; speechwriting

Special Skills and Personality Traits—Ability to think creatively; communication skills; detail-oriented; people skills; ability to stay calm

CAREER LADDER

```
┌─────────────────────────────────┐
│   Crisis Management Consultant   │
│   With Large Roster of Clients   │
└─────────────────────────────────┘

┌─────────────────────────────────┐
│   Crisis Management Consultant   │
└─────────────────────────────────┘

┌─────────────────────────────────┐
│    Public Relations Counselor    │
│  or Assistant Crisis Management   │
│      Counselor in Agency          │
└─────────────────────────────────┘
```

Position Description:

At one time or another businesses may run into situations that could negatively affect their business or their reputation. These situations may entail any number of scenarios depending on the specific business and ranging from life threatening to mildly problematic. Finding effective ways to deal with problematic issues and crises is essential to the reputation and bottom line of a business in trouble.

In some cases, corporate management decides that doing nothing would be their best bet. In others, the company's PR director or public relations agency takes over. Many larger companies call in Crisis Management Consultants. While crisis management is a part of public relations, there are people who specialize specifically in this area of the field.

Companies may need to use a Crisis Management Consultant for a variety of reasons. A hospital, for example, may find itself in the middle of a crisis when it is discovered that two babies were switched or when blood was not properly tested. A company producing food products would be in the middle of a crisis if it was found that its food was tainted with salmonella. Similarly, restaurants may need crisis management if food served resulted in people becoming ill with *E. coli*, or even if they received one or more critical violations when inspected by their local health department.

Crises are not always life-or-death situations, but they can negatively affect a company's reputation and bottom line. Layoffs, closings, corporate mergers, lower than expected earnings, corporate mismanagement, and bankruptcies are examples.

Crisis Management Consultants may handle a variety of functions ranging from crisis prevention to crisis response to crisis management depending on the specific situation. In some situations, a corporation may retain a Crisis Management Consultant *before* a crisis occurs. By getting in ahead of the problem, the consultant might either be able to prevent an impending crisis or prepare the company so that when the crisis hits, they are prepared to handle it swiftly.

The Crisis Management Consultant may execute a variety of functions to help prepare corporate management before a problem occurs. He or she may perform a risk analysis to determine the possibilities and identify issues of concern. What are the potential areas of weakness? Where are the potential flaws? Where is the company vulnerable? What are the potential problems? By identifying these issues, the consultant can help the company know where problems might exist.

The Crisis Management Consultant may also review the company's current preparedness for handling a crisis. Do they have a plan? Is it in writing? Who is authorized to speak to the media? Who is authorized to speak to employees? What are the crisis plans in place already?

After reviewing these situations, the Crisis Management Consultant will prepare a written report clarifying his or her findings. He or she is then responsible for developing a plan of recommendations for improvement.

Crisis Management Consultants provide crisis training and response techniques to key members of the corporate team. This is often accomplished through exercises in crisis simulation coupled with the appropriate response. The individual is also expected to make sure key management employees know how to prepare effective internal and external communications. These may include statements and press releases for the media, employees, stockholders, board members, and when necessary, the general public.

Part of the job of the consultant often involves training one or more of the key corporate management team in dealing effectively with media. This may include public speaking skills, appearing on camera, and answering questions in public forums.

Some companies do not use crisis management at all . . . until they have a crisis. Then, faced with a negative situation that needs to be attended to quickly, they call in a Crisis Management Consultant. This crisis response becomes a very important function of the Crisis Management Consultant.

In these situations, the individual must be able to think quickly, creatively, and calmly. He or she is expected to effectively handle damage control immediately. He or she is expected to find ways to stop rumors and get the company's message out.

In these cases, the Crisis Management Consultant may be the one who is preparing the statements and other communications to be given to the media, employees, and the public. The individual may also act as the company's spokesperson.

The key to success in this position is handling damage control and finding the most effective ways to minimize the negative impact of a crisis, problems, and bad news.

Salaries

Earnings are difficult to determine for Crisis Management Consultants. Compensation depends to a great extent on the number of clients individuals have and the professional reputation they have built. Some Crisis Management Consultants earn $30,000 annually, while other make $250,000 or more.

Individuals may work on an hourly basis, a per project basis, or be on a monthly retainer.

Employment Prospects

Employment prospects are fair for Crisis Management Consultants. While clients may be located throughout the country, individuals seeking this type of work may want to relocate to an area where there are a large number of major corporations for a potential client base.

Clients might include corporations in a vast array of areas as well as nonprofits, government agencies, and environmental agencies. There are also a number of Crisis Management Consultants who specialize in personal crisis management, handling individuals including politicians, entertainers, film and television stars, musicians, and sports figures.

Advancement Prospects

The most common method of career advancement in this field is for individuals to build either a large roster of clients or a roster of larger, more prestigious clients. If the consultant is good at what he or she does and builds a good professional reputation, this is often accomplished through word of mouth referrals.

Education and Training

A minimum of a bachelor's degree in public relations, communications, marketing, or a related field is usually necessary for success in this type of career. Courses and workshops in business, communications, public relations, and speechwriting will be helpful. There are a number of schools and institutes that offer intensive two-day programs in crisis management.

Experience, Skills, and Personality Traits

The most successful people in this field will be articulate, creative individuals with excellent communication skills. It is essential for a Crisis Management Consultant to be well-spoken and have a good command of the English language. The ability to think quickly is necessary.

In addition to a full working knowledge of public relations skills, the individual must also have the ability to be a compelling speechwriter. The ability to multitask without getting flustered is needed.

Unions and Associations

Crisis Management Consultants may be members of the Public Relations Society of America (PRSA). This organization is the most recognized in the public relations field, offering professional guidance and support to its members.

Tips For Entry

1. If you are still in school, look for an internship with a Crisis Management Consultant. You might also try to locate an internship with an agency that specializes in crisis management.
2. Take classes, workshops, and seminars in crisis management, communications, speechwriting, and public relations. In addition to honing your skills, they provide excellent networking opportunities.
3. If you are currently working in public relations and interested in branching out into crisis management, consider speaking about crisis management at local nonprofit and civic group meetings. When companies in your local area find the need for crisis management, they will often think of you first.
4. Consider placing an advertisement in your local business publication to help you obtain new clients.

MISCELLANEOUS OPPORTUNITIES

PRESS SECRETARY, GOVERNMENT/POLITICAL

CAREER PROFILE

Duties: Handle all press and media functions for a public or government official; write press releases; arrange press conferences, briefings, and photo opportunities; act as spokesperson

Alternate Title(s): Press Spokesperson; Spokesperson

Salary Range: $28,000 to $150,000+

Employment Prospects: Poor

Advancement Prospects: Good

Best Geographical Location(s): Washington, D.C. and state capitals offer the most opportunities.

Prerequisites

Education or Training—Four-year college degree required

Experience—Journalism, media, or public relations experience preferred; experience in politics and government helpful

Special Skills and Personality Traits—Understanding of politics; articulateness; good communication skills; ability to speak in front of groups of people; stamina; writing ability

CAREER LADDER

```
┌─────────────────────────────────────┐
│         Press Secretary for          │
│        More Prestigious Official     │
│                  or                  │
│      Public Relations, Media, or     │
│   Journalism Position in Prestigious │
│     Corporation or Publication       │
└─────────────────────────────────────┘

┌─────────────────────────────────────┐
│     Press Secretary, Government      │
└─────────────────────────────────────┘

┌─────────────────────────────────────┐
│      Public Relations, Media,        │
│                  or                  │
│        Journalism Position           │
└─────────────────────────────────────┘
```

Position Description

A Press Secretary working in government handles all press and media functions for the public official he or she is representing. The most prominent person in this field is the press secretary to the president of the United States. The individual may work for other public officials such as mayors or state or federal legislators. He or she might also represent cabinet officers or agencies on the federal, state, or local level. There are also Press Secretaries who handle this function for political candidates, who are in the process of running for office. All Press Secretaries have similar duties and functions, no matter which official, candidate, or agency they represent.

One of the basic functions of the Press Secretary is to respond to questions from the press and media. The individual may answer questions him- or herself on behalf of the official. The Press Secretary might also brief the official on the situation and have him or her respond to questions.

The Press Secretary schedules press conferences and press briefings. He or she may be responsible for making preparations for the conference, including setting up the location and checking on facilities for audiovisuals, microphones, podiums, seating, etc. The individual must prepare and distribute handouts for the media at these conferences. The Press Secretary may be in charge of opening informal press conferences. He or she may act as the moderator of the event, handling introductions, etc.

The Press Secretary works with the official or candidate in identifying subjects, issues, and topics for speeches, presentations, and awards. In some instances the Press Secretary is responsible for writing and/or editing speeches for the official.

In other cases the official may write the speech, or the task may be turned over to a professional speechwriter.

The Press Secretary is in charge of keeping the media informed about the official's activities and schedules photo opportunities for the media. He or she is responsible for writing and distributing press releases on both routine subjects and special informational matters or issues. The individual constantly strives to put and keep the official in the public eye in a positive manner.

The Press Secretary often acts as a buffer between the official and the press. When the official is unavailable or not ready to answer a media question, it is the Press Secretary who is responsible for holding reporters at bay. The Press Secretary also acts as a spokesperson for the official, at times reading statements or offering remarks.

The Press Secretary spends many long hours with the official. Together they decide how to improve the official's image, the cost effective ways to answer difficult policy questions, how to deal with the media, etc.

The Press Secretary does not work a typical nine-to-five day. Instead, he or she may work from early in the morning till late at night. The individual may also be required to work on weekends. The Press Secretary is responsible to the official. In cases where the Press Secretary is working on a political campaign, he or she may also be responsible to the campaign manager.

Salaries

A Press Secretary can expect to earn between $28,000 and $100,000 plus annually. Earnings vary for individuals depending on the government official with whom they are working. Federal positions have a maximum on the annual salary that can be paid to people in this job.

Press Secretaries working in local government may earn salaries on the lower end of the scale. Those working for governors, senators, representatives, etc. earn more.

Press Secretaries involved with political campaigns may earn $150,000 or more.

Employment Prospects

Employment prospects are poor for Press Secretaries in government. While the individual might act as a spokesperson for public officials, opportunities are limited.

Even though any city might hold employment prospects, the best geographic locations for these jobs are Washington, D.C. and state capitals across the country.

Advancement Prospects

Advancement prospects are good for Press Secretaries working in government. Once an individual has a job in this field, he or she can move up the career ladder in a number of ways. The Press Secretary may locate a similar job in state or federal government, which would result in increased earnings and prestige. For example, the individual may be the spokesperson for a city mayor. He or she may then be hired to be the Press Secretary for a state representative.

The Press Secretary may also advance his or her career by going into lobbying activities. Other possibilities for climbing the career ladder include a public relations job in an agency, large corporation, or the media.

Education and Training

Individuals looking for jobs in the political and governmental field should have a minimum of a four-year college degree. Good choices for majors for those aspiring to be Press Secretaries include public relations, marketing, English, liberal arts, communications, advertising, and political science.

Experience, Skills, and Personality Traits

The Press Secretary working in government must have a complete knowledge of the political process. He or she should be familiar with political policies, government regulations, and attitudes of constituents. The Press Secretary also needs to keep up with current affairs.

The individual in this position should be articulate with good communications skills. He or she should be comfortable speaking in front of large crowds of people as well as into a microphone or on television. The Press Secretary should be persuasive both in speaking and on paper.

The Press Secretary needs a lot of stamina. He or she frequently has to work long and irregular hours. The individual should have the ability to work on many different projects at once without getting flustered. The position of Press Secretary requires the ability to work under pressure a great deal of the time.

The Press Secretary needs to be able to perform all public relations functions. He or she must be adept at a variety of writing functions, from letters and memos to press releases and speeches.

One's success or failure in his or her job depends on the media. The individual must have a good working relationship with media people and try to remain accessible at all times.

Many Press Secretaries have worked in the media themselves as reporters, journalists, or editors. Others have worked in the political sphere in various capacities.

Unions and Associations

Press Secretaries do not belong to any type of union. Individuals may be members of any of a number of different public relations or communications trade associations. These include the National Association of Government Communicators (NAGC), the Association of House Democratic Press Assistants (AHDPA), the Republican Communications Association (RCA), the Public Relations Society of America (PRSA), Women In Communications (WIC),

National Federation of Press Women (NFPW), and the National Press Club (NPC).

Press Secretaries working in governmental and political situations usually belong to political associations and organizations.

Tips for Entry

1. This is one of those jobs where you have to be in the right place at the right time. A lot of luck is involved.
2. This is not the time to try to see if you can obtain a job on your own. Use every contact you have. If your mother has a friend who has a cousin who is a receptionist for the mayor, ask for an introduction. The more contacts you use, the better your chances of finding a job in this field.
3. Try to locate a political internship. This will give you the opportunity to make valuable contacts on your own.
4. Volunteer to work on a political campaign. This will give you hands-on experience working in the political world as well as giving you the chance to make professional contacts.
5. Contact your county political chairperson. He or she may know of a position open or may be able to give you a lead on whom to see to find a job in this field.

DIRECTOR OF PUBLIC AFFAIRS, COLLEGE/UNIVERSITY

CAREER PROFILE

Duties: Handle press and public relations functions for institution; prepare press releases; arrange press briefings and press conferences; write special-interest articles; respond to media requests for information

Alternate Title(s): News and Information Coordinator; News and Information Director; Public Relations Director; Public Affairs Director; Public Information Director

Salary Range: $30,000 to $100,000+

Employment Prospects: Fair

Advancement Prospects: Fair

Best Geographical Location(s): Positions may be located throughout the country

Prerequisites

Education or Training—Four-year college degree is required; graduate degree may be preferred.

Experience—Publicity, public relations, or journalism experience preferred

Special Skills and Personality Traits—Good writing skills; articulateness; ability to deal with many projects at one time; good communications skills; public speaking ability

CAREER LADDER

```
┌─────────────────────────────────┐
│   Director of Public Affairs     │
│     at a Larger Institution      │
│               or                 │
│       in Another Industry        │
└─────────────────────────────────┘

┌─────────────────────────────────┐
│   Director of Public Affairs     │
└─────────────────────────────────┘

┌─────────────────────────────────┐
│    Public Affairs Assistant      │
│               or                 │
│   Public Relations Assistant     │
└─────────────────────────────────┘
```

Position Description

The Director of Public Affairs working in a college or university is responsible for handling all press and public relations functions of the institution. The individual may work alone in the department or with an assistant or may supervise a staff.

The Director of Public Affairs, who might also be called the news and information coordinator, public relations director, public affairs coordinator, or public information director, performs a number of communications and writing functions. These include preparing press and media releases on a regular basis. He or she may write press releases regarding routine college activities and events or cover special events or programs the college is holding. The individual may also prepare releases on honors and awards received by college professors, administrators, or students.

Other writing responsibilities, depending on the institution and its structure, might include the preparation of event calendars, brochures, letters, marketing pieces, feature stories, special-interest articles, etc. He or she may be expected to write a column for the school or local paper about college happenings.

The Director of Public Affairs is responsible for publicizing special programs sponsored by the college. These might include extension and outreach programs or college/community affairs programs. The individual may, for example, publicize a new nursing program initiated, developed, and supported by a local hospital and offered by the college.

The director often works with other college departments in preparing publicity, developing programs, arranging interviews, etc. The individual might work with college alumni or the alumni relations department on a homecoming weekend or with the fund-raising and development department when raising funds for a new building. The Director of Public Affairs frequently works with student government and student activities directors handling the publicity for a theatrical event, concert, sports event, or other attraction. He or she may prepare press material or arrange speaking engagements or interviews for college professors, administrators, or the admissions department.

The individual is responsible for arranging for media coverage of noteworthy college events and functions. He or she may call media to inform them of events or send information to their offices.

The Director of Public Affairs is expected to handle inquiries and questions by the media. He or she may refer them to someone who can answer the question or may act as the college spokesperson him- or herself.

The individual may frequently be asked to speak on behalf of the college at local civic and community events, fund-raising functions, etc.

The Director of Public Affairs may arrange press conferences or press briefings. This might occur when a famous individual becomes a member of the teaching staff, a professor or administrator receives a special award or honor, or someone is donating a large sum of money. Press conferences might also be called to clarify the nature of a problem on campus or to announce its solution.

The individual is expected to work a normal eight-hour day. He or she may put in overtime to finish projects, write required releases, talk to media on the phone, etc. The Director of Public Affairs is responsible to the president of the institution.

Salaries

Individuals working as Directors of Public Affairs in college or university settings have salaries that range greatly. Compensation depends on a number of variables. These include the size, location, and prestige of the institution, its status (whether it is profit or nonprofit), and the experience and responsibilities of the individual.

Salaries range from $30,000 to $100,000 or more annually. Individuals are compensated on the lower end of the scale if they have limited experience or are working in a small college. Those with more experience or those working in larger colleges and universities earn between $45,000 and $70,000 a year. Individuals working in very large institutions earn up to $100,000 or more.

Many colleges and universities often offer valuable perks such as free tuition to those working in the school or to their spouses and children.

Employment Prospects

Employment prospects are fair for individuals seeking public affairs jobs. Almost every college, no matter how small, needs someone to fill this position. While the job may be called public information, public relations, or news and information, it fulfills the same functions. Opportunities may exist in local community colleges, state universities, private colleges, or large universities.

Jobs may be located throughout the country. In larger institutions there may be more than one person working in the news and information department. In smaller colleges the individual often works alone.

Smaller institutions such as community colleges may also offer an individual with a good education and résumé a position even though he or she has only limited experience.

Advancement Prospects

The Director of Public Affairs has fair advancement prospects. The individual may advance his or her career by locating a position in a larger, more prestigious university, resulting in advanced earnings. The Director may also climb the career ladder by becoming a public relations or public affairs director in another industry.

Education and Training

The Director of Public Affairs must have a four-year college degree. Good choices for majors include public relations, journalism, communications, English, marketing, and liberal arts.

Individuals might also find courses and seminars in public relations, publicity, or writing offered through trade associations or other groups useful in honing skills.

Experience, Skills, and Personality Traits

The Director of Public Affairs working in a college or university setting should have a good understanding and overview of college life and policies. The individual should be personable and have the ability to get along well with others.

He or she needs to have excellent writing skills. The individual will have to write press releases, calendars, articles, and feature stories. A thorough knowledge of word usage, grammar, and spelling is necessary.

The Director of Public Affairs should be confident and articulate and have good communication skills. He or she should be comfortable talking to the media as well as speaking in front of a microphone or before a group of people. The individual is often called on to be the college spokesperson.

The Director of Public Affairs should both understand and be able to implement public relations functions. He or she needs the ability to deal with a lot of details and many different projects at once.

Many individuals who currently hold this position previously worked as journalists, reporters, or in other publicity or public relations jobs. Others came into the job as an assistant or obtained experience as a trainee or intern. Individuals who have a good college education with relevant experience before graduation may get this position with little or no work experience.

Unions and Associations

People in this type of position do not belong to any bargaining union. Instead, they may belong to any of a number of trade associations. These groups are useful to the individual for a number of reasons. Many provide educational seminars, literature, trade journals, and job guidance.

Associations include the Public Relations Society of America (PRSA), International Association of Business Communications (IABC), Women In Communications, Inc. (WIC), National Federation of Press Women (NFPW), and the International Public Relations Association (IPRA).

Tips for Entry

1. Join trade associations. You will make valuable professional contacts. Attend meetings, ask for literature, and read their trade journals. A number of the groups offer student memberships.

2. Trade journals frequently advertise job openings. Look in the marketplace, help wanted, or classified section.

3. Jobs may also be advertised in local newspapers. Check out both the display and classified sections. Look under the heading classifications of "Education," "College," "University," "News and Information," "Publicity," "Public Affairs," or "Public Relations."

4. Try to obtain experience through an internship or training program offered by a corporation, trade association, or college.

5. If you are still in school, see if you can work out a program with your school's news and information or public affairs department. Even if you just volunteer some time, you will be gaining valuable hands-on experience that will be useful in helping land a job after graduation.

6. You may obtain experience by finding a college that has an assistant director of public affairs position.

7. Consider working in a journalism position to get experience writing.

SPORTS INFORMATION DIRECTOR, COLLEGE/UNIVERSITY

CAREER PROFILE

Duties: Publicize team and players; write press releases; provide media with information about team; respond to media questions; prepare biographies, press kits, and yearbooks; arrange press conferences and briefings

Alternate Title(s): Collegiate Sports Information Director; Sports Information Manager

Salary Range: $25,000 to $85,000+

Employment Prospects: Fair

Advancement Prospects: Fair

Best Geographical Location(s): Positions located throughout the country; areas that have colleges and universities with large sports teams hold most opportunities

Prerequisites

Education or Training—Four-year college degree required for most positions

Experience—Writing experience preferred

Special Skills and Personality Traits—Good writing skills; personability; articulateness; knowledge of sports; ability to deal with media

CAREER LADDER

```
┌─────────────────────────────────────┐
│     Sports Information Director      │
│            in Larger,                │
│    More Prestigious Institution      │
│                or                    │
│ Professional Sports Team Publicist   │
└─────────────────────────────────────┘

┌─────────────────────────────────────┐
│     Sports Information Director      │
└─────────────────────────────────────┘

┌─────────────────────────────────────┐
│   Sports Information Assistant,      │
│    Public Relations, Media,          │
│                or                    │
│     Journalism Position              │
│                or                    │
│          Entry Level                 │
└─────────────────────────────────────┘
```

Position Description

The Sports Information Director works with collegiate athletic teams publicizing both the teams and their players. The individual may work with one particular sport or may be required to handle the press and publicity functions for all sports played at the college.

The Sports Information Director has a number of writing responsibilities. He or she must write press releases on a variety of subjects. These include upcoming games, new additions to the team, coaches, players, etc. The Sports Information Director may also be required to send scores of games to the media. At times the individual writes feature stories and articles for use by either the general media or specialized publications.

Press releases, scores, and feature stories are sent to all local media by the Sports Information Director. This includes newspapers, magazines, other written publications, and television and radio stations. The Sports Information Director is expected to look for additional avenues to distribute this information. If the individual is working with a school whose team merits regional or national publicity, the Sports Information Director also sends information to sports editors in these area. He or she might also send press releases to media in a player's home town.

The Sports Information Director is responsible for interviewing each athlete and coach in order to prepare biographies of the players, the team, and the coaches. Depending on the size of the school and the emphasis on sports, this information may be put together in a folder, like a press kit; in a booklet, as a press guide; or in the form of a yearbook. It may also contain statistics and records of the team, photographs of the players and coaches, etc. The information is valuable to the Sports Information Director when writing press releases and feature stories or when answering questions from the media.

The Sports Information Director may be expected to take photographs or arrange for a professional photographer. This depends on the size and budget of the college. Photos of players individually and as a team are needed. Photos of games might also be required. If the individual is working in a situation where media coverage includes television, he or she might also arrange for video clips of the team.

The Sports Information Director is responsible for arranging, coordinating, and implementing press conferences and press briefings. Depending on the situation, these might be either formal affairs or informal events. The individual calls, sends, or delivers invitations to media informing them of the time, date, and location of the conference as well as of the reason for it. Press conferences may be held for a number of reasons. A valuable new player might have transferred to the school and its team; a player might have been injured during a game and is hospitalized; or a new coach from a prestigious school might have been hired. The important thing for the individual to remember is to make sure that there is a reason for a press conference. Otherwise, the next time he or she schedules one, the media might not show up.

The Sports Information Director's relationship with the media is important. A good working relationship with these people helps to make his or her job easier and more effective. The individual usually gets to know sports reporters, editors, and journalists. Many areas have collegiate sports reporters or sports sections devoted to the collegiate scene.

If the Sports Information Director has a good, honest relationship with the media, when he or she needs some publicity, the individual can just pick up a phone. Conversely, sports media people frequently need a story and will feel comfortable calling the Sports Information Director for a suggestion.

The individual is responsible for responding to inquiries from the general public and the media. There may be some situations in which the Sports Information Director is placed in a position where he cannot answer a specific question at a given time or must give a "no comment" type of response. This might be because of a delicate situation, confidentiality, etc. The individual must explain the situation to the media without breaking confidentiality, keeping the relationship intact.

The individual is responsible for collecting articles, newspaper and magazine clippings, stories, etc. about the team. Copies of radio or television stories might also be collected. He or she may perform this function, assign the task to an assistant, or retain the services of a media clipping service.

The Sports Information Director is especially busy on game days. He or she must make sure that the press has received passes to get in, are seated in good seats, and receive the latest press information. The individual also answers any questions reporters might have.

The Sports Information Director sees to it that school or local dignitaries have received complimentary passes and arranges for their seating. After the game he or she may arrange a press conference.

The individual in this job works long hours, frequently working at night and on weekends. The Sports Information Director is usually expected to attend all team games. Depending on the structure of the school, he or she may be responsible to the sports director, the athletic director, or the president of the college.

Salaries

Salaries for Sports Information Directors vary greatly. Variables include the size of the college or university, its enrollment, its budget, and the amount of emphasis the school puts on sports. Compensation also depends on the experience level of the individual and his or her responsibilities.

Salaries can range from $25,000 to $85,000 plus annually for full-time Sports Information Directors. Those working in smaller schools or those with limited experience receive earnings on the lower end of the scale. Individuals working in large colleges and universities with major sports programs earn higher salaries.

Employment Prospects

Larger schools may employ more than one individual in the sports information department. A college may hire one director and an assistant director. Schools may also hire a Sports Information Director for football, one for basketball, and one for other sports.

Smaller schools usually have only one Sports Information Director. In very small colleges the position may be only part time. There are also small colleges that don't employ anyone for this job, instead assigning the task to the college public affairs or public relations office. Other schools leave sports information functions to the coaches.

Individuals who are willing to relocate to find a position, willing to work in a small school, or willing to take a part-time position have fair employment prospects.

Advancement Prospects

Advancement prospects vary depending on how the individual wants to climb the career ladder. He or she may find a position as a Sports Information Director in a larger, more prestigious school. This will result in increased earnings, responsibilities, and visibility.

The Sports Information Director might advance by locating a position with a professional team. He or she might also work in public relations or publicity in another industry.

Education and Training

While there are rare cases of a high school graduate getting this job, the majority of these positions require a four-year college degree. In order to be prepared for a position as a

Sports Information Director the individual should take courses in public relations, publicity, marketing, journalism, English, writing, sports, studies, and physical education.

There are a number of seminars available throughout the country on obtaining publicity, writing press releases, and securing media exposure that would also prove useful.

Experience, Skills, and Personality Traits

It is necessary for the individual in this job to enjoy sports. He or she must watch games, work with coaches, and interact with players. It is also useful if the Sports Information Director has a knowledge of the various sports he or she is publicizing.

The Sports Information Director needs the ability to write well. He or she prepares press releases, booklets, leaflets, biographies, and feature stories. A good grasp of the English language is needed, as well as good spelling, word usage, and grammar.

The individual should be energetic. He or she works long hours. The Director should also be personable and enjoy dealing with people.

The Sports Information Director needs to be articulate, with the ability to communicate well. A pleasant phone manner is essential. The ability to speak before groups of people is often necessary.

The individual should be able to work on a lot of different projects at once and deal with details without getting flustered. He or she should have or be able to develop a good working relationship with the media.

Unions and Associations

The Sports Information Director working in a college or university may belong to any of a number of trade associations that can provide forums for those in the industry. The most prevalent in this field is College Sports Information Directors of America. The Sports Information Director might be a member of the National Sportscasters and Sportswriters Association.

Individuals might be members of any of a number of other public relations trade associations, including the public Relations Society of America (PRSA), Women In Communications, Inc. (WIC), and the National Federation of Press Women (NFPW).

Tips for Entry

1. Get experience working with the media. Volunteer to do publicity for a nonprofit group.
2. Consider a summer or part-time job writing for a newspaper.
3. If your school doesn't have a sports information department, offer to do publicity for school sports teams. You might see if you can write a column for your school or local paper on the college sports scene.
4. If your school does have such a department, see if you can become an intern, trainee, aide, assistant, typist, etc. Working in this department in any capacity will give you valuable hands-on experience as well as being useful for your résumé.
5. Join trade associations. Attend their meetings and subscribe to trade journals. These organizations will keep you abreast of trends in the industry.
6. Check out college and university Web sites. Many list employment opportunities.

APPENDIXES

APPENDIX I
DEGREE PROGRAMS

A. COLLEGES AND UNIVERSITIES OFFERING MAJORS IN ADVERTISING

The following is a listing of selected four-year schools granting degrees with majors in advertising. They are grouped by state. School names, addresses, phone numbers, Web addresses, and e-mail admission addresses are included when available.

The author does not endorse any one school over another. Use this list as a beginning. More colleges are beginning to grant degrees in this area every year. Check the newest edition of *Lovejoy's College Guide* (found in the reference section of libraries or in guidance counseling centers) for additional schools offering degrees in this field.

ALABAMA

Spring Hill College
4000 Dauphin Street
Mobile, AL 36608
Phone: (251) 380-3030
Fax: (251) 460-2186
E-mail: admit@shc.edu
http://www.shc.edu

University of Alabama
P.O. Box 870132
Tuscaloosa, AL 35487
Phone: (205) 348-5666
E-mail: uaadmit@enroll.ua.edu
http://www.ua.edu

ARIZONA

Northern Arizona University
P.O. Box 4084
Flagstaff, AZ 86011-4084
Phone: (205) 348-5666
Toll-free phone: (800) 933-BAMA
Fax: (205) 348-9046
E-mail: admissions@ua.edu
http://www.nau.edu

ARKANSAS

Harding University
P.O. Box 12255
Searcy, AR 72149
Phone: (501) 279-4407
Fax: (501) 279-4129
E-mail: admissions@harding.edu
http://www.harding.edu

University of Arkansas—Little Rock
South University Avenue
Little Rock, AR 72204
Phone: (501) 569-3127
Toll-free phone: (800) 482-8892
Fax: (501) 569-8915
http://www.ualr.edu

CALIFORNIA

Academy of Art University
79 New Montgomery Street
San Francisco, CA 94105
Phone: (415) 274-2222
Fax: (415) 263-4130
http://www.academyart.edu

Art Center College of Design
1700 Lida Street
Pasadena, CA 91103
Phone: (626) 396-2200
E-mail: admissions@artcenter.edu
http://www.artcenter.edu

Art Institute of California–San Diego
7650 Mission Valley Road
San Diego, CA 92108
Phone: (858) 598-1399 Ext. 1208 or
    (800) 591-2422-Ext. 3117
Fax: (619) 291-3206
E-mail: info@aii.edu

California State University, Fullerton
P.O. Box 6900
800 North State College Boulevard
Fullerton, CA 92834
Phone: (714) 278-2370
http://www.fullerton.edu

California State University, Hayward
25800 Carlos Bee Boulevard
Hayward, CA 94542
Phone: (510) 885-3248
Fax: (510) 885-3816
E-mail: adminfo@csuhayward.edu
http://www.csuhayward.edu

Chapman University
One University Drive
Orange, CA 92866
Phone: (714) 997-6711
Fax: (714) 997-6713
E-mail: admit@chapman.edu
http://www.chapman.edu

Notre Dame de Namur University
1500 Ralston Avenue
Belmont, CA 94002
Phone: (650) 508-3600
E-mail: admiss@ndnu.edu
http://www.ndnu.edu

Pepperdine University
Malibu, CA 90263-4392
Phone: (310) 506-4392
Fax: (310) 506-4861
http://www.pepperdine.edu

San Jose State University
One Washington Square
San Jose, CA 95192
Phone: (408) 924-1000
E-mail: info@soar.sjsu.edu
http://www.sjsu.edu

University of San Francisco
2130 Fulton Street
San Francisco, CA 94117-1046
Phone: (415) 422-6563
Fax: (415) 422-2217
E-mail: admission@usfca.edu
http://www.usfca.edu

COLORADO

Adams State College
Alamosa, CO 81102
Phone: (719) 587-7712
Fax: (719) 587-7522
E-mail: ascadmit@adams.edu
http://www.adams.edu

Art Institute of Colorado
1200 Lincoln Street
Denver, CO 80203
Phone: (303) 837-0825
Fax: (303) 860-8520
E-mail: aicinfo@aii.edu

University of Colorado—Boulder
Regent Admin. Center
Boulder, CO 80309
Phone: (303) 492-1411
E-mail: apply@colorado.edu
http://www.colorado.edu

CONNECTICUT

Quinnipiac University
Hamden, CT 06518
Phone: (203) 582-8600
Fax: 203-582-8906
E-mail: admissions@quinnipiac.edu
http://www.quinnipiac.edu

DISTRICT OF COLUMBIA

Howard University
2400 Sixth Street, NW
Washington, DC 20059
Phone: (202) 806-2763
E-mail: admission@howard.edu
http://www.howard.edu

University of the District of Columbia
4200 Connecticut Avenue, NW
Washington, DC 20008
Phone: (202) 274-6200
http://www.udc.edu

FLORIDA

Barry University
11300 N.E. Second Avenue
Miami Shores, FL 33161
Phone: (305) 899-3000
E-mail: admissions@mail.barry.edu
http://www.barry.edu

Florida Southern College
111 Lake Hollingsworth Drive
Lakeland, FL 33801

Phone: (800) 274-4131
E-mail: fscadm@flsouthern.edu
http://www.flsouthern.edu

Florida State University
Tallahassee, FL 32306
Phone: (850) 644-2525
E-mail: admissions@admin.fsu.edu
http://www.fsu.edu

Johnson & Wales University
1701 Northeast 127th Street
North Miami, FL 33181
Phone: (305) 892-7002
Fax: 305-892-7020
E-mail: admissions@jwu.edu

Northwood University
2600 North Military Trail
West Palm Beach, FL 33409
Phone: (561) 478-5500
E-mail: fladmit@northwood.edu
http://www.northwood.edu

University of Central Florida
4000 Central Florida Boulevard
Orlando, FL 32816
Phone: (407) 823-2000
E-mail: admission@mail.ucf.edu
http://www.ucf.edu

University of Florida
201 Criser Hall
Gainesville, FL 32611
Phone: (352) 392-3261
E-mail: freshman@ufl.edu
http://www.ufl.edu

University of Miami
P.O. Box 248025
Coral Gables, FL 33124
Phone: (305) 284-2211
E-mail: admission@miami.edu
http://www.miami.edu

GEORGIA

University of Georgia
212 Terrell Hall
Athens, GA 30602
Phone: (706) 542-3000
E-mail: undergrad@admissions.uga.edu
http://www.uga.edu

Wesleyan College
4760 Forsyth Road
Macon, GA 31210
Phone: (478) 757-5206
http://www.wesleyancollege.edu

HAWAII

Hawaii Pacific University
1164 Bishop Street
Honolulu, HI 96813
Phone: (808) 544-0200
E-mail: admissions@hpu.edu
http://www.hpu.edu

ILLINOIS

American Academy Of Art
332 South Michigan Avenue, Suite 300
Chicago, IL 60604-4302
Phone: (312) 461-0600
E-mail: stuartrnet@comcast.net
http://www.aaart.edu

Bradley University
1501 West Bradley Avenue
Peoria, IL 61625
Phone: (309) 676-7611
E-mail: admissions@bradley.edu
http://www.bradley.edu

Columbia College Chicago
600 South Michigan Avenue
Chicago, IL 60605
Phone: (312) 344-7130
Fax: (312) 344-8024
http://www.colum.edu

DePaul University
1 East Jackson Boulevard
Chicago, IL 60604
Phone: (312) 362-8300
E-mail: admitdpu@depaul.edu
http://www.depaul.edu/

**University of Illinois—
      Urbana–Champaign**
901 West Illinois
Urbana, IL 61801
Phone: (217) 333-1000
E-mail: admissions@oar.uiuc.edu
http://www.uiuc.edu

INDIANA

Ball State University
2000 University Avenue
Muncie, IN 47306
Phone: (765) 285-8300
E-mail: askus@bsu.edu
http://www.bsu.edu

University of Southern Indiana
8600 University Boulevard
Evansville, IN 47712
Phone: (812) 464-8600

E-mail: enroll@usi.edu
http://www.usi.edu

IOWA

Clarke College
1550 Clarke Drive
Dubuque, IA 52001
Phone: (319) 588-6300
E-mail: admissions@clarke.edu
http://www.clarke.edu

Drake University
2507 University Avenue
Des Moines, IA 50311
Phone: (515) 271-2011
E-mail: admitinfo@acad.drake.edu
http://www.drake.edu

Iowa State University of Science and Technology
100 Alumni Hall
Ames, IA 50011
Phone: (515) 294-4111
E-mail: admissions@iastate.edu
http://www.iastate.edu

St. Ambrose University
518 West Locust Street
Davenport, IA 52803
Phone: (563) 333-6300
E-mail: admit@sau.edu
http://www.sau.admissions

Simpson College
701 North "C" Street
Indianola, IA 50125
Phone: (515) 961-1624
E-mail: admiss@simpson.edu
http://www.simpson.edu

KANSAS

Pittsburg State University
Pittsburg, KS 66762
Phone: (620) 235-4251
Fax: 316-235-6003
E-mail: psuadmit@pittstate.edu

University of Kansas
1502 Iowa
Lawrence, KS 66045
Phone: (785) 864-2700
E-mail: adm@ukans.edu
http://www.ukans.edu

KENTUCKY

Murray State University
P.O. Box 9
Murray, KY 42071

Phone: (270) 762-3035
Fax: (270) 762-3050
E-mail: admissions@murraystate.edu

University of Kentucky
206 Administration Building
Lexington, KY 40506
Phone: (859) 257-2000
E-mail: admissio@pop.uky.edu
http://www.uky.edu

Western Kentucky University
One Big Red Way
Bowling Green, KY 42101
Phone: (270) 745-2551
Fax: (270) 745-6133
E-mail: admission@wku.edu
http://www.wku.edu

LOUISIANA

Louisiana College
1140 College Drive
Pineville, LA 71359
Phone: (318) 487-7259
Fax: (318) 487-7550
E-mail: admissions@lacollege.edu

MAINE

Saint Joseph's College of Maine
278 Whites Bridge Road
Standish, ME 04084
Phone: (207) 893-7746
E-mail: admission@sjcme.edu
http://www.sjcme.edu

MASSACHUSETTES

Boston University
121 Bay State Road
Boston, MA 02215
Phone: (617) 353-2000
E-mail: admissions@bu.edu
http://www.bu.edu

Eastern Nazarene College
Quincy, MA 02170
Phone: (617) 745-3711
E-mail: admissions@enc.edu
http://www.enc.edu

Emerson College
120 Boylston Street
Boston, MA 02116
Phone: (617) 824-8500
E-mail: admission@emerson.edu
http://www.emerson.edu

Endicott College
376 Hale Street
Beverly, MA 01915
Phone: (978) 927-0585
E-mail: admissio@endicott.edu
http://www.endicott.edu

Northeastern University
360 Huntington Avenue
Boston, MA 02115
Phone: (617) 373-2000
E-mail: admissions@neu.edu
http://www.neu.edu

Simmons College
300 The Fenway
Boston, MA 02115
Phone: (800) 345-8468
Fax: (617) 521-3190
http://www.simmons.edu

Western New England College
1215 Wilbraham Road
Springfield, MA 01119
Phone: (413) 782-3111
E-mail: ugradmis@wnec.edu
http://www.wnec.edu

MICHIGAN

Central Michigan University
Mount Pleasant, MI 48859
Phone: (989) 774-3076
E-mail: cmuadmit@cmich.edu
http://www.cmich.edu

Ferris State University
901 State Street
Big Rapids, MI 49307
Phone: (231) 591-2000
E-mail: admissions@ferris.edu
http://www.ferris.edu

Grand Valley State University
One Campus Drive
Allendale, MI 49401
Phone: (616) 895-6611
E-mail: go2gvsu@gvsu.edu
http://www.gvsu.edu

Michigan State University
250 Administration Building
East Lansing, MI 48824
Phone: (517) 355-8332
Fax: (517) 353-1647
E-mail: admis@msu.edu

Northwood University
4000 Whiting Drive
Midland, MI 48640

Phone: (989) 837-4273
http://www.northwood.edu

Western Michigan University
1201 Oliver Street
Kalamazoo, MI 49008
Phone: (616) 387-1000
E-mail: ask-wmu@wmich.edu
http://www.wmich.edu

MINNESOTA

Concordia College—Moorhead
901 South Eighth Street
Moorhead, MN 56562
Phone: (218) 299-4000
E-mail: admissions@cord.edu
http://www.cord.edu

Metropolitan State University
700 East 7th Street
St. Paul, MN 55106
Phone: (651) 793-1303
Fax: (651) 793-1310
E-mail: admissionsmetro@metrostate.
edu

Minneapolis College of Art and Design
2501 Stevens Avenue South
Minneapolis, MN 55404
Phone: (612) 874-3760
Fax: (612) 874-3701
E-mail: admissions@mcad.edu
http://www.mcad.edu

University of St. Thomas
2115 Summit Avenue
St. Paul, MN 55105
Phone: (651) 962-6150
Fax: (651) 962-6160
E-mail: admissions@stthomas.edu
http://www.stthomas.edu

Winona State University
P.O. Box 5838
Winona, MN 55987
Phone: (800) 342-5978
E-mail: admissions@vax2.winona.msus.
edu
http://www.winona.msus.edu

MISSISSIPPI

University of Mississippi
P.O. Box 1848
University, MS 38677
Phone: (662) 915-7211
E-mail: admissions@olemiss.edu
http://www.olemiss.edu

University of Southern Mississippi
P.O. Box 5167 Southern Station
Hattiesburg, MS 39406
Phone: (601) 266-4000
E-mail: admissions@USM.EDU
http://www.usm.edu

MISSOURI

Northwest Missouri State University
800 University Drive
Maryville, MO 64468
Phone: (660) 562-1146
Fax: (660) 562-1121
E-mail: admissions@acad.nwmissouri.edu
http://www.nwmissouri.edu

Southeast Missouri State University
Cape Girardeau, MO 63701
Phone: (573) 651-2590
Fax: (573) 651-5936
E-mail: admissions@semo.edu

Stephens College
1200 East Broadway
P.O. Box 2121
Columbia, MO 65215
Phone: (573) 442-2211
E-mail: apply@sc.stephens.edu
http://www.stephens.edu

University of Missouri—Columbia
305 Jesse Hall
Columbia, MO 65211
Phone: (573) 882-2121
E-mail: mu4u@missouri.edu
http://www.missouri.edu

Washington University in St. Louis
One Brookings Drive
St. Louis, MO 63130
Phone: (314) 935-6000
Fax: (314) 935-4290
E-mail: admissions@wustl.edu

Webster University
470 East Lockwood Avenue
St. Louis, MO 63119
Phone: (314) 961-2660
Fax: (314) 968-7115
E-mail: admit@webster.edu
http://www.webster.edu

William Woods University
1 University Avenue
Fulton, MO 65251
Phone: (573) 592-4221
E-mail: admissions@williamwoods.edu
http://www.williamwoods.edu

NEBRASKA

Hastings College
800 Turner Avenue
Hastings, NE 68901
Phone: (402) 461-7320
Fax: (402) 461-7490
E-mail: mmolliconi@hastings.edu
http://www.hastings.edu

University of Nebraska—Lincoln
14th and R Streets
Lincoln, NE 68588
Phone: (402) 472-7211
E-mail: nuhusker@unl.edu
http://www.unl.edu

University of Nebraska—Omaha
6001 Dodge Street
Omaha, NE 68182
Phone: (402) 554-2800
E-mail: unoadm@unomaha.edu
http://www.unomaha.edu

Wayne State College
1111 Main Street
Wayne, NE 68787
Phone: (402) 375-7234
Fax: (402) 375-7204
E-mail: admit1@wsc.edu
http://www.wsc.edu

NEVADA

University of Nevada, Reno
Reno, NV 89557
Phone: (775) 784-4700
E-mail: asknevada@unr.edu
http://www.unr.edu

NEW HAMPSHIRE

Franklin Pierce College
College Road, P.O. Box 60
Rindge, NH 03461
Phone: (603) 899-4000
E-mail: admissions@fpc.edu
http://www.fpc.edu

New England College
26 Bridge Street
Henniker, NH 03242-3297
Phone: (800) 521-7642
Fax: (603) 428-3155
E-mail: admission@nec.edu
http://www.nec.edu

New Hampshire College
2500 North River Road
Manchester, NH 03106

Phone: (603) 668-2211
E-mail: admission@nhc.edu
http://www.nhc.edu

NEW JERSEY

Rider University
2083 Lawrenceville Road
Lawrenceville, NJ 08648
Phone: (609) 896-5000
E-mail: admissions@rider.edu
http://www.rider.edu

Rowan University
Glassboro, NJ 08028
Phone: (856) 256-4200
E-mail: admissions@rowan.edu
http://www2.rowan.edu

Thomas Edison State College
101 West State Street
Trenton, NJ 08608
Phone: (888) 442-8372
Fax: (609) 984-8447
E-mail: admissions@call.tesc.edu
http://www.tesc.edu

NEW YORK

College of New Rochelle
Castle Place
New Rochelle, NY 10805
Phone: (914) 654-5000
E-mail: admission@cnr.edu
http://www.cnr.edu

CUNY—Baruch College
17 Lexington Avenue
New York, NY 10010
Phone: (646) 312-1400
Fax: (646) 312-1363
E-mail: admissions@baruch.cuny.edu
http://www.baruch.cuny.edu

Fashion Institute of Technology
Seventh Avenue at 27th Street
New York, NY 10001
Phone: (212) 217-7675
E-mail: fitinfo@fitnyc.edu
http://www.fitnyc.edu

Iona College
715 North Avenue
New Rochelle, NY 10801
Phone: (914) 633-2120
Fax: (914) 637-2778
E-mail: admissions@iona.edu
http://www.iona.edu

Marist College
3399 North Road
Poughkeepsie, NY 12601
Phone: (845) 575-3226
E-mail: admissions@marist.edu
http://www.marist.edu

New York Institute of Technology
P.O. Box 8000
Old Westbury, NY 11568
Phone: (516) 686-7516
E-mail: admissions@nyit.edu
http://www.nyit.edu

Pace University
1 Pace Plaza
New York, NY 10038
Phone: (800) 874-7223
Fax: (212) 346-1821
E-mail: infoctr@pace.edu
http://www.pace.edu

Rochester Institute of Technology
60 Lomb Memorial Drive
Rochester, NY 14623
Phone: (585) 475-6631
Fax: (585) 475-7424
E-mail: admissions@rit.edu
http://www.rit.edu

School of Visual Arts
209 East 23rd Street
New York, NY 10010
Phone: (212) 592-2100
Fax: (212) 592-2116
E-mail: admissions@sva.edu
http://www.schoolofvisualarts.edu

Syracuse University
201 Tolley Administration Building
Syracuse, NY 13244
Phone: (315) 443-1870
E-mail: orange@syr.edu
http://www.syracuse.edu

NORTH CAROLINA

Appalachian State University
Boone, NC 28608
Phone: (828) 262-2000
E-mail: admissions@appstate.edu
http://www.appstate.edu

Campbell University
P.O. Box 546
Buies Creek, NC 27506
Phone: (910) 893-1320
E-mail: adm@mailcenter.campbell.edu
http://www.campbell.edu

OHIO

Columbus College of Art and Design
107 North Ninth Street
Columbus, OH 43215
Phone: (614) 224-9101
E-mail: admissions@ccad.edu
http://www.ccad.edu

Kent State University
P.O. Box 5190
Kent, OH 44242
Phone: (330) 672-2121
E-mail: KENTADM@Admissions.Kent.
  edu
http://www.kent.edu

Marietta College
215 Fifth Street
Marietta, OH 45750
Phone: (740) 376-4643
E-mail: admit@marietta.edu
http://www.marietta.edu

Ohio University
Athens, OH 45701
Phone: (740) 593-1000
E-mail: FRSHINFO@ohiou.edu
http://www.ohiou.edu

University of Akron
302 Buchtel Common
Akron, OH 44325
Phone: (330) 972-7111
E-mail: InfoReq@uakron.edu
http://www.uakron.edu

Youngstown State University
One University Plaza
Youngstown, OH 44555
Phone: (330) 742-3000
E-mail: enroll@ysu.edu
http://www.ysu.edu

OKLAHOMA

Oklahoma Baptist University
P.O. Box 61174
Shawnee, OK 74804
Phone: (405) 878-2033
Fax: (405) 878-2046
E-mail: admissions@mail.okbu.edu

Oklahoma Christian University
P.O. Box 11000
Oklahoma City, OK 73136
Phone: (405) 425-5050
Fax: (405) 425-5208
E-mail: info@oc.edu

Oklahoma City University
2501 North Blackwelder
Oklahoma City, OK 73106
Phone: (405) 521-5050
E-mail: uadmissions@okcu.edu
http://www.youatocu.com

Oklahoma State University
324 Student Union
Stillwater, OK 74078
Phone: (405) 744-6858
Fax: (405) 744-5285
E-mail: admit@okstate.edu

University of Central Oklahoma
100 North University Drive, P.O. Box 151
Edmond, OK 73034
Phone: (405) 974-2338
Fax: (405) 341-4964
E-mail: admituco@ucok.edu

University of Oklahoma
1000 Asp Avenue
Norman, OK 73019
Phone: (405) 325-2151
Fax: 405-325-7124
E-mail: admrec@ou.edu
http://www.ou.edu

OREGON

Portland State University
P.O. Box 751
Portland, OR 97207
Phone: (503) 725-3000
E-mail: askadm@ess.pdx.edu
http://www.pdx.edu

University of Oregon
1217 University of Oregon
Eugene, OR 97403
E-mail: uoadmit@oregon.uoregon.edu
http://www.uoregon.edu

PENNSYLVANIA

Duquesne University
600 Forbes Avenue
Pittsburgh, PA 15282
Phone: (412) 396-6000
E-mail: admissions@duq.edu
http://www.duq.edu

Gannon University
109 University Square
Erie, PA 16541
Phone: (814) 871-7240
Fax: (814) 871-5803
E-mail: admissions@gannon.edu
http://www.gannon.edu

Marywood University
2300 Adams Avenue
Scranton, PA 18509
Phone: (570) 348-6211
E-mail: ugadm@ac.marywood.edu
http://www.marywood.edu

Mercyhurst College Admissions
501 East 38th Street
Erie, PA 16546
Phone: (814) 824-2202
E-mail: admissions@mercyhurst.edu
http://www.mercyhurst.edu

**Pennsylvania State University—
    University Park**
University Park Campus
University Park, PA 16802
E-mail: admissions@psu.edu
http://www.psu.edu

Point Park College
201 Wood Street
Pittsburgh, PA 15222
Phone: (800) 321-0129
E-mail: enroll@ppc.edu
http://www.ppc.edu

Temple University
Philadelphia, PA 19122
Phone: (215) 204-7200
E-mail: tuadm@temple.edu
http://www.temple.edu

Waynesburg College
51 West College Street
Waynesburg, PA 15370
Phone: (724) 627-8191
E-mail: admissions@waynesburg.edu
http://www.waynesburg.edu

Widener University
Office of Admissions
One University Place
Chester, PA 19013
Phone: (610) 499-4126
E-mail: admissions.office@widener.edu
http://www.widener.edu

RHODE ISLAND

Johnson & Wales University
8 Abbott Park Place
Providence, RI 02903
Phone: (401) 598-1000
Fax: (401) 598-4901
E-mail: petersons@jwu.edu
http://www.jwu.edu

SOUTH CAROLINA

**University of South Carolina—
    Columbia**
Columbia, SC 29208
Phone: (803) 777-7000
E-mail: admissions-ugrad@sc.edu
http://www.sc.edu

SOUTH DAKOTA

University of South Dakota
414 East Clark Street
Vermillion, SD 57069
Phone: (605) 677-5434
Fax: (605) 677-6753
E-mail: admiss@usd.edu

TENNESSEE

Belmont University
900 Belmont Boulevard
Nashville, TN 37212
Phone: (615) 460-6785
Fax: (615) 460-5434
E-mail: buadmission@mail.belmont.edu
http://www.belmont.edu

Milligan College
P.O. Box 210
Milligan College, TN 37682
Phone: (423) 461-8730
Fax: (423) 461-8982
E-mail: admissions@milligan.edu
    (general)
http://www.milligan.edu

Union University
1050 Union University Drive
Jackson, TN 38305
Phone: (901) 668-1818
E-mail: info@uu.edu
http://www.uu.edu

University of Tennessee—Knoxville
800 Andy Holt Tower
Knoxville, TN 37996
Phone: (865) 974-1000
E-mail: admissions@utk.edu
http://www.utk.edu

TEXAS

Abilene Christian University
ACU Station, P.O. Box 29000
Abilene, TX 79699-9000
Phone: (915) 674-2650
E-mail: info@admissions.acu.edu
http://www.acu.edu

Sam Houston State University
1700 Sam Houston Avenue
Huntsville, TX 77341
Phone: (936) 294-1111
E-mail: adm_jbc@shsu.edu
http://www.shsu.edu

Southern Methodist University
P.O. Box 750296
Dallas, TX 75275
Phone: (214) 768-2000
E-mail: ugadmission@smu.edu
http://www.smu.edu

Texas Christian University
2800 South University Drive
Fort Worth, TX 76129
Phone: (817) 257-7490
Fax: (817) 257-7268
E-mail: frogmail@tcu.edu
http://www.tcu.edu

Texas Tech University
P.O. Box 42013
Lubbock, TX 79409
Phone: (806) 742-2011
E-mail: nsr@ttu.edu
http://www.texastech.edu

Texas Woman's University
P.O. Box 425587
Denton, TX 76204
Phone: (940) 898-2000
E-mail: admissions@twu.edu
http://www.twu.edu

University of Houston
4800 Calhoun Road
Houston, TX 77004
Phone: (713) 743-1000

E-mail: admissions@uh.edu
http://www.uh.edu

University of Texas—Austin
Main Building, Room 7
Austin, TX 78712
Phone: (512) 471-3434
E-mail: frmn@uts.cc.utexas.edu
http://www.utexas.edu

West Texas A&M University
P.O. Box 60999
Canyon, TX 79016
Phone: (806) 651-2000
E-mail: apifer@mail.wtamu.edu
http://www.wtamu.edu

VIRGINIA

Hampton University
Hampton, VA 23668
Phone: (757) 727-5070
E-mail: admissions@hamptonu.edu
http://www.hamptonu.edu

Virginia Commonwealth University
821 West Franklin Street
Richmond, VA 23284
Phone: (804) 828-0100
E-mail: ugrad@vcu.edu
http://www.vcu.edu

WASHINGTON

Washington State University
French Administration Building
Pullman, WA 99164
Phone: (509) 335-5586
Fax: (509) 335-7468
E-mail: admiss@wsu.edu
http://www.wsu.edu

WEST VIRGINIA

Concord College
1000 Vermillion Street
Athens, WV 24712
Phone: (304) 384-3115
E-mail: admissions@concord.edu
http://www.concord.edu

West Virginia State College
P.O. Box 1000
Institute, WV 25112
Phone: (304) 766-3032
Fax: (304) 766-4158
E-mail: meeksjd@wvsc.edu

West Virginia University
P.O. Box 6009
Morgantown, WV 26506
Phone: (304) 293-2124
Fax: (304) 293-3080
E-mail: go2wvu@mail.wvu.edu

WISCONSIN

Marquette University
P.O. Box 1881
Milwaukee, WI 53201
Phone: (414) 288-7250
E-mail: admissions@marquette.edu
http://www.marquette.edu

University of Wisconsin–Madison
716 Langdon Street
Madison, WI 53706
Phone: (608) 262-3961
Fax: (608) 262-7706
E-mail: on.wisconsin@admissions.wisc.
edu

B. COLLEGES AND UNIVERSITIES OFFERING MAJORS IN PUBLIC RELATIONS

The following is a listing of selected four-year schools granting degrees with majors in public relations. They are grouped by state. School names, addresses, phone numbers, Web addresses, and e-mail admission addresses are included when available.

The author does not endorse any one school over another. Use this list as a beginning. More college are beginning to grant degrees in this area every year. Check the newest edition of *Lovejoy's College Guide* (found in the reference section of libraries or in guidance counseling centers) for additional schools offering degrees in this field.

ALABAMA

Alabama State University
915 South Jackson Street
Montgomery, AL 36104
Phone: (334) 229-4291
http://www.alasu.edu

Auburn University
202 Martin Hall
Auburn University, AL 36849
Phone: (334) 844-4080
E-mail: admissions@
auburn.edu
http://www.auburn.edu

Spring Hill College
4000 Dauphin Street
Mobile, AL 36608
Phone: (251) 380-3030
Fax: (251) 460-2186
E-mail: admit@shc.edu
http://www.shc.edu

University of Alabama
P.O. Box 870132
Tuscaloosa, AL 35487
Phone: (205) 348-5666
E-mail: uaadmit@enroll.ua.edu
http://www.ua.edu

ARIZONA

Northern Arizona University
P.O. Box 4084
Flagstaff, AZ 86011-4084
Phone: (205) 348-5666
Fax: (205) 348-9046
E-mail: admissions@ua.edu
http://www.nau.edu

ARKANSAS

Harding University
P.O. Box 12255
Searcy, AR 72149
Phone: (501) 279-4407
Fax: (501) 279-4129
E-mail: admissions@harding.edu
http://www.harding.edu

John Brown University
200 West University Street
Siloam Springs, AR 72761
Phone: (501) 524-7454
Fax: (501) 524-4196
E-mail: jbuinfo@acc.jbu.edu
http://www.jbu.edu

CALIFORNIA

California State Polytechnic University
3801 West Temple Avenue
Pomona, CA 91768
Phone: (909) 869-3210
http://www.csupomona.edu

California State University, Chico
400 West First Street
Chico, CA 95929
Phone: (530) 898-4879
Fax: (530) 898-6456
E-mail: info@csuchico.edu
http://www.csuchico.edu

California State University, Dominguez Hills
1000 East Victoria Street
Carson, CA 90747
Phone: (800) 344-5484
Fax: (310) 217-6800
http://www.csudh.edu

California State University, Fullerton
P.O. Box 6900
800 North State College Boulevard
Fullerton, CA 92834
Phone: (714) 278-2370
http://www.fullerton.edu

California State University, Hayward
25800 Carlos Bee Boulevard
Hayward, CA 94542
Phone: (510) 885-3248
Fax: (510) 885-3816
E-mail: adminfo@csuhayward.edu
http://www.csuhayward.edu

Chapman University
One University Drive
Orange, CA 92866
Phone: (714) 997-6711
Fax: (714) 997-6713
E-mail: admit@chapman.edu
http://www.chapman.edu

Pacific Union College
One Angwin Avenue
Angwin, CA 94508
Phone: (707) 965-6425
Fax: (707) 965-6432
E-mail: enroll@puc.edu
http://www.puc.edu

Pepperdine University
Malibu, CA 90263-4392
Phone: (310) 506-4392
Fax: (310) 506-4861
http://www.pepperdine.edu

San Diego State University
5500 Campanile Drive
San Diego, CA 92182
Phone: (619) 594-6886
Fax: (619) 594-1250
E-mail: admissions@sdsu.edu
http://www.sdsu.edu

San Jose State University
One Washington Square
San Jose, CA 95192
Phone: (408) 924-1000
E-mail: info@soar.sjsu.edu
http://www.sjsu.edu

University of Southern California
University Park
Los Angeles, CA 90089
Phone: (213) 740-1111
E-mail: admitusc@usc.edu
http://www.usc.edu

COLORADO

Colorado State University
Fort Collins, CO 80523
Phone: (970) 491-6909
http://www.colostate.edu

Colorado State University—Pueblo
2200 Bonforte Boulevard
Pueblo, CO 81001
Phone: (719) 549-2461
Fax: (719) 549-2419
E-mail: info@uscolo.edu
http://www.uscolo.edu

Mesa State College
1100 North Avenue
Grand Junction, CO 81501
Phone: (970) 248-1875
Fax: (970) 248-1973
E-mail: admissions@mesastate.edu
http://www.mesastate.edu

CONNECTICUT

Quinnipiac University
Hamden, CT 06518
Phone: (203) 582-8600
Fax: 203-582-8906
E-mail: admissions@quinnipiac.edu
http://www.quinnipiac.edu

DELAWARE

University of Delaware
Newark, DE 19716
Phone: (302) 831-8123
Fax: (302) 831-6905
E-mail: admissions@udel.edu
http://www.udel.edu

DISTRICT OF COLUMBIA

American University
4400 Massachusetts Avenue, NW
Washington, DC 20016
Phone: (202) 885-6000
Fax: (202) 885-1025
E-mail: afa@american.edu
http://www.admissions.american.edu

FLORIDA

Barry University
11300 N.E. Second Avenue
Miami Shores, FL 33161
Phone: (305) 899-3000
E-mail: admissions@mail.barry.edu
http://www.barry.edu

Florida Agricultural and Mechanical University
Tallahassee, FL 32307
Phone: (850) 599-3796
E-mail: admissions@famu.edu
http://www.famu.edu

Florida Southern College
111 Lake Hollingsworth Drive
Lakeland, FL 33801
Phone: (800) 274-4131
E-mail: fscadm@flsouthern.edu
http://www.flsouthern.edu

Florida State University
Tallahassee, FL 32306
Phone: (850) 644-2525
E-mail: admissions@admin.fsu.edu
http://www.fsu.edu

University of Florida
201 Criser Hall
Gainesville, FL 32611
Phone: (352) 392-3261
E-mail: freshman@ufl.edu
http://www.ufl.edu

University of Miami
P.O. Box 248025
Coral Gables, FL 33124
Phone: (305) 284-2211
E-mail: admission@miami.edu
http://www.miami.edu

GEORGIA

Berry College
P.O. Box 490159
2277 Martha Berry Highway, NW
Mount Berry, GA 30149
Phone: (706) 236-2215
Fax: (706) 290-2178
E-mail: admissions@berry.edu
http://www.berry.edu

Columbus State University
4225 University Avenue
Columbus, GA 31907
Phone: (706) 568-2035
Fax: (706) 568-5272
http://www.colstate.edu

Georgia Southern University
Forest Drive
Statesboro, GA 30460
Phone: (912) 681-5391
Fax: (912) 486-7240
E-mail: admissions@georgiasouthern.edu
http://www.georgiasouthern.edu

Shorter College
315 Shorter Avenue
Rome, GA 30165
Phone: (706) 233-7319
Fax: (706) 233-7224
E-mail: admissions@shorter.edu
http://www.shorter.edu

Toccoa Falls College
P.O. Box 800-899
Toccoa Falls, GA 30598
Phone: (706) 886-6831
Fax: (706) 282-6012
E-mail: admissions@tfc.edu
http://www.tfc.edu

University of Georgia
212 Terrell Hall
Athens, GA 30602
Phone: (706) 542-3000
E-mail: undergrad@admissions.uga.edu
http://www.uga.edu

Valdosta State University
Valdosta, GA 31698
Phone: (229) 333-5791
Fax: (229) 333-5482
E-mail: admissions@valdosta.edu
http://www.valdosta.edu

HAWAII

Hawaii Pacific University
1164 Bishop Street
Honolulu, HI 96813
Phone: (808) 544-0200
E-mail: admissions@hpu.edu
http://www.hpu.edu

IDAHO

Northwest Nazarene University
623 Holly Street
Nampa, ID 83686
Phone: (208) 467-8000
Fax: (208) 467-8645
E-mail: admissions@nnu.edu
http://www.nnu.edu

University of Idaho
Moscow, ID 83844
Phone: (208) 885-6326
Fax: (208) 885-9119
E-mail: carolynl@uidaho.edu
http://www.uidaho.edu

ILLINOIS

Bradley University
1501 West Bradley Avenue
Peoria, IL 61625

Phone: (309) 676-7611
E-mail: admissions@bradley.edu
http://www.bradley.edu

Columbia College Chicago
600 South Michigan Avenue
Chicago, IL 60605
Phone: (312) 344-7130
Fax: (312) 344-8024
http://www.colum.edu

Greenville College
315 East College Avenue
Greenville, IL 62246
Phone: (618) 664-7100
Fax: (618) 664-9841
E-mail: admissions@greenville.edu
http://www.greenville.edu

Illinois State University
Normal, IL 61790
Phone: (309) 438-2181
Fax: (309) 438-3932
E-mail: ugradadm@ilstu.edu
http://www.ilstu.edu

Lewis University
One University Parkway
Romeoville, IL 60446-2200
Phone: (800) 897-9000
E-mail: admissions@lewisu.edu
http://www.lewisu.edu

Monmouth College
700 East Broadway
Monmouth, IL 61462
Phone: (309) 457-2140
Fax: (309) 457-2141
E-mail: admit@monm.edu
http://www.monm.edu

North Central College
30 North Brainard Street
Naperville, IL 60540
Phone: (630) 637-5800
Fax: (630) 637-5819
E-mail: ncadm@noctrl.edu
http://www.northcentralcollege.edu

Quincy University
1800 College Avenue
Quincy, IL 62301
Phone: (217) 228-5210
E-mail: admissions@quincy.edu
http://www.quincy.edu

Roosevelt University
Chicago Campus
430 South Michigan Avenue
Chicago, IL 60605

Phone: 877-APPLY-RU
http://www.roosevelt.edu

INDIANA

Ball State University
2000 University Avenue
Muncie, IN 47306
Phone: (765) 285-8300
E-mail: askus@bsu.edu
http://www.bsu.edu

Indiana University Northwest,
    Hawthorne
3400 Broadway
Gary, IN 46408
Phone: (219) 980-6767
Fax: (219) 981-4219
E-mail: admit@iun.edu
http://www.iun.edu

Purdue University Fort Wayne
2101 East Coliseum Boulevard
Fort Wayne, IN 46805
Phone: (260) 481-6812
Fax: (260) 481-6880
E-mail: ipfwadms@ipfw.edu
http://www.ipfw.edu

Saint Mary-of-the-Woods College
Saint Mary-of-the-Woods, IN 47876
Phone: (812) 535-5106
Fax: (812) 535-4900
E-mail: smwcadms@smwc.edu
http://www.smwc.edu

Taylor University, Fort Wayne
1025 West Rudisill Boulevard
Fort Wayne, IN 46807
Phone: (219) 744-8689
Fax: (260) 744-8660
E-mail: admissions_f@tayloru.edu
http://www.tayloru.edu

University of Southern Indiana
8600 University Boulevard
Evansville, IN 47712
Phone: (812) 464-8600
E-mail: enroll@usi.edu
http://www.usi.edu

IOWA

Clarke College
1550 Clarke Drive
Dubuque, IA 52001
Phone: (319) 588-6300
E-mail: admissions@clarke.edu
http://www.clarke.edu

Coe College
1220 First Avenue, NE
Cedar Rapids, IA 52402
Phone: (319) 399-8500
Fax: (319) 399-8816
E-mail: admission@coe.edu
http://www.coe.edu

Drake University
2507 University Avenue
Des Moines, IA 50311
Phone: (515) 271-2011
E-mail: admitinfo@acad.drake.edu
http://www.drake.edu

St. Ambrose University
518 West Locust Street
Davenport, IA 52803
Phone: (563) 333-6300
E-mail: admit@sau.edu
http://www.sau.admissions

University of Iowa
Iowa City, IA 52242
Phone: (319) 335-3847
Fax: (319) 335-1535
E-mail: admissions@uiowa.edu
http://www.uiowa.edu

University of Northern Iowa
Cedar Falls, IA 50614
Phone: (319) 273-2281
Fax: (319) 273-2885
E-mail: admissions@uni.edu
http://www.uni.edu

University of Southern Indiana
8600 University Boulevard
Evansville, IN 47712
Phone: (812) 464-1765
Fax: (812) 465-7154
E-mail: enroll@usi.edu
http://www.usi.edu

Wartburg College
100 Wartburg Boulevard
P.O. Box 1003
Waverly, IA 50677
Phone: (319) 352-8264
Fax: (319) 352-8579
http://www.wartburg.edu

KANSAS

Fort Hays State University
600 Park Street
Hays, KS 67601
Phone: (785) 628-5830
E-mail: tigers@fhsu.edu
http://www.fhsu.edu

MidAmerica Nazarene University
2030 East College Way
Olathe, KS 66062
Phone: (913) 791-3380
Fax: (913) 791-3481
E-mail: admissions@mnu.edu
http://www.mnu.edu

Pittsburg State University
Pittsburg, KS 66762
Phone: (620) 235-4251
Fax: (316) 235-6003
E-mail: psuadmit@pittstate.edu
http://www.pittstate.edu

KENTUCKY

Eastern Kentucky University
521 Lancaster Avenue
Richmond, KY 40475
Phone: (859) 622-2106
Fax: (859) 622-8024
E-mail: admissions@eku.edu
http://www.eku.edu

Murray State University
P.O. Box 9
Murray, KY 42071
Phone: (270) 762-3035
Fax: 270) 762-3050
E-mail: admissions@murraystate.edu
http://www.murraystate.edu

Western Kentucky University
One Big Red Way
Bowling Green, KY 42101
Phone: (270) 745-2551
Fax: (270) 745-6133
E-mail: admission@wku.edu
http://www.wku.edu

LOUISIANA

University of Louisiana at Lafayette
P.O. Box 44652
Lafayette, LA 70504
Phone: (800) 752-6553
E-mail: enroll@louisiana.edu
http://www.louisiana.edu

MAINE

New England School of
    Communications
1 College Circle
Bangor, ME 04401
Phone: (207) 941-7176
Fax: (207) 947-3987
E-mail: info@nescom.edu
http://www.nescom.edu

MASSACHUSETTES

Assumption College
500 Salisbury Street
P.O. Box 15005
Worcester, MA 01609
Phone: (508) 767-7285
E-mail: admiss@assumption.edu
http://www.assumption.edu

Boston University
121 Bay State Road
Boston, MA 02215
Phone: (617) 353-2000
E-mail: admissions@bu.edu
http://www.bu.edu

Curry College
Milton, MA 02186
Phone: (617) 333-2210
Fax: (617) 333-2114
E-mail: curryadm@curry.edu
http://www.curry.edu

Emerson College
120 Boylston Street
Boston, MA 02116
Phone: (617) 824-8500
E-mail: admission@emerson.edu
http://www.emerson.edu

Framingham State College
100 State Street
P.O. Box 9101
Framingham, MA 01701
Phone: (508) 626-4500
E-mail: admiss@frc.mass.edu
http://www.framingham.edu

Salem State College
352 Lafayette Street
Salem, MA 01970
Phone: (978) 542-6200
E-mail: admissions@salemstate.edu
http://www.salemstate.edu

Simmons College
300 The Fenway
Boston, MA 02115
Phone: (800) 345-8468
Fax: (617) 521-3190
http://www.simmons.edu

Suffolk University
8 Ashburton Place
Boston, MA 02108
Phone: (800) 6-SUFFOLK
Fax: 617-742-4291
E-mail: admission@suffolk.edu
http://www.suffolk.edu

MICHIGAN

Andrews University
Berrien Springs, MI 49104
Phone: (800) 253-2874
Fax: (269) 471-3228
E-mail: enroll@andrews.edu
http://www.andrews.edu

Central Michigan University
Mt. Pleasant, MI 48859
Phone: (989) 774-3076
Fax: (989) 774-7267
E-mail: cmuadmit@cmich.edu
http://www.cmich.edu

Eastern Michigan University
Ypsilanti, MI 48197
Phone: (734) 487-3060
Fax: (734) -487-6559
E-mail: admissions@emich.edu
http://www.emich.edu

Ferris State University
901 State Street
Big Rapids, MI 49307
Phone: (231) 591-2000
E-mail: admissions@ferris.edu
http://www.ferris.edu

Grand Valley State University
One Campus Drive
Allendale, MI 49401
Phone: (616) 895-6611
E-mail: go2gvsu@gvsu.edu
http://www.gvsu.edu

Madonna University
36600 Schoolcraft Road
Livonia, MI 48150
Phone: (734) 432-5317
Fax: (734) 432-5393
E-mail: muinfo@smtp.munet.edu
http://www.munet.edu

Northern Michigan University
1401 Presque Isle Avenue
Marquette, MI 49855
Phone: (906) 227-2650
Fax: 906-227-1747
E-mail: admiss@nmu.edu
http://www.nmu.edu

Wayne State University
Detroit, MI 48202
Phone: (313) 577-3581
Fax: (313) 577-7536
E-mail: admissions@wayne.edu
http://www.wayne.edu

Western Michigan University
1201 Oliver Street
Kalamazoo, MI 49008
Phone: (616) 387-1000
E-mail: ask-wmu@wmich.edu
http://www.wmich.edu

MINNESOTA

Concordia College—Moorhead
901 South Eighth Street
Moorhead, MN 56562
Phone: (218) 299-4000
E-mail: admissions@cord.edu
http://www.cord.edu

Minnesota State University Mankato
Mankato, MN 56001
Phone: (507) 389-6670
Fax: (507) 389-1511
E-mail: admissions@mnsu.edu
http://www.mnsu.edu

Minnesota State University Moorhead
Moorhead, MN 56563
Phone: (218) 477-2161
Fax: (218) 236-2168

Northwestern College
3003 Snelling Avenue North
St. Paul, MN 55113
Phone: (651) 631-5209
Fax: (651) 631-5680
E-mail: admissions@nwc.edu
http://www.nwc.edu

St. Cloud State University
720 4th Avenue South
St. Cloud, MN 56301
Phone: (320) 308-2244
Fax: (320) 308-2243
E-mail: scsu4u@stcloudstate.edu
http://www.stcloudstate.edu/

Saint Mary's University of Minnesota
700 Terrace Heights #2
Winona, MN 55987
Phone: (507) 457-1700
Fax: (507) 457-1722
E-mail: admissions@smumn.edu
http://www.smumn.edu

University of St. Thomas
2115 Summit Avenue
St. Paul, MN 55105
Phone: (651) 962-6150
Fax: (651) 962-6160
E-mail: admissions@stthomas.edu
http://www.stthomas.edu

Winona State University
P.O. Box 5838
Winona, MN 55987
Phone: (800) 342-5978
E-mail: admissions@vax2.winona.msus.edu
http://www.winona.msus.edu

MISSOURI

Central Missouri State University
1401 Ward Edwards
Warrensburg, MO 64093
Phone: (660) 543-4290
Fax: (660) 543-8517
E-mail: admit@cmsuvmb.cmsu.edu

Concordia College
901 8th Street South
Moorhead, MN 56562
Phone: (218) 299-3004
Fax: (218) 299-3947
E-mail: admissions@cord.edu
http://www.cord.edu

Fontbonne University
6800 Wydown Boulevard
St. Louis, MO 63105
Phone: (314) 889-1400
Fax: (314) 719-8021
E-mail: pmusen@fontbonne.edu
http://www.fontbonne.edu

Lindenwood University
209 South Kings Highway
St. Charles, MO 63301
Phone: (636) 949-4949
Fax: (636) 949-4989
http://www.lindenwood.edu

Northwest Missouri State University
800 University Drive
Maryville, MO 64468
Phone: (660) 562-1146
Fax: (660) 562-1121
E-mail: admissions@acad.nwmissouri.edu
http://www.nwmissouri.edu

Rockhurst University
1100 Rockhurst Road
Kansas City, MO 64110
Phone: (816) 501-4100
Fax: (816) 501-4241
E-mail: admission@rockhurst.edu
http://www.rockhurst.edu

Southeast Missouri State University
Cape Girardeau, MO 63701
Phone: (573) 651-2590

Fax: (573) 651-5936
E-mail: admissions@semo.edu
http://www.semo.edu

Stephens College
Columbia, MO 65215
Phone: (573) 876-7207
Fax: (573) 876-7237
E-mail: apply@stephens.edu
http://www.stephens.edu

Webster University
470 East Lockwood Avenue
St. Louis, MO 63119
Phone: (314) 961-2660
Fax: (314) 968-7115
E-mail: admit@webster.edu
http://www.webster.edu

William Woods University
1 University Avenue
Fulton, MO 65251
Phone: (573) 592-4221
E-mail: admissions@williamwoods.edu
http://www.williamwoods.edu

MONTANA

Carroll College
1601 North Benton Avenue
Helena, MT 59625
Phone: (406) 447-4384
E-mail: admit@carroll.edu
http://www.carroll.edu

Montana State University—Billings
1500 University Drive
Billings, MT 59101
Phone: (406) 657-2158
Fax: (406) 657-2302
E-mail: admissions@msubillings.edu
http://www.msubillings.edu

NEBRASKA

Doane College
Crete, NE 68333
Phone: (402) 826-8222
Fax: (402) 826-8600
E-mail: admissions@doane.edu
http://www.doane.edu

Hastings College
800 Turner Avenue
Hastings, NE 68901
Phone: (402) 461-7320
Fax: (402) 461-7490
E-mail: mmolliconi@hastings.edu
http://www.hastings.edu

University of Nebraska—Omaha
6001 Dodge Street
Omaha, NE 68182
Phone: (402) 554-2800
E-mail: unoadm@unomaha.edu
http://www.unomaha.edu

NEVADA

University of Nevada, Reno
Reno, NV 89557
Phone: (775) 784-4700
E-mail: asknevada@unr.edu
http://www.unr.edu

NEW HAMPSHIRE

New England College
26 Bridge Street
Henniker, NH 03242-3297
Phone: (800) 521-7642
Fax: (603) 428-3155
E-mail: admission@nec.edu
http://www.nec.edu

NEW JERSEY

Rider University
2083 Lawrenceville Road
Lawrenceville, NJ 08648
Phone: (609) 896-5000
E-mail: admissions@rider.edu
http://www.rider.edu

Rowan University
Glassboro, NJ 08028
Phone: (856) 256-4200
E-mail: admissions@rowan.edu
http://www.rowan.edu

NEW YORK

Buffalo State College
1300 Elmwood Avenue
Buffalo, NY 14222
Phone: (716) 878-4017
Fax: (716) 878-6100
E-mail: admissions@buffalostate.edu
http://www.buffalostate.edu

Hofstra University
Hempstead, NY 11549
Phone: (516) 463-6700
Fax: (516) 463-5100
http://www.hofstra.edu

Ithaca College
Ithaca, NY 14850

Phone: (800) 429-4274
E-mail: admission@ithaca.edu
http://www.ithaca.edu

Long Island University, C.W. Post Campus
720 Northern Boulevard
Brookville, NY 11548
Phone: (516) 299-2900
Fax: (516) 299-2137
E-mail: enroll@cwpost.liu.edu
http://www.liu.edu

Marist College
3399 North Road
Poughkeepsie, NY 12601
Phone: (845) 575-3226
E-mail: admissions@marist.edu
http://www.marist.edu

Mount Saint Mary College
330 Powell Avenue
Newburgh, NY 12550
Phone: (845) 569-3248
E-mail: mtstmary@msmc.edu
http://www.msmc.edu

State University of New York College at Brockport
350 New Campus Drive
Brockport, NY 14420
Phone: (585) 395-2751
Fax: (585) 395-5452
E-mail: admit@brockport.edu
http://www.brockport.edu

Utica College
1600 Burrstone Road
Utica, NY 13502
Phone: (315) 792-3006
E-mail: admiss@ucsu.edu
http://www.utica.edu

NORTH CAROLINA

Appalachian State University
Boone, NC 28608
Phone: (828) 262-2000
E-mail: admissions@appstate.edu
http://www.appstate.edu

Campbell University
P.O. Box 546
Buies Creek, NC 27506
Phone: (910) 893-1320
E-mail: adm@mailcenter.campbell.edu
http://www.campbell.edu

University of North Carolina at Pembroke
One University Drive
Pembroke, NC 28372
Phone: (910) 521-6262
Fax: (910) 521-6497
E-mail: admissions@uncp.edu
http://www.uncp.edu

Wingate University
Wingate, NC 28174
Phone: (704) 233-8200
Fax: (704) 233-8110
E-mail: admit@wingate.edu
http://www.wingate.edu

OHIO

Bowling Green State University
110 McFall Center
Bowling Green, OH 43403
Phone: (419) 372-BGSU
Fax: (419) 372-6955
E-mail: choosebgsu@bgnet.bgsu.edu
http://www.bgsu.edu

Capital University
2199 East Main Street
Columbus, OH 43209
Phone: (614) 236-6101
Fax: (614) 236-6926
E-mail: admissions@capital.edu
http://www.capital.edu

Cleveland State University
1983 East 24th Street
Cleveland, OH 44115
Phone: (216) 523-5139
Fax: (216) 687-9210
E-mail: admissions@csuohio.edu
http://www.csuohio.edu

Columbus College of Art and Design
107 North Ninth Street
Columbus, OH 43215
Phone: (614) 224-9101
E-mail: admissions@ccad.edu
http://www.ccad.edu

Defiance College
701 North Clinton Street
Defiance, OH 43512
Phone: (419) 783-2359
Fax: (419) 783-2468
E-mail: admissions@defiance.edu
http://www.defiance.edu

Heidelberg College
310 East Market Street
Tiffin, OH 44883

Phone: (419) 448-2330
Fax: (419) 448-2334
E-mail: adminfo@heidelberg.edu
http://www.heidelberg.edu

Kent State University
P.O. Box 5190
Kent, OH 44242
Phone: (330) 672-2121
http://www.kent.edu

Malone College
515 25th Street, NW
Canton, OH 44709
Phone: (330) 471-8145
E-mail: admissions@malone.edu
http://www.malone.edu

Marietta College
Marietta, OH 45750
Phone: (800) 331-7896
E-mail: admit@marietta.edu
http://www.marietta.edu

Otterbein College
Westerville, OH 43081
Phone: (614) 823-1500
E-mail: uotterb@otterbein.edu
http://www.uotterb@otterbein.edu

Ohio Northern University
Ada, OH 45810
Phone: (888) 408-4668
Fax: (419) 772-2313
E-mail: admissions-ug@onu.edu
http://www.onu.edu

Ohio University
Athens, OH 45701
Phone: (740) 593-4100
E-mail: admissions.freshmen@ohiou.edu
http://www.ohiou.edu

University of Dayton
300 College Park
Dayton, OH 45469
Phone: (937) 229-4411
E-mail: admission@udayton.edu
http://www.admission.udayton.edu

University of Findlay
1000 North Main Street
Findlay, OH 45840
Phone: (419) 434-4732
E-mail: admissions@findlay.edu
http://www.findlay.edu

University of Rio Grande
Rio Grande, OH 45674
Phone: (740) 245-7208

Fax: (740) 245-7260
E-mail: elambert@rio.edu
http://www.rio.edu

Ursuline College
2550 Lander Road
Pepper Pike, OH 44124
Phone: (440) 449-4203
Fax: (440) 684-6138
E-mail: admission@ursuline.edu
http://www.ursuline.edu

Xavier University
3800 Victory Parkway
Cincinnati, OH 45207
Phone: (513) 745-3301
E-mail: xuadmit@xavier.edu
http://www.xavier.edu

Youngstown State University
One University Plaza
Youngstown, OH 44555
Phone: (330) 941-2000
Fax: (330) 941-3674
E-mail: enroll@ysu.edu
http://www.ysu.edu

OKLAHOMA

Cameron University
2800 West Gore Boulevard
Lawton, OK 73505
Phone: (580) 581-2837
Fax: (580) 581-5514
E-mail: admiss@cua.cameron.edu
http://www.cameron.edu

Northwestern Oklahoma State University
709 Oklahoma Boulevard
Alva, OK 73717
Phone: (580) 327-8550
Fax: (580) 327-8699
E-mail: smmurrow@nwosu.edu
http://www.nwosu.edu

Oklahoma Baptist University
500 West University
Shawnee, OK 74804
Phone: (405) 878-2033
Fax: (405) 878-2046
E-mail: admissions@mail.okbu.edu
http://www.okbu.edu

Oklahoma City University
2501 North Blackwelder
Oklahoma City, OK 73106
Phone: (405) 521-5050
E-mail: uadmissions@okcu.edu
http://www.youatocu.com

Oral Roberts University
7777 South Lewis Avenue
Tulsa, OK 74171
Phone: (918) 495-6518
Fax: (918) 495-6222
E-mail: admissions@oru.edu
http://www.oru.edu

University of Central Oklahoma
100 North University Drive
Edmond, OK 73034
Phone: (405) 974-2338
Fax: (405) 341-4964
E-mail: admituco@ucok.edu
http://www.ecok.edu

University of Oklahoma
1000 Asp Avenue
Norman, OK 73019
Phone: (405) 325-2151
Fax: (405) 325-7124
E-mail: admrec@ou.edu
http://www.ou.edu

OREGON

George Fox University
Newberg, OR 97132
Phone: (800) 765-4369
E-mail: admissions@georgefox.edu
http://www.georgefox.edu

Marylhurst University
17600 Pacific Highway
P.O. Box 261
Marylhurst, OR 97036
Phone: (503) 699-6268
Fax: (503) 635-6585
E-mail: admissions@marylhurst.edu
http://www.marylhurt.edu

University of Oregon
1217 University of Oregon
Eugene, OR 97403
E-mail: uoadmit@oregon.uoregon.edu
http://www.uoregon.edu

PENNSYLVANIA

Gwynedd-Mercy College
1325 Sumneytown Pike
P.O. Box 901
Gwynedd Valley, PA 19437
Phone: (800) DIAL-GMC
E-mail: admissions@gmc.edu
http://www.gmc.edu

La Salle University
1900 West Olney Avenue
Philadelphia, PA 19141

Phone: (215) 951-1500
Fax: (215) 951-1656
E-mail: admiss@lasalle.edu
http://www.lasalle.edu

Marywood University
2300 Adams Avenue
Scranton, PA 18509
Phone: (570) 348-6211
E-mail: ugadm@ac.marywood.edu
http://www.marywood.edu

Mansfield University of Pennsylvania
Mansfield, PA 16933
Phone: (570) 662-4813
Fax: (570) 662-4121
E-mail: admissions@mansfield.edu
http://www.mansfield.edu

Mercyhurst College Admissions
501 East 38th Street
Erie, PA 16546
Phone: (814) 824-2202
E-mail: admissions@mercyhurst.edu
http://www.mercyhurst.edu

Point Park College
201 Wood Street
Pittsburgh, PA 15222
Phone: (800) 321-0129
E-mail: enroll@ppc.edu
http://www.ppc.edu

Seton Hill University
Seton Hill Drive
Greensburg, PA 15601
Phone: (724) 838-4255
Fax: (724) 830-1294
E-mail: admit@setonhill.edu
http://www.setonhill.edu

Susquehanna University
514 University Avenue
Selinsgrove, PA 17870
Phone: (570) 372-4260
Fax: (570) 372-2722
E-mail: suadmiss@susqu.edu
http://www.susqu.edu

Temple University
Philadelphia, PA 19122
Phone: (215) 204-7200
E-mail: tuadm@temple.edu
http://www.temple.edu

University of Pittsburgh at Bradford
300 Campus Drive
Bradford, PA 16701
Phone: (814) 362-7555
http://www.upb.pitt.edu

Westminster College
New Wilmington, PA 6172
Phone: (800) 942-8033
E-mail: admis@westminster.edu
http://www.westminster.edu

York College of Pennsylvania
York, PA 17405
Phone: (717) 849-1600
Fax: 717-849-1607
E-mail: admissions@ycp.edu
http://www.ycp.edu

RHODE ISLAND

Johnson & Wales University
8 Abbott Park Place
Providence, RI 02903
Phone: (401) 598-1000
Fax: (401) 598-4901
E-mail: petersons@jwu.edu
http://www.jwu.edu

SOUTH CAROLINA

University of South Carolina—Columbia
Columbia, SC 29208
Phone: (803) 777-7000
E-mail: admissions-ugrad@sc.edu
http://www.sc.edu

SOUTH DAKOTA

University of Sioux Falls
1101 West 22nd Street
Sioux Falls, SD 57105
Phone: (605) 331-6600
Fax: (605) 331-6615
E-mail: admissions@usiouxfalls.edu
http://www.usiouxfalls.edu

University of South Dakota
414 East Clark Street
Vermillion, SD 57069
Phone: (605) 677-5434
Fax: (605) 677-6753
E-mail: admiss@usd.edu
http://www.usd.edu

TENNESSEE

Freed-Hardeman University
158 East Main Street
Henderson, TN 38340
Phone: (731) 989-6651
Fax: (731) 989-6047
E-mail: admissions@fhu.edu
http://www.fhu.edu

Lambuth University
705 Lambuth Boulevard
Jackson, TN 38301
Phone: (731) 425-3223
E-mail: admit@lambuth.edu
http://www.lambuth.edu

Lipscomb University
3901 Granny White Pike
Nashville, TN 37204
Phone: (615) 269-1000
Fax: (615) 269-1804
E-mail: admissions@lipscomb.edu
http://www.lipscomb.edu

Middle Tennessee State University
1301 East Main Street
Murfreesboro, TN 37132
Phone: (615) 898-2111
Fax: (615) 898-5478
E-mail: admissions@mtsu.edu
http://www.mtsu.edu

Milligan College
P.O. Box 210
Milligan College, TN 37682
Phone: (423) 461-8730
Fax: (423) 461-8982
E-mail: admissions@milligan.edu
http://www.milligan.edu

Union University
1050 Union University Drive
Jackson, TN 38305
Phone: (800) 33-UNION
E-mail: info@uu.edu
http://www.uu.edu

University of Tennessee at Martin
Martin, TN 38238
Phone: (731) 587-7032
Fax: (731) 587-7029
E-mail: jrayburn@utm.edu
http://www.utm.edu

TEXAS

Howard Payne University
1000 Fisk Avenue
Brownwood, TX 76801
Phone: (325) 649-8027
Fax: (325) 649-8901
E-mail: enroll@hputx.edu

Sam Houston State University
1700 Sam Houston Avenue
Huntsville, TX 77341
Phone: (936) 294-1111
E-mail: adm_jbc@shsu.edu
http://www.shsu.edu

Southern Methodist University
P.O. Box 750296
Dallas, TX 75275
Phone: (214) 768-2000
E-mail: ugadmission@smu.edu
http://www.smu.edu

Texas State University—San Marcos
San Marcos, TX 78666
Phone: (512) 245-2364
Fax: (512) 245-8044
E-mail: admissions@txstate.edu
http://www.txstate.edu

Texas Tech University
P.O. Box 42013
Lubbock, TX 79409
Phone: (806) 742-2011
E-mail: nsr@ttu.edu
http://www.texastech.edu

University of Houston
4800 Calhoun Road
Houston, TX 77004
Phone: (713) 743-1000
E-mail: admissions@uh.edu
http://www.uh.edu

University of Texas at Arlington
P.O. Box 19111
701 South Nedderman Drive
Arlington, TX 76019
Phone: (817) 272-6287
Fax: (817) 272-3435
E-mail: admissions@uta.edu

University of Texas—Austin
Main Building, Room 7
Austin, TX 78712
Phone: (512) 471-3434
E-mail: frmn@uts.cc.utexas.edu
http://www.utexas.edu

UTAH

University of Utah
201 South Presidents Circle
Salt Lake City, UT 84112
Phone: (801) 581-8761
Fax: (801) 585-7864
E-mail: admissions@sa.utah.edu
http://www.utah.edu

Weber State University
1137 University Circle
3750 Harrison Boulevard
Ogden, UT 84408-1137
Phone: (801) 626-6050
Fax: (801) 626-6744

E-mail: admissions@weber.edu
http://www.weber.edu

VERMONT

Champlain College
163 South Willard Street
P.O. Box 670
Burlington, VT 05402
Phone: (802) 860-2727
Fax: (802) 860-2767
E-mail: admission@champlain.edu
http://www.champlain.edu

VIRGINIA

Hampton University
Tyler Street
Hampton, VA 23668
Phone: (757) 727-5070
E-mail: admissions@hamptonu.edu
http://www.hamptonu.edu

Mary Baldwin College
Frederick and New Streets
Staunton, VA 24401
Phone: (540) 887-7221
Fax: (540) 887-7292
E-mail: admit@mbc.edu
http://www.mbc.edu

WASHINGTON

Central Washington University
400 East University Way
Ellensburg, WA 98926
Phone: (509) 963-1211
Fax: (509) 963-3022
E-mail: cwuadmis@cwu.edu
http://www.cwu.edu

Eastern Washington University
Cheney, WA 99004
Phone: (509) 359-2397
Fax: 509-359-6692

E-mail: admissions@mail.ewu.edu
http://www.ewu.edu

Gonzaga University
Spokane, WA 99258
Phone: (800) 322-2584
E-mail: mcculloh@gu.gonzaga.edu
http://www.gonzaga.edu

Seattle University
900 Broadway
Seattle, WA 98122
Phone: (206) 296-2000
E-mail: admissions@seattleu.edu
http://www.seattleu.edu

Walla Walla College
204 South College Avenue
College Place, WA 99324
Phone: (509) 527-2327
Fax: (509) 527-2397
E-mail: info@wwc.edu
http://www.wwc.edu

Washington State University
French Administration Building
Pullman, WA 99164
Phone: (509) 335-5586
Fax: (509) 335-7468
E-mail: admiss@wsu.edu
http://www.wsu.edu

WEST VIRGINIA

West Virginia Wesleyan College
59 College Avenue
Buckhannon, WV 26201
Phone: (304) 473-8510
E-mail: admission@wvwc.edu
http://www.wvwc.edu

WISCONSIN

Cardinal Stritch University
6801 North Yates Road

Milwaukee, WI 53217
Phone: (414) 410-4040
E-mail: admityou@stritch.edu
http://www.stritch.edu

Carroll College
100 North East Avenue
Waukesha, WI 53186
Phone: (262) 524-7220
E-mail: ccinfo@cc.edu
http://www.cc.edu

Mount Mary College
2900 North Menomonee River
    Parkway
Milwaukee, WI 53222
Phone: (414) 256-1219
Fax: (414) 256-0180
E-mail: admiss@mtmary.edu
http://www.mtmary.edu

Marquette University
P.O. Box 1881
Milwaukee, WI 53201
Phone: (414) 288-7250
E-mail: admissions@marquette.edu
http://www.marquette.edu

University of Wisconsin–Madison
716 Langdon Street
Madison, WI 53706
Phone: (608) 262-3961
Fax: (608) 262-7706
E-mail: on.wisconsin@admissions.wisc.
    edu
http://www.wisc.edu

University of Wisconsin—River Falls
410 South Third Street
River Falls, WI 54022
Phone: (715) 425-3500
Fax: (715) 425-0676
E-mail: admit@uwrf.edu
http://www.uwrf.edu

APPENDIX II
INTERNSHIPS IN ADVERTISING AND PUBLIC RELATIONS

The following is a selected listing of agencies, associations, and corporations offering internships in advertising and/or public relations. Many associations, agencies, nonprofit organizations, radio and television stations, and corporations throughout the country offer programs of this type. This is by no means a complete listing. Use it to get started.

You might also contact agencies, associations, hospitals, television and radio stations, advertising agencies, public relations firms, sports teams, and other corporations to see if they offer internships or if they would be willing to create a program.

Keep in mind that some internships will be paid positions while others will not offer remuneration. Often these programs are used for college credit.

While we have included phone numbers for your information, be aware that many companies prefer not to be called regarding internship programs, instead requesting applicants to contact them by mail.

Write and inquire about eligibility requirements and application procedures. They will differ from company to company. You might address your correspondence to the "Internship Coordinator." It will be easier, using this procedures, for your letter to be routed to the correct person. Contact companies early. Many receive hundreds of requests, each of which must be considered. It is acceptable to check the status of your application if you are not contacted within a reasonable amount of time.

This listing is for your information. It is offered to help you find programs of interest. The author does not endorse any specific programs and is not responsible for subject content.

Adcom Communications
3040 North 44th Street
Phoenix, AZ 85018
Phone: (602) 258-9100
http://www.adcom1.com

American Advertising Federation
Education Services Department
1101 Vermont Avenue, NW
Washington, DC 20005
Phone: (202) 898-0089
Fax: (202) 898-0159
http://www.aaf.org

American Association of Advertising Agencies
405 Lexington Avenue
New York, NY 10174
Phone: (212) 682-2500
Fax: (212) 953-5665
http://www.aaaa.org

Amway Corporation
7575 Fulton Street, East
Ada, MI 49355
Phone: (616) 787-6000
Fax: (616) 682-4000
http://www.amway.com

Bates North America
498 Seventh Avenue
New York, NY 10018

Phone: (212) 297-7000
Fax: (212) 986-0270
http://www.batesusa.com

Bernstein-Rein Advertising Inc.
4600 Madison Avenue
Kansas City, MO 64112
Phone: (816) 756-0640
Fax: (816) 756-1753

Burson-Marsteller
230 Park Avenue South
New York, NY 10003
Phone: (212) 614-4000
Fax: (212) 598-6928
http://www.bm.com

Cairns and Associates
3 Park Avenue
New York, NY 10016
Phone: (212) 421-9770
Fax: (212) 413-1799

Campbell-Ewald Company
30400 Van Dyke Avenue
Warren, MI 48093
Phone: (810) 574-3400
http://www.campbell-ewald.com

Canaan Public Relations
114 East 32nd Street
New York, NY 10016

Phone: (212) 223-0100
Fax: (212) 223-3737
http://www.canaanpr.com

CBS News
524 West 57th Street
New York, NY 10019
Phone: (212) 975-2114
Fax: (212) 975-6699

Chenoweth & Falkner
100 East Madison Street
Tampa, FL 33602
Phone: (813) 224-0011
http://www.chenoweth.com

Chicago Magazine
435 North Michigan Avenue
Chicago, IL 60611
http://www.chicagomag.com

Cronin and Company
50 Nye Road
Glastonbury, CT 06033
Phone: (860) 659-0514
http://www.cronin-co.com

D'Arcy Masius Benton and Bowles, Inc.
1675 Broadway
New York, NY 10019
Phone: (212) 468-3622
Fax: (212) 468-4385

Davis Elen Advertising, Inc.
865 South Figueroa Street
Los Angeles, CA 90017
Phone: (213) 688-7000
Fax: (213) 688-7288
http://www.daviselen.com

DDB Worldwide Communications Group, Inc.
437 Madison Avenue
New York, NY 10022
Phone: (212) 415-2000
http://www.ddbn.com

Douglas Cohn & Wolfe
8730 Sunset Boulevard
Los Angeles, CA 90069
Phone: (310) 967-2900

E.B. Lane Marketing Communications
733 West McDowell Road
Phoenix, AZ 85007
Phone: (602) 258-5263
http://www.eblane.com

Escada-USA
1412 Broadway
New York, NY 10018
Phone: (212) 852-5500
Fax: (212) 852-5595
E-mail: internships@escadausa.com
http://www.escadausa.org

Foote, Cone and Belding
100 West 33rd Street
New York, NY 10001
Phone: (212) 885-3000
Fax: (212) 885-2803
http://www.fcb.com

Franco Public Relations Group
400 Renaissance Center
Detroit, MI 48243
Phone: (313) 567-2300
Fax: (313) 567-4486
http://www.franco.com

Goldforest Advertising
112 Northeast 41st Street
Miami, FL 33137
Phone: (305) 573-7370
http://www.goldforest.com

Hill and Knowlton, Inc.
466 Lexington Avenue
New York, NY 10017
Phone: (212) 885-0300
Fax: (212) 885-0570
http://www.hillandknowlton.com

International Advertising Association (IAA)
521 Fifth Avenue
New York, NY 10175
Phone: (212) 557-1133
Fax: (212) 983-0455
http://www.iaaglobal.org

John F. Kennedy Center for the Performing Arts
Vilar Institute for Arts Management Internships
The Kennedy Center
Washington, DC 20566
http://www.kennedy-center.org/education/vilarinstitute/internships/

J. Walter Thompson Company
466 Lexington Avenue
New York, NY 10017
Phone: (212) 210-7000
Fax: (212) 210-7299
http://www.jwt.com

KCSA Public Relations Worldwide
800 Second Avenue
New York, NY 10017
Phone: (212) 682-6300
Fax: (212) 697-0910
http://www.kcsa.com

Ketchum, Inc.
711 Third Avenue
New York, NY 10017
Phone: (646) 935-3900
Fax: (646) 935-4499
http://www.ketchum.com

Lowe and Partners Worldwide
1114 Avenue of the Americas
New York, NY 10036
Phone: (212) 704-1200
Fax: (212) 704-1201

Magnet Communictions
110 Fifth Avenue
New York, NY 10011
Phone: (212) 367-6800
Fax: (212) 367-7154
http://www.magnetcom.com

Makovsky and Company, Inc.
575 Lexington Avenue
New York, NY 10022
Phone: (212) 508-9600
Fax: (212) 751-9710
http://www.makovsky.com

Manning, Selvage and Lee, Inc.
1675 Broadway
New York, NY 10019
Phone: (212) 468-4200
Fax: (212) 447-5462
http://www.mslpr.com

Martin Agency Inc.
1 Shockoe Plaza
Richmond, VA 23219
Phone: (804) 698-8204
Fax: (804) 698-8001

mPRm Public Relations
5670 Wilshire Boulevard
Los Angeles, CA 90036
Phone: (323) 933-3399

N.W. Ayer Inc.
825 Eighth Avenue
New York, NY 10019
Phone: (212) 474-5000
Fax: (212) 474-5400
http://www.nwayer.com

Oregon Public Broadcasting
7140 Southwest Macadam Avenue
Portland, OR 97219
Phone: (503) 244-9900
http://www.opb.org

Peak Biety, Inc.
1715 North Westshore Boulevard
Tampa, FL 33607
Phone: (813) 289-8006
Fax: (813) 289-7898
http://www.pbpb.com

The Phelps Group
901 Wilshire Boulevard
Santa Monica, CA 90401
Phone: (310) 752-4400
Fax: (310) 752-4444
http://www.thephelpsgroup.com

Porter Novelli, Inc.
450 Lexington Avenue
New York, NY 10017
Phone: (212) 601-8000
Fax: (212) 601-8101
http://www.porternovelli.com

Promotion Marketing Association of America
257 Park Avenue South
New York, NY 10010
Phone: (212) 420-1100
Fax: (212) 533-7622

Public Relations Society of America (PRSA)
33 Maiden Lane
New York, NY 10038
Phone: (212) 460-1400
Fax: (212) 995-0757
http://www.prsa.org

Rogers and Cowan
640 Fifth Avenue
New York, NY 10019
Phone: (212) 445-8400
Fax: (212) 445-8290
http://www.rogersandcowan.com

Rogers and Cowan, Inc.
1888 Century Park East
Los Angeles, CA 90067
Phone: (310) 201-8849
Fax: (310) 788-6611
http://www.rogersandcowan.com

Ruder Finn, Inc.
301 East 57th Street
New York, NY 10022

Phone: (212) 593-6423
http://www.ruderfinn.com

Shandwick Miller Technologies
4 Copley Plaza
Boston, MA 02116
Phone: (617) 536-0470
Fax: (617) 536-2772

Sports Illustrated
Time and Life Building
New York, NY 10020
Phone: (212) 522-1212
Fax: (212) 522-0320

TBWA\Chiat\Day New York
488 Madison Avenue
New York, NY 10022
Phone: (212) 804-1000
Fax: (212) 804-1200
http://www.tbwachiat.com

U.S. Olympic Committee (USC)
One Olympic Plaza

Colorado Springs, CO 80909
Phone: (719) 632-5551

Verónica León Memorial Internship
3102 Oak Lawn
Dallas, TX 75219
http://www.aaf.org/college/leonscholar_app.doc

Weber Shandwick, Inc.
640 Fifth Avenue
New York, NY 10019
Phone: (212) 445-8000
http://www.webershandwick.com

Wilson, Elser, Moskowitz, Edelman and Dicker
150 East 42nd Street
New York, NY 10017
Phone: (212) 490-3000
Fax: (212) 490-3038
http://www.wemed.com

APPENDIX III
SEMINARS, WORKSHOPS, ETC.

The following is a selected listing of associations and companies offering workshops, seminars, and courses and the general subjects they cover. This is by no means a complete listing. Many associations, schools, agencies, and companies offer programs.

As subject matter changes frequently, many of the organization running these workshops and seminars did not wish to have their programs listed. You may want to contact associations dealing with the employment areas in which you are interested to obtain more information on programs.

This listing is for your information. It is offered to help you find programs of interest. The author does not endorse any specific programs and is not responsible for subject content.

Advertising Club of New York (ACNY)
235 Park Avenue South
New York, NY 10003
Phone: (212) 533-8080
Fax: (212) 533-1929
http://www.theadvertisingclub.org
The Advertising Club of New York sponsors many different seminars and courses in advertising and marketing throughout the year.

Advertising Research Foundation (ARF)
641 Lexington Avenue
New York, NY 10022
Phone: (212) 751-5656
Fax: (212) 319-5265
E-mail: Arf@thearf.org
http://www.arfsite.org
The Advertising Research Foundation conducts a number of conferences and seminars throughout the year on advertising and marketing research.

Advertising Women of New York (AWNY)
25 West 45th Street
New York, NY 10036
Phone: (212) 221-7969
Fax: (212) 221-8296
E-mail: liz@awny.org
http://www.awny.org
Advertising Women of New York holds an annual career conference for college students interested in advertising, marketing, public relations, merchandising, research, and promotion. They also offer career development and guidance.

American Advertising Federation (AAF)
1101 Vermont Avenue, NW
Washington, DC 20005
Phone: (202) 898-0089
Fax: (202) 898-0159
E-mail: aaf@aaf.org
http://www.aaf.org
The American Advertising Federation offers seminars on advanced advertising management as well as a variety of other educational services.

American Institute of Graphic Arts
164 Fifth Avenue
New York, NY 10010
Phone: (212) 807-1990
Fax: (212) 807-1799
E-mail: Publications@aiga.org
http://www.aiga.org
The American Institute of Graphic Artists conducts a variety of educational activities via chapters found throughout the country in various areas of graphic design.

American Management Association (AMA)
1601 Broadway
New York, NY 10019-7420
Phone: (212) 586-8100
Fax: (212) 903-8168
E-mail: customerservice@amanet.org
http://www.amanet.org
The American Management Association offers a variety of educational opportunities throughout the country on an array of different business, management, and public relations skills.

Art Directors Club (ADC)
106 West 29th Street
New York, NY 10001
Phone: (212) 643-1440
Fax: (212) 643-4266
E-mail: classifieds@adcny.org
http://www.adcny.org
The Art Directors Club offers programs for members in the graphic arts.

Association of National Advertisers (ANA)
708 Third Avenue
New York, NY 10017-4270
Phone: (212) 697-5950
Fax: (212) 661-8057
http://www.ana.net
The Association of National Advertisers offers seminars throughout the year in an array of subjects related to advertising.

Business Marketing Association (BMA)
400 North Michigan Avenue
Chicago, IL 60611
Phone: (312) 822-0005:
(800) 664-4262 (toll free)
Fax: (312) 822-0054
E-mail: bma@marketing.org
http://www.marketing.org
The Business Marketing Association offers seminars, workshops, and conferences in marketing and communications.

Direct Marketing Association (DMA)
1120 Avenue of the Americas
New York, NY 10036-6700
Phone: (212) 768-7277
Fax: (212) 302-6714
E-mail: president@the-dma.org
http://www.the-dma.org
The Direct Marketing Association offers educational programs, seminars, and workshops for those interested in direct marketing and response.

National Investor Relations Institute (NIRI)
8020 Towers Crest Drive
Vienna, VA 22182
Phone: (703) 506-3570
Fax: (703) 506-3571
E-mail: info@niri.org
http://www.niri.org

The National Investor Relations Institute holds professional development seminars in the areas of investor relations.

National Society of Fund Raising Executives

c/o Ann L. Woodfield, Executive Director
250 West 57th Street
New York, NY 10107
Phone: (212) 265-7838
Fax: (212) 265-4974
http://www.nsfre.org
The National Society of Fund Raising Executives holds seminars, conferences, and workshops on all aspects of fund raising.

Professional Society for Sales and Marketing Training (SMT)

180 North LaSalle Street
Chicago, IL 60601
Phone: (312) 551-0768
Fax: (312) 551-0815
E-mail: smt@rmygroup.com
http://www.smt.org
The Professional Society For Sales and Marketing Training offers educational conferences and clinics in sales training to help improve sales, marketing, and customer relations.

Promotion Marketing Association of America (PMAA)

257 Park Avenue South
New York, NY 10010
Phone: (212) 420-1100
Fax: (212) 533-7622
E-mail: pma@pmaalink.org
http://www.praalink.org
The Promotion Marketing Association of America conducts seminars for those interested in the use of premiums in marketing, sales, and promotion.

Public Affairs Council (PAC)

2033 K Street
Washington, DC 20036
Phone: (202) 872-1790
Fax: (202) 835-8343
E-mail: pac@pac.org
http://www.pac.org

The Public Affairs Council conducts clinics and sponsors annual public affairs conferences.

Public Relations Society of America (PRSA)

33 Maiden Lane
New York, NY 10038
Phone: (212) 460-1400
Fax: (212) 995-0757
http://www.prsa.org
The Public Relations Society of America (PRSA) offers seminars, conferences, and workshops, on a variety of public relations–oriented subjects.

Radio Advertising Bureau (RAB)

261 Madison Avenue
New York, NY 10016
Phone: (212) 681-7200; (800) 232-3131 (toll free)
Fax: (972) 753-6727
http://www.rab.com
The Radio and Advertising Bureau sponsors conferences and programs for training radio advertising salespeople.

Retail Advertising and Marketing Association

325 7th Street, NW
Washington, DC 20004
Phone: (202) 661-3052
Fax: (202) 661-3049
E-mail: perweilerp@rama-nrf.com
http://www.rama-nrf.org
The Retail Advertising and Marketing Association holds an annual conference dealing with advertising in retail.

Shelly Field Motivational Programs and Seminars

SFO Booking Office
P.O. Box 711
Monticello, NY 12701
Phone: (845) 794-7312
http://www.shellyfield.com
Shelly Field offers a variety of motivational programs, seminars, and keynote presentations to corporations throughout the country on a wide array of subjects including careers, human recruitment and retention,

empowerment, stress management, obtaining public relations, and publicity.

Society of Consumer Affairs Professionals in Business (SOCAP)

675 North Washington Street
Alexandria, VA 22314
Phone: (703) 519-3700
Fax: (703) 549-4886
E-mail: socap@socap.org
http://www.socap.org
The Society of Consumer Affairs Professionals in Business offers a variety educational programs throughout the year to individuals interested in the consumer affairs profession.

Society of Illustrators

128 East 63rd Street
New York, NY 10021
Phone: (212) 838-2560
Fax: (212) 838-2561
E-mail: Si1901@aol.com
http://www.societyillustrators.org
The Society of Illustrators offers a number of different seminars and classes to those interested in art careers.

Stress Busters Seminars and Keynote Presentations

SFO Booking Office
P.O. Box 711
Monticello, NY 12701
Phone: (845) 794-7312
http://www.shellyfield.com
Stress Busters Seminars offers programs, workshops, and keynote presentations on managing stress to corporate executives at conventions, conferences, and corporations throughout the country.

Television Bureau of Advertising (TVB)

3 East 54th Street
New York, NY 10022
Phone: (212) 486-1111
Fax: (212) 935-5631
E-mail: info@tvb.org
http://www.tvb.org
The Television Bureau of Advertising holds sales training courses for television sales representatives.

APPENDIX IV
TRADE ASSOCIATIONS, UNIONS, AND OTHER ORGANIZATIONS

The following is a listing of trade associations, unions, and organizations discussed in this book. There are also a number of other associations listed that might be of use to you.

The names, addresses, phone numbers, fax numbers, Web addresses, and e-mail addresses are included when available to help you easily get in touch with any of the organizations.

Many of the associations have branch offices located throughout the country. Organization headquarters can get you the contact information of the closest local branch.

Actors Equity Association (AEA)
165 West 46th Street
New York, NY 10036
Phone: (212) 869-8530
Fax: (212) 719-9815
E-mail: info@actorsequity.org
http://www.actorsequity.org

Advertising and Marketing International Network (AMIN)
c/o B. Vaughn Sink
12323 Nantucket
Wichita, KS 67235
Phone: (316) 722-2535
Fax: (316) 722-8353
E-mail: vaughn_sink@shscom.com
http://www.aminworldwide.com

Advertising Club of New York (ACNY)
235 Park Avenue South
New York, NY 10003
Phone: (212) 533-8080
Fax: (212) 533-1929
http://www.theadvertisingclub.org

Advertising Council (AC)
261 Madison Avenue
New York, NY 10016
Phone: (212) 922-1500;
   (800) 933-7727 (toll free)
Fax: (212) 922-1676
E-mail: info@adcouncil.org
http://www.adcouncil.org

Advertising Production Club of New York (APC)
60 East 42nd Street
New York, NY 10165
Phone: (212) 983-6042
Fax: (212) 983-6043
E-mail: adprodclub@aol.com
http://www.apc-ny.org

Advertising Research Foundation
641 Lexington Avenue
New York, NY 10022
Phone: (212) 751-5656
Fax: (212) 319-5265
E-mail: Arf@thearf.org
http://www.thearf.org

Advertising Women of New York (AWNY)
25 West 45th Street
New York, NY 10036
Phone: (212) 221-7969
Fax: (212) 221-8296
E-mail: liz@awny.org
http://www.awny.org

American Advertising Federation (AAF)
1101 Vermont Avenue, NW
Washington, DC 20005
Phone: (202) 898-0089
Fax: (202) 898-0159
E-mail: aaf@aaf.org
http://www.aaf.org

American Advertising Federation Education Services
1101 Vermont Avenue, NW
Washington, DC 20005
Phone: (202) 898-0089;
   (800) 999-AAF1 (toll free)
Fax: (202) 898-0159
http://www.aaf.org

American Artists Professional League (AAPL)
47 Fifth Avenue
New York, NY 10003
Phone: (212) 645-1345
Fax: (212) 645-1345
http://www.american
   artistsprofessionalleague.org

American Association of Advertising Agencies (AAAA)
405 Lexington Avenue
New York, NY 10174
Phone: (212) 682-2500
Fax: (212) 682-8391
E-mail: obd@aaaa.org
http://www.aaaa.org

American Association of Retired Persons (AARP)
601 East Street, NW
Washington, DC 20049
Fax: (202) 434-2320
E-mail: member@aarp.org
http://www.aarp.org

American Chamber of Commerce Executives (ACCE)
4875 Eisenhower Avenue
Alexandria, VA 22304
Phone: (703) 998-0072
Fax: (703) 212-9512
E-mail: mfleming@acce.org
http://www.acce.org

American Federation of Musicians of the United States and Canada (AFM)
1501 Broadway
New York, NY 10036
Phone: (212) 869-1330
Fax: (212) 764-6134
E-mail: info@afm.org
http://www.afm.org

American Federation of Television and Radio Artists (AFTRA)
260 Madison Avenue
New York, NY 10016
Phone: (212) 532-0800
Fax: (212) 532-2242
E-mail: aftra@aftra.com
http://www.aftra.com

American Film Marketing Association (AFMA)
10850 Wilshire Boulevard
Los Angeles, CA 90024
Phone: (310) 446-1000
Fax: (310) 446-1600
E-mail: info@afma.com
http://www.afma.com

American Guild of Musical Artists (AGMA)
1430 Broadway
New York, NY 10018
Phone: (212) 265-3687
Fax: (212) 262-9088
E-mail: agma@musicalartists.org
http://www.musicalartists.org

American Guild of Variety Artists (AGVA)
363 Seventh Avenue
New York, NY 10001
Phone: (212) 675-1003
Fax: (212) 633-0097
http://americanguildofvarietyartistsagva.
visualnet.com

American Institute of Graphic Arts
164 Fifth Avenue
New York, NY 10010
Phone: (212) 807-1990
Fax: (212) 807-1799
E-mail: Publications@aiga.org
http://www.aiga.org

American Management Association (AMA)
1601 Broadway
New York, NY 10019-7420
Phone: (212) 586-8100
Fax: (212) 903-8168
E-mail: customerservice@amanet.org
http://www.amanet.org

American Marketing Association
311 South Wacker Drive, Suite 5800
Chicago, IL 60606
Phone: (312) 542-9000;
    (800) 262-1150 (toll free)
Fax: (312) 542-9001
E-mail: info@ama.org
http://www.ama.org

American Society for Training and Development (ASTD)
1640 King Street
P.O. Box 1443
Alexandria, VA 22313
Phone: (703) 683-8100
Fax: (703) 683-0250
http://www.astd.org

American Society of Artists
P.O. Box 1326
Palatine, IL 60078-1326
Phone: (312) 751-2500
E-mail: Asoa@webtv.net

American Teleservices Association (ATA)
1620 I Street, NW
Washington, DC 20006
Phone: (317) 816-9336;
    (877) 779-3974 (toll free)
Fax: (202) 463-8498
E-mail: ata@moinc.com
http://www.ataconnect.org

The ARF – Advertising Research Foundation (ARF)
641 Lexington Avenue
New York, NY 10022
Phone: (212) 751-5656
Fax: (212) 319-5265
E-mail: jim@theARF.org
http://www.theARF.org

Art Directors Club, New York
106 West 29th Street
New York, NY 10009
Phone: (212) 643-1440
Fax: (212) 643-4293
E-mail: messages@adcny.org
http://www.adcny.org

Association for Business Communication (ABC)
Baruch College
Communication Studies
One Bernard Baruch Way
Box B8-240
New York, NY 10010
Phone: (646) 312-3726
Fax: (646) 349-5297
E-mail: abcrjm@cs.com
http://www.businesscommunication.org

AACSB International-The Association to Advance Collegiate Schools of Business
600 Emerson Road
Street Louis, MO 63141
Phone: (314) 872-8481
Fax: (314) 872-8495

Association for Healthcare Philanthropy (AHP)
313 Park Avenue
Falls Church, VA 22046
Phone: (703) 532-6243
Fax: (703) 532-7170
E-mail: anp@ahp.org
http://www.ahp.org

Association for Women in Communications
780 Ritchie Highway
Severna Park, MD 21146
Phone: (410) 544-7442
Fax: (410) 544-4640
E-mail: pat@womcom.org
http://www.womcom.org

Association of Fundraising Professionals (AFP)
1101 King Street
Alexandria, VA 22314
Phone: (703) 684-0410
Fax: (703) 684-0540
E-mail: mnilsen@afpnet.org
http://www.afpnet.org

Association of Hispanic Advertising Agencies (AHAA)
8201 Greensboro Drive, Suite 300
McLean, VA 22102
Phone: (703) 610-9014
Fax: (703) 610-9005
E-mail: info@ahaa.org
http://www.ahaa.org

Association of House Democratic Press Assistants (AHDPA)
House of Representatives
P.O. Box 007
Washington, DC 20515
Fax: (202) 226-8843

Association of Independent Commercial Producers (AICP)
3 West 18th Street
New York, NY 10011
Phone: (212) 929-3000
Fax: (212) 929-3359
E-mail: info@aicp.com
http://www.aicp.com

Association of National Advertisers (ANA)
708 Third Avenue
New York, NY 10017-4270
Phone: (212) 697-5950
Fax: (212) 661-8057
http://www.ana.net

Association of Promotion Marketing Agencies Worldwide (now Marketing Agencies Association Worldwide (MAA)
1031 US Highway 22 West
Bridgewater, NJ 08807
Phone: (908) 595-6924
Fax: (908) 707-0407

E-mail: vincentsottosanti@maaw.org
http://www.maaw.org

Association of Retail Marketing
    Services Inc.
244 Broad Street
Red Bank, NJ 07701-2003
Phone: (732) 842-5070
Fax: (732) 219-1938
E-mail: Info@goarms.com

Association of Sales & Marketing
    Companies
1010 Wisconsin Avenue, NW
Washington, DC 20007-3603
Phone: (202) 337-9351
Fax: (202) 337-4508
E-mail: info@asmc.org
http://www.asmc.org

Association of Teachers of Technical
    Writing (ATTW)
c/o Brenda Sims
University of North Texas
P.O. Box 311307
Denton, TX 76203
Phone: (940) 565-2115
E-mail: sims@unt.edu
http://www.attw.org

Association of Theatrical Press Agents
    and Managers (ATPAM)
1560 Broadway
New York, NY 10036
Phone: (212) 719-3666
Fax: (212) 302-1585
E-mail: atpam@erols.com
http://www.atpam.com

Association of Travel Marketing
    Executives (ATME)
28 North Avenue
Larchmont, NY 10538
Phone: (973) 835-1340;
    (800) 526-0041 (toll-free)
E-mail: admin@atme.org
http://www.atme.org

Baptist Communicators Association
    (BCA)
c/o BCA Administrative Coordinator
BCA 1715-K South Rutherford
    Boulevard
Murfreesboro, TN 37130
Phone: (615) 904-0152
Fax: (615) 904-0183
E-mail: bca.office@att.net
http://www.baptistcommunicators.org

BDA
2029 Century Park East
Los Angeles, CA 90067
Phone: (310) 712-0040
Fax: (310) 712-0039
E-mail: keren@promax.tv
http://www.bda.tv

Business Marketing Association (BMA)
400 North Michigan Avenue
Chicago, IL 60611
Phone: (312) 822-0005; (800) 664-4262
    (toll-free)
Fax: (312) 822-0054
E-mail: bma@marketing.org
http://www.marketing.org

Cabletelevision Advertising Bureau
    (CAB)
830 Third Avenue
New York, NY 10022
Phone: (212) 508-1200
Fax: (212) 832-3268
http://www.cabletvadbureau.com

College Sports Information Directors
    of America (CoSIDA)
c/o Jeff Hodges
UNA P.O. Box 5038
Wesleyan Avenue
Keller Hall 385
Florence, AL 35632
Phone: (256) 765-4659
Fax: (512) 592-0389
E-mail: sportsinfomation@una.edu
http://www.cosida.com

Communications Media Management
    Association (CMMA)
P.O. Box 227
Wheaton, IL 60189
Phone: (630) 653-2772
Fax: (630) 653-2882
E-mail: cmma@cmma.net
http://www.cmma.net

Council for Advancement and Support
    of Education
1307 New York Avenue, NW
Washington, DC 20005
Phone: (202) 478-5616;
    (800) 554-8536 (toll-free)
Fax: (202) 387-4973
E-mail: Books@case.org
http://www.case.org/books

Council of American Survey Research
    Organizations (CASRO)
3 Upper Devon

Port Jefferson, NY 11777
Phone: (631) 928-6954
Fax: (631) 928-6041
E-mail: casro@casro.org
http://www.casro.org

Direct Mail Fundraisers Association
    (DMFA)
224 Seventh Street
Garden City, NY 11530-5771
Phone: (516) 746-6700
Fax: (516) 294-8141
E-mail: info@dmfa.org
http://www.dmfa.org

Direct Marketing Association (DMA)
1120 Avenue of the Americas
New York, NY 10036-6700
Phone: (212) 768-7277
Fax: (212) 302-6714
E-mail: president@the-dma.org
http://www.the-dma.org

Direct Marketing Association Catalog
    Council (DMACC)
1120 Avenue of the Americas
New York, NY 10036
Phone: (212) 768-7277
Fax: (212) 302-6714
E-mail: Presiden@the-dma.org
http://www.the-dma.org

Direct Marketing Club of New York
    (DMCNY)
224 Seventh Street
Garden City, NY 11530
Phone: (516) 746-6700
Fax: (516) 294-8141
E-mail: info@dmcny.org
http://www.dmcny.org

Direct Marketing Educational
    Foundation (DMEF)
1120 Avenue of the Americas
New York, NY 10036-6700
Phone: (212) 768-7277
Fax: (212) 302-6714
E-mail: dmef@the-dma.org
http://www.the-dma.org/dmef

Direct Marketing Insurance and
    Financial Services Council (IFSC)
c/o Direct Marketing Association
1120 Avenue of the Americas
New York, NY 10036-6700
Phone: (212) 768-7277
Fax: (212) 302-6714
E-mail: hr@the-dma.org
http://www.the-dma.org

Electronic Retailing Association (ERA)
2101 Wilson Boulevard
Arlington, VA 22201
Phone: (703) 841-1751; (800) 987-6462
    (toll-free)
Fax: (703) 841-1860
E-mail: jcavarretta@retailing.org
http://www.retailing.org

Food Marketing Institute (FMI)
655 15th Street, NW
Washington, DC 20005
Phone: (202) 452-8444
Fax: (202) 429-4519
E-mail: fmi@fmi.org
http://www.fmi.org

Graphic Artists Guild
90 John Street
New York, NY 10038
Phone: (212) 791-3400
Fax: (212) 791-0333
http://www.gag.org

**Grocery Manufacturers of America
    (GMA)**
1010 Wisconsin Avenue, NW
Washington, DC 20007
Phone: (202) 337-9400
Fax: (202) 337-4508
E-mail: info@gmabrands.com
http://www.gmabrands.com

**Healthcare Marketing and
    Communications Council**
1525 Valley Center Parkway
Bethlehem, PA 18017
Phone: (610) 868-8299
Fax: (610) 868-8387
E-mail: info@hmc-council.org
http://www.hmc-council.org

**Hospitality Sales and Marketing
    Association International**
1300 L Street, NW
Washington, DC 20005
Phone: (202) 789-0089
Fax: (202) 789-1725
http://www.hsmai.org

Institute for Public Relations (IPR)
University of Florida
P.O. Box 118400
Gainesville, FL 32611-8400
Phone: (352) 392-0280
Fax: (352) 846-1122
E-mail: iprre@grove.ufl.edu
http://www.instituteforpr.com

**International Advertising Association
    (IAA)**
521 Fifth Avenue, Suite 1807
New York, NY 10175
Phone: (212) 557-1133
Fax: (212) 983-0455
E-mail: iaa@iaaglobal.org
http://www.iaaglobal.org

**International Association of Business
    Communicators (IABC)**
1 Hallidie Plaza
San Francisco, CA 94102
Phone: (415) 544-4700
Fax: (415) 544-4747
E-mail: Service_centre@iabc.com
http://www.iabc.com

**International Association of Business
    Communicators—Dallas Chapter**
c/o Robin McCasland
P.O. Box 172935
Arlington, TX 76003
http://www.dallasiabc.com

**International Brotherhood of Electrical
    Workers (IBEW)**
1125 15th Street, NW
Washington, DC 20005
Phone: (202) 833-7000
Fax: (202) 467-6316
E-mail: web@isbew.org
http://www.ibew.org

**International Communications
    Association (ICA)**
3530 Forest Lane
Dallas, TX 75234
Phone: (214) 902-3632
Fax: (877) 902-6521
E-mail: information@icanet.com

**International Council of Shopping
    Centers**
1221 Avenue of the Americas
New York, NY 10022
Phone: (646) 728-3800
Fax: (212) 589-5555
http://www.icsc.org

**International Council – National
    Academy of Television Arts and
    Sciences (IC/NATAS)**
142 West 57th Street
New York, NY 10019
Phone: (212) 489-6969
Fax: (212) 489-6557
E-mail: info@iemmys.tv
http://www.iemmys.tv

**International Newspaper Marketing
    Association (INMA)**
10300 North Central Expressway
Dallas, TX 75231-8621
Phone: (214) 373-9111
Fax: (214) 373-9112
http://www.inma.org

**Library Public Relations Council
    (LPRC)**
2565 Broadway, No. 532
New York, NY 10025
E-mail: info@libraryprcouncil.org
http://www.libraryprcouncil.org

**Mailing and Fulfillment Service
    Association (MFSA)**
1421 Prince Street
Alexandria, VA 22314
Phone: (703) 836-9200
Fax: (703) 548-8204
E-mail: mfsa-mail@MFSAnet.org
http://www.mfsanet.org

**Mail Order Association of America
    (MOAA)**
1877 Bourne Court
Wantagh, NY 11793
Fax: (516) 221-5697

**Manufacturers Representatives
    Educational Research Foundation
    (MRERF)**
P.O. Box 247
Geneva, IL 60134
Phone: (630) 208-1466
Fax: (630) 208-1475
E-mail: info@mrerf.org
http://www.mrerf.org

**Manufacturers Representatives of
    America (MRA)**
P.O. Box 150229
Arlington, TX 76015
Phone: (817) 561-7272
Fax: (817) 561-7275
E-mail: assnhqtrs@aol.com
http://www.mra-reps.com

**Marketing Agencies Association
    Worldwide (MAA)**
1031 US Highway 22 West, 3rd Floor
Bridgewater, NJ 08807
Phone: (908) 595-6924
Fax: (908) 707-0407
E-mail: vincentsottosanti@maaw.org
http://www.maaw.org

Marketing Research Association (MRA)
1344 Silas Deane Highway
P.O. Box 230

Rocky Hill, CT 06067
Phone: (860) 257-4008
Fax: (860) 257-3990
E-mail: email@mra-net.org

**National Academy of Television Arts
and Sciences (NATAS)**
111 West 57th Street
New York, NY 10019
Phone: (212) 586-8424
Fax: (212) 246-8129
E-mail: natashq@aol.com
URL: http://www.emmyonline.org

**National Advertising Division Council
of Better Business Bureaus (NAD)**
4200 Wilson Boulevard
Arlington, VA 22203
Phone: (703) 276-0100
Fax: (703) 525-8277
http://www.bbb.org

**National Association Broadcast
Employees and Technicians–
Communications Workers of
America (NABET-CWA)**
501 3rd Street, NW
Washington, DC 20001
Phone: (202) 434-1254
Fax: (202) 434-1426
E-mail: nabet@nabetcwa.org
http://www.nabetcwa.org

**National Association of County
Relations Officials**
c/o National Association of Counties
440 1st Street, NW
Washington, DC 20001
Phone: (202) 393-6226
Fax: (202) 393-2630
http://www.naco.org

**National Association of Government
Communicators (NAGC)**
10301 Democracy Lane
Fairfax, VA 22030
Phone: (703) 691-0037
Fax: (703) 706-9583
E-mail: alexgroup@alexandriagroup.com
http://www.nagc.com

**National Association of Home Based
Businesses (NAHBB)**
10451 Mill Run Circle
Owings Mills, MD 21117
Phone: (410) 363-3698
E-mail: nahbb@msn.com
http://www. homebusiness.com

National Association of Manufacturers
1331 Pennsylvania Avenue, NW
Washington, DC 20004
Phone: (202) 637-3000 or
(800) 637-3005
Fax: (202) 637-3182
http://www.nam.org

National Child Safety Council
c/o K C Wilkinson
4065 Page Avenue
Jackson, MI 49204-1368
Phone: (517) 764-6070

**National Council of County Association
Executives (NCCAE)**
c/o National Association of Counties
440 1st Street, NW
Washington, DC 20001
Phone: (202) 942-4208
Fax: (202) 942-4203
E-mail: tgoodman@naco.org
http://www.naco.org

**National Federation of Federal
Employees (NFFE)**
1016 16th Street, NW
Washington, DC 20036
Phone: (202) 862-4400
Fax: (202) 862-4432
E-mail: rcrandall@nffe.org
http://www.nffe.org

**National Federation of Music Clubs
(NFMC)**
1336 North Delaware Street
Indianapolis, IN 46202
Phone: (317) 638-4003
Fax: (317) 638-0503
E-mail: nfmc@nfmcmusic.org
http://www.nfmc-music.org

**National Federation of Press Women
(NFPW)**
P.O. Box 5556
Arlington, VA 22205
Phone: (703) 534-2500 or
(800) 780-2715
Fax: (703) 534-5750
E-mail: presswomen@aol.com
http://www.nfpw.org

**National Investor Relations Institute
(NIRI)**
8020 Towers Crest Drive
Vienna, VA 22182
Phone: (703) 506-3570
Fax: (703) 506-3571
E-mail: info@niri.org
http://www.niri.org

National Press Club (NPC)
National Press Building
529 14th Street, NW
Washington, DC 20045
Phone: (202) 662-7500
Fax: (202) 662-7512
E-mail: info@npcpress.org
http://www.press.org

National Retail Federation
325 7th Street, NW
Washington, DC 20004
Phone: (202) 783-7971 or
(800) 673-4692
Fax: (202) 737-2849
http://www.nrf.com

National Safety Council (NSC)
1121 Spring Lake Drive
Itasca, IL 60143
Phone: (630) 285-1121 or
(800) 621-7619
Fax: (630) 285-1315
E-mail: customerservice@nsc.org
http://www.nsc.org

**National School Public Relations
Association**
15948 Derwood Road
Rockville, MD 20855
Phone: (301) 519-0496
Fax: (301) 519-0494
E-mail: Nspra@nspra.org
http://www.napra.org

**National Sportscasters and
Sportswriters Association (NSSA)**
322 East Innes Street
Salisbury, NC 28144
Phone: (704) 633-4275
Fax: (704) 633-2027

National Tour Association (NTA)
546 East Main Street
Lexington, KY 40508
Phone: (859) 226-4444 or
(800) 682-8886
Fax: (606) 226-4414
E-mail: questions@ntastaff.com
http://www.ntaonline.com

National Writers Association (NWA)
3140 South Peoria Street
Aurora, CO 80014-3155
Phone: (303) 841-0246
Fax: (303) 841-2607
E-mail: ExecDirSandyWhelchel@
nationalwriters.com
http://www.nationalwriters.com

Newspaper Association of America (NAA)
1921 Gallows Road
Vienna, VA 22182
Phone: (703) 902-1600
Fax: (703) 917-0636
http://www.naa.org

The Newspaper Guild (TNG-CWA)
501 3rd Street, NW
Washington, DC 20001
Phone: (202) 434-7177 or 800-585-5tng
Fax: (202) 434-1472
E-mail: guild@cwa-union.org
http://www.newsguild.org

North American Agriculture Marketing Officials (NAAMO)
California Department of Food and
Agriculture
1220 North Street
Sacramento, CA 95814
E-mail: info@naamo.org
http://www.naamo.org

Outdoor Advertising Association of America (OAAA)
1850 M Street, NW
Washington, DC 20036
Phone: (202) 833-5566
Fax: (202) 833-1522
E-mail: info@oaaa.org
http://www.oaaa.org

Point-of-Purchase Advertising International (POPAI)
1660 L Street, NW
Washington, DC 20036
Phone: (202) 530-3000
Fax: (202) 530-3030
E-mail: info@popai.com
http://www.popai.com

Printing Industries of America (PIA)
100 Daingerfield Road
Alexandria, VA 22314-2888
Phone: (703) 519-8100 or (800) 742-2666
Fax: (703) 548-3227
E-mail: gain@printing.org
http://www.gain.net

Professional Hockey Writers' Association (PHWA)
c/o Sherry L. Ross
1480 Pleasant Valley Way
West Orange, NJ 07052
Phone: (973) 669-8607
Fax: (973) 669-8607

Professional Society for Sales and Marketing Training (SMT)
180 North LaSalle Street
Chicago, IL 60601
Phone: (312) 551-0768
Fax: (312) 551-0815
E-mail: smt@rmygroup.com
http://www.smt.org

Promotional Products Association International
c/o G. Stephen Slagle, CAE Pres./CEO
3125 Skyway Circle, North
Irving, TX 75038
Phone: (972) 258-3090
Fax: (972) 258-3016
E-mail: steves@ppa.org
http://www.ppa.org

Promotion Marketing Association of America (PMAA)
257 Park Avenue South
New York, NY 10010
Phone: (212) 420-1100
Fax: (212) 533-7622
E-mail: pma@pmalink.org
http:/www.pmalink.org

Public Affairs Council (PAC)
2033 K Street, NW
Washington, DC 20036
Phone: (202) 872-1790
Fax: (202) 835-8343
E-mail: pac@pac.org
http://www.pac.org

Public Relations Society of America (PRSA)
33 Irving Place, 3rd Floor
New York, NY 10003-2376
Phone: (212) 995-2230
E-mail: hq@prsa.org
http://www.prsa.org

Radio Advertising Bureau (RAB)
261 Madison Avenue
New York, NY 10016
Phone: (212) 681-7200 or
(800) 232-3131
Fax: (972) 753-6727
http://www.rab.com

Religion Communicators Council (RCC)
475 Riverside Drive
New York, NY 10115
Phone: (212) 870-2985
Fax: (212) 870-3578
http://www.religioncommunicators.org

Retail Advertising and Marketing Association (RAMA)
325 7th Street, NW
Washington, DC 20004
Phone: (202) 661-3052
Fax: (202) 661-3049
E-mail: perweilerp@rama-nrf.com
http://www.rama-nrf.org

Sales and Marketing Executives
6767 West Greenfield Avenue
Milwaukee, WI 53214
Phone: (414) 475-7005

Sales and Marketing Executives International
P.O. Box 1390
Sumas, WA 98295-1390
Phone: (312) 893-0751 or
(800) 999-1414
Fax: (604) 855-0165
http://www.smei.org

Screen Actors Guild (SAG)
5757 Wilshire Boulevard
Los Angeles, CA 90036
Phone: (323) 954-1600
Fax: (323) 549-6603
http://www.sag.org

Society for Healthcare Strategy and Market Development of the American Hospital Association
1 North Franklin
Chicago, IL 60606
Phone: (312) 422-3888 (312) 422-3739
Fax: (312) 422-4579
E-mail: stratsoc@aha.org
http://www.stratsociety.org

Society for Technical Communication (STC)
901 North Stuart Street
Arlington, VA 22203
Phone: (703) 522-4114
Fax: (703) 522-2075
E-mail: stc@stc.org
http://www.stc.org

Society of Consumer Affairs Professionals in Business (SOCAP)
675 North Washington Street

Alexandria, VA 22314
Phone: (703) 519-3700
Fax: (703) 549-4886
E-mail: socap@socap.org
http://www.socap.org

Society of Illustrators
128 East 63rd Street
New York, NY 10021
Phone: (212) 838-2560
Fax: (212) 838-2561
E-mail: Si1901@aol.com

Television Bureau of Advertising (TVB)
3 East 54th Street
New York, NY 10022
Phone: (212) 486-1111
Fax: (212) 935-5631
E-mail: info@tvb.org
http://www.tvb.org

Toastmasters International (XI TI)
23182 Arroyo Vista
P.O. Box 9052
Rancho Santa Margarita, CA 92688
Phone: (949) 858-8255
Fax: (949) 858-1207
E-mail: tminfo@toastmasters.org
http://www.toastmasters.org

Type Directors Club (TDC)
60 East 42nd Street

New York, NY 10165
Phone: (212) 983-6042
Fax: (212) 983-6043
E-mail: director@tdc.org
http://www.tdc.org

Utility Communicators International
17610 128th Trail North
Jupiter, FL 3347
E-mail: eboardman@aesp.org
http://www.uci-online.com

Web Printing Association/Printing Industries of America
100 Daingerfield Road
Alexandria, VA 22314
Phone: (703) 519-8156
Fax: (703) 519-7109
http://www.gain.net

Women Executives in Public Relations (WEPR)
P.O. Box 7657
FDR Station
New York, NY 10150
Phone: (212) 896-1281
Fax: (212) 697-0910
E-mail: info@wepr.org
http://www.wepr.org

World Organization of Webmasters
9580 Oak Parkway
Folsom, CA 95630

Phone: (916) 608-1597
Fax: (916) 987-3022
E-mail: info@joinwow.org
http://www.joinwow.org

Women in Direct Marketing International (WDMI)
c/o Hoke Communications
224 7th Street
Garden City, NY 11530
Phone: (516) 746-6700
Fax: (516) 294-8141
E-mail: info@wdmi.org
http://www.wdmi.org

Writers Guild of America, East, Inc. (WGAE)
555 West 57th Street
New York, NY 10019
Phone: (212) 767-7800
Fax: (212) 582-1909
E-mail: info@wgaeast.org
http://www.wgaeast.org

Writers Guild of America, West (WGAW)
7000 West Third Street
Los Angeles, CA 90048
Phone: (323) 951-4000
Fax: (323) 782-4800
E-mail: website@wga.org
http://www.wga.org

APPENDIX V
ADVERTISING AGENCIES

The following is a selected listing of advertising agencies throughout the country. Space limitations make it impossible to list every agency. Companies are listed with their main addresses and phone numbers. Many agencies have branch offices in other parts of the country as well as all over the world. Company names, addresses, phone numbers, fax numbers, Web sites, and e-mail addresses are listed when available.

If you would like more information about any of the agencies listed or require names and addresses of other companies, look in the *Standard Directory of Advertising* *Agencies* (also known as the "Agency Red Book"), located in most larger libraries.

The author does not endorse any one agency over another. The inclusion or exclusion does not imply the author's approval or disproval of an agency in this listing. Use this list to get started locating internships, training programs, summer employment, or to send your résumé when you are ready to go job hunting.

Remember to check out agency Web sites. Many post employment opportunities.

Arher/Malmo Advertising, Inc.
65 Union Avenue
Memphis, TN 38103
Phone: (901) 523-2000
Fax: (901) 573-7654
E-mail: hcollins@archermalmo.com
http://www.archermalmo.com

Arnold Worldwide
101 Huntington Avenue
Boston, MA 02199
Phone: (617) 587-8000
Fax: (617) 587-8070
http://www.arn.com

Avrett, Free and Ginsberg Advertising, Inc.
800 Third Avenue
New York, NY 10022
Phone: (212) 832-3800
Fax: (212) 759-9603
http://www.afg-adv.com

Baublizt Advertising
20 West Market Street
York, PA 17401
Phone: (717) 854-3040
Fax: (717) 852-4864
http://www.baublitz.com

BBDO Worldwide Inc.
1285 Avenue of the Americas
New York, NY 10019
Phone: (212) 459-5000
Fax: (212) 459-6645
http://www.bbdo.com/new

Bernard Hodes Group, Inc.
555 Madison Avenue
New York, NY 10022

Phone: (212) 750-5200
http://www.hodes.com

Burrell Communications Group, Inc.
233 North Michigan Avenue
Chicago, IL 60602
Phone: (312) 297-9600
Fax: (312) 297-9601
http://www.burrell.com

Campbell-Ewald Company
30400 Van Dyke Avenue
Warren, MI 48093
Phone: (810) 574-3400
http://www.campbell-ewald.com

Carat North America
3 Park Avenue South
New York, NY 10016
Phone: (212) 252-0050
Fax: (212) 252-1250
http://www.carat-na.com

Carlson Marketing Group
1405 Xenium Lane North
Minneapolis, MN 55441
Phone: (763) 212-4520
Fax: (763) 212-4580
E-mail: cmgsolutions@carlson.com
http://www.carlsonmarketing.com

Cliff Freeman and Partners
375 Hudson Street
New York, NY 10014
Phone: (212) 463-3200
Fax: (212) 463-3225
http://www.clifffreeman.com

Corinthian Media, Inc.
214 West 29th Street
New York, NY 10001

Phone: (212) 279-5700
Fax: (212) 239-1882
E-mail: corinthian@mediabuying.com
http://www.mediabuying.com

Dailey and Associates, Inc.
8687 Melrose Avenue
West Hollywood, CA 90069
Phone: (310) 360-3100
Fax: (310) 360-0810
http://www.daileyads.com

DDB Worldwide Communications Group, Inc.
437 Madison Avenue
New York, NY 10022
Phone: (212) 415-2000
E-mail: mail@ddb.com
http://www.ddbn.com

DraftWorldwide, Inc.
633 North St. Clair Street
Chicago, IL 60611
Phone: (312) 944-3500
Fax: (312) 944-3566
E-mail: info@draftworld.com
http://www.draftworldwide.com

Equity Marketing
6330 San Vicente Boulevard
Los Angeles, CA 90048
Phone: (323) 932-4300
Fax: (323) 932-4400
http://www.equity-marketing.com

Foote, Cone and Belding
100 West 33rd Street
New York, NY 10001
Phone: (212) 885-3000

Fax: (212) 885-2803
E-mail: info@fcb.com
http://www.fcb.com

Goodby, Silverstein and Partners
720 California Street
San Francisco, CA 94108
Phone: (415) 392-0669
http://www.goodbysilverstein.com

Gotham Group, Inc.
100 Fifth Avenue
New York, NY 10011
Phone: (212) 414-7000
Fax: (212) 414-7095
E-mail: infor@gothaminc.com
http://www.gothaminc.com

Grey Global Group, Inc.
777 Third Avenue
New York, NY 10017
Phone: (212) 546-2000
Fax: (212) 546-1495
E-mail: webmaster@grey.com
http://www.greyglobalgroup.com

Hill, Holiday, Connors, Cosmpolulos, Inc.
200 Clarendon Street
Boston, MA 02116
Phone: (617) 437-1600
Fax: (617) 572-3400
E-mail: info@hhcc.com
http://www.hhcc.com

Interpublic Group of Companies, Inc.
1271 Avenue of the Americas
New York, NY 10020
Phone: (212) 399-8000
Fax: (212) 399-8130
http://www.interpublic.com

J. Walter Thompson Company
466 Lexington Avenue
New York, NY 10017
Phone: (212) 210-7000
Fax: (212) 210-7299
http://www.jwt.com

Klemtner Advertising, Inc.
375 Hudson Street
New York, NY 10014
Phone: (212) 463-3400
Fax: (212) 463-3456

Kraus-Anderson, Inc.
525 South 8th Street
Minneapolis, MN 55404
Phone: (612) 332-7281

Fax: (612) 332-0271
E-mail: info@k-a-c.com
http://www.krausanderson.com

Leo Burnett Worldwide
35 West Wacker Drive
Chicago, IL 60601
Phone: (312) 220-5959
Fax: (312) 220-3299
http://www.leoburnett.com

Lowe and Partners Worldwide
1114 Avenue of the Americas
New York, NY 10036
Phone: (212) 704-1200
Fax: (212) 704-1201
E-mail: info@loweworldwide.com
http://www.loweworldwide.com

Marc USA, Inc.
4 Station Square
Pittsburgh, PA 15219
Phone: (412) 562-2000
Fax: (412) 562-1680
E-mail: contact@marcadv.com
http://www.marcadv.com

Margeotes/Feritta and Partners L.L.C
411 Lafayette Street
New York, NY 10003
Phone: (212) 979-6600
Fax: (212) 979-5490
http://www.margeotes.com

McCann-Erickson USA
750 Third Avenue
New York, NY 10017
Phone: (212) 697-6000
Fax: (212) 867-5177
http://www.mccann.com

Medicus Group International
1675 Broadway
New York, NY 10019
Phone: (212) 468-3636
Fax: (212) 468-3208
http://www.medicusgroup.com

Menasha Corp.
1645 Bergstrom Road
Neenah, WI 54956
Phone: (920) 751-1000
Fax: (920) 751-1236
E-mail: info@measha.com
http://www.menasha.com

Monster Worldwide, Inc.
622 Third Avenue
New York, NY 10017

Phone: (212) 351-7000
Fax: (646) 658-0541
http://www.monsterworldwide.com

Nationwide Advertising Service
One Infinity Corporate Centre Drive
Cleveland, OH 44125
Phone: (216) 478-0300
Fax: (216) 468-8280

Ogilvy and Mather Worldwide, Inc.
309 West 49th Street, Worldwide Plaza
New York, NY 10019
Phone: (212) 237-4000
Fax: (212) 237-5123
http://www.ogilvy.com

Omnicom Group, Inc.
437 Madison Avenue
New York, NY 10022
Phone: (212) 415-3600
Fax: (212) 415-3530
http://www.omnicomgroup.com

Publicis, New York, New York
4 Herald Square
950 Sixth Avenue
New York, NY 10001
Phone: (212) 279-5550
Fax: (212) 279-5560
http://www.publicis-usa.com

Sudler and Hennessey
230 Park Avenue South
New York, NY 10003
Phone: (212) 614-4100
Fax: (212) 598-6915
http://www.sudler.com

TBWA\Chiat\Day New York
488 Madison Avenue
New York, NY 10022
Phone: (212) 804-1000
Fax: (212) 804-1200
http://www.tbwachiat.com

Team One Advertising
1960 East Grand Avenue
El Segundo, CA 90245
Phone: (310) 615-2000
http://www.teamoneadv.com

Ted Thomas Associates, Inc.
210 West Washington Square
Philadelphia, PA 19106
Phone: (215) 238-8500
Fax: (215) 592-4287
http://www.voxmedica.com

Tierney and Partners, Inc.
200 South Broad Street
Philadelphia, PA 19102
Phone: (215) 790-4100
Fax: (215) 790-4363
E-mail: presscontact.tc@tierneyagency.
    com
http://www.tierneyagency.com

True North Communications
101 East Erie Street
Chicago, IL 60611
Phone: (312) 425-6500
Fax: (312) 425-5010
http://www.truenorth.com

**Tucker, Hampel, Stefanides and
    Partners**
551 Madison Avenue
New York, NY 10022
Phone: (212) 994-6700
Fax: (212) 994-6699
http://www.tuckerhs.com

Uniworld Group, Inc.
100 Avenue of the Americas
New York, NY 10013
Phone: (212) 219-1600

Fax: (212) 274-8565
http://www.uniworldgroup.com

Vermont Media Corp.
P.O. Box 310
West Dover, VT 05356
Phone: (802) 464-3388
Fax: (802) 464-7255
http://www.dvalnews.com

Vertis, Inc.
250 West Pratt Street
Baltimore, MD 21201
Phone: (410) 528-9800
Fax: (410) 528-9288
http://www.vertisinc.com

Visions USA, Inc.
17 Executive Park Drive
Atlanta, GA 30329
Phone: (404) 320-1818
Fax: (404) 320-1880
E-mail: info@visionsusa.net
http://www.visionsusa.net

Western International Media Corp.
8544 Sunset Boulevard
Los Angeles, CA 90069

Phone: (310) 659-5711
Fax: (310) 659-8590

WPP Group USA, Inc.
125 Park Avenue
New York, NY 10017
Phone: (212) 632-2000
Fax: (212) 632-2249
http://www.wpp.com

Wunderman
285 Madison Avenue
New York, NY 10017
Phone: (212) 210-3000
Fax: (212) 490-9073
http://www.wunderman.com

Young and Rubicam, Inc.
285 Madison Avenue
New York, NY 10017
Phone: (212) 210-3000
Fax: (212) 490-9073
http://www.yr.com

APPENDIX VI
PUBLIC RELATIONS AGENCIES

The following is a selected listing of public relations agencies throughout the country. Space limitations make it impossible to list every agency. Companies are listed with their main addresses and phone numbers. Many agencies have branch offices in other parts of the country as well as all over the world. Company names, addresses, phone numbers, fax numbers, Web sites, and e-mail addresses are listed when available.

If you would like more information about any of the agencies listed or require names and addresses of other companies consult the *Public Relations Society of America Register* or *O'Dwyer's PR Directory*.

The author does not endorse any one agency over another. The inclusion or exclusion does not imply the author's approval or disapproval of an agency in this listing Use this list to get started locating internships, training programs, summer employment, or to send your résumé when you are ready to go job hunting.

Remember to check out agency Web sites. Many post employment opportunities.

Access Communications
245 Fifth Avenue
New York, NY 10016
Phone: (917) 522-3500
E-mail: ny@accesspr.com
http://www.accesspr.com

Access Communications
101 Howard Street
San Francisco, CA 94106
Phone: (415) 904-7070
E-mail: sf@accesspr.com
http://www.accesspr.com

Bader Rutter and Associates, Inc.
13845 Bishop's Drive
Brookfield, WI 53005
Phone: (262) 784-7200
Fax: (262) 938-5595
http://www.baderrutter.com

Baker Winokur Ryder Public Relations, Inc.
9100 Wilshire Boulevard
Beverly Hills, CA 90212
Phone: (310) 550-7776
Fax: (310) 550-1701

Barnhart/CMI Inc.
1819 Wazee Street
Denver, CO 80202
Phone: (303) 626-7200
Fax: (303) 892-4991
E-mail: contact@barnhartcmi.com
http://www.barnhartcmi.com

Bender/Helper Impact
11500 West Olympic Boulevard
Los Angeles, CA 90064

Phone: (310) 473-4147
Fax: (310) 478-4727
E-mail: bhimpact@impact.com
http://www.bhimpact.com

Black, Rogers, Sullivan, Goodnight, Inc.
701 Brazos
Austin, TX 78701
Phone: (512) 320-8511
Fax: (512) 320-8990
http://www.brsg.com

Brodeur Worldwide
855 Boylston Street
Boston, MA 02116
Phone: (617) 587-2800
Fax: (617) 587-2828
http://www.brodeur.com

Brownstein Group
215 South Broad Street
Philadelphia, PA 19107
Phone: (215) 735-3470
Fax: (215) 735-6298
http://www.brownsteingroup.com

Burrell Communications Group L.L.C
233 North Michigan Avenue
Chicago, IL 60601
Phone: (312) 297-9600
Fax: (312) 297-9601
http://www.burrell.com

Burson-Marsteller
230 Park Avenue South
New York, NY 10003
Phone: (212) 614-4000
Fax: (212) 598-6928
http://www.bm.com

Citigate Dewe Rogerson, Inc.
630 Third Avenue
New York, NY 10017
Phone: (212) 687-8080
Fax: (212) 687-6344
http://www.citigatedewerogerson.com

Clark and Weinstock
52 Vanderbilt Avenue
New York, NY 10017
Phone: (212) 953-2550
Fax: (212) 953-2564
E-mail: info@cwnyc.com
http://www.clarkandweinstock.com

Clarke and Company
535 Boylston Street
Boston, MA 02116
Phone: (617) 536-3003
Fax: (617) 536-8524
E-mail: info@clarkeco.com
http://www.clarkeco.com

Clayton-Davis and Associates, Inc.
777 Bonhomme Avenue
St. Louis, MO 63105
Phone: (314) 862-7800
Fax: (314) 721-5171
http://www.claytondavis.com

ClientLogic Corp.
2 American Center
3102 West End
Nashville, TN 37203
Phone: (615) 301-7100
Fax: (615) 301-7150
E-mail: pr@clientlogic.com
http://www.clientlogic.com

Cole Henderson Drake, Inc.
426 Marietta Street
Atlanta, GA 30313
Phone: (404) 892-4500
Fax: (404) 892-4522
http://www.chdatlanta.com

Cronin and Company
50 Nye Road
Glastonbury, CT 06033
Phone: (860) 659-0514
Fax: (860) 659-3455
http://www.cronin-co.com

Daniel J. Edelman Public Relations Worldwide, Inc.
200 East Randolph Drive
Chicago, IL 60601
Phone: (312) 240-3000
Fax: (312) 240-2900
E-mail: chicago@edelman.com
http://www.edelman.com

Dan Klores Communications
386 Park Avenue South
New York, NY 10016
Phone: (212) 685-4300
Fax: (212) 685-9024
http://www.dkcnews.com

Doe-Anderson Advertising and Public Relations
620 West Main Street
Louisville, KY 40202
Phone: (502) 589-1700
Fax: (502) 587-8349
E-mail: info@doeanderson.com
http://www.doeanderson.com

Duffy Communications, Inc.
3379 Peachtree Road, NE
Atlanta, GA 30326
Phone: (404) 266-2600
Fax: (404) 266-3198
E-mail: info@duffy.com
http://www.duffey.com

Earle Palmer Brown Cos.
685 Third Avenue
New York, NY 10017
Phone: (212) 986-4122
Fax: (212) 986-4955
http://www.epb.com

Entertainment Marketing, Inc.
360 North Michigan Avenue
Chicago, IL 60601
Phone: (312) 444-9100
Fax: (312) 444-9116
http://www.entertainment-marketing.com

Financial Relations Board, Inc.
676 North St. Clair
Chicago, IL 60611
Phone: (312) 266-7800
Fax: (312) 266-2874
http://www.frbinc.com

Fleishman-Hillard, Inc.
200 North Broadway
St. Louis, MO 63102
Phone: (314) 982-1700
Fax: (314) 231-2313
http://www.fleishman.com

Franco Public Relations Group
400 Renaissance Center
Detroit, MI 48243
Phone: (313) 567-2300
Fax: (313) 567-4486
http://www.franco.com

Frix Group
6 Concourse Parkway
Atlanta, GA 30328
Phone: (770) 396-6206
Fax: (770) 396-0207
http://www.frixgroup.com

Gard and Gerber
209 Southwest Oak Street
Portland, OR 97204
Phone: (503) 221-0100
Fax: (503) 221-0100
http://www.gardandgerber.com

Glennon Company, Inc.
707 North Second Street
St. Louis, MO 63102
Phone: (314) 436-5455
Fax: (314) 436-0359
http://www.glennon.com

Golin/Harris International
111 East Wacker Drive
Chicago, IL 60601
Phone: (312) 729-4000
Fax: (312) 729-4010
http://www.golinharris.com

Hammond Farrell, Inc.
257 Park Avenue South
New York, NY 10010
Phone: (212) 995-5680
Fax: (212) 995-5696
http://www.hammondfarrell.com

Hill and Knowlton, Inc.
466 Lexington Avenue
New York, NY 10017

Phone: (212) 885-0300
Fax: (212) 885-0570
http://www.hillandknowlton.com

HMS Partners Ltd.
250 Civic Centers Drive
Columbus, OH 43215
Phone: (614) 221-7667
Fax: (614) 222-2596

IW Group, Inc.
633 West 5th Street
Los Angeles, CA 90071
Phone: (213) 622-6513
Fax: (213) 627-4476
http://www.iwgroupinc.com

Ketchum, Inc.
711 Third Avenue
New York, NY 10017
Phone: (646) 935-3900
Fax: (646) 935-4499
E-mail: on-line@ktechum.com
http://www.ketchum.com

Laughlin/Constable, Inc.
207 East Michigan Street
Milwaukee, WI 53202
Phone: (414) 272-2400
Fax: (414) 270-7140
http://www.laughlin.com

Lehman Millet, Inc.
60 Canal Street
Boston, MA 02114
Phone: (617) 722-0019
Fax: (617) 722-6099
http://www.lminc.com

Levinson and Hill, Inc.
717 North Harwood Street
Dallas, TX 75201
Phone: (214) 880-0200
Fax: (214) 880-0630
http://www.levensonandhill.com

Lois Paul and Partners
152 Presidential Way
Woburn, MA 01801
Phone: (781) 782-5000
Fax: (781) 782-5999
http://www.loispaul.com

Lopez Negrete Communications, Inc.
5615 Kirby Drive
Houston, TX 77005
Phone: (713) 877-8777
Fax: (713) 877-8796
http://www.lopeznegrete.com

Magnet Communications
110 Fifth Avenue
New York, NY 10011
Phone: (212) 367-6800
Fax: (212) 367-7154
http://www.magnetcom.com

Makovsky and Company, Inc.
575 Lexington Avenue
New York, NY 10022
Phone: (212) 508-9600
Fax: (212) 751-9710
http://www.makovsky.com

Manning, Selvage and Lee, Inc.
1675 Broadway
New York, NY 10019
Phone: (212) 468-4200
Fax: (212) 447-5462
http://www.mslpr.com

Marc USA, Inc.
4 Station Square
Pittsburgh, PA 15219
Phone: (412) 562-2000
Fax: (412) 562-1680
http://www.marcadv.com

Martz and Associates, Inc.
14500 North Northsight Boulevard
Scottsdale, AZ 85260
Phone: (480) 998-3154
Fax: (480) 998-7985
http://www.martzagency.com

Matlock and Associates, Inc.
1545 Peachtree Street, NE
Atlanta, GA 30309
Phone: (404) 872-3200
Fax: (404) 876-4929
E-mail: info@matlock-adpr.com
http://www.matlock-adpr.com

Matthews Marks
225 Broadway
San Diego, CA 92101
Phone: (619) 238-8500
Fax: (619) 238-8505
http://www.matthewsmark.com

McKinley Communications, Inc.
3675 South Noland Road
Independence, MO 64055
Phone: (816) 833-8100
Fax: (816) 833-8188
http://www.mckinleycommunications.
   com

**McNeely Pigott and Fox Public
    Relations L.L.C.**
611 Commerce
Nashville, TN 37203
Phone: (615) 259-4000
Fax: (615) 259-4040
http://www.mpf.com

Media Logic
1520 Central Avenue
Albany, NY 12205
Phone: (518) 456-3015
Fax: (518) 456-4279
http://www.mlinc.com

Ninyo and Moore
5710 Ruffin Road
San Diego, CA 92123
Phone: (858) 576-1000
Fax: (858) 576-9600
http://www.ninyoandmoore.com

Ogilvy and Mather Worldwide, Inc.
309 West 49th Street
Worldwide Plaza
New York, NY 10019
Phone: (212) 237-4000
Fax: (212) 237-5123
http://www.ogilvy.com

**Peppers and Rogers Group/Marketing
    1to1**
20 Glover Avenue
Norwalk, CT 06850
Phone: (203) 642-5151
Fax: (203) 642-5126
http://www.marketingonetoone.com

Phelps and Associates, Inc.
901 Wilshire Boulevard
Santa Monica, CA 90401
Phone: (310) 752-4400
Fax: (310) 752-4444
E-mail: info@thephelpsgroup.com
http://www.phelpsgroup.com

Podesta Associates, Inc.
1001 G Street, NW
Washington, DC 20001
Phone: (202) 393-1010
Fax: (202) 393-5510
E-mail: podesta@podesta.com
http://www.podesta.com

Porter Novelli, Inc.
450 Lexington Avenue
New York, NY 10017
Phone: (212) 601-8000
Fax: (212) 601-8101
http://www.porternovelli.com

Publicis, New York, New York
4 Herald Square
New York, NY 10001
Phone: (212) 279-5550
Fax: (212) 279-5560
http://www.publicis-usa.com

**R.J. Dale Advertising and Public
    Relations, Inc.**
211 East Ontario Street
Chicago, IL 60611
Phone: (312) 644-2316
Fax: (312) 644-2688
http://www.rjdale.com

Rogers & Cowan, Inc.
1888 Century Park East
Los Angeles, CA 90067
Phone: (310) 201-8849
Fax: (310) 788-6611
http://www.rogersandcowan.com

Howard J. Rubenstein Associates, Inc.
1345 Avenue of the Americas
New York, NY 10105
Phone: (212) 489-6900
Fax: (212) 843-9200
E-mail: info@rubinstein.com
http://www.rubenstein.com

Rubenstein Associates Inc.
1345 Avenue of the Americas
New York, NY 10105
Phone: (212) 843-8000
Fax: (212) 843-9200
E-mail: info@rubenstein.com
http://www.rubenstein.com

Ruder Finn, Inc.
301 East 57th Street
New York, NY 10022
Phone: (212) 593-6423
E-mail: finnp@ruderfinn.com
http://www.ruderfinn.com

Schraff Group
4621 Teller Avenue
Newport Beach, CA 92660
Phone: (949) 833-3400
Fax: (949) 833-3474
http://www.schraff.com

Schwartz Communications, Inc.
230 Third Avenue
Waltham, MA 02451
Phone: (781) 684-0770
Fax: (781) 684-6500
http://www.schwartz-pr.com

Shandwick Miller Technologies
4 Copley Place
Boston, MA 02116
Phone: (617) 536-0470
Fax: (617) 536-2772

Shelly Field Organization
P.O. Box 711
Monticello, NY 12701
http://www.shellyfield.com

Smith, Dawson and Andrews
1000 Connecticut Avenue, NW
Washington, DC 20036
Phone: (202) 835-0740
Fax: (202) 775-8526
http://www.sda-inc.com

Stephan and Brady, Inc.
1850 Hoffman Street
Madison, WI 53704
Phone: (608) 241-4141

Fax: (608) 241-4246
http://www.stephanbrady.com

Thompson and Company, Inc.
50 Peabody Place
Memphis, TN 38103
Phone: (901) 527-8000
Fax: (901) 527-3697
http://www.thompson-co.com

Weber Shandwick, Inc.
640 Fifth Avenue
New York, NY 10019
Phone: (212) 445-8000
E-mail: gheimann@webershandwick.
   com
http://www.webershandwick.com

Weightman Group
2129 Chestnut Street
Philadelphia, PA 19103
Phone: (215) 977-1700

Fax: (215) 977-1827
E-mail: mail@weightman.com
http://www.weightman.com

Weyforth-Haas
10561 Barkley Street
Overland Park, KS 66212
Phone: (913) 648-8333
Fax: (913) 648-5024
E-mail: info@marketingcomm.com
http://www.weyforth-haas.com

Widmeyer Communications
1825 Connecticut Avenue, NW
Washington, DC 20009
Phone: (202) 667-0901
Fax: (202) 667-0902
http://www.widmeyer.com

APPENDIX VII
ADVERTISING AND PUBLIC RELATIONS RECRUITING AGENCIES

The following is a listing of recruiting and "head-hunter" agencies specializing in finding people for jobs in advertising and public relations and related communications fields. This is by no means a complete listing. You may find additional agencies of this type in the yellow pages of telephone directories or in trade journals, publications, and newspapers as well as the Internet. Despite the location of the specific recruiting agency, jobs may be located nationwide.

This listing is provided for your information. The author does not endorse any particular company and is not responsible for policies of any company listed The inclusion or exclusion of a company does not imply the author's approval or disapproval of any particular agency in this listing.

Abbott Executive Search
500 Commercial Street
Manchester, NH 03101
Phone: (603) 669-9909
Fax: (603) 606-5502
E-mail: info@abbottsearch.com
http://www.abbottsearch.com

Acquient Search
2070 Chain Bridge Road
Vienna, VA 22182
Phone: (703) 356-8200
Fax: (703) 356-6930
http://www.acquientsearch.com

Adow Professionals
36 East Fourth Street
Cincinnati, OH 45202
Phone: (513) 721-2369
Fax: (513) 721-3724
http://www.adow.com

Advertising Recruitment Specialists
16700 Sequoia Street
Fountain Valley, CA 92708
Phone: (714) 775-3910
Fax: (714) 775-3911
E-mail: recruiter@adrecruiters.com
http://www.adrecruiters.com

Alexander & Company
8308 Barber Oak Drive
Plano, TX 75025
Phone: (877) 495-8300

Allen Austin
4543 Post Oak Place
Houston, TX 77027
Phone: (713) 355-1900
Fax: (713) 355-1901

E-mail: resumes@allenaustinsearch.com
http://www.allenaustinsearch.com

The Amy Burack Company, Inc.
444 North Michigan Avenue
Chicago, IL 60611
Phone: (312) 527-2505
Fax: (312) 527-2445
E-mail: amyburack@amyburack.com
http://www.amyburack.com

Ann H. Ross Executive Search
2662 North Burling Street
Chicago, IL 60614
Phone: (773) 525-7879
Fax: (773) 525-8175

Ariel Recruitment Associates, Inc.
141 East 89th Street
New York, NY 10128
Phone: (212) 348-9600
Fax: (212) 348-9666
E-mail: info@arielassociates.com
http://www.arielassociates.com

Artemis Search
2064 Antioch Court
Oakland, CA 94611
Phone: (510) 339-4191
Fax: (510) 339-4195
http://www.artemissearch.com

Aquent
711 Boylston Street
Boston, MA 02116
Phone: (617) 535-5000
Fax: (617) 535-5005
E-mail: questions@aquent.com
http://www.aquent.com

Baywood Consulting
1395 Bolton Drive
Morro Bay, CA 93442
Phone: (805) 772-4170
Fax: (805) 771-8076
E-mail: info@baywoodconsulting.com
http://www.baywoodconsutling.com

Bishop Partners, LLC
8029 Forsyth Boulevard
St. Louis, MO 63105
Phone: (314) 863-7755
Fax: (314) 863-7765
http://www.bishop-partners.com

Blue Notebook LLC
555 Fifth Avenue
New York, NY 10017
Phone: (212) 377-2080
Fax: (212) 214-0431
E-mail: anna@bluenotebook.com
http://.www.bluenotebook.com

Boreham Search International, Inc.
245 Park Avenue
New York, NY 10167
Phone: (212) 792-4333
Fax: (212) 792-4001
http://www.borehamsearch.com

The Briarwood Group
P.O. Box 1374
Hermitage, PA 16149
Phone: (724) 981-0240
Fax: (724) 981-6670
E-mail: briarwoodgroup@att.net
http://www.briarwoodgroup.com

BrickWork Consulting
230 West 13th Street
New York, NY 10011

Phone: (212) 741-9669
Fax: (212) 741-9681
E-mail: info@bwcon
http://www.bwcon.com

The Cantor Concern, Inc.
315 West 57th Street
New York, NY 10019
Phone: (212) 333-3000
Fax: (212) 245-1012
http://www.cantorconcern.com

Career Forum, Inc.
165 South Union Boulevard
Lakewood, CO 80228
Phone: (303) 279-9200
Fax: (303) 279-9296
E-mail: inquiries@careerforum.com
http://www.careerforum.com

Career Group
150 East 52nd Street
New York, NY 10022
Phone: (212) 750-8188
Fax: (212) 751-8328
http://www.careergroupinc.com

CC Burke, Ltd.
P.O. Box 30
New York, NY 10156
Phone: (212) 481-1941
Fax: (212) 725-7116

**Chuck Zimering Advertising
    Recruitment**
170 West End Avenue
New York, NY 10023
Phone: (212) 724-7904
Fax: (212) 724-7163

Collins Associates
2395 Stoney Glen Drive
Orange Park, FL 32003
Phone: (904) 278-6333
Fax: (904) 278-6555
http://www.collinsassociates.net

Compro Search
28202 Cabot Road
Laguna Niguel, IA 92677
Phone: (949) 365-5615
http://www.comprosearch.com

CorPeople, Inc.
2001 Union Street
San Francisco, CA 94123
Phone: (415) 771-3725
Fax: (415) 771-4860
E-mail: greatpeople@CorPeople.com
http://www.CorPeople.com

CPS, Inc.
One Westbrook Corporate Center
Westchester, IL 60154
Phone: (708) 562-0001
http://www.cps4jobs.com

The Creative Network, Inc.
2334 Northwest 22nd Circle
Camas, WA 98607
Phone: (360) 834-0802
http://www.creativenetworkinc.com

Creative Sourcing
3338 North Lincoln Avenue
Chicago, IL 60657
Phone: (773) 296-0167
Fax: (773) 296-6511
http://www.creativesourcing.com

Cross-Jordan
5961 Sunlight Garden Way
Las Vegas, NV 89118
Phone: (702) 248-1936

David Gomez & Associates, Inc.
20 North Clark Street
Chicago, IL 60602
Phone: (312) 346-5525
Fax: (312) 279-2077
E-mail: info@dgai.com
http://www.dgai.com

DCA Professional Search
175 Georgian Drive
Coppell, TX 75019
Phone: (214) 626-0149
Fax: (214) 745-1616
E-mail: info@dcaprosearch.com
http://www.dcaprosearch.com

Eric Kercheval & Associates
15 South First Street
Minneapolis, MN 55401
Phone: (612) 670-2278
Fax: (509) 479-1179
E-mail: eric@ekassoc.com
http://www.ekassoc.com

ERx Recruiters
5340 Alla Road
Los Angeles, CA
Phone: (310) 578-7373
Fax: (310) 578-5005

The Esquire Staffing Group, Ltd.
1 South Wacker Drive
Chicago, IL 60606
Phone: (312) 795-4300
Fax: (312) 795-4329
http://www.esquirestaffing.com

Excellence in HR
P.O. Box 844
Campbell, CA
Phone: (408) 376-0212
Fax: (408) 376-4276
http://www.excellenceinhr.com

The Executive Alliance Group
1875 Century Park East, Suite H2560
Los Angeles, CA 90067
(310) 291-9889
E-mail: info@EAgroup.biz
http://www.EAgroup.biz

Executive Resources, Ltd.
3816 Ingersoll Avenue
Des Moines, IA 50312
Phone: (515) 287-6880
Fax: (515) 255-9445
E-mail: iaexercres@aol.com
http://www.executiveresourcesltd.com

Executive Search Network
2607 West Sunrise Drive
Phoenix, AZ 85041
Tel: (602) 276-9030
Fax: (602) 305-9531
E-mail: marysnow@executivesearch
    network.com
http://www.executiveserarchnetwork.com

Executive Staffers
6360 LBJ Freeway
Dallas, TX 75240
Phone: (214) 265-9343
E-mail: info@executivestaffers.com
http://www.executivestaffers.com

Exhibit Recruiter
3787 Cliff Crest Drive
Smyrna, GA 30080
Phone: (770) 319-6141
Fax: (770) 319-6142
E-mail: infor@exhibitrecruiter.com
http://www.exhibitrecruiter.com

Filcro Media Staffing
342 Madison Avenue
New York, NY 10017
Phone: (212) 599-0909
http://www.executivesearch.tv

Forbes & Company
7088 Stonebridge Road
Newburgh, IN 47639
Phone: (812) 853-9325
Fax: (812) 853-1953
http://www.jobsforadpros.como

Ford & Ford
105 Chestnut Street
Needham, MA 02492
Phone: (781) 449-8200
Fax: (781) 444-7335
http://www.logonajob.com

Fristoe & Carleton
77 Milford Drive
Hudson, OH 44236
Phone: (330) 655-3535
Fax: (330) 655-3585
http://www.adjob.com

The Fry Group
369 Lexington Avenue
New York, NY 10017
Phone: (212) 557-0011
Fax: (212) 557-3449
http://www.frygroup.com

Greenberg and Associates, Inc.
1133 Broadway
New York, NY 10010
Phone: (212) 463-0020

The Gumbinner Company
509 Madison Avenue
New York, NY 10022
Phone: (212) 688-0129
Fax: (212) 688-0504

Gundersen Partners, L.L.C.
30 Irving Place
New York, NY 10003
Phone: (212) 677-7660
Fax: (212) 358-0275
E-mail: lpm@gpllc.com
http://www.gunderstenpartners.com

The Hanna Group
12140 Fowlers Mill Road
Chardon, OH 44024
Phone: (440) 285-2468
Fax: (440) 285-2066
http://www.hannagroup.com

Hayden Resources
9 Ivy Ridge Court
Mount Kisco, NY 10549
Phone: (914) 244-1129
Fax: (914) 244-5953
info@haydenresources.com
http://www.haydenresrourses.com

Heyman Associates, Inc.
11 Penn Plaza
New York, NY 10001
Phone: (212) 784-2717

Fax: (212) 244-9648
E-mail: info@heymanassociates.com
http://www.heymanassociates.com

Howard Executive Resources Corp.
111 West 57th Street
New York, NY 10019
Phone: (212) 246-1001
Fax: (212) 246-5268

Howard Sloan Koller Group
300 East 42nd Street
New York, NY 10016
Phone: (212) 661-5250
Fax: (212) 557-9178
E-mail: hsk@hsksearch.com
http://www.hsksearch.com

Hunter, Rowan & Crowe
9843 Treasure Cay
Bonita Springs, FL 34135
Phone: (239) 495-1389
Fax: (239) 992-7517

Insearch Worldwide Corporation
One Landmark Square
First Floor
Stamford, CT 06901
Phone: (203) 355-3000
Fax: (203) 355-8580
E-mail: info@insearchworldwide.com
http://www.insearchworldwide.com

Integrated People Solutions
10901 West 120th Avenue
Broomfield, CO 80021
Phone: (303) 998-0100
Fax: (303) 998-0400
E-mail: info@ipeplesolutions.com
http://www.ipeoplesolutions.com

JBS International
11966 Prince Charles Court
Cape Coral, FL 33991
Phone: (239) 283-9019
http://www.jbsinternational.com

JFK Search
7013 Ximines Lane North
Minneapolis, MN 55369
Phone: (612) 332-8082
Fax: (763) 424-1809
Email: jkmsp@comcast.net
http://www.jfksearch.com

Jobs Market
902 Greensboro Road
High Point, NC 27260
Phone: (336) 889-0118

Fax: (336) 889-7794
E-mail: tjmadmin@jobsmarket.com
http://www.jobsmarket.com

Lynn Hazan & Associates, Inc.
55 East Washington
Chicago, IL 60602
Phone: (312) 863-5401
Fax: (312) 863-5404
E-mail: lhazan@lynnhazanandassociates.
    com
http://www.lynnhazanandassociates.com

Konrad Associates
P.O. Box 8725
San Jose, CA 95155
Phone: (408) 920-0101
E-mail: info@Konradassociates.com
http://www.konradassociates.com

The Lane Group
735 North Water Street
Milwaukee, WI 53202
Phone: (412) 226-2400
Fax: (412) 226-2421
E-mail: info@thelanegroup.net
http://www.thelanegroup.net

Lucas Group
441 Lexington Avenue
New York, NY 10017
Phone: (212) 599-2200
http://www.lucascareers.com

Management Recruiters
9515 Deereco Road
Timonium, MD 21093
Phone: (410) 252-6616
Fax: (410) 252-7076
http://www.mribaltimore.com

MarketPro, Inc.
235 Peachtree Street
Atlanta, GA 30303
Phone: (404) 222-9992
Fax: (404) 222-9999
http://www.marketproinc.com

Martin Brinbach & Associates
15150 Preston Road
Dallas, TX 75248
Phone: (972) 490-5627
Fax: (972) 490-4606
E-mail: mba@executiverecruiter.com
http://www.executiverecruiter.com

Martin Kartin and Company
211 East 70th Street
New York, NY 10021

Phone: (212) 628-7676
Fax: (212) 628-8838
http://www.martinkartin.com

Matteson Partners, Inc.
Two Ravinia Drive
Atlanta, GA 30346
Phone: (770) 392-7170
Fax: (770) 392-7180
http://www.mattesonpartners.com

Melinda Holm & Associates
676 North LaSalle Drive
Chicago, IL 60610
Phone: (312) 654-9391
Fax: (312) 654-9392
E-mail: info@mhajobs.com
http://www.mhajobs.com

Moyer, Sherwood Associates, Inc.
1285 Avenue of the Americas
New York, NY 10019
Phone: (212) 554-4008
E-mail: research@moyersherwood.com
http://www.moyersherwood.com

New Career Personnel Services, Inc.
364 Parsippany Road
Parsippany, NJ 07054
Phone: (973) 884-1920
Fax: (973) 884-9329
E-mail: newcareer1@aol.com
http://www.newcareerpersonnel.com

Pailin Group Professional Search
Center City Plaza
1412 Main Suite 601
Dallas, TX 75202
Phone: (214) 752-6100
Fax: (214) 752-6100
E-mail: pailingrouppsc@compuserve.
   com
http://www.pailingroup.com

Paradigm Staffing
104 West Branch Street
Arroyo Grande, CA 93420
Phone: (805) 473-3112
Fax: (805) 473-3143
E-mail: info@paradigmstaffing.com
http://www.paradigmstaffing.com

Patch & Associates
600 Townsend Street
San Francisco, CA 94103
Phone: (415) 352-0272
Fax: (415) 503-3985
http://www.patchassociates.com

The Pennmor Group Executive Search
25 Chestnut Street
Haddonfield, NJ 08033
Phone: (856) 354-1414
Fax: (856) 354-7660
E-mail: info@pennmore.com
http://www.pennmor.com

Personnel Management Solutions, Inc.
1080 Kirts Boulevard
Troy, MI 48084
Phone: (800) 266-1143
Fax: (248) 269-8364
http://www.pmsirecruiting.com

Phyllis Solomon Executive Search
230 Sylvan Avenue
Englewood Cliffs, NJ 07632
Phone: (201) 947-8600
Fax: (201) 947-8600
http://www.solomonsearch.com

Peter Gray Staffing
1 Bank Street
Stamford, CT 06901
Phone: (203) 348-2216
Fax: (203) 348-2259

PLA, Inc.
12108 North 56th Street
Tampa, FL 33617
Phone: (813) 983-1855
Fax: (813) 983-1845
http://www.pla-inc.com

Procard International
6709 West 119th Street
Overland Park, KS 66209
Phone: (913) 287-8995
E-mail: careers@procardinternational.
   com
http://www.procardinternational.com

Profiler Digital Media Recruiters
10474 Santa Monica Boulevard
Los Angeles, CA 90025
Phone: (310) 446-8343
Fax: (310) 968-0468
http://www.profilerusa.com

Raskin Executive Search, LLC
275 Madison Avenue
New York, NY 10016
Phone: (212) 213-6381
Fax: (212) 94906146
http://www.raskinexecsearch.com

Recruiters, Inc.
One Liberty Plaza
New York, NY 10006

Phone: (212) 201-5424
E-mail: info@recruitersinc.com
http://www.recruitersinc.com

Results Staffing
40 Exchange Place
New York, NY 10005
Phone: (212) 284-8505
Fax: (212) 797-9203
http://www.resultsstaffing.com

RitaSue Siegel Resources
20 East 46th Street
New York, NY 10017
Phone: (212) 682-2100
Fax: (212) 682-2946
E-mail: ritasues@ritasue.com
http://www.ritasuesiegelresources.com

RPA Inc.
951 Westminster Drive
Williamsport, PA 17701
Phone: (800) 922-9277
Fax: (570) 321-7160
E-mail: email@rpainc.org
http://www.rpainc.org

Salem Associates
504 Hamburg Turnpike
Wayne, NJ 07470
Phone: (973) 389-7858
Fax: (973) 389-7818
http://www.salemsearch.com/

Salem Executive Search
275 Madison Avenue
New York, NY 10016
Phone: (212) 213-2600
Fax: (212) 213-2728
E-mail: jsalem@salemsearch.com
http://www.salemsearch.com

Salesstars.com
12165 North 102nd street
Scottsdale, AZ 85260
Phone: (602) 312-6802
Fax: (602) 296-0240
http://www.salesstars.com

SHS, Inc.
711 DeLasalle Court
Naperville, IL 60565
Phone: (630) 718-1704
Fax: (630) 718-1709
http://www.shsinc.com

Stephen Bradford Search
1140 Avenue of the Americas
New York, NY 10036

Phone: (212) 221-6333
http://www.stephenbradford.com

Strategic Resources
3380 146th Place Southeast
Bellevue, WA 98007
Phone: (425) 688-1151
Fax: (425) 688-1272
E-mail: corporate@strategicresources.
  com
http://www.strategicresources.com

The Sultan Moore Agency
1300 Clay Street
Oakland, CA 94612
Phone: (510) 446-7880
Fax: (425) 944-6967
E-mail: info@sultanmoore.com
http://www.sultanmoore.com

Tesar-Reyne
500 North Michigan Avenue
Chicago, IL 60611
Phone: (312) 661-0700
Fax: (312) 661-1598

Thomas & Associates, Inc.
6 East 39th Street
New York, NY 10016
Phone: (212) 779-7059
Fax: (212) 779-7096
E-mail: recruiters@artstaffing.com
http://www.artstaffing.com

T.K. Sutphin & Associates
8601 Six Forks Road
Raleigh, NC 27615
Phone: (919) 676-5284
Fax: (919) 870-9165
E-mail: kemsutphin@tksutphin.com
http://www.tksutphin.com

Travaille
1720 Rhode Island Avenue, NW
Washington, DC 20036
Phone: (202) 463-6342
Fax: (202) 331-7922

TSC Management Services Group, Inc.
112 Wool Street
Barrington, IL 60010
Phone: (847) 381-0167
Fax: (847) 381-1977
E-mail: infomaiton@TSCsearch.com
http://www.tscearch.com

Viscusi Group, Inc.
2095 Broadway
P.O. Box 261
New York, NY 10023
Phone: (212) 595-3811
http://www.viscusigroup.com

Vojta & Associates
102 Hobson Street
Stamford, CT 06902
Phone: (203) 357-8022

Fax: (203) 357-8262
E-mail: resume@optonline.net

The Ward Group
Eight Cedar Street
Woburn, MA 01801
Phone: (781) 938-4000
Fax: (781) 938-4100
E-mail: info@wardgroup.com
http://www.wardgroup.com

Wennik & Motta
23 Main Street
Andover, MA 01810
Phone: (978) 475-30322
http://www.wennikandmotta.com

Wills Consulting
Two Sound View Drive
Greenwich, CT 06830
Phone: (203) 622-4930
Fax: (203) 622-4931
http://www.wca-search.com

Yaekle & Company
P.O. Box 615
Granville, OH 43023
Phone: (740) 587-7366
Fax: (740) 587-1973
http://www.yaekleco.com

GLOSSARY

The following is a list of abbreviations, acronyms, and lingo that will prove helpful to individuals interested in advertising and public relations. Entries are listed alphabetically.

4A's   American Association of Advertising Agencies

AAF   American Advertising Federation

ABC   Audit Bureau of Circulations

ABCA   American Business Communication Association

ABWA   Associated Business Writers of America

AC   Advertising Council

ACCE   American Chamber of Commerce Executives

account executive   The individual who supervises the planning and preparation of an advertising or public relations account in an agency.

account   Refers to the client of an advertising or public relations agency; may refer to a client placing advertising with the media.

ACNY   Advertising Club of New York

AD   Art Director

ADACS   Art Directors & Artists Club of Sacramento

ADC   Art Directors Club, Inc.

ADCLA   Art Directors Club of Los Angeles

ADCMW   Art Directors Club of Metropolitan Washington

addressable advertising   A type of advertising that gives television programmers and advertisers the ability to deliver targeted television commericals to individual households based on specific criteria.

advertiser   Person or business who sells, manufactures, develops, or distributes products or services that need to be advertised in order to sell.

AE   Account executive

AEF   Advertising Educational Foundation

affiliate   A broadcast station that belongs to a network. For example, WABC in New York and KABC in Los Angeles are both affiliates of the ABC network.

AFM   Advertising Federation of Minnesota

AFM   American Federation of Musicians

AFTRA   American Federation of Television and Radio Artists

AGC   Artists Guild of Chicago

Agency Red Book   *Standard Directory of Advertising Agencies.* This book contains names, addresses, and phone numbers of most of the advertising agencies in the world as well as how much business each agency does, heads of departments, etc.

AGMA   American Guild of Musical Artists

AGVA   American Guild of Variety Artists

AHDPA   Association of House Democratic Press Assistants

AHPR   Academy of Hospital Public Relations

AICP   Association of Independent Commercial Producers

A.I.C.P. form   A form used by production companies that are members of the Association of Independent Commercial Producers to estimate the cost of a television commercial.

AIGA   American Institute of Graphic Arts

AJPRS   American Jewish Public Relations Society

AMA   American Management Association

AMA   American Marketing Association

ANA   Association of National Advertisers, Inc.

ANPAF   American Newspaper Publishers Association Foundation

APG   American Publicist Guild

Arbitron Ratings   A television and radio rating service that indicates what percentage of people are viewing or listening to a particular show or station. Commercial rates are often based on these ratings.

ARF   Advertising Research Foundation

ASHPR   American Society for Hospital Public Relations

ATA   American Telemarketing Association

ATAA   Advertising Typographers Association of America

ATME   Association of Travel Marketing Executives

ATPAM   Association of Theatrical Press Agents and Managers, AFL-CIO

AWNY   Advertising Women of New York, Inc.

banner ad   A graphic Web advertising unit.

B & W glossy   Used by publicists, press agents, and public relations people when putting together press kits, it is an 8 × 10 glossy photograph of their client that can be used for reproduction purposes in newspapers or magazines.

BDA   Broadcast Designers Association

B/PAA   Business/Professional Advertising Association

billboard   A large panel used in outdoor advertising.

bio   A biography put together by press agents, publicists, public relations people, etc. on a client.

bleed   Printing something to the very edge of the page.

book   A portfolio or book is a collection of samples done by someone in either the art or writing field to show prospective employers an applicant's potential.

BPA   Broadcasters' Promotion Association

BPRA   Baptist Public Relations Association

brand manager   A brand manager is in charge of advertising and promotion for specific brands of products within a company.

bullpen   The bullpen in an agency is a section of the art department where pasteups and mechanicals are done.

CAB   Cabletelevision Advertising Bureau

calendar listing   Dated listings sent to the media by publicists regarding upcoming events and programs. They are designed to bring the events to the attention of the public as well as newspeople and other editors.

camera ready   Everything in an ad is ready for a printer to produce a print of the advertisement. Nothing has to be retouched.

campaign   A series of advertisements used to promote and advertise a product or group of products.

campaign   An advertising concept complete with a series of advertisements put together for a client.

CASE   Council for the Advancement and Support of Education

CASRO   Council of American Survey Research Organizations

casting   Choosing and hiring the actors, actresses, announcers, etc. to star in a commercial.

CCS   Council of Communication Societies

CD   Creative director

circulation   The number of copies of a newspaper or magazine distributed.

column inch   Unit of publication space one column wide and one inch deep.

commission   A percentage of money spent to place an advertisement in the media is paid to the agency in the form of a commission.

comp   Short for comprehensive; it is a rough layout of an advertisement used to illustrate what the ad will look like.

copywriter   The person who develops the words used in advertisements, brochures, marketing and promotional pieces, etc.

CSA   Casting Society of America

CSIDA   College Sports Information Directors of America

CSPA   Council of Sales Promotion Agencies

dateline   Location information provided at the beginning of a news release indicating the specific town, city, etc. where the press or news release originated. In some instances the date may also be included.

demographics   The way an area or population is characterized, such as age, income, sex, race, religion, education, etc. Used to help determine where advertising can be most effective.

direct mail advertising   Advertisements and promotional pieces mailed directly to consumers.

direct response advertising   Advertising that uses either a mail-in coupon or a toll-free telephone number for responding immediately to an advertisement.

DMA   Direct Marketing Association

DMCG   Direct Marketing Creative Guild

DRTV   direct response television.

ECGA   Educational Council of the Graphic Arts

Equity   Actors Equity Association

FCC   Federal Communications Commission

Five Ws   Who, What, When, Where, and Why—used by press people to gather and write the basic news story.

font   Used to describe different typefaces in printing.

FPRRE   Foundation for Public Relations Research and Education

frequency   Describes number of times an ad will be running.

GAG   Graphic Artists Guild

graphics   The artwork, pictures, photographs, etc. used in advertisements.

house organ   A publication issued for a business's employees.

HSMAI   Hotel Sales and Marketing Association International

hype   Extensive publicity used to promote people, products, events, etc. Hype is not always true.

IAA   International Advertising Association

IABC   International Association of Business Communicators

IBEW   International Brotherhood of Electrical Workers

ICA   International Communications Associations

ICC   Industrial Communications Council

ICMA   International Circulation Managers Association

INAME   International Newspaper Advertising and Marketing Executives

infomercial   Short or regular length television programs that combine information with a suggestion or sales pitch to purchase a particular product or service.

INPA   International Newspaper Promotion Association

IOA   Institute of Outdoor Advertising

IPRA   International Public Relations Association

jingle   A musical tune in a commercial.

layout   The way an advertisement or promotional piece is put together.

lead   The opening lines of a news release or feature designed to attract reader interest.

local   The local in a union is the local affiliation in a particular geographic area of a national or international union; may also refer to a local television or radio station in relation to a national station.

location shoot   A place other than a studio where a commercial or photo for an advertisement or promotional piece is filmed or photographed.

log   An hourly record of all programs and commercials aired by a TV or radio station.

long form   Television commercials that are longer than two minutes; also called infomercial.

LPRC   Library Public Relations Council

market   Refers to a geographical location in television or radio; may refer to a specific size or style of audience market, such as small-market radio, major-market television, etc.

market research   Research dealing with the opinions of people about a product or service.

MASAI   Mail Advertising Service Association International

MRA   Marketing Research Association

NAB   National Association of Broadcasting

NAB   Newspaper Advertising Bureau

NABET   National Association of Broadcast Employees and Technicians

NACIO   National Association of Counties Information Officers

NAGC   National Association of Government Communicators

NAHD   National Association of Hospital Development

NAM   National Association of Manufacturers

NAPCRO   National Association of Police Community Relations Officers

NATAS   National Academy of Television Arts and Sciences

NBPRS   National Black Relations Society

NEJA   National Entertainment Journalists Association

Net   The Internet.

network   A group of TV or radio stations affiliated and interconnected for simultaneous broadcast of the same programming.

NFFE   National Federation of Federal Employees

NFMC   National Federation of Music Clubs

NFPW   National Federation of Press Women

Nielsen ratings   A television rating service.

NIRI   National Investors Relations Institute

NORC   National Opinion Research Center

NPC   National Press Club

NSFR   National Society of Fund Raising Executives

NSPRA   National School Public Relations Association

NSSA   National Sportscasters and Sportswriters Association

NTA   National Tour Association

online   Connected to the Internet.

PAC   Public Affairs Committee

PAC   Public Affairs Council

PAC   Publisher's Ad Club

photo caption   The story line accompanying a photograph, identifying the people in the photo and/or telling the story about the photo.

photo cropping   Trimming a photograph (manually or by electronic means) to reduce unnecessary and distracting elements; used to make a photo visually suitable to accompany a related story.

PIOA   Printing Industries of America

PMAA   Promotion Marketing Association of America

P.O.P.   Point of purchase; displays or posters used in stores to advertise a specific product or group of products.

portfolio   A collection of sample pieces done by someone in the creative field (either a writer or artist) put together in a book so that prospective employers can get an idea of a person's potential.

PPA   Publisher's Publicity Association, Inc.

P.R.   Public relations

press kit   A promo kit containing publicity, photographs, and other promotional materials used by publicists, press agents, and public relations people to help publicize a client.

promo   Promotion.

PRSA   Public Relations Society of America

PRSSA   Public Relations Student Society of America

publicity peg   An interesting piece of information designed to grab the attention of a news editor.

RAB   Radio and Advertising Bureau

rate card   A card listing rates for space or time and providing mechanical requirements for advertisements.

RCA   Republican Communications Association

RPRC   Religious Public Relations Council

SAAI   Specialty Advertising Association International

SAG   Screen Actors Guild

scale   Minimum wages that can be paid to a union member.

search the net   To look for information on the Internet.

SEG   Screen Extras Guild

ship date   The actual date a manufacturer ships a product.

shoot   The filming of a television commercial.

short form   Direct response television commercials that are less than two minutes in length.

SILA   Society of Illustrators of Los Angeles

site   Web site.

SMEGNY   Sales and Marketing Executives of Greater New York

SMEI   Sales and Marketing Executives International

SMPS   Society for Marketing Professional Services

SOCAP   Society of Consumer Affairs Professionals in Business

SOI   Society of Illustrators

SPGA   Society of Professional Graphic Artists

sponsor   An advertiser who pays for program time in relation to just one commercial.

STA   Society of Typographic Arts

STC   Society for Technical Communications

stock   Various types and weights of paper on which advertising or promotional pieces might be printed.

storyboard   A group of sketches with copy in parallel sequence to illustrate the layout of a television commercial.

surf the net   going online; visiting various sites on the Internet.

TDC   Type Directors Club

TNG   The Newspaper Guild

TOC   The One Club

trades   Magazines and newspapers that deal with specific industries.

TvB   Television Bureau of Advertising

union card   A card that is used to identify members of specific unions.

WADC   Western Art Directors Club

WDC   Women in Design of Chicago

WDRG   Women's Direct Response Group

Web   The World Wide Web.

Web site   A "place" on the World Wide Web

WEPR   Women Executives in Public Relations

WGA   Writers Guild of America East

WGA   Writers Guild of America West

WIC   Women In Communications, Inc.

WWW   World Wide Web

YPD   Young Professionals Division

BIBLIOGRAPHY

A. BOOKS

There are thousands of books written on all aspects of advertising and public relations. The books listed below are separated into general categories with the subject matter in many overlapping into other categories.

These books can be found in bookstores or libraries. If your local library does not have the books you want, you might ask your librarian to order them for you through the interlibrary loan system.

This list is meant as a beginning. For other books that might interest you, consult the business section of bookstores and libraries. You can also check *Books In Print* (found in the reference section of libraries) for other books on the subject.

ADVERTISING

Berger, Arthur Asa. *Media Analysis Techniques.* Thousand Oaks, Calif.: Sage Publications, 1998.

Berlin Press and Zwangsleitner, Klaus. *Best Rejected Advertising.* London: Trolley Press, 2005.

Hackley, Chris. *Advertising and Promotion: Communicating Brands.* Thousand Oaks, Calif.: Sage Publications, 2005.

Haig, Matt. *Brand Failures: The Truth About the 100 Biggest Branding Mistakes of All Time.* London: Kogan Page, 2003.

Heimann, Jim, ed. *All American Ads of the 80's.* New York: Taschen, 2005.

Kaplan, Linda and Robin Koval. *Bang! Getting Your Message Heard in a Noisy World.* New York: Currency, 2005.

Lasalle, Diana and Terry A Britton. *Priceless: Turing Ordinary Products Into Extraordinary Experiences.* Boston: Harvard Business School Press, 2002.

Ogilvy, David. *Ogilvy on Advertising.* New York: Vintage, 1985.

Pricken, Mario and Thames Hudson. *Creative Advertising: Ideas and Techniques from the World's Best Campaigns.* New York: Thames and Hudson, 2004.

Roman, Kenneth and Jane Mass. *How to Advertise.* New York: St. Martin's Griffin, 2005.

Steele, Jon. *Truth, Lies and Advertising: The Art of Account Planning.* Hoboken, N.J.: Wiley, 1998.

Sullivan, Luke. *Hey, Whipple, Squeeze This: A Guide to Creating Great Ads, Second Edition.* Hoboken, N.J.: Wiley, 2003.

Wells, William, D., John Burnett, and Sandra Moriarty. *Advertising Principles and Practice, Sixth Edition.* Upper Saddle River, N.J.: Prentice Hall, 2005.

Wheeler, Alina. *Designing Brand Identity: A Complete Guide To Creating, Building and Maintaining Strong Brands.* Hoboken, N.J.: Wiley, 2003.

Yeshin, Tony. *Advertising.* Washington, D.C.: Thomson Business Press, 2005.

Zaltman, Gerald. *How Customers Think: Essential Insights into the Mind of the Market.* Boston: Harvard Business School Press, 2003.

ADVERTISING AGENCIES

Beal, Stanley and David Beal. *Agency Compensation: A Guidebook.* New York: Association of National Advertisers, 2001.

Hameroff, Eugene J. *The Advertising Agency Business.* New York: McGraw-Hill, 1998.

Jaffee, Andrew. *Casting For Big Ideas: A New Manifesto For Agency Managers.* Hoboken, N.J.: Wiley, 2003.

Solomon, Robert. *Art of Client Service.* Chicago: Dearborn Trade, 2003.

CORPORATE AND INDUSTRY

Alsop, Ron. *The 18 Immutable Laws of Corporate Reputation: Creating, Protecting, and Repairing Your Most Valuable Asset.* New York: Free Press, 2004.

Caris, Melinda. *The New Culture of Desire: 5 Radical New Strategies That Will Change Your Business and Your Life.* New York: Free Press, 2001.

Fombrun, Charles, J. and Van Riel, Cees. *Fame and Fortune: How Successful Companies Build Winning Reputations.* Upper Saddle River, N.J.: Financial Times Prentice Hall, 2003.

Kobliski, Kathy. *Advertising Without an Agency.* Irvine, Calif.: Entrepreneur Press, 2005.

Neumeier, Marty. *The Brand Gap: How to Bridge the Distance Between Business Strategy and Design.* Berkeley, Calif.: New Riders Press, 2003.

Yohalem, Kathy, C. *Thinking Out of the Box: How to Market Your Company into the Future.* Hoboken, N.J.: Wiley, 1997.

CONSULTING AND FREELANCE

Augustine, Dennis F. *How to Market Your Professional Services: A Professional's Guide to Advertising & Public Relations.* Saratoga, Calif: Golden Gates Publications, 1993.

Banks, Michael A. *How to Become a Fulltime Freelance Writer: A Practical Guide to Setting Up a Successful Writing Business at Home.* New York: Watson-Guptill Publications, 2003.

Biech, Elaine. *The Consultant's Quick Start Guide: An Action Plan for Your First Year in Business.* Ontario, Canada: Pfeiffer, 2001.

Bowerman, Peter. *The Well-Fed Writer: Financial Self-Sufficiency as a Freelance Writer in Six Months or Less.* Atlanta: Fanove Publishing, 2000.

Formichelli, Linda and Diana Burrell. *The Renegade Writer: A Totally Unconventional Guide to Freelance Writing Success.* Salem, Ore.: Marion Street Press, 2003.

Shenson, Howard. *The Contract and Fee-Setting Guide for Consultants and Professionals.* Hoboken, N.J.: Wiley, 1990.

Slaunwhite, Steve. *Start and Run a Copywriting Business.* Bellingham, Wash.: Self-Counsel Press, 2001.

Weiss, Alan. *How to Acquire Clients: Powerful Techniques for the Successful Practitioner.* Toronto, Canada: Pfeiffer, 2002.

———. *Million Dollar Consulting: The Professional's Guide to Growing a Practice.* New York: McGraw-Hill, 2002.

CREATIVE

Canfield, Jon and Tim Grey. *Photo Finish: The Digital Photographer's Guide to Printing, Showing, and Selling Images.* Alameda, Calif.: Sybex 2004.

Krause, Jim. *Layout Index.* Cincinnati, Ohio: Northlight Books, 2001.

Thomas, Gregory. *How to Design Logos, Symbols and Icons: 24 Internationally Renowned Studios Reveal How They Develop Trademarks for Print and New Media.* Cincinnati, Ohio: How Design Books, 2003.

Walker, Sandra C., ed. *Image Buyers' Guide: An International Directory of Sources for Slides and Digital Images for Art and Architecture.* Englewood, Colo.: Libraries Unlimited, 1999.

Wheeler, Alina. *Designing Brand Identity: A Complete Guide to Creating, Building, and Maintaining Strong Brands.* Hoboken, N.J.: Wiley, 2003.

DIRECT MARKETING/DIRECT RESPONSE

Bly, Robert, W. *Complete Idiot's Guide to Direct Marketing.* New York: Penguin Putnam, 2001.

Geller, Lois. *Direct Marketing Techniques: Building Your Business Using Direct Mail and Direct Response Advertising.* Menlo Park, Calif.: Crisp Publications, 1998.

Nash, Edward. *Direct Marketing: Strategy, Planning, Execution.* New York: McGraw-Hill, 2000.

Stone, Bob and Ron Jacobs. *Successful Direct Marketing Methods.* New York: McGraw Hill, 2001.

IMAGE BUILDING

Adatto, Kiku. *Picture Perfect: The Art and Artifice of Public Image Making.* Collingdale, Pa.: Diane Publishing, 1999.

Alsop, Ronald. *The 18 Immutable Laws of Corporate Reputation: Creating, Protecting, and Repairing Your Most Valuable Asset.* New York: Free Press, 2004.

Fombrun, Charles, J. and Cees Van Riel. *Fame and Fortune: How Successful Companies Build Winning Reputations.* Upper Saddle River, N.J.: Financial Times Prentice Hall, 2003.

Gaines-Ross, Leslie. *CEO Capital: A Guide To Building CEO Reputation and Company Success.* Hoboken, N.J.: Wiley, 2002.

Gee, Bobbie. *Creating A Million Dollar Image For Your Business.* Berkeley, Calif.: Pagemill Press, 1996.

———. *Winning the Image Game: A Ten Step Masterplan for Achieving Power, Prestige, and Profit.* Berkeley, Calif.: Pagemill Press, 1994.

INTERNET AND WEB ADVERTISING, PUBLIC RELATIONS, AND MEDIA

Bly, Robert W., Michelle Fait, and Steve Roberts. *Internet Direct Mail: The Complete Guide to Successful E-Mail Marketing Campaigns.* New York: McGraw-Hill, 2000.

Giguere, Eric. *Google Advertising: Making the Most of Google's AdWords and AdSense.* Berkeley, Calif.: Peachpit Press, 2005.

Kennedy, Dennis. *Winning on the Web: Net Marketing for Lawyers.* New York: American Lawyers Media, 2005.

Lewis, Herschell Gordon. *Effective E-Mail Marketing: The Complete Guide to Creating Successful Campaigns.* New York: AMACOM, 2002.

Lynn, Jacquelyn. *Make Big Profits on Ebay: The Ultimate Guide for Building a Business on Ebay.* Irvine, Calif.: Entrepreneur Press, 2005.

O'Keefe, Steve. *Complete Guide to Internet Publicity: Creating and Launching Successful Online Campaigns.* Hoboken, N.J.: Wiley, 2002.

Seda, Catherine. *Search Engine Advertising: Buying Your Way to the Top to Increase Sales.* Indianapolis, Ind.: Pearson Education, 2004.

MARKETING

Beckwith, Harry. *Selling The Invisible: A Field Guide To Modern Marketing.* New York: Warner Business Books, 1997.

Jaffe, Joseph. *Life After the 30-Second Spot: Ten Fresh Ways to Reach Customers That Are Transforming the Marketing Game.* Hoboken, N.J.: Wiley, 2005.

Keller, Kevin Lane. *Strategic Brand Management.* Upper Saddle River, N.J.: Prentice Hall, 2002.

Kotler, Phillip. *Marketing Management.* Upper Saddle River, N.J.: Prentice Hall, 2002.

Nagle, Thomas, T. and Reed K. Holden. *The Strategy and Tactics of Pricing: A Guide To Profitable Decision Making* (3rd ed.). Upper Saddle River, N.J.: Prentice Hall, 2002.

Phillips, Michaels and Salli Rasberry. *Marketing Without Advertising: Inspire Customers to Rave about Your Business & Create Lasting Success.* Berkeley, Calif.: Nolo.com, 2005.

Schor, Juliet. *Born to Buy: Marketing and the Transformation of Childhood and Culture.* New York: Scribner, 2005.

MEDIA RELATIONS

Goldberg, Bernard. *Bias: A CBS Insider Exposes How the Media Distort the News,* Washington, D.C.: Regnery, 2001.

Hart, Hal. *Successful Spokespersons Are Made, Not Born: How to Control the Direction of Media Interviews & Deliver Winning Presentations.* Bloomington, Ind.: Authorhouse, 2000.

Howard, Carole M. and Wilma, K. Mathews. *On Deadline: Managing Media Relations.* Prospect Heights, Ill.: Waveland Press, 2003.

Jones, Clarence. *Winning with the News Media : A Self-Defense Manual When You're the Story.* Pomona, Calif.: Winning News Media, 2001.

Stewart, Sally. *Media Training 1001: A Guide to Meeting the Press.* Hoboken, N.J.: Wiley, 2003.

Stauffer, Dennis. *Mediasmart: How to Handle a Reporter by a Reporter.* Minneapolis, Minn.: MinneApplePress, 2004.

MUSIC PUBLIC RELATIONS, PUBLICITY, MARKETING AND PROMOTION

Baker, Bob. *Guerrilla Music Marketing Handbook: 201 Self-Promotion Ideas for Songwriters, Musicians & Bands.* Colorado Springs, Colo.: Spotlight Publishing, 2001.

Britt, Shawnassey Howell. *The Independent Record Label's Plain and Simple Guide to Music Promotion.* Jackson, Miss.: One Horse Publishing, 2004.

Field, Shelly. *Career Opportunities in the Music Industry.* New York: Facts On File, 2004.

Fisher, Jeffrey P. *Ruthless Self-Promotion In the Music Industry.* Overland Park, Kans.: Primedia Business Magazines & Media, 1999.

Kalmar, Veronika. *Label Launch: A Guide to Independent Record Recording, Promotion, and Distribution.* New York: St. Martin's Press, 2002.

Karmen, Steve. *Who Killed The Jingle.* Milwaukee, Wis.: Hal Leonard, 2004.

Lathrop, Ted. *This Business of Music Marketing and Promotion, Revised and Updated Edition.* New York: Billboard Books, 2003.

Letts, Richard. *The Art of Self-Promotion: Successful Promotion by Musicians.* Crows Nest, Australia: Allen & Unwin, 1997.

Pettigrew, Jim. *The Billboard Guide to Music Publicity.* New York: Billboard Books, 1997.

Summers, Jodi. *Making and Marketing Music.* New York: Allworth Press, 2004.

NONPROFIT

Bonk, Kathy, Henry Griggs, and Emily Tynes. *The Jossey-Bass Guide to Strategic Communications for Nonprofits: A Step-by-Step Guide to Working with the Media to Generate Publicity, Enhance Fundraising.* San Francisco: Jossey-Bass, 1998.

Conners, Gail. *Good News!: How to Get the Best Possible Media Coverage for Your School.* Thousand Oaks, Calif.: Corwin Press, 2000.

Field, Edwin and Selma Field. *Publicity Manual For Law Enforcement Agencies.* Bridgewater, N.J.: Replica Books, 2000.

———. *Publicity Manual For Libraries.* Bridgewater, N.J.: Replica Books, 1999.

McLeish, Barry J. *Successful Marketing Strategies For Nonprofit Organizations* Hoboken, N.J.: Wiley, 1995.

POLITICAL

Faucheux, Ron. *Running for Office: The Strategies, Techniques, and Messages Modern Political Candidates Need to Win Elections.* New York: M. Evans, 2002.

———. *Winning Elections: Political Campaign Management, Strategy & Tactics.* New York: M. Evans, 2003.

Shea, Daniel M. and Michael John Buron. *Campaign Craft: The Strategies, Tactics, and Art of Political Campaign Management.* Westport, Conn.: Praeger Paperback, 2001.

PUBLIC RELATIONS, PROMOTION AND PUBLICITY

Abott, Susan. *Fine Art Publicity: The Complete Guide for Artists, Galleries And Museums.* New York: Allworth Press, 2005.

Breakenridge, Deidre and Thomas J. DeLoughry. *The New PR Toolkit: Strategies for Successful Media Relations.* Upper Saddle River, N.J.: Financial Times Prentice Hall, 2003.

Conners, Gail. *Good News!: How to Get the Best Possible Media Coverage for Your School.* Thousand Oaks, Calif.: Corwin Press, 2000.

Crilley, Jeff. *Free Publicity: A TV Reporter Shares The Secrets For Getting Covered On The News.* Wellesley, Mass.: Brown Publishing, 2002.

De La Cruz, Melissa and Karen Robinovitz. *How to Become Famous in Two Weeks or Less.* New York: Ballantine Books, 2003.

Doty, Dorothy. *Publicity & Public Relations.:* Hauppauge, N.Y.: Barron's Educational Series, 2001.

Fletcher, Tana. *Getting Publicity.* Bellingham, Wash.: Self-Counsel, 2000.

Godin, Seth. *Free Prize Inside.* New York: Penguin, 2004.

Guth, David W. *Adventures In Public Relations: Case Studies and Critical Thinking.* Old Tappan, N.J.: Allyn & Bacon, 2004.

Kohl, Susan. *Getting Attention: Leading-Edge Lessons for Publicity and Marketing.* Boston: Butterworth Heinemann, 2002.

Laermer, Richard. *Full Frontal PR: Building Buzz About Your Business, Your Product or You.* Princeton, N.J.: Bloomberg Press, 2004.

Levine, Michael. *Guerrilla PR Wired: Waging a Successful Publicity Campaign Online, Offline, and Everywhere In Between.* New York: McGraw-Hill Trade, 2003.

Levinson, Jay Conrad, Rick Frishman, and Jill Lubin. *Guerrilla Publicity: Hundreds of Sure-Fire Tactics to Get Maximum Sales for Minimum Dollars.* Avon, Mass.: Adams Media, 2002.

McIntyre, Catherine. *Writing Effective News Releases...: How to Get Free Publicity for Yourself, Your Business, or Your Organization.* Colorado Springs, Colo.: Piccadilly Books, 1992.

Parsons, Patricia. *Ethics Public Relations.* London: Kogan Page, 2004.

Rein, Irving J., Philip Kotler, and Martin Stoller. *High Visibility: The Making and Marketing of Professionals into Celebrities.* New York: McGraw-Hill, 1997.

Stauber, John and Sheldon Rampton. *Trust Us We're Experts: How Industry Manipulates Science and Gambles with Your Future.* New York: Penguin Putnam, 2002.

Theaker, Alison. *The Public Relations Handbook.* New York: Routledge, 2004.

Van Yoder, Steven. *Get Slightly Famous: Become A Celebrity In Your Field and Attract More Business With Less Effort.* Berkeley, Calif.: Bay Tree Publishing, 2003.

Yale, David R. and Andrew J. Carothers. *The Publicity Handbook, New Edition: The Inside Scoop from More than 100 Journalists and PR Pros on How to Get Great Publicity Coverage.* New York: McGraw-Hill, 2001.

Yudkin, Marcia. *6 Steps to Free Publicity: "For Corporate Publicists or Solo Professionals, Including ... Publishers, Consultants, Conference Planners, Politicians, Inventors.* Franklin Lakes, N.J.: Career Press, 2003.

PUBLISHING

Blanco, Jodee. *The Complete Guide To Book Publicity.* New York: Allworth Press, 2004.

Cole, David. *The Complete Guide To Book Marketing.* New York: Allworth Press, 2004.

Deval, Jacqueline. *Publicize Your Book!: An Insider's Guide to Getting Your Book the Attention It Deserves.* New York: Penguin Group, 2003.

Reiss, Fern. *The Publishing Game: Bestseller In 30 Days.* Newton, Mass.: Peanut Butter & Jelly Press, 2003.

Warren, Lisa. *The Savvy Author's Guide to Book Publicity.* New York: Carroll & Graf, 2004.

RADIO ADVERTISING

Ingram, Andrew and Mark Barber. *Advanced Level Radio Advertising.* Hoboken, N.J.: Wiley, 2005.

RESEARCH

Dominick, Wimmer. *Mass Media Research.* Florence, Ky.: Wadsworth, 2005.

SALES PROMOTION

Chandler, Steve. *The Joy of Selling: Breakthrough Ideas that Lead to Success In Sales.* Richmond, Calif: Maurice Basset, 2004.

Galician, Mary-Lou. *Handbook of Product Placement in the Mass Media: New Strategies in Marketing Theory, Practice, Trends, and Ethics.* Binghamton, N.Y.: Haworth Press, 2004.

Schultz, Don E. *How to Sell More Stuff: Promotional Marketing That Really Works.* Chicago: Dearborn Trade, 2004.

SPORTS AND ENTERTAINMENT ADVERTISING AND PUBLIC RELATIONS

Field, Shelly. *Career Opportunities in the Sports Industry.* New York: Facts On File, 2004.

———. *Career Opportunities in Theater and the Performing Arts.* New York: Facts On File, 1999.

Graham, Stedman, Lisa Delpy Neirotti, and Joe Jeff Goldblatt. *The Ultimate Guide To Sports Marketing.* New York: McGraw Hill, 2001.

Helitzer, Melvin. *The Dream Job: Sports Publicity, Promotion and Marketing.* Athens, Ohio: University Sports Press, 1999.

Jackson, Steven, J. and David L. Andrews. *Sport, Culture and Advertising: Identities, Commodities and the Politics of Representation.* New York: Routledge, 2005.

Schaaf, Phil. *Sports Marketing: It's Not Just a Game Anymore.* Amherst, N.Y.: Prometheus Books, 1995.

Stotlar, David K. *Developing Successful Sport Sponsorship Plans.* Morgantown, W.Va.: Fitness Information Technology, 2002.

WRITING

Blake, Gary and Robert W. Bly. *The Elements of Copywriting: The Essential Guide to Creating Copy that Gets the Results You Want.* New York: Longman, 1998.

Bly, Robert W. *The Copywriter's Handbook: A Step-By-Step Guide to Writing that Sells.* New York: Owl Books, 1990.

———. *Everything You Need to Know to Write Electronic Copy that Sells.* New York: McGraw-Hill, 2003.

Eisenberg, Bryan, Jeffrey Eisenberg, and Lisa T. Davis. *Persuasive Online Copywriting: How to Take Your Words to the Bank.* Buda, Tex.: Wizard Academy Press, 2002.

Gabay, Johathan J. *Teach Yourself Copywriting.* New York: McGraw-Hill, 2003.

Higgins, Dennis. *The Art of Writing Advertising: Conversations with Masters of the Craft: David Ogilvy, William Bernbach, Leo Burnett, Rosser Reeves.* New York: McGraw-Hill, 2003.

Lewis, Herschell Gordon. *On the Art of Writing Copy.* Evanston, Ill.: Racom Communications, 2003.

Price, Jonathan and Lisa Price. *Hot Text: Web Writing that Works.* Brussels, Belgium: New Riders Press, 2002.

Usborne, Nick. *Net Words: Creating High-Impact Online Copy.* New York: McGraw-Hill, 2001.

B. PERIODICALS

Magazines, newspapers, membership bulletins, and newsletters may be helpful for finding information about a specific job category, finding a job in a specific field, or giving you insight into what certain jobs entail.

As with the books in the previous section, this list should serve as a beginning. There are many periodicals that are not listed because of space limitations. The subject matter of some periodicals may overlap with others. Periodicals also tend to come and go. Look in your local library or in the newspaper/magazine shop for other periodicals that might interest you.

Names, addresses, phone numbers, Web sites and e-mail addresses have been included when available.

ADVERTISING—GENERAL INTEREST

Adweek
VNU Business Media
770 Broadway
New York, NY 10003
Phone: (646) 654-5000
http://www.adweek.com

Adweek/Midwest
VNU Business Publications, Inc.
200 West Jackson Boulevard
Chicago, IL 60606
Phone: (312) 583-5500
Fax: (312) 583-5502
http://www.adweek.com

Adweek/New England
Adweek L.P.
100 Boylston Street
Boston, MA 02116
Phone: (617) 482-0876
Fax: (617) 482-2921
http://www.adweek.com

Adweek Western Edition
VNU Business Media USA
770 Broadway
New York, NY 10003
Phone: (646) 654-5000
http:www.adweek.com

Advertising Age
Crain Communications, Inc.
711 Third Avenue
New York, NY 10017
Phone: (212) 210-0100
Fax: (212) 210-0244
http://www.advertisingage.com

Brandweek Directory
ADWEEK Magazines
770 Broadway
New York, NY 10003
Phone: (646) 654-5115
Fax: (646) 654-5351
http://www.brandweek.com

Journal of Advertising
American Academy of Advertising
Iowa State University
Department of Marketing
300 Carver Hall
Ames, IA 50011

ADVERTISING RESEARCH

Journal of Advertising Research
Advertising Research Foundation
641 Lexington Avenue
New York, NY 10022
Phone: (212) 751-5656
Fax: (212) 319-5265

CREATIVE (ARTISTS, ART DIRECTORS, ETC.)

AIGA Journal of Graphic Design
American Institute of Graphic Arts
164 Fifth Avenue
New York, NY 10010
Phone: (212) 807-1990
Fax: (212) 807-1799

American Artist
VNU Business Media USA
770 Broadway
New York, NY 10003
Phone: (646) 654-5000
http://www.myamericanartist.com

American Artist Directory of Art Schools and Workshops Issue
VNU Business Publications
575 Prospect Avenue
Lakewood, NJ 08701
Phone: (732) 363-5679
Fax: (732) 363-0338

Communication Arts Magazine
Communication Arts
110 Constitution Drive
Menlo Park, CA 94025
Phone: (650) 326-6040
Fax: (650) 326-1648
http://www.commarts.com/advertising

Creative
Magazines/Creative, Inc.
42 West 38th Street
New York, NY 10018
Phone: (212) 840-0160
Fax: (212) 819-0945
http://www.creativemag.com

Gain
American Institute of Graphic Arts
164 Fifth Avenue
New York, NY 10010
Phone: (212) 807-1990
Fax: (212) 807-1799
http://www.gain.aiga.org

Trace: AIGA Journal of Design
American Institute of Graphic Arts
164 Fifth Avenue
New York, NY 10010
Phone: (212) 807-1990
Fax: (212) 807-1799

ENTERTAINMENT

Alternative Press
6516 Detroit Avenue
Cleveland, OH 44102
Phone: (216) 631-1510
Fax: (216) 631-1016
http://www.altpress.com

Amusement Business
VNU Business Publications
P.O. Box 24970
Nashville, TN 37202
Phone: (615) 321-4250
Fax: (615) 327-1575
http://www.amusementbusiness.com

Back Stage West
VNU Business Media
770 Broadway
New York, NY 10003
Phone: (646) 654-5000
http://www.backstage.com

Billboard
770 Broadway
New York, NY 10003
Phone: (646) 654-4400
Fax: (646) 654-4681
http://www.billboard.com

Blender
1040 Avenue of the Americas
New York, NY 10018
Phone: (212) 302-2626
Fax: (212) 302-9671
http://www.blender.com

Daily Variety
Reed Business Information
249 West 17th Street
New York, NY 10011
Phone: (212) 337-6900
Fax: (212) 337-6977
http://www.variety.com

Electronic Musician
Primedia Business
6400 Hollis Street
Emeryville, CA 94608
Phone: (510) 653-3307
Fax: (510) 653-5142
http://www.emusician.com

The Hollywood Reporter
5055 Wilshire Boulevard
Los Angeles, CA 90036
Phone: (323) 525-2000
Fax: (323) 525-2377
http://www.hollywoodreporter.com

International Musician
American Federation of Musicians
1501 Broadway
New York, NY 10023
Phone: (212) 869-1330
Fax: (212) 302-4374

Music Clubs Magazine
1336 North Delaware Street
Indianapolis, IN 46202
Phone: (317) 638-4003
Fax: (317) 638-0503

Music Monthly
Maryland Musician Publications
1144 York Road
Lutherville, MD 21093
Phone: (410) 494-0566
Fax: (410) 494-0565
http://www.musicmonthly.com

Radio and Records
Radio and Records, Inc.
10100 Santa Monica Boulevard
Los Angeles, CA 90067
Phone: (310) 553-4330
Fax: (310) 203-9763
http://www.radioandrecords.com

Recording
Music Maker Publications, Inc.
5412 Idylwild Trail
Boulder, CO 80301
Phone: (303) 516-9118
Fax: (303) 516-9119
http://www.recordingmag.com

Record Retailing Directory
VNU Business Media
770 Broadway
New York, NY 10003
Phone: (646) 654-5000
Fax: (646) 654-5487

Variety
Reed Business Information
5700 Wilshire Boulevard
Los Angeles, CA 90036
Phone: (323) 857-6600
Fax: (323) 965-2475
http://www.variety.com

Variety Deal Memo
Baskerville Communications Corp.
7286 Woodvale Court
West Hills, CA 91307
Phone: (818) 461-9660
Fax: (818) 461-9661

INVESTOR RELATIONS

Investor Relations Guide
National Investor Relations Institute
  (NIRI)
8020 Towers Crescent Drive
Vienna, VA 22182
Phone: (703) 506-3570
Fax: (703) 506-3571
E-mail: bcarty@niri.org
http://www.niri.org

Investor Relations Newsletter
Kennedy Information, Inc.
One Pheonix Mill Lane
Peterborough, NH 03458
Phone: (603) 924-1006
Fax: (603) 924-4034
E-mail: bookstore@kennedyinfo.com

Strategic Investor Relations
Aspen Publishers
3133 Connecticut Avenue, NW
Washington, DC 20008
Phone: (202) 483-0828
Fax: (202) 483-0828

MARKETING

Advertising and Marketing Review
CSC Publishing
622 Gardenia Court
Golden, CO 80401
Phone: (303) 277-9840
Fax: (303) 278-9909
http://www.ad-mkt-review.com

Direct Marketing
Hoke Communications, Inc.
224 7th Street
Garden City, NY 11530
Phone: (516) 746-6700
Fax: (516) 294-8141

Direct Marketing Association-Direct Line
Direct Marketing Association, Inc.
1120 Avenue of the Americas
New York, NY 10036
Phone: (212) 768-7277
Fax: (212) 302-6714
http://www.the-dma.org

Direct Marketing Hints and Secrets
145 East 27th Street
New York, NY 10016
Phone: (212) 689-0772
Fax: (212) 481-0552

Direct Marketing List Source
SRDS
1700 East Higgins Road
Des Plaines, IL 60018
Phone: (847) 375-5000
Fax: (847) 375-5001
E-mail: contact@srds.com
http://www.srds.com

Direct Marketing Market Place
LexisNexis Group
121 Chanlon Road
New Providence, NJ 07974
Phone: (908) 464-6800
Fax: (908) 771-7704
http://www.dirmktgplace.com

Direct Response
Creative Direct Marketing Group
2360 Plaza Del Amo
Torrance, CA 90501
Phone: (310) 212-5727
Fax: (310) 212-5773
http://www.directmarketingcenter.net

Inside Mass Marketing
Direct Marketing Association, Inc.
1120 Avenue of the Americas
New York, NY 10036-6700
Phone: (212) 768-7277
Fax: (212) 302-6714

Journal of Direct and Interactive Marketing
John Wiley and Sons, Inc.
111 River Street
Hoboken, NJ 07030

Phone: (201) 748-6000
Fax: (201) 748-6088
E-mail: subinfo@wiley.com

Journal of Business to Business Marketing
The Haworth Press, Inc.
Baruch College—City University of New York
1 Bernard Baruch Way
P.O. Box 12-240
New York, NY 10010
Phone: (646) 312-3281
Fax: (646) 312-3271
http://www.haworthpress.com/web/JBBM

Journal of Food Products Marketing
The Haworth Press, Inc.
Dept. of Food Marketing
St. Joseph's University
5600 City Avenue
Philadelphia, PA 19131
Phone: (610) 660-1607
Fax: (215) 660-1604
E-mail: getinfo@haworthpress.com
http://www.haworthpress.com/web/JFPM

Journal of Global Marketing
The Haworth Press, Inc.
International Business Press
P.O. Box 399
Middletown, PA 17057
Phone: (717) 566-3054
Fax: (717) 566-8589
E-mail: getinfo@haworthpress.com
http://www.haworthpress.com/web/JGM

Journal of Hospital Marketing and Public Relations
The Haworth Press, Inc.
57 Pembrook Loop
Staten Island, NY 10309
Phone: (718) 390-3182
E-mail: getinfo@haworthpress.com
http://www.haworthpress.com/web/JHMPR

PCS Direct Marketing Newsletter
PCS Mailing List Company
39 Cross Street
Peabody, MA 01960
Phone: (978) 532-7100
Fax: (978) 532-9181
E-mail: info@pcslist.com

Target Marketing
North American Publishing Co.
Pierce Financial Corporation
837 Villa Ridge Road

Falls Church, VA 22046
Phone: (215) 238-5482
Fax: (215) 238-5412
E-mail: customerservice@napco.com

MEDIA

Cap Communications—Contacts
CAP Communications
35-20 Broadway
Astoria, NY 11106
Phone: (718) 721-0508
Fax: (718) 274-3387
E-mail: contactspr@aol.com

News Media Update
Reporters Committee for Freedom of the Press
1815 North Fort Myer Drive
Arlington, VA 22209
Phone: (703) 807-2100
Fax: (703) 807-2109

Partyline Newsletter
Partyline Publishing Company
35 Sutton Place
New York, NY 10022
Phone: (212) 755-3487
Fax: (212) 755-4859
http://www.partylinepublishing.com

NEWSLETTERS

The Newsletter On Newsletters
20 West Chestnut Street
Rhinebeck, NY 12572
Phone: (845) 876-5222
Fax: (845) 876-4943

NONPROFITS

Foundation Grants Index
Foundation Center
79 Fifth Avenue
New York, NY 10003
Phone: (212) 620-4230
Fax: (212) 691-1828
http://www.fdncenter.org/marketplace

Journal of Nonprofit and Public Sector Marketing
The Haworth Press, Inc.
Dept. of Management & Marketing
Christopher Newport University
Newport News, VA 23606
Phone: (757) 594-7692
Fax: (334) 244-3792
E-mail: getinfo@haworthpress.com
http://www.haworthpress.com/web/JNPSM

News From The Foundation Center
Foundation Center
79 Fifth Avenue
New York, NY 10003
Phone: (212) 807-3690
Fax: (212) 807-3691
http://www.fdncenter.org/newsletters

PHOTOGRAPHY AND COMMERCIAL PRODUCTION

Focus On Imaging
PLM Publishing, Inc.
1312 Lincoln Boulevard
P.O. Box 1700
Santa Monica, CA 90401
Phone: (310) 451-1344
Fax: (310) 395-9058

Photo News
Beacon Newspapers, Inc.
220 Deer Park Avenue
P.O. Box 670
Babylon, NY 11702

Shoot Directory For Commercial Production and Post Production
VNU Business Publications
575 Prospect Avenue
Lakewood, NJ 08701
Phone: (732) 363-5679
Fax: (732) 363-0338
E-mail: maze@cahners.com
http://www.shootonline.com/shootonline/
   directory/index.jsp

PUBLIC RELATIONS/ PUBLICITY AND PROMOTION—GENERAL

Bulldog Reporter – Eastern Edition
Infocom Group
5900 Hollis Street
Emeryville, CA 94608
Phone: (510) 596-9300
Fax: (510) 596-9331
http://www.infocomgroup.com

Bulldog Reporter – Western
Infocom Group
5900 Hollis Street
Emeryville, CA 94608
Phone: (510) 596-9300
Fax: (510) 596-9331
http://www.infocomgroup.com

Contacts: The Media Pipeline for PR People
Mercomm, Inc.
550 Executive Boulevard
Ossining, NY 10562
Phone: (914) 923-9400
Fax: (914) 923-9484

O'Dwyer's Directory of Public Relations Firms
J.R. O'Dwyer Company, Inc.
271 Madison Avenue
New York, NY 10016
Phone: (212) 679-2471
Fax: (212) 683-2750
E-mail: sales@odwyerpr.com
http://www.odwyerpr.com/index.html

PR Intelligence Report
Lawrence Ragan Communications, Inc.
316 North Michigan Avenue
Chicago, IL 60601
Phone: (312) 960-4100
Fax: (312) 960-4105

PR News
PBI Media, LLC
1201 Seven Locks Road
Potomac, MD 20854
Phone: (301) 354-2000 or
   (888) 707-5812
Fax: (301) 762-4196
E-mail: clientservices@pbimedia.com

PR Quarterly
Howard Penn Hudson Associates, Inc.
P.O. Box 311
Rhinebeck, NY 12572
Phone: (845) 876-2081
Fax: (845) 876-2561

PR Reporter
PR Publishing Company, Inc.
Dudley House
P.O. Box 600
Exeter, NH 03833
Phone: (603) 778-0514
Fax: (603) 778-1741
E-mail: prr@prpublishing.com

PR Review
University of California Press
38091 Beach Road
P.O. Box 180
Coltons Point, MD 20626
Phone: (301) 769-3899

PR Tactics
Public Relations Society of America (PRSA)
33 Maiden Lane
New York, NY 10038
Phone: (212) 460-1400
Fax: (212) 995-0757
http://www.prsa.org

PR Watch
Center for Media & Democracy, Inc.
520 University Avenue
Madison, WI 53703
Phone: (608) 260-9713
Fax: (608) 260-9714
E-mail: editor@prwatch.org
http://www.prwatch.org

Ragan's PR Intelligence Report
Lawrence Ragan Communications, Inc.
316 North Michigan Avenue
Chicago, IL 60601
Phone: (312) 960-4100
Fax: (312) 960-4106

The Strategist
Public Relations Society of America (PRSA)
33 Maiden Lane
New York, NY 10038
Phone: (212) 460-1400
Fax: (212) 995-0757
http://www.prsa.org

PUBLISHING

Magazine and Bookseller
North American Publishing Company
837 Villa Ridge Road
Falls Church, VA 22046-3665
Phone: (215) 238-5482
Fax: (215) 238-5412
http://www.magazinebookseller.com

Publishers Weekly
360 Park Avenue South
New York, NY 10010
Phone: (646) 746-6758
Fax: (646) 746-6631
http://www.publishersweekly.com

RADIO AND TELEVISION

Cable TV Facts
Cabletelevision Advertising Bureau
830 Third Avenue
New York, NY 10022
Phone: (212) 508-1200
Fax: (212) 832-3268

Country Airplay Monitor
VNU Business Media USA
770 Broadway
New York, NY 10003
Phone: (646) 654-5000
E-mail: bmcomm@vnuinc.com
http://www.vnubusinessmedia.com

R&B Airplay Monitor
VNU Business Media USA
770 Broadway
New York, NY 10003
Phone: (646) 654-5000
E-mail: bmcomm@vnuinc.com
http://www.vnubusinessmedia.com

Radio-TV Interview Report
Bradley Communications Corporation
135 East Plumstead Avenue
P.O. Box 1206
Lansdowne, PA 19050
Phone: (610) 259-0707
Fax: (610) 284-3704
http://www.rtir.com

Rock Airplay Monitor
VNU Business Media USA
770 Broadway
New York, NY 10003
Phone: (646) 654-5000

E-mail: bmcomm@vnuinc.com
http://www.vnubusinessmedia.com

Top 40 Airplay Monitor
VNU Business Media USA
770 Broadway
New York, NY 10003
Phone: (646) 654-5000
E-mail: bmcomm@vnuinc.com
http://www.vnubusinessmedia.com

C. DIRECTORIES

The following is a listing of advertising, public relations, general information, and media directories that you will find useful both in your search for a job and in career advancement. Directories are used to locate information sources. They contain addresses, phone numbers, Web sites, and other contact information of companies and media sources.

Many directories are revised annually or even biannually. Some online directories may be revised more often. When checking for information, try to locate the newest version. While most of these books are quite expensive, they can usually be located in most public libraries.

ADWeek Directory
ADWEEK Magazines
770 Broadway
New York, NY 10003
Phone: (646) 654-5115
Fax: (646) 654-5351
http://www.adweek.com/directories

Associations Unlimited
The Gale Group
27500 Drake Road
Farmington Hills, MI 48331
Phone: (248) 699-4253
Fax: (248) 699-8065
E-mail: galeord@gale.com
http://www.galenet.gale.com

Business Publication Advertising Source
SRDS
1700 East Higgins Road
Des Plaines, IL 60018
Phone: (847) 375-5000
Fax: (847) 375-5001
E-mail: contact@srds.com
http://www.srds.com

Community Publication Advertising Source
SRDS
1700 East Higgins Road
Des Plaines, IL 60018

Phone: (847) 375-5000
Fax: (847) 375-5001
E-mail: contact@srds.com
http://www.srds.com

Consultants and Consulting Organizations Directory
27500 Drake Road
Farmington Hills, MI 48331
Phone: (248) 699-4253
Fax: (248) 699-8065
http://www.gale.com

Co-Op Advertising Programs Sourcebook
LexisNexis Group
121 Chanlon Road
New Providence, NJ 07974
Phone: (908) 464-6800
Fax: (908) 771-7704
http://www.co-opsourcebook.com

Directory of Business To Business Catalogs
Grey House Publishing
P.O. Box 860
Millerton, NY 12546
Phone: (518) 789-8700
Fax: (518) 789-0556
E-mail: books@greyhouse.com
http://www.greyhouse.com

Corporate Directory of U.S. Public Companies
Walker's Research L.L.C.
1650 Borel Place
San Mateo, CA 94402
Phone: (650) 341-1110
Fax: (650) 341-2351
E-mail: walkersres@aol.com
http://www.walkersresearch.com

Directory of Minority-Owned Professional and Personal Service Consultants
San Francisco Redevelopment Agency
770 Golden Gate Avenue
San Francisco, CA 94102
Phone: (415) 749-2400
Fax: (415) 749-2500

Directory of Special Libraries and Information Centers
The Gale Group
27500 Drake Road
Farmington Hills, MI 48331
Phone: (248) 699-4253
Fax: (248) 699-8065
E-mail: galeord@gale.com
http://www.galegroup.com

*Encyclopedia of Business Information
    Sources*
The Gale Group
27500 Drake Road
Farmington Hills, MI 48331
Phone: (248) 699-4253
Fax: (248) 699-8065
E-mail: galeord@gale.com
http://www.gale.com

*Encyclopedia of Governmental Advisory
    Organizations*
The Gale Group
27500 Drake Road
Farmington Hills, MI 48331

Phone: (248) 699-4253
Fax: (248) 699-8065
E-mail: galeord@gale.com
http://www.galenet.gale.com

*Hollywood Reporter Blu-Book Film, TV
    and Commercial Production
    Directory*
The Hollywood Reporter
5055 Wilshire Boulevard
Los Angeles, CA 90036
Phone: (323) 525-2000
Fax: (323) 525-2377
http://www.hollywoodreporter.com/thr/
    thrblu/letter.jsp

*O'Dwyer's Directory of Corporate
    Communications*
J.R. O'Dwyer Company, Inc.
271 Madison Avenue
New York, NY 10016
Phone: (212) 679-2471
Fax: (212) 683-2750
E-mail: sales@odwyerpr.com

Ulrich's Periodicals Directory
R.R. Bowker
630 Central Avenue
New Providence, NJ 07974
Phone: (908) 286-1090
http://www.bowker.com

D. MEDIA DIRECTORIES

Alabama News Media Directory
P.O. Box 316
Mount Dora, FL 32756
Phone: (800) 749-6399
Fax: (866) 586-7020
E-mail: NewsMedia@comcast.net

Alaska Media Directory
6828 Cape Lisburne
Anchorage, AK 99504
Phone: (907) 338-7288
Fax: (907) 338-8339
E-mail: akmedia@ak.net

American College Media Directory
Vineberg
P.O. Box 205
Westhampton, NY 11977
Phone: (631) 288-6933
Fax: (631) 288-7953
E-mail: collegemedia@vineberg
    communications.com
http://www.amercollegemedia.com

Bacon's Media Calendars
Bacon's Information, Inc.
332 South Michigan Avenue
Chicago, IL 60604
Phone: (312) 922-2400
Fax: (312) 987-9773
E-mail: directories@bacons.com
http://www.bacons.com

Bacon's Metro California Media
Bacon's Information, Inc.
332 South Michigan Avenue
Chicago, IL 60604
Phone: (312) 922-2400
Fax: (312) 987-9773

E-mail: directories@bacons.com
http://www.bacons.com

*Bacon's Newspaper and Magazine
    Directories*
Bacon's Information, Inc.
332 South Michigan Avenue
Chicago, IL 60604
Phone: (312) 922-2400
Fax: (312) 987-9773
E-mail: directories@bacons.com
http://www.bacons.com

Bacon's New York Publicity Outlets
Bacon's Information, Inc.
332 South Michigan Avenue
Chicago, IL 60604
Phone: (312) 922-2400
Fax: (312) 987-9773
E-mail: directories@bacons.com
http://www.bacons.com

*Bacon's Radio/TV/Cable
    Directory*
Bacon's Information, Inc.
332 South Michigan Avenue
Chicago, IL 60604
Phone: (312) 922-2400
Fax: (312) 987-9773
E-mail: directories@bacons.com
http://www.bacons.com

*Burrelle's Chesapeake Bay Media
    Directory*
Burrelle's Information Services
75 East Northfield Road
Livingston, NJ 07039
Phone: (973) 992-6600

Fax: (973) 992-7675
E-mail: directory@burelles.com
https://www.burrelles.com

Burrelle's Media Directory
Burrelle's Information Services
75 East Northfield Road
Livingston, NJ 07039
Phone: (973) 992-6600
Fax: (973) 992-7675
E-mail: directory@burelles.com
https://www.burrelles.com

Burrelle's Midwest Media Directory
Burrelle's Information Services
75 East Northfield Road
Livingston, NJ 07039
Phone: (973) 992-6600
Fax: (973) 992-7675
E-mail: directory@burelles.com
https://www.burrelles.com

Burrelle's Minnesota Directory
Burrelle's Information Services
75 East Northfield Road
Livingston, NJ 07039
Phone: (973) 992-6600
Fax: (973) 992-7675
E-mail: directory@burelles.com
https://www.burrelles.com

*Burrelle's New England Media
    Directory*
Burrelle's Information Services
75 East Northfield Road
Livingston, NJ 07039
Phone: (973) 992-6600
Fax: (973) 992-7675
E-mail: directory@burelles.com
https://www.burrelles.com

Burrelle's New Jersey Media Directory
Burrelle's Information Services
75 East Northfield Road
Livingston, NJ 07039
Phone: (973) 992-6600
Fax: (973) 992-7675
E-mail: directory@burelles.com
https://www.burrelles.com

Burrelle's New York Media Directory
Burrelle's Information Services
75 East Northfield Road
Livingston, NJ 07039
Phone: (973) 992-6600
Fax: (973) 992-7675
E-mail: directory@burelles.com
https://www.burrelles.com

Burrelle's Pennsylvania Media Directory
Burrelle's Information Services
75 East Northfield Road
Livingston, NJ 07039
Phone: (973) 992-6600
Fax: (973) 992-7675
E-mail: directory@burelles.com
https://www.burrelles.com

Burrelle's Southeast Media Directory
Burrelle's Information Services
75 East Northfield Road
Livingston, NJ 07039
Phone: (973) 992-6600
Fax: (973) 992-7675
E-mail: directory@burelles.com
https://www.burrelles.com

Burrelle's Texas Media Directory
Burrelle's Information Services
75 East Northfield Road
Livingston, NJ 07039
Phone: (973) 992-6600
Fax: (973) 992-7675
E-mail: directory@burelles.com
https://www.burrelles.com

Burrelle's West Coast Media Directory
Burrelle's Information Services
75 East Northfield Road
Livingston, NJ 07039
Phone: (973) 992-6600
Fax: (973) 992-7675
E-mail: directory@burelles.com
https://www.burrelles.com

Business Media Directory
Bacon's Information, Inc.
332 South Michigan Avenue
Chicago, IL 60604
Phone: (312) 922-2400 or (800) 621-0561
Fax: (312) 987-9773
E-mail: directories@bacons.com
http://www.bacons.com/research/
    businessmedia.htm

Computer/Hi-Tech Media Directory
Bacon's Information, Inc.
332 South Michigan Avenue
Chicago, IL 60604
Phone: (312) 922-2400 or (800) 621-0561
Fax: (312) 987-9773
E-mail: directories@bacons.com
http://www.baconsinfo.com

**Gale Directory of Publications and
    Broadcast Media**
The Gale Group
27500 Drake Road
Farmington Hills, MI 48331
Phone: (248) 699-4253
Fax: (248) 699-8065
http://www.galegroup.com

Gebbie Press All-in-One Directory
Gebbie Press, Inc.
P.O. Box 1000
New Paltz, NY 12561
Phone: (845) 255-7560
Fax: (845) 256-1239
E-mail: gebbie@pipeline.com
http://www.gebbieinc.com

**Hudson's Washington New Media
    Contact Directory**
Howard Penn Hudson Associates, Inc.
P.O. Box 311
Rhinebeck, NY 12572
Phone: (845) 876-2081
Fax: (845) 876-2561
E-mail: hudsonsdir@aol.com
http://www.hudsonsdirectory.com

North America Senior Media Directory
630 North Rosemead Boulevard
Pasadena, CA 91107
Phone: (626) 794-0288
Fax: (626) 794-7298

Senior Media Directory
Creative Ink, Inc.
P.O. Box 22383
Eagan, MN 55122
Phone: (952) 894-6720
Fax: (952) 894-1066

Tennessee News Media Directory
P.O. Box 316
Mount Dora, FL 32756
Phone: (800) 749-6399
Fax: (866) 586-7020
E-mail: NewsMedia@comcast.net

TV and Cable Source
1700 East Higgins Road
Des Plaines, IL 60018
Phone: (847) 375-5000 or
    (800) 851-7737
Fax: (847) 375-5001
E-mail: contact@srds.com
http://www.srds.com

TV News
Community Publications of America, Inc.
55 West 14th Street
New York, NY 10011
Phone: (212) 243-6800
Fax: (212) 243-7457

Ulrich's Periodicals Directory
R.R. Bowker L.L.C.
630 Central Avenue
New Providence, NJ 07974
Phone: (908) 286-1090
Fax: (908) 219-0098
E-mail: info@bowker.com
http://www.ulrichsweb.com

Vermont Media Directory
212 Battery Street
Burlington, VT 05401
Phone: (802) 862-8261
Fax: (802) 863-4724
E-mail: info@ksvc.com
http://www.vermontmediadirectory.com

INDEX

ABOUT THE AUTHOR

Shelly Field is a nationally recognized motivational speaker, career expert, stress specialist, and author of more than 25 best-selling books in the business and career fields.

Her books instruct people on how to obtain jobs in a wide array of areas including the hospitality, music, sports and communications industries, casinos and casino hotels, advertising, public relations, theater, the performing arts, entertainment, animal rights, health care, writing and art; and choosing the best career for the new century.

She is a frequent guest on local, regional, and national radio, cable, and television talk, information, and news shows and also does numerous print interviews and personal appearances.

Field is a featured speaker at conventions, expos, casinos, corporate functions, employee training and development sessions, career fairs, spouse programs, and events nationwide. She speaks on empowerment, motivation, careers, gaming, and human resources; attracting, retaining, and motivating employees; customer service; and stress reduction. Her popular seminars, *"STRESS BUSTERS: Beating The Stress In Your Work and Your Life"* and *"The De-Stress Express"* are favorites around the country.

President and CEO of The Shelly Field Organization, a public relations and management firm handling national clients, she also does corporate consulting and has represented celebrities in the sports, music, and entertainment industries as well as authors, businesses, and corporations.

For information about personal appearances or seminars contact The Shelly Field Organization at P.O. Box 711, Monticello, NY 12701, or log on to www.shellyfield.com.